ELECTORAL REFORMS

ELECTORAL REFORMS
Why and How

Editors

K. Raman Pillai
R.K. Suresh Kumar
P. Sukumaran Nair

KALPAZ

Electoral Reforms: Why and How

K. Raman Pillai, R.K. Suresh Kumar,
P. Sukumaran Nair

ISBN : 978-81-7835-957-1

Published in 2013 in India by
Kalpaz Publications
C-30, Satyawati Nagar,
Delhi - 110052
E-mail: kalpaz@hotmail.com

Laser Type Setting : Sanya Computers, Delhi
Printed at : G. Print Process.Delhi

Dedicated to the memory of
C.K. Chandrappan, the spirit behind the
organisation of the National Seminar on
Electoral Reforms

Contents

Acknowledgements

We are grateful to all the contributors for their encouraging participation in the debate on Electoral Reforms. It was their whole hearted co-operation that enabled us to publish this volume. Work for the related seminar this book and has been supported by grants from Indira Gandhi National Open University, New Delhi (IGNOU) and the Indian Council of Social Science Research (ICSSR) New Delhi. We thank these institutions. Our special thanks are due to Prof. (Dr.) V.N. Rajasekharan Pillai, former Vice-Chancellor, IGNOU for his inspiring involvement and material support. The Executive Committee and Staff of the C. Achutha Menon Foundation were part of this shared experience. We are indebted to N. Shanmughom Pillai, Treasurer of the Foundation for his total commitment and help in bringing out this Volume. Sincere thanks are also due to Ms. Bindu. N, for typing the manuscript.

K. Raman Pillai
R.K. Suresh Kumar
P. Sukumaran Nair

Introduction

Elections are an integral part of a democratic system of government. Democracy and free and fair elections go together and one cannot exist without the other. Free and fair elections can be ensured if the machinery which conducts the election is independent and the law under which the elections are conducted is faultless.

The election laws of our country are embodied in Articles 324 to 329 of the Constitution of India and in the two statutes viz the Representation of People Act 1950 and 1951.

The first serious attempt at electoral reforms led to the appointment of a joint parliamentary committee on amendment to election law in pursuance of motions adopted in the Lok Sabha and Rajya Sabha in June 1971. The committee under the chairmanship of Jagannath Rao submitted its report in March 1972. The reforms recommended by the committee were "by no means of a radical nature". A bill was introduced in the Lok Sabha in December 1973 incorporating some of the recommendations with a view to amending the Representation of People Act of 1950 and 1951 but it was not passed.

The first people's movement for electoral reforms was launched by Jaya Prakash Narayan. As President of the Citizens for Democracy, he set up in August 1974 a committee under the chairmanship of Justice V.M. Tharkunde to study and report on a scheme for electoral reforms with particular reference to the use of money power, the misuse of official authority and machinery and other forms of corrupt practices. The committees report was presented by Jaya Prakash Narayan to the Presiding officers of both Houses of Parliament at the conclusion of a massive demonstration but nothing happened.

In September 1983, the then Chief Election Commissioner R.K. Trivedi proposed certain electoral reforms. However the country went to polls in 1984 without any electoral reforms.

The national front government led by V.P. Singh (1989) convened a meeting of the representatives of political parties in Parliament in January 1990 to discuss various aspects of electoral reforms. It constituted a committee on electoral reforms under the chairmanship of the Law Minister Dinesh Goswamy. The committee submitted its report in May 1990. The government introduced four bills in Parliament to give effect to such recommendations which it accepted. However, the government resigned from office in November 1990 before these bills could be passed.

Prime Minister, Narasimha Rao introduced two bills on electoral reforms at a special session of Parliament. In fact the government had to withdraw the bills at the Zero hour.

The Indrajit Gupta Committee report on state funding of elections is lying with the central government just like other reports. In fact, neither the central government nor the political parties are sincere about their commitment to introduce electoral reforms aimed at ensuring free and fair elections. Be that as it may, there is no going away from the fact that there is an urgent need to introduce electoral reforms in our country.

Agenda for Electoral Reforms

The objective of any electoral reform needs to be the deepening of the democratic process, strengthening the instruments of public accountability and guaranteeing opportunity for meaningful voter participation.

Reforming the Electoral System

The nature of the electoral system in our country is such that it does not reflect the wishes of the people adequately. We have adopted the single choice plurality method common to British-American two-party systems without having a two party system. In the first past- the –post system that we have adopted vulnerability is the major criterion for the selection of candidates. Hence considerations such as religion, region, caste, money and muscle power are used in the selection process. This system results in giving the plurality party a disproportionate number of seats both in the Legislatures and Parliament and reduce the number of seats and percentage of votes to the small parties. There is no representation of minority social groups. It encourages fragmentation and wastage of votes. Electoral record for the Lok Sabha election shows that in the past five general elections the number of winning candidates who secured 50% or more of the valid votes polled has varied between 121 and 221, it was 121 in 2009. Earlier the Venkata Cheliah Commission had surveyed the record of three general elections to conclude that over two-thirds of the members of the Lok Sabha and almost 90% of members of some legislative assemblies were elected on a minority vote.

Proportional representation would ensure representation to important groups and factions. This system is supposed to produce approximately the same percentage of legislative seats for each party as its relative voting strength justifies. There are two outstanding systems of Proportional Representation—the single transferable vote (Hare) system and the List system.

Under the single transferable vote system, the voter is given a preferential ballot *i.e.,* he may indicate his order of preference by writing in the numbers 1, 2, 3 etc. A quota is then determined which when obtained will entitle the candidate to a seat. The quota is determined by dividing the total number of votes cast by the number of seats in the district plus one and adding one to the result. Candidates receiving the particular number of first preference votes would be declared elected. If the requisite number is not obtained on the basis of first preference, then the excess ballots of the elected candidates will be distributed among others according to second preference. The advantage is that a party whose supporters steadfirstly vote the party ticket will find it easier to get a seat since the quota is much easier to reach than a majority or even a plurality of the total vote. This method is used in electing members of the Irish Diet, the Australian and South African Senates and members of the Indian Rajya Sabha.

List system of proportional representation is by far the most frequently used electoral system. While the Hare system attempts to achieve proportionality by making the individual candidates the unit of representation, the list system views the political party as the basic unit. Each party prepares and submits the list of candidates. The lists are printed on the ballot paper with the candidates listed in the same order that they appear in the list submitted by the parties. This means that the candidate at the top of the list is the party's first choice of filling any of the seats it may win. The remaining candidates in the order they appear on the list are the party's additional preferences for filling the additional seats allotted to it. This system exists in West Germany, Israel, Switzerland, Luxemburg, Sweden and Norway.

Advocates of proportional representation claim that it is a more realistic gauge of public opinion since its alternatives the majority principle rests on the assumption of an absolute two party system which does not really exist in many countries. It permits a greater variety of interest to be directly represented. A number of European countries have electoral system which represents a compromise between proportional representation and the majority plurality method. In India, we can try this method. S.L. Shakdher, the former Chief Election Commissioner suggested that 50% of the seats should be allowed to various political parties in proportion to the votes polled by them in each state to remedy the situation. This would restore some balance between the votes polled and the seats won by various political parties. The former Chief Election Commissioner J.M. Lyngdoh has said that switching over to proportional representation of the electoral system will help curb the influence of money power in the long term. In a proportional representation system, the parties would be competing against each other and not candidates and so much money is not going to be spent. Alternatively we can think of introduction of a two round system with the second round conducted between two leading candidates in each constituency on the day after the first round.

Money Power and Muscle Power in Elections

In India the two pernicious elements eating into the vitals of the electoral system are money power and muscle power. Money power brings muscle power and the two work havoc with the electoral process. With large constituencies, multiplicity of parties and candidates, absence of ideology, politicisation of caste and communal identities and building of vote banks, elections have become very expensive, thereby generating corruption and black money and leading to criminalisation of politics.

The explanation to section 77 (1) of the Representation of People

Act had put a ceiling on election expenditure incurred by the candidate or his agent, not by his party or any one else. Under the guise of this provision, big money bags could freely spend for the candidate or parties which they do so after obtaining guarantees for adequate returns. This has not only affected the level playing ground between parties and candidates but also the very economic system since those who spend money for candidates expect adequate returns.

The statutory ceilings are patently unrealistic and inadequate to cover even a small portion of expenses actually incurred. The actual expenditure incurred by a candidate does not bear any relation to the maximum limits laid down. More or less open admissions have been made of substantial sums of money, several times the ceiling fixed for a particular election, being spent by the candidates. Where does this money come from and on what terms and how is the debt repaid is anybody's guess.

In 1974, the Supreme Court clearly expressed itself against the unchecked use of 'party money' for candidates in the elections. The congress government promptly promulgated an ordinance to nullify the effect of the Supreme Court verdict while the Janata Party vacillated and failed to ensure compliance with the courts' views. In another Judgment, the Supreme Court observed. "If the campaign runs bersek and expenses unlimited become the rule, general elections become national nightmares and the fabric of our freedom shakes". Again in August 1994, the Supreme Court in its judgment in C. Narayanaswamy vs Jaffer Sherif, observed. "If the call for purity of elections is not to be reduced to a lip service, then the persons investing funds in furtherance of the prospect of election of a candidate must be identified and listed". It is reported that "as the law stands in India today anybody including a smuggler, criminal or any other anti social element may spend any amount on the election for which no account is to be maintained".

In fact, there are ways and means to reduce the influence of money power in Indian elections. We can take lessons from foreign countries in this regard. In Britain, part of the election expenses of political parties is met by the government. Free postal delivery is allowed to candidates. In France, candidates get a certain amount of free publicity. In Russia, the state bears all the election and campaign expenses. In

Germany, assurance of state financial assistance to candidates or parties that have secured minimum prescribed percentage of votes in the previous elections have encouragd smaller splinter parties to join the mainstream political parties thereby avoiding political fragmentation.

During the Constituent Assembly debates, K.T. Shah said: "All expenses in connection with election to Parliament of all candidates shall be defrayed out of the public treasury in accordance with a scale prescribed by parliament provided that any candidate securing less than 10% of the votes cast at an election shall not be entitled to claim such expenses." The Joint Parliamentary Committee in its report of 1972 recommended that election expenses must be met from public exchequer and that all recognised parties must get equal opportunities for canvassing.

The use of vehicles on polling day to provide free conveyance to voters to and from the polling stations is another corrupt practice associated with elections. The plying of all vehicles on polling day except those connected with election assignments, police, hospitals etc should be completely prohibited.

There are all types of laws regulating expenditure on elections, most of them only on paper. The legal framework is not strong enough to correct the distortions, which crept into the polity. Alternatives have been proposed, but the political class seem reluctant to reform the system which may empower the voter as against the power they enjoy at present in manipulating the system.

In fact, electoral competition leads to criminalisation of politics. Elections cost money and require vast organisation to reach up to one million voters. Criminals have come forward to offer both. Political competition has ensured that the offer is seldom turned down. Almost anyone who can contribute money or muscle power to help a politician win an election has been able to carve a niche for himself within the political system and buy immunity from the law. Most political activity is carried out with black money which is by definition generated by crime. The entire political system is afloat on a sea of crime. The criminals seek, demand and secure short term gains in return for favours done to their political patrons. Gradually their appetite gets further whetted by the influence they wield and this leads them to aspire for and succeed in becoming candidates for Parliament/ Assembly/ local bodies. Criminals, contest, win elections and become legislators so that they can enjoy the privileges and perpetuate their nefarious activities with more impunity. Cases against them may remain pending for years, witness against them may not turn up, may turn hostile or may get eliminated and finally the cases may be dropped.

The Representation of People Act does contain provisions to disqualify a person from contesting the elections if he is convicted of any of the many offences listed in section 8 (1) and (2). Subsection (3) proceeds to disqualify a person convicted of an offence, other than the ones so listed, for which he is sentenced to imprisonment for not less than two years. Accordingly the Election Commission ordered the returning officers to reject the nomination papers of such candidates who are covered under section 8. But the law was diluted to such an extent that criminals continued to flourish in electoral politics. In the 14th Lok Sabha there were 125 members ie 23% of the total members with criminal background involving serious charges of murder, rape, kidnapping, extortion etc. The development of the nexus among criminals including smugglers of arms and narcotics, extortions, mafia gangs, terrorists and politicians, police, bureaucrats and businessmen in running the state apparatus forbodes the demise of the democratic system in our country unless urgent measures are adopted by the government to stop this malaise.

The home ministry has prepared certain guidelines to prevent the entry of criminals in the election fray. According to the recommendations of the home ministry, any person intending to contest an election must file an affidavit to the effect that he has neither been punished by a court of law for criminal offences during the last ten years nor charge sheeted (as an accused). He should also submit before the returning officer before ten days of filing nomination that there is no case against him pending before a court. These affidavits must be endorsed by the chief of the State Crime Records Bureau. In case incorrect information is given, it would involve imprisonment, fine or disqualification for six years. The candidate should further file an affidavit that there is no case pending against him for corruption, deceit, breach of trust or FERA violation. He should also submit a statement showing the assets including movable and immovable property in his name as well as in the name of his close relations. The home ministry has submitted these proposals to the Election Commission. It is up to the Election Commission to accept them and enforce them.

The committee on electoral reforms set up by the Union Ministry of Law and Justice recently has proposed to disqualify persons accused of an offence punishable with imprisonment for five years or more from contesting elections, even when the trial was pending, provided charges have been framed by a competent court. It has also recommended banning door to door campaigning 48 hours before the polls since money changed hands during this period. Another important proposal was on banning opinion as well as exit polls, since they lacked credibility. As regards state funding of elections, the then Chief Election Commissioner S.Y. Quraishi said that the commission was against the "shortcut solution" of having state funded elections. That would just put thousands of crores of public money into the hands of political parties without the guarantee that expenditure ceilings will be respected. He has suggested that the accounts of political parties be audited by the Comptroller and Auditor General of India.

The influence of money power and muscle power in elections cannot be completely eliminated, but it can be reduced by adopting the following measures.

1. The ceiling on the election expenditure by a candidate must be realistically and reasonably fixed by law and no one should be allowed to spend more than the amount specified. Those who are found to have spent more should be disqualified from contesting the elections for a specified period.

2. Part of the election expenses of all candidates who secure a minimum percentage of votes must be defrayed out of the public exchequer in accordance with a formula prescribed by parliament. Former Chief Election Commissioner S.L. Shakdher proposed the creation of an election fund with contributions from the central and state government expenses on 50:50 basis to meet not only of government expenses on the conduct of elections but also of the expenses incurred by candidates and political parties.

The Goswami Committee has proposed that to start with State assistance in kind should be provided only to candidates of recognized political parties in respect of three or four items *viz,* provision of prescribed quantity of fuel or petrol to vehicles used by candidates, supply of additional copies of electoral rolls, payment of the charges for prescribed number of microphones used by candidates and distribution of voter identity slips. In 1998, following an all-party meeting, a seven member committee headed by Indrajit Gupta was constituted to make specific recommendations regarding the introduction of state funded elections. This report, like the reports of other commissions is also lying with the central government.

3. There should be a total ban on political donations by companies. The big business houses, the contactors, black marketeers and liquor barons who donate liberally to the election funds of political parties do it not for nothing. They know how to reap the harvest in terms of licence, permits or quota. The political leaders who accept the donations go often out of the way to placate the donors. No political party in India is free from such offence. The earlier it is reduced, the better it would be for the country.

4. Compulsory voting must be introduced in India. Compulsory voting is practised in Australia, Belgium, Netherlands, Greece, Italy, Chile, Egypt and other countries. Political parties campaigning for election no longer have to spend part of the campaign funds for getting the voters to the polling booth. What is aimed at is that majority of the electorate should not keep away from exercising the franchise and the selection of legislators should not be left exclusively in the hands of professional politicians.

5. Criminals must not be allowed to contest elections. Political parties must not give tickets to persons with criminal background.

Code of Conduct for Political Parties

It is high time that in India a code of conduct is evolved for political parties to refrain from exploitation of communal, caste and religious prejudices and maintain some minimum ethics in public life to cleanse the Indian society of many evil influences that have crept into it.

The All-India Conference of Presiding officers, leaders of political parties, Ministers of Parliamentary affairs and Whips held in September 1992 resolved to evolve and observe a code of conduct for legislators. The resolution did not materialise because those in power could not muster enough courage. There is a case for prescribing certain minimum qualifications for contesting the election and holding the posts of legislators. There should be no court cases or convictions not only for the candidates but any member in the family that should suffice to disqualify the candidate.

The first and foremost step towards an untainted electoral system would be to make political parties function on democratic lines. In the words of Shakdher, "political parties make strong demands for the conduct of free and fair elections to legislative bodies but choose to ignore the application of the same principle when it comes to the functioning of their own party organs".

Defections must not be encouraged. The home ministry has suggested that those who defect must seek a fresh mandate of the electorate within one year. Until they are reelected they should not hold any official position. This will definitely prevent defections.

Equally important is the need to curb acts of violence and unruly behavior on the floor of the House by the elected representatives of the people. MPs and MLAs indulging in such unparliamentary practices which is a slur on the democratic process must be debarred from attending the House for a period of six months. Those who defect should not be offered ministerial berths by other parties.

Another aspect is the role played by the media in elections. Whether this role is constructive or otherwise is a matter of debate. Of late, the role played by the media during elections has come in for severe criticism. The 2009 elections to the Lok Sabha and to some state legislatures saw a spate of complaints as millions of rupees were spent by powerful political parties and candidates to plant "paid news" in sections of the media. Shocked by the pernicious practice of publishing "paid news" by Newspapers and TV channels, the Editors guild of India has strongly condemned the practice, "which whittles down the foundations of Indian Journalism". Taking cognisance of "paid news" at its annual meeting on 22 December 2009, the Guild said "Both the media organisations and editors who indulge in it, and the customers who offer payment for such "paid news" are guilty of undermining the free and fair press, for which every citizen of India is entitled to". The guild has decided to approach the Election Commission to suggest reforms in the election laws as "paid news" was being used by political parties to circumvent the strict limits on poll expenditure. The Election Commission has ordered the setting up of "district level committees for scrutiny of "paid news" during election period."

Restructuring the Election Commission

The power and authority as also the independence and credibility of the Election Commission are of such importance to the electoral process that any scheme of electoral reform would remain incomplete without having regard to these aspects. The state election commission has to be integrated with the National Election Commission and the appointment of the National Election Commissioners and the state election commissioners has to be done through a uniform procedure. Under the existing law, the Chief Election Commissioner and other election commissioners are appointed by the President which in effect means the union political executive. This has given rise to certain misgivings about the CEC especially in matters falling within his discretionary powers. Any such misgivings could easily be avoided if the CEC is appointed in consultation with the Chief Justice of India and the leader of the opposition. For the appointment of other election commissioners the CEC should also be consulted besides others.

In view of the increasing workload of the Election Commission and the necessity of supervising the functioning of the Electoral machinery in the states, the appointment of regional commissioners even on an adhoc basis as recommended by the Goswamy Committee need be considered seriously. They should also be given statutory recognition and be endowed with statutory powers.

Reforms of Electoral Laws

In order to ensure free and fair polls a number of changes have to be introduced in the electoral laws especially the Representation of People Act 1950 and 1951. Some of the important changes to be introduced are indicated below.

1. Unless a candidate secures 1/5th of the total votes polled his security deposit must be forfeited by the government. Such candidates should be debarred from contesting elections for the next six years.
2. The nomination fee for contesting the Lok Sabha and the State Assembly Polls should be increased to discourage candidates who are not serious about elections and files nomination for the sake of enjoying some temporary benefits and sometimes in anticipation of some favour either in cash or kind from the candidates of the major political parties.
3. The norms for recognizing political parties should be streamlined. No political party should be recognized unless it gets at least 10% of the votes cast. Only those political parties which have registered themselves with the Election Commission be permitted to field candidates if they aim at forming the government. Non-party individuals may contest on their own but cannot form or join the government. This will eventually reduce the number of independent candidates contesting the elections and thereby reduce election expenditure.
4. No one should be allowed to contest from more than one constituency.
5. All candidates must submit an audited account of the election expenses within 30 days of the poll to the Election Commission.
6. Places of worship should not be used for election propaganda.
7. Ministers should not combine their official visits with electioneering or use the official machinery or personnel for poll related work. They should be prevented from using government transport including official aircraft in furtherance of the interest of the party in power. The ruling party must be prevented from issuing advertisements at the cost of public

exchequer in newspapers and electronic media. The party in power should not be allowed to lay foundation stones for projects and to make adhoc appointments on the eve of the elections.

8. A minimum educational qualification must be prescribed for those contesting the elections to the Parliament and State Legislatures. Election Commission's proposal to fix matriculation as the minimum qualification for candidates contesting elections has found favour with 80% of the people surveyed by the Centre for Media and Cultural Research.

Electoral Reforms to make the democratic polity of India more vibrant and resilient are much too important to be left exclusively to governments, political parties or the Election Commission. Each citizen has to actually engage himself in the electoral reform process and must not leave the development and implementation of the agenda to reform the electoral process in the hands of few people. The quality of electoral process determines the quality of democracy. The initiative of the civil society in the process is of paramount importance. Any attempt to ensure free and fair elections should also ensure that responsible sections of civil society are closely associated with every stage of the electoral process.

It is in pursuit of the above objective that a three day national seminar on 'Electoral Reforms' was organized by C. Achutha Menon Study Centre and Library in July 2010 at Thiruvananthapuram. The seminar focused on five important themes viz., the Electoral System in India, Role of money power and muscle power in elections, political parties and elections, media, civil society and elections and agenda for electoral reforms. The wide participation of scholars in the seminar motivated us to bring out this volume consisting of selected papers presented in different sessions. The papers have been arranged theme wise to enable the readers to comprehend the various dimensions of the issue. The larger objective is to make the Indian electoral democracy a vibrant one.

II

The papers included in Part I of this volume takes a critical look at the existing electoral system in India. The papers focus on important issues related to the strength and weakness of our electoral democracy. Dr Hamid Ansari questions the 'representativeness of our elected representatives' and stresses the need for meaningful electoral reforms. He makes it clear that democracy is not just a mechanism of forming and running a government but represents a matrix of relations between citizens which allows for every citizen to live his/her life to the fullest, in dignity, and able to develop, exert and enjoy his/her capabilities. For this there should be change in politics as it is practised today. Society at large should encourage a politics defined by 'what you believe in' and 'what you want to achieve' instead of 'who you are' and 'where you live'. He also cautions us against mechanistic analyses and suggestions relating to electoral reforms.

Dr N.R. Madhava Menon considers our electoral system as the largest endeavour ever in democratic governance. He gives full credit for the successful conduct of the general elections to the people of India and to the strength of its political institutions. Enumerating the inadequacies of the existing electoral system, he raises the pertinent question whether it has succeeded in putting into place persons who can actually legislate? He reminds us of the flaws of the first – past – the post system and the increasing criminalisation of politics. To him, the laws regulating expenditure on elections remain only on paper. The Election Commission, inspite of its handicaps, has proved its effectiveness under the leadership of strong Election Commissioners. He cautions that unless the appointment of the Commissioners is freed from politics, the sanctity of the 'free will' of the individual voter will be in danger of losing its status.

Justice K.T. Thomas in his paper demands that the verdict should be a true reflection of the choice of the electorate. He argues for the rectification of the present system of 'fictious representation' through the adoption of preferential voting. He is of the view that by-elections and mid term elections are not suited to a vast country like India. Alternative methods can be worked out based on the lessons and experience of other big countries.

P.D.T. Achary points out that electoral reforms became a subject of discussion with the eclipse of the monolithic character of the premier political formation in India. The realisation that many undemocratic practices have crept into electioneering also necessitated electoral reforms. To the author, criminals becoming law makers is an all India phenomenon. The law in this regard is toothless as disqualification is possible only after 'conviction' of the law breaker. He finds merit in the recommendation of the Election Commission that a person facing trial on a serious offence should not be allowed to contest. But he is doubtful of the practicability of the proposition that only those who get 50% plus votes should be declared elected. However, carefully crafted electoral reforms can make democracy more meaningful.

Dr S.N. Sangita in his paper examines the electoral process with the objective of finding out how far it has been able to promote inclusive governance. He analyses the electoral practices and functioning of political parties by focusing on their capability to provide effective and responsive leadership.

According to ProfVijayabalan and Lekshmi Vijayabalan the challenge to revamp the electoral system has to be taken up by each citizen. The authors advocate measures like ceiling on campaign expenses, stringent laws for excluding criminals, restriction on paid news, banning the parade of celebrities during campaign, preventing the proliferation of political parties, regulation of the electronic media, allowing NRIs to exercise their franchise, encouraging citizen engagement in the political process and a proactive role by the Election Commission.

Dr A.D. Damodaran's paper deals with the larger issue of the mounting challenges of our democratic governance. He argues that though we have recognised the principle of one man one vote and one vote one value in politics, it is denied in the social and economic realms. He envisages electoral reforms within a total perspective, and not just through bits and pieces. The reforms should cover the three structures of governance in synergic model.

The constitutionality and propriety of electoral disqualification on the ground of holding office of profit is discussed by Dr K.C. Sunny in his informative paper. He states that since the constitution did not define the term 'office of profit' it has become the duty of the Judiciary to interpret what is an office of profit and what is not, depending on the practical situations of each and every case.

Dr P.L. Dharma poses the fundamental question in this regard when he asks 'Are we for reforms'? He asserts that democratic experiments are not a set of activities that could be achieved overnight in a complicated society like India where different modes of inequality prevail. He feels that electoral reforms are infact attempts at democratizing our polity. Electoral reforms need to prioritize the fact that social reforms can create a meaningful base to political reform in general and electoral reforms in particular.

III

It is true that balloting is essential for a functioning democracy but not a sufficient condition. The authenticity of balloting is what gives sanctity to peoples, verdict. But there are many hindrances to it. Part II of this volume consists of six scholarly articles relating to the role of money power and muscle power in elections.

The first paper authored by Dr J. Prabhash reminds us that the core problem involved in representation is the relationship that exists between the representatives and the represented. Though this relationship is predominantly anchored on the legal foundation of citizen rights it also rests partially on the ideology and clarity of moral language of the political society. From 1970's onwards politics took a new turn in India with the weakening of the congress party and the resultant 'regionalisation' and 'ethnicisation' of the party system. There was tremendous pressure on the electoral system when the political space became a highly contested one. The elections have ceased to be a contest of ideas and public policies. No wonder, malpractices were resorted to by political parties and dubious politicians. The paper systematically analyses the extent and role of money power and muscle power in Indian elections. The arguments are backed by authentic facts and figures. The scholar identifies depoliticization as the main reason for the existing state of affairs and wants to counter it through the counter logic of politicization.

The influence of money and muscle power in elections mainly focusing on Lok Sabha polls forms the central theme of Dr K.M. George's paper. He notes that a change in the financing of political parties by the business houses has occurred since liberalization in the form of making payments per deal in place of the earlier practice of regular financing. The business houses themselves have entered into election contest rather than depending on their protégées. The gulf between representatives and the represented has also widened. There is ambiguity surrounding the expression 'conviction' relating to disqualification of persons with criminal background. He correctly observes that the existing justice system was designed to deal with individual crimes and as such helpless in dealing with organized crimes by mafia. He recommends reforms like restriction of poll expenses, inner democracy in political parties, auditing of party accounts, effective measures to check malpractice of political parties and amendments in the criminal judicial system.

Dr M.A. Hussain and Dr Venkatesula Reddy in their paper argues for the introduction of 'compulsory voting' to sustain our representative democracy. While acknowledging the work done by the Election commission so far, they want it to go for more speedy reforms. The Commission should initiate action for introducing the fifty plus criteria, proportional representation and compulsory voting.

Dr T.M. Joseph and Dr Jos Chathukulam in their jointly authored paper probes the unrepresentative character of the existing first-past-the-post system and advances certain alternative models. Under the existing system the votes of those (often a majority) who voted for the defeated candidates go unrepresented. To the authors this amounts to their votes being wasted and at the national level, this leads to a disproportionality between the percentage of votes polled by political parties and the number of seats won by parties. In order to rectify this the scholars undertakes an analysis of the alternative models of electoral systems and suggests the Mixed Member Proportional System as the suitable one for India.

A scholarly analysis of the unruly behaviour of our elected representatives in legislature and how it has played havoc with the system of parliamentary democracy is the theme skillfully discussed by Dr K. Suryaprasad in his thought provoking paper titled "Pernicious Behaviour of Elected Representatives – An Unresolved Challenge to Indian Democracy". With serious concern he observes that what started some time ago as a spontaneous action by a few members, especially from minority parties, to make their voice heard in parliament on sensitive issues is now seen by political parties as an ordinary form of protest. The most unfortunate aspect is that even if a single member wants to disturb the proceedings he can hold the House to ransom. He strongly argues that there is a valid case for prescribing minimum educational qualifications for contesting elections. It is also essential to bring in a law to disqualify those who indulge in unruly behavior in the House and thereby disturb parliamentary proceedings. He rightly feels that this will make it necessary to define the term 'pernicious behaviour'. His other proposals are also worth considering. The presiding officers should discharge their duties effectively. He wants the responsibility for the smooth conduct of the house to be made a collective responsibility along with the right to recall. He also recommends training and apprenticeship for the new entrants and positive criticism by the mass media. Towards the end of his paper the author thoughtfully observes that the 'major difference appears to be that while earlier, serving the nation was seen as a privilege and attracted many well-meaning people now it is the privilege that attracts the politicians.'

The democratic objective as desired by the Indian Constitution will be realized only when the interests of the impoverished people get priority in our governance agenda. A joint article by C.E. Ajith Kumar and Dr M. Lathika examines whether elections in India has positively contributed towards making our democratic polity an inclusive one. Their forceful contention is that no government in a democracy holds the moral authority to continue for the next term, if a substantial number of its citizens are not salvaged from their deprivation of capabilities for a decent living, livelihood, nutrition, health and education. The electoral system according to them should address this serious issue.

IV

In every political system political parties perform the function of interest aggregation. As such their role in election assumes special importance. Part III of the volume debates this role under the title 'Political Parties and Elections'. Commenting on our electoral system M.Vijaya Kumar observes that in India the space for popular participation is declining as the system is twisted and turned by people with money and muscle power. What is required is to bring people back to politics. Political parties should take up this responsibility. Electoral reforms should also aim at politicizing people. Participation of people in politics should come up as an instinct. It can check the efforts at depoliticizing the entire governance process. The author boldly brushes aside the argument that politics should be subservient to economic issues.

The big deficiency in Indian democracy, observes Sudhakar Reddy, is the inability of any ruling party to poll 50+1% of the vote in elections to the Lok Sabha. Parties come to power with less than 35% of the votes. Giving suggestions for a better electoral system, he bats for a modified type of proportional representation which allows for 50% through proportional representation and 50% through direct election. Dwelling on state funding of the elections, he comments that it can prevent the illegitimate spending by multi-millionaires to some extent. He favours the adoption of a law that bans retired election commissioners from accepting any political or administrative responsibility for ten years after their retirement. Adoption of stringent laws that can prevent the entry of corporate house magnates to parliament need to be thought of. He laments over the fact that unfortunately the media in India has become part of the big business activity and as such has lost its freedom.

The need for comprehensive reforms in the electoral system becomes imperative if we take into consideration the challenges faced by the Election Commission to conduct free and fair elections in India. After this initial observation D. Raja argues for corrective action by the Election Commission and political parties in this regard. An interesting observation is that changes or amendment in electoral system is slow since the parties in power do not want to change a system that has been returning them. The author extends his support for the adoption of proportional representation system, state funding of political parties and steps against criminalization of politics.

In a scholarly article examining the feasibility of constitutional changes for electoral reforms and for the functioning of political parties, Dr. RLM Patil rejects proposals for recall, proportional representation and presidential system of government. The Election Commission should be given the power to register and de-register political parties. He reminds us that though the Indian constitution does not specify anywhere that we have to follow the British parliamentary path, we are pursuing that path without following the spirit of it. As the coalition governments have entered a confusing phase of flux and uncertainty, he advocates a radical step to allow major political parties to rule for a period proportionate to the percentage of seats won by them in the House. He also makes it clear that it is not the electoral outcome that forms the corner stone of democracy, but an alert public opinion, strong judiciary and independent media.

Dr Aruna Sivakami asserts that India should have a system of proportional representation as it has a multi-party system. She is right in pointing out that under the present system a big party which polls less than 45% votes like the congress party gets a comfortable majority in the House while a smaller party like the Socialists who polled 10% of the votes secures only a negligible number of seats. This results in under representation of minority social groups in terms of class, race and gender. The present electoral system as it encourages fragmentation and wastage of votes should have reduced the number of minor and small parties, but it has not. She wants reforms that would secure socially responsible and ethical political parties.

M.N. Prasad convinces us that electoral reforms for immunizing local bodies against party politics is a logical step since in the local bodies all elected members are co-sharers of the power to rule including planning and implementation of welfare and development programmes. He is correct in stating that political ideologies are of no real consequence at this level as policy making is absent in its functioning. Our experience is that party politics affects team work and impede their effective and transparent functioning.

V

Part IV of the volume consists of six articles under the rubric "Media, Civil Society and Elections". Highlighting the role of media on the democratic process, Sashi Kumar asserts that the free press is sine qua non of a true democracy and that Gandhiji was always alive to the power of the press. The freedom of the Indian media arises from fundamental rights part dealing with freedom of expression, freedom of movement and freedom to practise any profession unlike in USA, where the first amendment specifies that Congress shall make no laws which abridge the freedom of the press. In India it is widely accepted that censoring of the press would amount to curtailing democracy.

The article brushes aside the thinking that free press is a mismatch in a socialist society. The author is inimical of liberal democracies with free markets as they have ceased to be safe havens for press freedom. The paper cautions the public against games that party controlled TV channels play in India today. Looking ahead, the paper concludes with the idea that the news media in India should gain credibility by being accountable to the readers.

According to BRP Bhaskar, Indians have a misconception that election constitutes the most important element in the whole democratic process. He draws our attention to the fact that people have only little role during the inter election period. There was a close relationship between media and the political parties from the beginning of the freedom movement. News paper owners and editors were elected to our parliament supported by leading political parties. The 'paid news' phenomenon can be viewed as the continuation of such a relationship. Today we also see the entry of the political parties into the media business. But they also have their limitations in influencing the elections. The message that emanates from the paper is that the country needs a new media model which balance its profit motive.

T.N. Gopakumar, in his interesting paper "Elections and the Journalist's Dilemma" sounds critical when he states that the media often ignores issues of primary concern to people. In election reporting also such concerns do not find a place in the main stream. This is because of the various compulsions on the media. As the television is still a very young medium in India the tremendous pressure on media men has put them in a dilemma.

In another article on media and elections in India, Dr. Mirza Asmer Beg points to the growing phenomenon of elected representatives funding their poll campaigns with corporate backing. Temptations for manipulating the media are on the increase as today the popular culture is media culture. The last elections saw the culture of 'cover package' which meant no money, no news coverage. The scholar cites many instances to prove that money can get the better of ideology in elections. The paper sheds light on the urgency of dealing with the malaise of "paid news" which has spread deep into India's body politic.

After identifying the distressing trends in Indian politics like the growing cynicism about politics and political parties, Dr S.S. Sreekumar examines the role of the civil society in the electoral process of the country. As parliamentary democracy is not merely representative democracy but also participatory democracy the role of civil society can not be ignored or avoided as it helps making the right decision and rational choice. It can work as a vigil to the working of electoral process. The paper addresses issues like restructuring of electoral process, reform of the Election Commission, electoral expenses, poll related violence, multiplicity of contestants and duplication of names in electoral rolls.

The idea that any electoral reform aiming at widening the base of democracy should invariably lead to human rights protection and human development is articulated in the paper contributed by Dr P.S. Vijaya Natharaj. He points out that every election in India starts and ends with varying degrees of violation of human rights. He wants concrete steps for cleaning India's public life through a comprehensive amendment to the electoral law.

VI

The last part of the volume deals with the central theme "Agenda for Electoral Reforms". Dr P.J. Alexander rightly notes that electoral reform in India is not the result of a single piece of legislation, but the outcome of sustained pressure and persuasion put up by activists and civil society groups over the years. It is also an unfinished agenda. There is an earnest appeal from the author for carrying forward the struggle for electoral reforms. He notes with concern that in our legislature today we have more rich people than poor. The flow of money into election along with muscle power has ensured that there is today no level playing ground in the electoral contest. It is in this context that the paper looks at the viability of the suggestions for state funding of elections and disqualification of men with criminal records. The author affirms that short circuiting the judicial process has become all too common. Other important areas where attention should be paid according to the scholar are the stage of pre-poll arrangements and challenge in polling booths. The initiative of the civil society in electoral reforms is of utmost importance.

Dr Jaya Prakash Narayanan feels that for nurturing and sustaining our values through laws we require institutional mechanisms which would enforce values. Prevalence of competitive elections, political freedom, toleration of the defeated and the elected government functioning as the real executive are the positive traits of our democracy. Our staunch belief that we can do much better, make us seek further reforms. Naturally this urge motivates us to fight the play of illegitimate funds in elections, role of criminals in Politics, casteism, communalism, regionalism and linguism. For the people, elections have become meaningless because of our failure to demonstrate that electoral outcomes can make difference to their life in a significant way. The author comes up with the controversial statement that the Election Commission is an over glorified institution and that it is not the answer to India's political problems. The media in India is also not competent enough to expose the truth. He boldly states that the finances are not part of a political party's internal affairs. In the prevailing first-past-the-post system, there is a mad chase for the decisive marginal votes compelling politicians to resort to illegitimate practices. He feels that what is needed is to make it possible for people to get into power through legitimate means. The present situation also demands that legislators be freed from functioning as disguised executives. As a serious political activist, the scholar is convinced of the usefulness of independent anti-corruption institutions and feels that if people can get things done legitimately then it will root out criminalisation. The article ends with the positive observation that India is now ready for a fundamental transformation.

In India, there has been no dearth of government committees which went in to the issue of electoral reforms. From 1990 to 2010 eight committees were entrusted with this job beginning with the Goswami committee on Electoral Reforms (1990). Joining the public discourse on this subject Dr D. Jeevan Kumar in his well crafted paper highlights the four critical areas i.e. criminalisation of politics, financing elections, curbing electoral offences and malpractices and regulation of political parties. The scholar sounds serious when he observes that "deeper systemic reforms may need to be pursued to transform our procedural democracy in to a genuine one."

The best thing about electoral reforms is that it is a way to achieve the fruits of democracy. Dr. Midatala Rani in her paper on "An Agenda for Reforms" considers our democratic deficit more serious than budget deficit. While setting an agenda for electoral reforms she notes that elections in India have almost become a policing system.

Dr R. Sreekantan Nair points out the immeasurable distance between promise and performance with regard to the Indian electoral system. He notes with concern that we are regular in the periodic conduct of elections but ignore the essence and spirit of democratic election. The author demands a fixed term for representatives along with the preparation of a performance chart to be published periodically so that people can evaluate the performance of their representatives.

C.P. John takes a timely and critical look at the electoral system and the conduct of election through the prism of quality of democracy. He recalls the UN millennium declaration emphasising the quality of democratic elections and raises concern about its neglect in India. He points out that "freeness" and "fairness" constitutes the major fundamentals of the quality of democracy and that the concept of free and fair election can be applied to any election any where in the world. We also need to precisely define 'quality of election' in the Indian context as it faces stiff challenges from various sources. The author identifies state funding of elections, proper media support, auditing of party accounts, and amendment to the Representation of People Act as concrete steps towards attaining this goal.

Dr M. Kunhaman in his thought provoking paper boldly raises the question whether the electoral system as it exists today must continue? Inspite of the frank and scathing criticism, the author also offers a list of revolutionary reforms to bring in some order in the existing system. To him, the increasing tendency to abstain from voting shows the disillusionment of the people with electoral politics. He sounds realistic in stating that there is a disconnection between promises and performance by political parties. He craftfully sketches how in parliamentary democracy elections become more important than politics. To him, parliamentary democracy and equality won't go together – due to the caste – class – patriarchy axis existing in our country. It is indeed saddening that while the rich manage to elect the representatives of their liking, the poor do no get the leaders they deserve. The interim remedial measures suggested by him are revolutionary in content.

The consensus of the debate on Electoral Reforms seems to be that we cannot continue to live in the present state of affairs without radical reforms. The papers bring home to us the implications of subverting free and fair election in our democracy. It is not surprising that different scholars put forward different solutions, but all of them agree that the present system is no panacea. The task was to bring to focus the need for urgent electoral reforms. As we do not want to limit this important debate to academic circles alone we are presenting this to a wider circle with the hope that the citizens start reflecting on the ideas. We, on our part consider ourselves to be privileged to be part of such an endeavour.

Editors

List of Contributors

M. Hamid Ansari	Hon'ble Vice-President of India Prof (Dr) N.R. Madhava Menon Former Vice-Chancellor, National Juridical University, Kolkata, and Chairman, Dr S. Radhakrishnan Chair on Parliamentary Studies (Rajya Sabha).
Justice K.T. Thomas	Former Judge, Supreme Court of India.
P.D.T. Achary	Secretary General, Lok Sabha, India.
S.N. Sangita	Professor, Centre for Political Institutions, Governance and Development, Institute for Social and Economic Change, Nagarabhavi, Bangalore.
V. Vijayabalan	Former Principal, Government Law College, Thiruvananthapuram and Former Member Kerala State Public Service Commission.
Lekshmi Vijayabalan	BSc, LLM, MC, Halifax, Canada
A.D. Damodaran	Eminent Scientist and Social Activist and Former Director, Regional Research Laboratory, Thiruvananthapuram.
K.C. Sunny	Head, Department of Law, University of Kerala, Kariavattom, Thiruvananthapuram.
P.L. Dharma	Professor of Political Science, University of Mangalore, Mangalore
J. Prabhash	Professor of Political Science and Pro-Vice Chancellor, University of Kerala, Thiruvananthapuram.
K.M. George.	Associate Professor of Economics, Government Law College, Kozhikode, Kerala.
M.A. Hussain	Former Professor, Department of Political Science, S.V. University, Tirupati, Andhra Pradesh.
B. Venkatesula Reddy	Academic Consultant, Department of Political Science and Public

	Administration, S.V. University, Tirupati, Andhra Pradesh.
T.M. Joseph	Principal, Newman College, Thodupuzha, Kerala.
Jos Chathukulam	Director, Centre for Rural Management, Kottayam, Kerala.
K. Suryaprasad	Assistant Librarian, University of Kerala, Thiruvananthapuram.
C.E. Ajithkumar	Department of Agricultural Extension, College of Agriculture, Vellayani, Thiruvananthapuram.
M. Lathika	Associate Professor of Economics, N.S.S. College for Women, Karamana, Thiruvananthapuram
M. Vijaya Kumar	Hon'ble Minister for Parliamentary Affairs, Government of Kerala.
S. Sudhakar Reddy	Former MP and Deputy General Secretary, Communist Party of India.
D. Raja	Member of Parliament, (Rajya Sabha) and Secretary, Communist Party of India.
R.L.M. Patil	Former Professor and Chairman, Department of Political Science, Bangalore University and Member, Karnataka State Council for Higher Education.
Aruna Sivakami	Vice-Chancellor, Mother Teresa Women's University, Kodaikanal, Tamil Nadu.
M.N. Prasad	Former Chairman, Railway Board, Government of India.
Sashi Kumar	Chairman, Media Development Foundation and Asian College of Journalism, Chennai.
P.R.P. Bhaskar	Veternan Journalist and Social Activist.
T.N. Gopakumar	Vice-President, Asianet.
Mirza Asmer Beg	Professor, Department of Political Science, Aligarh Muslim University, Aligarh.
S.S. Sreekumar	Associate Professor, PG Department of Political Science, JNM Government College, Port Blair.

P.S. Vijaya Natharaj	Associate Professor and Head, Department of Political Science, Sree Narayana College, Chempazhanthi, Thiruvananthapuram, Kerala.
P.J. Alexander	Former Professor and Director, Institute of Management in Government and Director General of Police, Kerala.
Jayaprakash Narayanan	Leading Political Analyst and Chairman, Lok Satta Party, Andhra Pradesh.
Jeevan Kumar	Professor of Political Science and Director, Centre for Gandhian Studies, Bangalore University, Bangalore.
Midatala Rani	Professor, Department of Studies in Political Science, University of Mysore, Manasa Gangothri, Mysore.
R. Sreekantan Nair	Associate Professor of Political Science, VTM NSS College, Dhanuvachapuram, Thiruvananthapuram.
C.P. John	Member, State Planning Board, Kerala.
M. Kunhaman	Professor and Dean, School of Rural Development, Tata School of Social Science, Tuljapur, Maharashtra.

Part I

Electoral System in India : A Critique

1 Revisiting the Debate on Electoral Reforms*

M. Hamid Ansari

This valuable seminar focuses on a theme vital to the functioning of our democracy. The subject matter of the debate intersects the domains of theory and practice and has implications for both. There is also a need to revisit the concepts, premises, definitions and domains since systematic restatements do help in clarifying the form of facts under scrutiny.

Political scientists may recall debate initiated way back in 1967 by the publication of Hanna Pitkin's thesis on the idea of representation as a public institutionalised arrangement where representation emerges not from any single action by any one participant, but from the overall structure and functioning of the system. For this reason political representation is different from private representation; the former is intrinsically and inevitably transformative and creates for a dispersed and diffused constituency an interest or a principle that did not pre-exist the act of representation. Political representation could take different forms; it could be formalistic, symbolic, descriptive or substantive. Any of these puts in place a set of markers, of authorisation and accountability, to assess the efficacy and success of the exercise of representative democracy thus undertaken.

II

It is relevant to recall the Objectives Resolution moved by Jawaharlal Nehru in the Constituent Assembly on 13th December, 1946, stressed that 'all power and authority of this Sovereign Independent India, its constituent parts and organs of government, are derived from the people'. Pursuant to this "We the people of India' resolved in the Preamble of the Constitution to constitute India as a Republic dedicated to the attainment of justice, liberty, equality and fraternity. The text spelt out the essential detail: a representative, parliamentary democracy based on adult franchise;

* (From the Inaugural Address of Hon'ble Vice President of India Shri M. Hamid Ansari at the National Seminar on Electoral Reforms organised by C. Achyutha Menon Study Centre and Library on 8th July 2010 at Kanakakkunnu Palace, Thiruvananthapuram)

the sub-text anchored it in Rule of Law. Judicial pronouncements have amplified and highlighted four elements pertaining to these essentials:

1. A democratic set up is a part of the basic structure of the Constitution. It proceeds on the capacity of the people to elect their representatives and faith in the representatives to represent the people.

2. Democracy proceeds on the basic assumptions of popular sovereignty where the country is governed by the representatives of the people and that there exists equality among citizens in arriving at decisions affecting them.

3. There can be no democracy without periodical elections to ascertain popular will. These should be free and fair, in reality and form.

4. Democracy is not just a mechanism of forming and running a government but represents a matrix of relations between citizens which allows for every citizen to live his/her life to the fullest, in dignity, and able to develop, exert and enjoy his/her capabilities.

The various dimensions of electoral reforms have been debated in governmental and non-governmental fora. Many suggestions have been made. Some have been incorporated in the framework of rules; others remain on the table. The debate, to my mind, is selective rather than comprehensive.

Our founding fathers adopted specific electoral systems for specific institutions of the state. While elections to the Lower Houses of the Central and State legislatures were on the basis of adult suffrage and first-past-the-post in delimited constituencies, elections to the Upper Houses was on the basis of proportional representation through a single transferable vote. A similar electoral system of proportional representation through a single transferable vote with different electorates has also been prescribed for the elections of the president and the vice-president.

Since every decision has a context, a re-look at the occasion and the legislative intent is educative. The issue of representativeness came up for discussion in the Constituent Assembly in the Report on Minority Rights that was submitted on 8th August, 1947. In the debate that followed, one Member moved an amendment suggesting qualified joint electorates and stipulating that a scheduled caste candidate before being declared elected "shall have secured not less than 35 per cent of the votes polled by the Scheduled Castes in the elections for the reserved seat". He argued that it was important to demonstrate the scheduled caste representativeness of a victor in a seat reserved for scheduled castes. Another member argued that "there should be confidence in the minds of the minorities that their views are properly represented in the legislature by persons in whom they have confidence and in whose election they have a reasonably fair voice". Yet another proposal was for abolition of reserved constituencies and introduction of a system of proportional representation with multi member constituencies by means of cumulative vote for election to the lower houses of legislature.

In response, Dr Ambedkar gave three reasons for preferring the first-past-the-post system over the proportional representation system:

- Absence of a high level of literacy essential for proportional representation.
- Apprehension of a fragmented legislature that would impede stable government and maintenance of law and order.
- Disruption of the agreement already arrived at between the various minority communities and the majority community.

It would be recalled that the Two-Member Constituencies (Abolition) Act of January, 1961, abolished the two-member and three-member constituencies to which elections took place in the 1952 and 1957 general elections.

How well has the first-past-the-post system worked? Electoral record for the Lok Sabha elections shows that in the past five general elections the number of winning candidates who secured 50 per cent or more of the valid votes polled has varied between 121 and 221; it was 121 in 2009. Earlier, the Venkatachaliah Commission had surveyed the record of three general elections to conclude that over two-thirds of the members of the Lok Sabha and almost 90 per cent of the members of some state legislative assemblies were elected on a minority vote.

A perceptive observer of our electoral scene has rightly focused on what he calls the 'paradox' of a deepening representative democracy coexisting with a thinning of the very idea of representation. This paradox, he adds, plays out differently in different domains of the democratic arena and most commonly takes the form of an encounter between a dynamic political process and an inflexible institutional response.

III

Given this record and six decades after these formational structure were put in place, a few questions unavoidably come to mind :

- What is the representative-ness of the elected representative? Our system works on the principles of *plurality* rather than of *majority*.
- Why has the electoral system of first-past-the-post to the lower houses of legislature produced fragmented legislature and systemic instability since the third decade of the Republic, of a nature that was associated with the proportional representation system?
- Has the dis-proportionality between the share of votes obtained and the share of legislative seats won, eroded credibility and representativeness of our legislators?
- Is there merit in the suggestion that the government and the Election Commission conduct a careful and full examination of the introduction of a two-round system, with the second round conducted between the two leading candidates in each constituency on the day after the first round? Is the time opportune now to conduct such an examination in consultation with all political parties?
- Does the current electoral system encourage a politics defined by 'who you are' and 'where you live' rather than 'what you believe in' and 'what you want to achieve'?
- What can be done to address the grievance of under-representation and unequal access to political power emanating from the Muslims? The data is compelling and disturbing.
- How are we to overcome the implications, in terms of the principle of one person, one vote, one value, of the 84th Amendment that froze the number of seats in the Lok Sabha and the state legislative assemblies till the year 2026?

Electoral Systems are important because they translate the votes of people into legislative seats and hence into exercise of political power. Their credibility and representativeness are critical elements in bringing about stable polities that are essential for socio-economic progress.

Electoral system also have an undue influence on the evolution of party systems, their role and their cohesion. They can encourage inner-party democracy or can suppress dissent. Electoral systems can also influence the nature of political mobilisation, alliance formation and societal accommodation. They can spark societal conflict or facilitate conflict management.

It is thus important for us to consider our electoral system in the context of our experience of the last six decades, the mandate of our constitutional framework and the future outcomes that we desire from our polity.

Any debate on the question of electoral system reform must look at enhancing representativeness, promoting societal accommodation and conciliation, incorporating constitutional and international safeguards to vulnerable groups, providing accountable, stable and efficient governance, enhancing legislative oversight and encouraging the evolution and development of effective and internally-democratic political parties.

This paper has highlighted some dimensions of electoral reforms which, I believe, have not been sufficiently addressed. I believe we should also guard against mechanistic analyses and suggestions for electoral reform. One analyst has opined that reforms "cannot be introduced by legislative fiat, but require the hard labour of politics and self-transformation". Are our polity, political parties, their leaderships and our elected representatives ready and prepared for this hard labour of politics and self-transformation?

2 Electoral System : Massive Experiment in Democracy

N.R. Madhava Menon

By all standards the electoral system in India is the largest endeavour ever in democratic governance involving over 600 million voters and a massive machinery of men and material of unprecedented proportions. Seeing the initial hiccups of violence, booth capturing and low voter turnout, a keen foreign observer of Indian elections once remarked in 1980s that the Republic would not be able to sustain the system which might possibly end with the eighth or ninth general Elections! It is to the credit of the Indian people and the strength of its political institutions that the country has had many more general Elections since then, each time improving the standards of fairness and inclusiveness in the process. Therefore, any objective assessment must first acknowledge the positive and endearing features of the system before criticizing the gaps and inadequacies which however persist in varying degrees.

What Makes the Electoral System?

'A system; is defined as an organised complex and inter-connected process with a common structure and function. It has to have clear objectives and guidelines set out in the form of norms and standards guiding all the constituent parts. In the case of the electoral system, they constitute the electoral laws and procedures. To make a good working system, the laws have to be clear, specific and widely accepted as binding conduct for all concerned. If there are gaps and ambiguities, distortions in implementation may occur which lead to the malfunctioning of the system affecting its efficiency, purity and purpose.

The second important limb of 'a system' is the set of institutions or organisations which are set up under the laws to administer them for the purpose for which laws are made. In the case of the electoral system these include the Delimitation Commission, the electoral rolls, the Election Commission, the Election Tribunal, the independent observers etc.

Finally, the third limb of 'a system' is the personnel who man the institutions, whose competence and character determine the quality of outcome and the efficiency of the system.

In the above context, if one were to probe the electoral system one could focus on the electoral laws or the structures and institutions involved or the personnel who manage it or on all of them. The agenda of this national seminar is largely around the institutions and actors taking the electoral laws as given. Should the election be based on a two-party system or on proportional representation or on first-past-the-poll system or on compulsory voting or with freedom to case negative vote or to be financed by the State and similar questions seem to be outside the given law. These issues raise fundamental questions as to how representative are the elected representatives and how effective is the individual's right of franchise to determine the nature of government in Indian democracy.

The Indian Constitution has a part of six Articles (Articles 324 to 329) devoted entirely to 'Elections'. It vests the power to manage elections in an independent Election Commission with wide-ranging powers and freedom from the executive government. It gurantees universal adult franchise with the voter having the option to vote or not. Parliament and State Legislatures are empowered to make laws with respect to all matters relating to, or in connection with elections to either house of parliament or either house of the legislature of a state including the preparation of electoral rolls, the delimitation of constituencies and all other matters necessary for securing the due constitution of such House or Houses. Even courts are barred in electoral matters except by an election petition in such manner as may be provided for by law made by the appropriate Legislature.

The law enacted by Parliament (The Representation of the People Act, 1951) provides for periodic elections, single member constituencies with first-past-post winners and a number of norms and procedures intended to secure free and fair polls.

A Critique of Election Law

Election is not an end in itself. It is hailed as a means to ensure a representative, inclusive, efficient and participatory government. Does the existing election law and procedure enable that?

This is what a senior journalist-cum-parliamentarian has to say in this regard: ... "We must judge an electoral and political system on certain criteria. Is it putting into place persons who can actually legislate? Is it putting into office persons who can actually administer a country of a billion people?"

The standard argument for a first-past-the-post system over, say, that of proportional representation is that the former yields secure majorities, and, therefore, decisive governments. The latter is supposed to provide an incentive for progressive fragmentation of the electorate and of parties. Our experience is the exact opposite. The first-past-the-post system has given the maximum inducement to splinter the electorate, and to go on fragmenting parties….. It is supposed to induce the growth of a two party system and encourage large parties to broad-base their appeal. It is supposed to give the people a greater say in the selection of candidates. Yet, in every particular, in India it is leading to the opposite…. In a word, 99 per cent of the members got into the Lok Sabha by getting less than half the electors to vote for them. Almost 60 per cent got in with the endorsement of less than 30 per cent of electors in their constituencies. Even if we consider only the electors who actually turned out to vote, 60 per cent of the members got in on a minority vote. The unrepresentativeness of governments and legislators in the States is even greater… Pointing to this alarming feature, the Constitution Review Commission observed, 'In some cases those who would otherwise have forfeited their security deposit have been declared elected as they had obtained the highest number of votes amongst the candidates'. Is this representativeness? (Arun Shourie, The Parliamentary System, Rupa 25-32)

If candidates get elected with a woeful minority of votes, how representative the system is? Does the election law address this fundamental issue?

Let me move on to another drawback in our electoral system, the issue of criminals in politics and criminalisation of politics. In August 1997 the then Election Commissioner Mr G.V.G. Krishnamurthy released a press note entitled *Sample Profile of Criminalisation of Politics* in which he disclosed that a large chunk of sitting MPs and MLAs are people against whom serious criminal cases are pending. Nearly 1500 of the 13,000 candidates who contested the preceding elections had a criminal record of either murder or dacoity or rape-history sheeters in police language! One former Prime Minister (I.K. Gujral) even lamented the fact that in Parliament 'we are rubbing our shoulders with persons with whom we would be ashamed to be seen outside.'

The representation of the People Act does contain provisions to disqualify a person from contesting an election if he is convicted of any of the many offences listed in section 8(1) and (2). Sub-section (3) proceeds to disqualify a person convicted of an offence, other than the ones so listed, for which he was sentenced to imprisonment for not less than two years. Accordingly the Election Commission ordered the returning officers to reject the nomination papers of such candidates who are covered under Section 8. The issue was agitated both in Parliament and in the Supreme Court and the law was diluted to such an extent that criminals continued to flourish in electoral politics. Does our electoral system help us to get a clean parliament to represent the world's largest democracy?

Same has been the fate of the law debarring candidates who promote feelings of enemity or hatred between citizens on ground of religion, place of birth, language or caste to win elections. The penal code punishes such activity. Organisations can be banned for such acts. Yet elections and electioneering are dividing people on narrow loyalties and weakening the very concept of secularism which keeps the republic united and strong.

The devastating effect of money power in elections is now well documented. There are all types of laws regulating expenditure on elections, most of them only on paper.

Election Commission and Commissioners : A Critique

Electiòns being a contest for capturing power between opposing parties, it is important that its organisations and management are not only fair and free but also appear to be so. The Indian Constitution attempts to secure it by creating an autonomous Election Commission totally independent of the executive of the day. However, the Constitutional status by itself could not secure the independence as later events have shown. For one thing, as noted earlier, the special law enacted for the conduct of elections had so many loopholes which made the Commission helpless in many respects. Many of the proposals of the Election Commission for electoral law reform were not acceptable to government or parliament.

However, the Commission came up with a "model code of conduct" for electioneering which in the hands of strong Election Commissioners proved to be an effective instrument to redeem the purity and fairness of elections. The Code eventually assumed the force of law and political parties came to fear it the most. The role of Mr. T.N. Seshan, the powerful Election Commissioner of 1990s is remarkable in this regard. It was Seshan who asserted the power of the Commission over all election workers from whatever government they were on loan and refused to accept the executive's attempt to keep bureaucratic discipline over them during election campaigns. A similar confrontation with government and politicians marked the delineation of the "electoral period" during which the Commission's model code of conduct would be in effect which, Seshan argued should begin with the official announcement of the date of elections. Ultimately his argument had to be accepted despite resistance from a variety of sources. In all these challenges to its authority, the Election Commission used the courts to ventilate the constitutional foundations of its special powers during "electoral time". The Model Code was put to good use by employing immediate punishments against violators. Government largesse of any sort, which could be interpreted as an attempt to sway votes was open to close scrutiny during election campaigns. To give teeth to his expansive interpretation of the model code, Mr. Seshan issued orders claiming authority to "de-recognise" any party that blatantly violated the Code under the terms of the 1968 Election Symbols Ordinance.

Seshan's tenure at the Election Commission demonstrated how, in spite of resistance from central and state governments, the Commission could exercise its constitutional power to ensure free and fair polls and thereby give importance to the free choice of the voter. The electoral system of the country may not have changed significantly but certainly assumed a place in public consciousness ever since Seshan's activism of the 1990s. The executive was so disturbed that it forced him to share authority with two additional Election Commissioners. The character and loyalties of the persons appointed as Election Commissioners became crucial both for the Govenrment and the opposition and controversies followed in the public domain. Today, the Election Commission's own politics is a matter of public debate. The question of popular sovereignty and the sanctity of the "free will" of the individual voter are in danger of losing its status if the appointment of election commissioners is not freed from manipulation by political forces. More importantly, those appointed have to rise above narrow loyalties and political ambitions if the system, inherently imperfect, were to deliver to the advancement of democracy and constitutional morality.

Article 324(2) says : "The Election Commission shall consist of the Chief Election Commissioner and such number of other Election Commissioners, if any, as the president may from time to time fix and the appointment shall, *subject to the provisions of any law made in that behalf by Parliament,* be made by the President". (emphasis added). Apparently the Constitution did not want to leave the matter to the discretion of the executive. However, no law was enacted under clause (2) to regulate the power of appointment, though many proposals were advanced to bring in an advisory committee including the leader of the opposition, the Speaker and the Chief Justice of India. In appointing the other election commissioners, the Chief Election Commissioner was also to be consulted. But why should the executive government curb its own powers by law if that can be avoided?

Conclusion

While India can take pride in the smooth transfer of power through conduct of periodic elections which indeed is a massive exercise of popular sovereignty, there are many gaps in the system which undermines the freedom of the individual voter. The legal framework is not strong enough to correct the distortions which crept into the polity. Alternatives have been proposed, but the political class seem reluctant to reform the system which may empower the voter as against the power they enjoy at present in manipulating the system.

Independent and fearless election commissioners can still direct the system to perform; but a system cannot sustain itself on the chance of getting enlightened persons in leadership positions who are prepared to take risks. As such, reform of electoral law is a felt necessity; the earlier it is done, the better for Indian democracy.

3 Elections in India—Should be Choice of the Electorate

Justice K.T. Thomas

The Constitution of India envisages India to be a democratic Republic, which means the government, both at the centre and of the states, should be elected by the people of India. To ensure that fair elections shall be held for that purpose, the Constitution has created an independent body called "Election Commission". The Indian Parliament has passed legislation for governing elections both to parliament and to the state legislatures. Representatives of people came to be elected subsequently. Political parties were not contemplated in the Constitution in the Representation of the Peoples Act at the original stage. But through the introduction of the 10th Schedule of the Constitution and through various amendments of the Representation of the Peoples Act, provisions relating to political parties were also made.

With all the above provisions I do not agree that the elected person from each constituency is the true representative of the electorate of that constituency. In other words, a vast majority of the elected representatives got elected with far less than 50% of the total electorate, and in many cases they secure only less than 50% of even the total votes polled. Today when three or four candidates are contesting from the constituency and percentage of polling does not cross 65 on an average, in many instances candidates securing even 20 to 25% of the total electorate would get declared elected. By a fiction he is treated as the representative of the people of his constituency.

According to my perception, the above fictitious representation makes only a farce of the reality to make a person representative of the people. The defective system can be rectified if the present leaders would make a serious effort. A system of preferential voting should be introduced in the present place. It is in the preferential system of voting, the President of India is elected today. I find that by computerisation of the election process such as polling and counting, it is far easier today for introducing the system of preferential voting than it could have been done before. During counting, the candidate securing the lowest number of votes can be eliminated and his second preference votes could be counted easily through the computer. Like that the candidate securing more than 50% of the votes can be identified.

Voting should be made compulsory and non-voting should be made an offence. Those voters who are unable to reach the polling booth on account of valid reasons, whatsoever, should be provided facility to exercise their franchise.

Thirdly, the galloping expenses for election campaign must also be curtailed drastically. Otherwise elections would become monopoly of the rich and democracy will transform into plutocracy. One of the methods which can be suggested by me is this: Elections to local bodies, state assemblies and Lok Sabha shall be held on the same day. There is no necessity of holding by elections in any constituency, because death of the elected person must enable the President, or Governor or Election Commission to choose another person recommended by the political party whose candidate won the election at the first instance. If the candidate who died happened to be an independent, then the choice can be given to the president or the Governor to nominate any one from the constituency in his place as for the remaining period.

Another measure to curtail the election expenses is to drastically reduce the interval between the clearance of nomination papers and the date of polling.

In fact, the above suggestions were mooted years ago by a seasoned statesman B.K.Nehru. It is unfortunate that his suggestions were not even considered or discussed at the national level.

Another suggestion which can be made is that mid-term elections should be averted. Today the President can appoint Prime Minister and Governor can appoint a Chief Minister subject to the condition that he should enjoy the confidence of the Parliament or the State Legislature as the case may be. If a vote of no confidence is moved, the resolution for that purpose shall be worded peremptorily one for declaring that the house has no confidence in the present incumbent but has confidence in 'X'. Such a procedure can easily be brought in even without an amendment of the Constitution. In fact, a recommendation in that line was made by the Law Commission of India headed by Justice Jeevan Reddy. Only the rules of the Lok Sabha or the state assembly need be amended to make this possible.

By-elections and mid term elections are the legacies of British democracy. Britain can afford it being a tiny country in size. But a vast country like USA does not allow by-elections or mid-term elections for which they have incorporated necessary provisions. India is a vast country and also the largest democracy in the world. We should learn lessons from other democracies in respect of achieving stability and for averting frequent intermittent elections.

4 Revisiting Electoral System in India

P.D.T. Achary

India is hailed as the largest democracy in the world. Introduction of Parliamentary democracy and popular elections based on adult franchise are the boldest experiments done by the founding fathers of the Republic. Boldest experiments because, at the dawn of independence, the Indian society was not yet ready to comprehend the dynamics of a democratic polity based on universal adult franchise. It is the vision and determination of the great men who led the nation into freedom which made it possible for India to become a functioning democracy.

Free and fair elections are the life blood of democracy. Through periodic elections the people not only choose their representatives to govern themselves but also sustain democracy. The Constitution of India lays out the structure of the polity with institutionalized arrangements for the growth of democracy. Parliament of India under the command of the Constitution enacted the whole corpus of election laws which govern the conduct of free and fair elections in the country. The election laws constitute a code by itself which has been further strengthened by the various pronouncements of the judiciary from time to time.

The most prominent feature of elections in India is the first-past-the-post system where whoever gets the highest number of votes gets elected. All elections in India since 1952 have been held under this system. Electoral reforms became a subject of discussion since the late sixties when problems basically unconnected with the electoral system began to arise. When the monolithic character of the premier political formation in India began to change, a radical transformation in Indian politics began to take place with unforeseen consequences. The rise of political formations based on regional aspirations or cultural separateness and the progressive shrinkage of national perspective and the sharpening of adversarial nature of politics which slowly changed the tone and tenor of political interactions were the noteworthy features of this transformational stage. The successive decades saw many more radical changes in the Indian political scene which sharpened the awareness of the need to take a serious look at the electoral system. The most serious development and I must say the most tragic development which took place in the Indian electoral scene is the realisation among the political class that the appeal of ideology or nationalism or policies and programmes was not strong enough to secure the support of the people. Thus money and muscle entered the electoral scene and became a major factor in the democratic elections in India. Indian democracy thus entered a new phase in its evolution. Right thinking people believe that democracy in India needs a course correction. Therefore, the demand for electoral reforms became more and more strident. The political class responded to this demand with committees. We had the Jagannath Rao led Joint Parliamentary Committee, the Tarkunde Committee, the Dinesh Goswamy Committee, the Indrajit Gupta Committee and so on. All these Committees recommended various steps to reform the electoral system. But these recommendations were not very radical. Some recommendations related mainly to the date from which election expenses are to be counted, prohibition of contributions by companies to political parties and audit of accounts of candidates is and parties. Some other committees on the other hand recommended that election expenses by political parties or individuals other than the candidate or his agent should not be taken into account. One of the committees recommended the introduction of a partially proportional representation system and some limited financial assistance to political parties by the state. The government responded to these recommendations by incorporating some of them by way of amendments in the Representation of People Act.

The problems which afflict the elections in India are too complex to be tackled by these recommendations and amendments. One thing which at once comes to the notice of an observer of the election scene is that changes in the election law have been slow and few. The ruling parties showed no alacrity in bringing about far reaching reforms. So the debate on electoral reforms continues endlessly.

A major problem which the Indian democratic system is facing today is the increasing criminalization of politics. Legislators with criminal records adorning the benches in the Legislatures is not a very happy sight. Legislators being brought to the House straight from jails to attend the sessions of assemblies or parliament under Police escort is not a rare sight in India. There was a member in the 13th and 14th Lok Sabha who was involved in as many as 33 criminal cases involving murder, dacoity and rape. That member was defeated in the 15th Lok Sabha but the member who defeated him is seeking security cover from the government because he fears that he will be killed by that man. There may be many such cases in the Assemblies. Statistics show that the percentage of legislators with criminal record is increasing. Criminals becoming lawmakers is an entirely Indian phenomenon which throws up many disturbing questions about the credibility of the democratic system. The fact that these men are being elected by the voters points to another disturbing aspect of Indian democracy. In a fight between a decent man and a criminal, the criminal will most probably get elected. The political class has not looked at this problem with the seriousness it deserves.

The Representation of People Act provides for disqualification of a person for becoming and for being a member of a legislature if he has been convicted of an offence and sentenced to imprisonment for not less than six months in certain cases and in other cases not less than two years. The catch lies in the word 'conviction'. Disqualification will not arise unless conviction takes place. Criminals are entering the legislatures including Parliament taking advantage of this loophole. A criminal is innocent until convicted by a court of law as per the principle of jurisprudence. The resourceful criminals ensure that his case never reaches the stage of conviction. So he can stand for election and with his tremendous muscle power and money win the election and enter the assembly or parliament. The Law Commission had addressed this issue in its 170th report and made a recommendation that a person should be disqualified unless he files a declaration whether any charge in respect of an offence listed in section 8 (b) of the Representation of People Act, 1951, has been framed. The Election Commission has suggested in one of its reports to the Government that any person who is accused of any offence punishable with imprisonment for five years or more should be disqualified provided that the competent court of law has taken cognizance of the offence and framed the charges against him. In the opinion of the Election Commission a person who is facing trial in a serious offence should be kept out of the electoral fray in the greater public interest.

In my view there is great merit in this recommendation of the Commission. Under Section 228 of the Code of Criminal Procedure, a charge is framed only after consideration of the record of the case and the documents thereof and after hearing the accused and the prosecution by the Court. Thus framing of charge is an important stage in the trial of a criminal case where the court applies its mind to the material and documents on record to find out whether the facts emerging therefrom disclose the existence of all the ingredients of the offence. The Commission, therefore, rightly thought that if charge framed against an accused who is involved in a serious crime, he should be disqualified from contesting an election. But no action has been taken on this recommendation. If this recommendation had been acted upon perhaps many of the criminal elements would not have entered the legislatures. We must be able to make a choice between the right of a criminal to be treated as innocent until proved guilty and the sanctity of a legislature. We can't have both.

There is a general impression that elections in India have become the game of the rich and the powerful and are in the danger of losing their democratic character. Enormous amount of money is spent in the elections by parties and individuals. The Election Commission itself made some calculation about it some time ago. Billions of rupees are spent in a general election to the House of the People. I don't really understand why so much money is required to be spent in an election. The law permits a candidate to spend a maximum of Rs 25 lakh in a Parliamentary election and if a candidate is proved to have spent more than that his election will be set aside by the Court. If you work out the total permissible expenditure of Lok Sabha it comes to Rs 135 crores. But the actual expenditure is in astronomical figures. There is no minimum and no maximum. But why do people spend so much money to get elected? There is no guarantee that one will win the elections if a huge amount of money is spent. This naked use of money power corrupts the mind of the voters and degrades democracy.

Some of the Committees referred to earlier had suggested State funding of elections to curb the excessive use of money power. But this idea has not been examined seriously so far. The basic question is why should elections be so expensive as to become totally unaffordable to an ordinary citizen? Can't elections be fought with minimum of resources? I have come across members of parliament who have claimed that their election expenses were really within the permissible limits. It is possible and it should also be possible to curb the vulgar display of money. That is the duty of the election authorities. Tough measures to monitor and curb the ostentatious display of money are required. Is it necessary to organise a motorcade of 20 or 30 cars and block the traffic to get the votes? Is it necessary to change the posters every day to get the votes? I don't think it is necessary. I have always felt that the intellectual content in the public speeches during an election is shrinking. All this situation is the result of a wrong perception of the thinking of the public. I don't think that the people are very much impressed by the vulgar display of money or the traffic block. As regards the State funding of elections, I feel that it deserves to be seriously examined. There is no sense in rejecting this idea without examining it.

Political parties are the key operators of the political system. The Constitution of India did not contain any reference to political parties till the 10th Schedule was added to it. This schedule accords an important place for the political parties. But the proliferation of political parties introduces a comic element in the Indian elections. In the Lok Sabha itself there are 38 parties. In the context of electoral reforms, should we not take a look at this scene and seriously think of measures to discourage the proliferation of political parties and slowly move towards some kind of consolidation of parties. Indian society is truly a very complex one. At the subterranean level there is bewildering sectarianism. Narrow loyalties form the base of its hierarchical layers and therefore a comprehensive, holistic social perspective becomes almost impossible. Democracy which is based on the concept of egalitarianism is no guarantee that these hidden tendencies will not resurface in a forceful way and make India just an aggregate of nationalities. To avoid this danger of balkanisation, a serious examination of available options is necessary. I do not propose to specify these options. However, I feel that some rational criteria should be laid down to determine the eligibility of political formations to contest elections to Parliament. This will ultimately lead to a healthy consolidation of political parties and stabilisation of political system.

One of the serious deficiencies of the Indian electoral system is the shrinking vote base of the winning candidates. A large percentage of winning candidates get elected on a minority of votes. As per statistics only 3 out of 543 MPs secured more then 50 per cent of the votes polled. This means majority of candidates who get elected do not in the real sense represent the majority of voters. Political thinkers and columnists have suggested that law should be amended to provide that only those who get 50% plus votes should be declared elected. This, on the face of it, looks an attractive proposition. But, I am not sure how practical it would be. In fact multiplicity of parties in a constituency results in the fragmentation of votes. So in most cases the candidates who get elected poll less than 50 per cent votes.

Carefully crafted electoral reforms make democracy more meaningful and relevant to the changing times. But unfortunately a lot of confusion prevails in this area in India. Conflicting and contradictory suggestions and recommendations have been made by committees and individuals. There is a need to bring about greater clarity into the debate on electoral reforms. There is almost a consensus that there is urgent need to bring about reforms. But there is no agreement on the substance of the reforms. I don't think the proportional representation is an answer to the problems we are facing in this area. The objects of any electoral reforms in India should be *(i)* to stop criminals from contesting elections *(ii)* to eliminate the play of big money and thereby restore sanity in the electoral contest and *(iii)* bring back programmes and policies to the centre stage of elections. No comprehensive measures have ever been taken to achieve these objects. We keep groping in the dark. Any attempts at reform without keeping these objects in view will be non-productive and an exercise in self-delusion.

Any system can survive only if the people have faith in it. With all its imperfections, democracy has taken roots in India. Electoral reforms should be a process which could make every citizen feel that his opinion matters. Any attempt to manipulate or corrupt his mind can only weaken democracy.

Therefore it is high time that the enlightened citizens and serious minded political parties pay attention to the issue of electoral reforms seriously and generate strong public opinion in favour of it.

5 Electoral Process and Inclusive Governance

S.N. Sangita

India is one of the few developing countries, which has retained and nourished the parliamentary democracy for the last six and half decades. Elections are held regularly and governments are changed periodically. Human rights are protected and many welfare programmes are undertaken. However, its performance in promoting inclusive governance (responsive, transparent and accountable) and improving the quality of life is not at the desired level. A large percentage of population are poor, malnourished and illiterate. The elected governments (federal, state and local) are insensitive to the needs and aspirations of people. Increasing scams and scandals in public places has eroded people's faith in the integrity and credibility of the government. The emergence of parallel governments (private armies, buying of jobs, transfers, licenses, permits, and building plans) and parallel economies (black money or tainted money generated from tax evaders, land grabbers, smugglers, excise and other contractors), along with spread of the insurgent, radical and terrorist movements reflect people's helplessness, frustration and anger with the government.

The non-responsiveness of the elected governments to the people can be attributed to the electoral system and functioning of political parties, which have profound influence on the quality of the leadership (choice of representatives and leaders) and policies. Both electoral system and political parties are responsible for election of increasing number of leaders with money, muscle and communal (religion and caste) power over the years. Added to this, the election of majority leaders by minority vote has further undermines the credibility of the leaders because a large percent of them do not enjoy the confidence of the people.

This paper analyses the electoral practices and functioning of political parties with a view to electing responsive and accountable leaders in promoting inclusive governance in India. The paper also deals with the electoral process and political parties in India. The experiences of India's elections and the problems in selecting responsive leaders over the last six and half decades are discussed. The influence of money, criminal and communal power in elections is also examined.

I

Electoral Processes

Background

India is the second largest country in terms of population after china and the largest democracy in the world. India is a constitutional democracy with a parliamentary system of government at the federal, state and sub state levels. General elections to Lok Sabha and state legislative assemblies in India are held under the supervision, direction and control of a constitutional body—the Election Commission of India[1], while elections to the sub state level local bodies—panchayats and nagarpalikas—are the responsibility of State Election commission. 15 general elections and a number of elections at the state and sub state levels are organised ever since the modern Indian nation state came into existence on 15th of August 1947[2].

Laws Governing Elections

India has a comprehensive structure of laws to administer and conduct its elections. The formal legal framework for all these elections rests on certain provisions of the Constitution, the Representation of the People Act 1950, the Representation of the People Act 1951, the presidential and vice-presidential Elections Act 1952, the Delimitation Act 1972, and the various rules and regulations framed and orders issued under these statutes. In addition, certain provisions of the Indian Penal Code and a few other acts are relied upon to provide for punishment as well as disqualification of candidates and members of the various houses[3].

Indian Elections—Scale of Operation

The world's largest democracy holds general election once in five years to the Lok Sabha, state legislative assemblies, and to the office of the president and vice president. It may be worthwhile to note some significant features regarding the mammoth election exercise in India. The number of voters has gone up from 17.32 crore in 1952 to 60.23 crore in 1998. During the same period, the number of polling stations has gone up from 1.96 lakh to 7.65 lakh. As many as 85 lakh to 9 lakh polling booths had to be erected in the general elections in 1999, and 45 to 50 lakh personnel had to be deployed. Around 67.5 crore people caste their votes in the 1999 general election. The Election Commission employed almost 50 lakh polling personnel and over 10.7 crore electronic voting machines. A vast number of civilian police and security forces including home guards, National Cadet Corps (NCC) and para military personnel were deployed to carry out the elections peacefully. The government expenditure on holding elections has gone up steeply from just Rs.11 crore in 1952 elections to Rs 626 crore in 1998 and a staggering figure of Rs 900 crore in 1999. It was around Rs 1000 crore in the 2004 elections.

The number of candidates contesting each election has also steadily increased. The average number of candidates in each constituency rose-up to 26.3 in 1996 from 3.8 in 1952 (Table 5.1).

It was 16.7 in 1991 election. In Modakurichi assembly constituency of Tamil Nadu, 1033 candidates contested in the election to the Legislative Assembly in 1996. The ballot papers were in the form of a booklet. However this number has come down significantly due to amendments to the act by increasing the size of the deposit and making the number of people who have to nominate a candidate larger (Election Commission of India, 2004).

As on 1998, there were seven national parties, and 35 state parties, and 620 registered unrecognised parties. A look at the results of the last five general elections reveals that there is a decline in the performance of the national parties taken together both in terms of total number of seats won as well as their vote share (Table 5.2).

State parties and other registered parties gained at the cost of national parties during this period. This is one of the factors that have contributed to federal coalition governments in the recent past.

All the state parties, put together, could get only 27 seats in 1989 elections. They improved their tally to 51 in 1991 and 129 in the 1996 elections. But there was a decline in seat share to 101 in 1998 and subsequently an increase to 158 in the 1999 election. There was a corresponding increase in their vote share also. In the 1989 election their vote share was 9.28 per cent of the total valid votes polled. In 1991 they improved by a clear margin of 3.7 percent taking it to 12.98 per cent. In the 1996 elections they got 22.43 per cent of votes. In the 1998 election their vote share declined marginally to 18.79 per cent but increased again to 26.93 per cent in the 1999 polls.

Registered parties together had 19, 4, 4, 49 and 10 representatives in the last five Lok Sabhas respectively. Their vote share was 6.13 per cent in 1989, 2.19 per cent in 1991, 3.22 per cent in 1996, 10.87 per cent in

Table 5.1. Year-wise Polled Votes in Parliamentary Election in India

Sl. No.	Years	Total Seats	Candidates constested	Contestants per Lok Sabha Seat	Total Votes	Percent-age polled	Election Expenditure
1	1952	489	1864	3.8	173213635	47.00	
2	1957	494	1591	3.2	193652069	47.00	
3	1962	494	1985	4.0	216372215	49.00	
4	1967	520	2369	4.6	24903334	49.00	1796900
5	1971	518	2784	5.4	274094493	49.00	116087450
6	1977	542	2439	4.5	321174327	49.00	233368000
7	1980	542	4620	8.5	355590700	51.00	547739000
8	1984	542	5481	10.2	399816294	51.00	815134000
9	1989	543	6160	11.6	498906429	48.00	1542200000
10	1991	543	8699	16.7	*514126380	53.00	3591024679
11	1996	543	13952	26.3	592572288	53.00	5973441000
12	1998	543	**4693	8.6	605307962	61.81	*6662216000
13	1999	543	4648	11.68	619536847	59.99	**8800000000
14	2004	542	5398	10.04	671524934		

Source: EC of India.

Note: * excluding Jammu & Kashmir, ** excluding three seats in Jammu and Kashmir.

Table 5.2. Party-wise Seats in Lok Sabha during 1950-2004 (Seats Won)

Sl. No.	Party's Name	1952-57	1957-62	1962-67	1961-67	1971-77	1977-79	1980-84	1985-90	1989-91	1991-95	1995-98	1999-04	2004	2009
1.	Congress	364	371	361	283	366	154	366	420	198	231	140	114	145	206
2.	BJP	3	4	14	35	22			2	86	119	161	182	138	116
3.	Communist	16	27	29	46	48	29	47	28	45	49	32	38	53	
4.	Socialist	21	19	18	36	5									
5.	Janata Party						297	72	10	143	59				
6.	Regional Parties				28				30	2	24				
7.	Other Parties	44	72	41	81	74	20					159	313	205	
8.	Independents & Others	41	30	24	42	-	40	39	22	36	38				
	Total	489	523	487	551	515	540	524	512	510	520	492	647	541	

Source: EC of India.

Note: Communist CPI (M), CPI, CPI (IL), the Parties including Congress Allied Parties and BJP and Allied Parties.

1998 and 3.22 per cent in 1999. In the case of the Independent members, the figures were 12 in 1989, one in 1991, nine in 1996 and six each in 1998 and 1999 Lok Sabha elections. Their performance in terms of vote share was 5.25% in 1989, 3.92% in 1991, 6.28 per cent in 1996, 2.37 per cent in 1998 and 2.74 per cent in 1999 elections.

Major Issues for Democratic Electoral Practice

The non-responsive governance can be attributed to three major factors. They are electoral mal practice, election of leaders by minority vote, and poor functioning of political parties. Firstly, the electoral malpractices occur when politicians make use of three powers (*viz.,* money power, muscle power and mafia power) and 4cs, (*viz.,* criminalisation, corruption, communalism, and casteism) instead of fair means enshrined in the electoral laws. Secondly, the election of a majority of our representatives to federal, state, and local level legislative bodies by minority votes also questions the representative character and their credibility. Thirdly, the fragmentation of political parties and their non-democratic behaviour also undermines the effective functioning of Indian democracy.

Huge Election Expenses

Financing of political parties and candidates is a major issue facing the Indian electoral system. The election expenses are very high. The candidate spends 15-30 times higher than the limit prescribed by our electoral laws. For instance it was estimated that the contestants spent between Rs. 2 to 3 crore in the 1999 election. It was Rs. 1.3 crore in the 1998 elections. In the Lok Sabha elections held a few years ago, a chief minister reportedly gave a minimum of Rs. 50 lakhs to every candidate of his party. And even more - upto Rs. 2 crore depending upon the candidate's personal loyalty and caste affiliation. Where did this money come from? Often the expenditure is 10 to 15 times higher than the legal ceiling prescribed. In some States, the expenditure of Rs.1 crore for assembly election and Rs. 3 - 4 crores for Lok Sabha is common. The expenditure of major parties in the general election for Lok Sabha and Legislative Assembly in Andhra Pradesh in 1999 has been estimated (anecdotal evidence) at about Rs. 600 crores. The expenditure of candidates for the municipal elections in AP in 2000 was estimated at Rs.100 crores.

Illegal expenses also add high cost to the existing elections. It is believed that the political parties and candidates are spending money on intermediaries to buy votes, distributing liquor and other goodies. Some of them even hire rowdies and "goondas" of the locality to win the elections. Besides this, leaders also spend on illegitimate purposes in bribing election officials or police personnel for favours and partisan conduct, and hiring hoodlums and 'workers' to indulge in large-scale, booth capturing and rigging. Often criminal gangs are hired to browbeat the voters or prevent them from voting. On an average about Rs. 0.5 to 1 lakh has to be paid to a ten member gang to capture booths, says former Bihar Assembly speaker S.C. Jha (India Today, 31 March 1996). In some states, candidates are known to spend big sums to supply free liquor, blankets, silk sarees and stainless steel utensils to woo the voters.

Implications of Money Power on Governance

Huge election expenses have serious implications on the quality of governance on four counts. Firstly contesting elections is becoming a very costly affair, which keeps many good candidates away from politics. The entry of honest citizens into political and electoral arena is rendered almost impossible. Candidates are often chosen on the basis of their capacity to spend in elections rather than their ability to serve the public. Good candidates with limited means are discouraged from seeking public office.

Secondly, the high cost of election has made political parties and candidates excessively dependent on big business and wealthy individuals. Such interests, typically, seek rents as a *quid pro quo* for political donations. This (system of election fund-raising) ultimately give excessive power to wealthy individuals and big business. M.C. Chagala, former Supreme Court judge observed that elected members in India do not represent the people; they represent money power. Similarly the former Planning Commission member, and economist, Raj Krishna, was right when he said that Indian politics was becoming increasingly capital intensive.

Thirdly, the fund collection drive promoters corruption in the political arena and the resultant poor performance. The business groups expect a high return on their investment in terms of kickbacks or commissions. It also leads to unbridled corruption. The uncorroborated reports suggest that a large amount of tainted money from highly questionable sources is flowing into party coffers. Many scandals regarding political corruption in India can be attributed to such fund raising efforts. The Jain hawala scandal (payoffs from illegal foreign exchange transactions to politicians and to major political parties for raising election funds in 1996) and the *Tehelka.com* website's expose of corruption in arms deals in 2001 for collection of funds are a few examples.

Fourthly, the excesses of election expense also forces political parties to depend on black money. Contributions to parties by cheques are exceptional and the bulk of the funding is undisclosed (In fact, no party is believed to insist on accepting contributions only by cheques. Some time ago, BJP made an announcement that they would like to accept contributions by cheques. But it is believed that most contributions after that were undisclosed). Businessmen prefer to contribute in unaccounted cash *i.e.,* black money generated through tax evasion, smuggling, bootlegging, and other illegal activities.

A new class has also came into being and they consider themselves as above the law. Criminal elements first entered politics as fund raisers or providers. But over the years, the political parties' dependence on criminals grew by leaps and bounds. Thus lawbreakers of all sorts entered into a special relationship with the political leaders and parties. The National Institute of Public Finance and Policy, in its report, *Aspects of Black Money in India*, has shown their influence and role of black money in the Indian political system[4].

This has made the former chief election commissioner, S.L. Shakdhar to say that, "there is an atmosphere, too thick for anyone to ignore, that elections are tainted with money illegally obtained. This creates a doubt as to whether elections are indeed free, fair and pure. One of the recommendations of the Direct Taxes Enquiry Committee (Wanchoo Committee) Report, 1971 was the demonetisations of high value currency notes. In the ultimate analysis, the reality seems to be that political party and serious contenders have a single point agenda: "to win" the election and then to remain in power. Everything else, issues of good governance included or even long term national interest is secondary.

Criminalisation of Politics

Criminalisation of politics has of late been on the rise. It exists and operates mainly in three forms in politics: Entry of criminals and their money in politics (legislators with criminal background and tainted money in elections) poll rigging and malpractices and pre and post election violence. It is generally believed that criminals (underworld lords, smugglers, land grabbers, and black marketer), finance political parties to fight elections. The nexus between politicians, bureaucrats and criminals always exist.

Poll Rigging and Malpractices

Poll rigging includes exclusion of names from the voter's list, impersonation and intimidation. Cadre based parties enrol their supporters and at times exclude their opponents. This was one allegation often made against the Marxist government in West Bengal and the Janata Dal in Bihar. Impersonation and bogus voting is very common, if there is no strong opponent. Instances of high percentage of polling in some villages by intimidation or bogus voting in connivance with the polling officers are common in some elections. In some cases, voters are prevented from voting and someone else exercises their franchise. It is widely known that on the day of polling, the coercion of citizens to vote for a particular party, or to stay away from the polling booth, is a tactic for which political parties use anti-social elements.

Booth Capturing

Booth capturing and tearing up of ballot papers is common in some states. Pre and post election killings are also reported in the media. There is strong evidence available in many parts of the country that there is a growing nexus between some political parties and individuals with proven criminal records and muscle power that influence the outcome of elections. Two frequent crimes committed by thugs on the eve of elections, at the instigation of some political elements, are 'murder' and 'kidnapping'. In fact the pre and post election killings are increasing over the years. Five MLAs were murdered in Bihar between 1990 and 1998. The police reported that during the same period 371 political workers were also murdered in 302 separate incidents.

"Criminalisation of politics is worrying because parliament is losing its credibility," observed Indrajit Gupta, the CPI leader and former Union Home Minister in the United Front government. So nobody is surprised when an MP reveals a glimpse of his real self: *Wahan aakar dant tod doonga* (I will come there and break your teeth) snarled an MP (BJP) at his Janata Dal counterparts during a Lok Sabha debate.

What about the morale of the police, who had to provide security to undesirables like Kalpnath Rai, Phoolan Devi, Pappu Yadav, Anand Mohan Singh, Updesh Singh Chauhan, etc., when they became MPs. According to former UP Governor Satyanarayan Reddy, the state government is protecting an amazing 958 politicians. And out of these, 222 are either history sheeters or under trials in cases ranging from extortion, kidnapping, rape to even murder.

Although allegations regarding the influence of muscle power in Indian politics has long been a fact of political life since the First general elections of 1952, the intensity and frequency of such allegations have increased in recent times, along with the criminalisation of politics and the number persons known to have criminal past becoming legislators and ministers. It has not only become very common, but also spread throughout the country and is openly being defended by the party leaders. A stage has now reached when the politicians openly boast of their criminal connections. A Bihar minister's statement in the assembly that he patronised and would continue to patronise gangsters to fight and win election is a pointer to the Elections Commission and voters for taking a corrective measures.

Earlier in the 1960s, the criminals were content with playing second fiddle to the politicians for enabling them to win the elections and in turn they would get protection from them. Now it is a different case altogether. The Vohra Committee Report (1993) highlighted the nexus between politicians, administrators and criminals. The report says "It is apparent that crime syndicates and mafia organisations have established themselves in various parts of the country and have developed significant muscle and money power and established linkages with governmental functionaries, political leaders and others to be able to operate with impunity. The criminal gangs according to the report enjoyed the patronage of local politicians and the protection of government functionaries, in states like Bihar, Haryana and U.P. The dependence of politicians on crime syndicates for financial support to fight elections enhanced the latter's clout in dealing with the official machinery".

Criminals in Political Parties

Criminals are entering into politics in a large scale. Their number has been increased over the years. Inspite of taking oath, political parties are not able to deny tickets to the criminals for contesting elections. For instance in the 11th Lok Sabha a large number of MPs had criminal charges against them.

In the current Lok Sabha, nearly one fifth of the members irrespective of the political party have criminal records. RJD leads in the proportion of criminal cases (43.5 per cent). Biju Janata Dal has the smallest proportion of MPs with criminal cases. In respect of criminal cases with severe penalties (*i.e.,* five or more years' imprisonment), RJD leads with 34.8 per cent of MPs, BSP with 27.8 per cent and Samajwadi Party with 19.4 per cent. The proportion of Congress MPs who fall into this category account for 7.6 per cent of there total number and BJP MPs account for 10.9 per cent. Though the Shiva Sena has the highest percentage of members with criminal cases, no member has a case liable for the highest penalty, in other words, there are no criminal cases against 83 per cent of the Congress MPs and 80 per cent of the BJP MPs.

Communalism

The influence of communalism in electoral politics has been on the increase in recent times. It is mainly in three forms: distribution of government resources, selection of ministers and government functionaries and building of vote banks on the basis of religion, caste and region. Reservations in educational institutions and government jobs on the basis of the caste, religion comes under the first category while the appointment of ministers comes under the second category. These two categories are not discussed here.

In the same way, political parties build vote banks. The Congress and the Janata Dal build a political base or practise communalism in the name of secularism: the BJP, the Akali Dal and the DMK on sectarian lines. This sort of party divides society into majority and minority for electoral gains. By denying the legal right to Muslim women to please Muslim fundamentalists the Congress party government had enacted law i.e. Muslim Personal Law Special Act (1987). The declaration of the Prophet's birthday as a holiday by the Janata Dal is another example. However, this trend has been on the increase in recent times by both secular and communal parties. Mandal (reservation of seats and jobs for backward classes) and Mandir (construction of a temple in the place of a mosque to get Hindu votes) were the central issues in the 1991 parliamentary elections. Even the victory of the Samajwadi Party and the Bahujan Samajwadi Party in the 1992 UP Assembly elections can be attributed to this policy stand of the above parties.

Thus, political parties use religion and caste for electoral victory in spite of the fact that there is a specific provision in the Representation of the People Act of 1951 for forbidding political parties, which resort to raising religious sentiments. According to these provisions, misuse of religion in elections etc. is punishable and person can be sent to jail for upto three years, besides nullifying his or her seat in Parliament or the Assembly. Unfortunately, these provisions are not effectively enforced because of lack of political will and prolonged legal battles and litigation. Moreover, the laws are applicable only to the winning candidates. On the other hand, there is no provision to deter those who violate election laws before the elections.

The Question of Representation and Winning on Minority Vote

The multiplicity of political parties, combined with our Westminster based first-past-the-post system results in a majority of legislators and parliamentarians getting elected on a minority vote. In other words, they usually win by obtaining less than 50 per cent of the total votes and even the total number of votes in the election. This clearly reflects that there are more votes cast against them than in their favour. There are States where 85 to 90 per cent of the legislators have won on a minority vote (i.e., by having obtained less than 50 per cent of the votes cast). In many cases candidates have won by getting less than 20 per cent of the total votes cast in their constituency. To quote a few examples: in Uttar Pradesh, over the last three assembly elections an average of only 11 per cent legislators won on a majority vote. In other words, almost 90 per cent legislators won on a minority vote. The same proportion for Bihar is 18 per cent to 82 per cent; for Madhya Pradesh it is 40 per cent to 60 per cent; for Assam 29 per cent to 71 per cent and for Karnataka 31 per cent to 69 per cent. Only Tamil Nadu displays a different characteristic where a large proportion of legislators have won on a majority vote –1991 - 90 per cent, 1985 - 83 per cent.

At the national level, the proportion of MPs who have won on a minority vote is over 67 per cent at an average for the last three Lok Sabha elections. This means that at an average, at least two-thirds of our legislators all over India win on the basis of a minority vote.

Limits on Contributions

Limits on contributions of individuals and organizations have been introduced primarily to address the problem of equality of opportunity by lessening dependence on a small number of wealthy donors and making candidates more responsible to the grassroots. Ceilings on contributions may apply both to donors and recipients, that is, recipient parties and candidates may face limits on amounts that they receive from certain categories of donors and/or from any single donor, forcing them to broad base their fund-raising efforts. Potential donors may face limits on how much they can contribute per candidate, per party or per year. Tight legal limits are imposed on the amount of money a candidate can spend during the election campaign. The law prescribes that the total election expenditure shall not exceed the maximum limit prescribed under Rule 90 of the Conduct of Election Rules, 1961. It would also amount to a corrupt practice under sec 123 (6) of R.P. Act, 1951.

In some countries, like the United States, there may be bans on certain organisations (like corporations and trade unions) from making election contributions to parties or candidates. However, intermediary organizations, like political action committees (PACs) in the United States, may be allowed to receive and channel corporate political contributions, though they too may face limits on amounts per donor as recipients and amounts per candidate as donors.

Legal Limits

Limits are fixed by the EC from time to time taking reasonable costs into account. At present the limit of expenditure for a parliamentary constituency in bigger states like U.P., Bihar, Andhra Pradesh, Madhya Pradesh is Rs. 25 lakhs). It is Rs 10 lakhs for most assembly constituencies. Elected candidate has to submit election expenses to the Election Officer/ Returning Officer within 30 days of result of the election. If a candidate does not file his account of election expenses, the EC can disqualify him for a period of three years from membership of the legislative house.

Inspite of this clause (non-submission and irregular submission of election accounts); no action has been taken by EC for violating this law by many candidates. The EC took a lenient view and the disqualification was not enforced in many cases (J K Singh, Electoral Reforms). For instance, in the 1951-52 general election, the EC reported that out of 27,195 candidates and 3,187 election agents as many as 7,724 candidates and 855 election agents failed to submit their returns in due time and in proper manner and accordingly incurred the disqualification under section 7(c) and 143 of the Representation of the People Act, 1951. In the 1977 Lok Sabha Elections 360 candidates did not submit their account out of 2439 contested (EC Report on the sixth General Election in India, 77, Vol. 1, New Delhi, 77, p.127).

In the EC Report of 1962, the EC was of the view that the legal provision relating to election expenses as they stand at present are of no use and call for drastic changes. This expenditure ceiling does not include into the main limitation the expenditure incurred by the party or an association or a friend because it would be violative according to an ordinance in 1969 which was later made into law in 1974. This clause was misused by many and incurred huge expenditure. Goswami Committee (1990) did not include spending by independent supporters in the election expenditure limit but made such unauthorized spending a penal offence.

The second important development was the Supreme Court's order of 4 April, shortly before the general elections, interpreting it and giving Explanation 1 of Section 77(1) of the RPA that such election expenditure by a political party would not be clubbed with that of a candidate for the purposes of the spending ceiling only if the party had submitted audited accounts of its income and expenditures, something that no party had done. This constrained conspicuous party spending on behalf of the candidate during the 1996 campaign.

Limits on Company Donations

In 1950s and 1960s company donations to political parties to a limited extent were legally permitted and payments were made mostly by cheques (Section 293 of the Indian Companies Act). Such contributions could be up to 5 percent of the profit with the approval of the board of directors and unlimited with the approval of the shareholders.

In 1969, company contributions were banned. In 1985, again companies were permitted to contribute up to 5 percent of the profit. A Company, which receives state subsidy or has a decision or contract or licence pending with government, shall not contribute. In reality, these are believed to be huge undisclosed and unaccounted corporate contributions to political parties and candidates.

Corporate sector does play its legitimate role in the functioning of the Indian democracy, within the defined norms. The Dinesh Goswami Committee was of the view that the donations made by companies to political parties be completely banned. However, the Indrajit Gupta Committee left the decision in this regard to the wisdom of parliament and the government. The corrupting influence of money in politics has, however, not abated despite these legislative remedies.

Reporting and disclosure of expenditure requirements have been implemented simultaneously with limits on election expenditures and/or political contributions, and public subsidies to parties/candidates. This necessitates the institutionalization of legal requirements for disclosure of party/candidate's income and expenditures. The general trend is towards greater transparency. The reporting interval is every campaign (especially in countries which subsidise or regulate elections rather than parties), and/or annual.

Expenditures are required to be reported to EC in all cases. In most cases contributions, audit of accounts of political parties' and/or candidates' campaigns is generally required to be reported but not all the time. Most countries have the further requirement of disclosure, that is, it is not sufficient to file audited statements of accounts to the appropriate public authority in confidence (similar to the requirement of filing of income tax returns by parties in India). These records must be made publicly available, including to the press and political rivals.

The examination of electoral and party finance regulation reveals three patterns upon which one can draw to devise a system of political finance regulation for India. One is a minimalist pattern, another a maximalist pattern and in between are various mixed patterns.

Parties and Money Power

Parties with ideology and strong cadre depend less on money particularly on illegal money. For instance, the Congress party before independence would raise small money, the important part of its funds from the four-anna membership dues, and the bulk from Indian businessmen who wanted the party to support their demand for protection from imports duties. After independence, the party's need for funds grew dramatically because it had to fight elections, but the four-anna membership declined as the fervour aroused by the independence movement waned.

Cadre based party spends very less on elections. For instance, Chitta Basu, Forward Block leader and veteran parliamentarian from West Bengal who died in 1997, reminisced in an interview to The Sunday Observer in 1991 that for the 1957 election, he had campaigned almost entirely alone on a bicycle, carrying a megaphone to address impromptu roadside meetings and village gathering. Such instances were perhaps rare even in those days and possible only for candidates of cadre-based parties, but all old timers recall with nostalgia that during the 1950s and 60s elections generated a great deal of popular participation and candidates relied more on direct contact with voters than the costly hype and hoopla they take recourse to in these days. As Pius Tirkey, a long-standing revolutionary socialist party MP from West Bengal told A Surya Prakash, that "when I first entered parliament in 1977 even the security deposit was paid by my party. I spent five rupees on my first election!" Even today, an average left party contestant spends much less than his counterparts in other organisations since cadres can be relied upon to do most of the campaign for them.

Prevention of election expenditures requires transparency of finances of the political parties as abuse of power is common in raising resources or organising political rallies and meetings. Party finances are neither regulated nor transparent. Party workers are no longer volunteers inspired by ideology, great leaders or good goals, but hired supporters. In the absence of strict disclosure norms, parties are not inclined to receive contributions openly. Almost always political contributions are obtained through extortion or received as a consideration for past or future favors out of turn.

Thanks to the mandatory disclosure rules because there is more demand from the public that the information on candidates engaged in the current contests should be made public. The onus is clearly on the party leaders to field cleaner and more capable candidates.

Parties are bound by laws to maintain accounts regularly and disclose the names of all donors contributing more than Rs.10, 000 and have the accounts audited by a qualified accountant as defined in Section 288(2) of the IT Act. In 1978, Section 139(4B) was added to the Income Tax Act (IT Act). This provision must be read with Section 13A, which makes it mandatory for the political party to furnish return of income every year. Section 13A of the IT Act exempts from taxes the income of a party from house property, other sources and voluntary contributions. Legal penalty for not filing election expenditure returns is disqualification for three years. If the expenditure exceeds the ceiling prescribed, the penalty is six years' disqualification. Every major party is said to have violated this statutory requirement of furnishing returns if its income exceeded the normal taxable limit. Political parties are supposed to file returns to the income tax department. Many political parties had failed to submit the income tax returns till the intervention of Supreme Court which issued notices to political parties in 1996 January to file the Income Tax returns in response to a public interest petition filed by a private citizens' group, prior to this the parties did not respond to notices issued by the income tax department. This forced parties, none of which had filed for all the years since 1979 as required, to do so. However, they did only for 1994-95. In future this will place some transparency constraints on parties finances although the income tax returns filed are not open to public scrutiny.

The press reported that as per the Supreme Count's directives on a public interest litigation filed by the Delhi-based Common Cause Group, the income tax officials have sent notice to all political parties to file tax returns disclosing the receipts and sources of contributions.

Goswami Committee did not include spending by independent supporters in the election expenditure limit but made such unauthorized spending a penal offence. Goswami Committee also advocated a ban on company donations to political parties. In 1993, the Confederation of Indian Industry (CII) set up a task force, which recommended that corporate contributions be made tax-deductible and that board decisions should be required to be confirmed by shareholders. The CII has also recommended state funding of elections, the funds to be either raised by a cess on excise duty or by contributions by industry to an election fund pool managed by the state, from which money should be distributed to parties by formula; in effect, an election tax on industry.

The Goswami Committee (1990) and Gupta committee suggested limited state funding /support in kind for vehicle fuel (usually the main campaign expense), microphones, issue of voter identity slips and additional copies of the electoral rolls. The Indrajit Gupta Committee (1998) recommended partial state funding mainly in kind. The NEA '99 study of the CSDS, to be released, finds a strong correlation between the wealth and income of candidates and their prospects for getting major party nomination.

V.A. Pai Panandiker, Director for Policy Research, New Delhi in his article (India Today, 31 March 1996) said : The state should pay. If legitimate money is not available to political parties, they are bound to find illegitimate sources of money. The former Chief Election Commissioners L. Shakdher suggested for creation of Rs.100 crore fund to finance the elections in order to prevent corrupt practices.

There was a proposal to establish election-funding trust by some large business houses (Tata group' in 1997) from which contributions would be made to all qualifying political parties in a transparent manner. The objective is to make political contributions in a manner that is transparent, non-discriminatory and non-discretionary in order to create a climate where business and industry can be carried on more economically and efficiently. This would facilitate to reduce extortionate demands on individual business houses. The Tata's groups made a genuine effort to create a fund for campaign contributions. However, in the absence of an enabling climate, and the difficulty in providing corporate funding to all parties on objective criteria, the initiative did not make any progress. Efforts were on to provide state funding. Free time was allocated to 7 national and 34 state parties, totaling 61 hours on state owned television (Doordarshan) and radio (All India Radio) on the basis of a formula in 1998 elections. This was further enhanced in the 1999 election and a total of 126 hours was allotted to 6 national and 48 state parties.

Criminals in Politics

The EC has recommended that a person against whom a charge has been framed under certain sections of the IPC should be barred from contesting elections. Such a person framed under the unlawful Activities (Prevention) Act, 1967, the Narcotic Drugs and Psychotropic Substances Act, 1985 or any other offence punishable with imprisonment for life or death under any law, 'shall be disqualified for a period of five years from the date of framing the charge, provided he is not acquitted of the said charge before the date of scrutiny notified under Section 36 of the Act'.

Political Parties

The parties should strictly adhere to their constitution in regard to the holding of organisational elections at all levels. Each party should maintain day-to-day accounts, which should be opened for inspection and independent audit by auditors named by the EC. The audited accounts should be submitted annually to the EC together with a declaration that elections to the party organs have been held periodically. The EC should be armed with powers to derecognise a party in the event of a failure to observe the proposed law. The EC, in turn, should forward a yearly-consolidated report together with a copy of the audited accounts of each party to the speaker of the Lok Sabha in the case of recognised national parties and to the speaker of the state assembly in the case of recognised state parties.

Internal Democracy in Political Parties

Most of the Parties have become arbitrary, autocratic and unaccountable over the years. They are not representing dreams and aspirations of the people. The leadership often tightly and arbitrarily controls entry into a party. No objective and uniform norms are adopted to admit the members. In some parties the leadership denies membership to those who have the potential to challenge their position. Similarly, persons utterly opposed to party's stated ideology are admitted as members when it suits the whims and fancies of the leadership. Disciplinary powers are invoked and expulsions are resorted to habitually so as to safeguard the position of leadership of a party. No healthy debate and democratic dissent are tolerated. Democratic voting rarely makes leadership choices at various levels. In most parties the internal party elections are rarely held or if held then they are perfunctory. Even membership rolls are not available. Party leadership is utterly unaccountable to its members as well as the public regarding contributions made and expenditure incurred.

Choice of candidates is left to the discretion of the party bosses. There are no democratic procedures of member choice and secret ballot for candidate selection. Party policies are rarely debated or decided in party fora. Members have no role in shaping party's policies. Manifestoes are written in a cavalier fashion and if the party is elected to office then the promises are disregarded with impurity.

Reforming the Political Parties

Membership of a party should be open to all citizens of India, subject to their subscription to the party philosophy. Rules governing membership of the party and registers of current members should be available and open to inspection by any member of the party or the representatives of EC. There shall be internal mechanisms for adjudicating disputes within the party, including those concerning the interpretation of the party constitution. Disciplinary action shall not be initiated on the grounds that a member has opposed the leadership or espoused a view contrary to the leadership's view. The party constitution should contain provisions such as: *(a)* the name, registered office and activities of the party *(b)* the admission and resignation of members, *(c)* the rights and duties of members *(d)* admissible disciplinary measures against members and their exclusion from the party, *(e)* the general organisation of the party, *(f)* composition and powers of the executive committees and other organisations *(g)* The preconditions, time limits for convening meetings of members representatives and the official recording of resolutions must be made compulsory, *(h)* Matters which may only be decided upon by a meeting of members and representatives through an overall vote by members. Further, there should be procedures to be adopted when the party convention has passed a resolution to dissolve a party or merge with another party. The result of the overall vote determines whether the resolution is in order or not.

A member may only be expelled from the party if he or she deliberately infringes the statutes or acts in a manner contrary to the principles or discipline of the party and thus seriously impairs its standing in the polity of the country. The EC decides upon appeals on expulsion from the party. The rights to appeal in a higher court must be guaranteed.

There shall be democratic election by members through secret ballot for filling all vacancies of office bearers and the highest executive body. The executive committees at various levels shall be elected at least every second calendar year. All decision making in party organs shall be by majority vote and the ballots shall be secret at the executive committee levels, delegates level and representatives levels. Voting at other levels shall be secret if the members ask for it.

Candidates for election to any public office must be chosen by secret ballot. The nomination procedure shall be governed by the party statutes. A person may only be named as party candidate in a constituency if he or she has been selected as the official candidates for an assembly constituency in a special general assembly of representatives elected for this purpose. The candidates and the representatives for the assemblies of representatives shall be selected by secret ballot. Selection of candidates for other public offices shall be by secret ballot at the appropriate level.

A provision similar to Article 21 of the German basic law should be incorporated in the constitution so as to facilitate effective regulation of parties. Article 21(1) of the German basic law states that all the political parties shall participate in the formation of the political will of the people. They may be freely established. Their internal organization must conform to democratic principles. They must publicly account for their assets and for the sources and use of their funds.

Conclusion

In the light of the foregoing analysis, we would argue that comprehensive state funding of elections could be a working formula for reducing/preventing corruption and looting of public money. It should be complemented by the limits on expenditure, implementation of the reporting and disclosure requirements, enforcement of the existing laws regarding criminals and ensuring the transparent functioning of political parties.

All these would indirectly help in reducing the entry of criminals and remove barriers for the potential candidates who would find it difficult to win party nominations due to lack of resources.

NOTES

1. EC is a three-member body headed by the chief election commissioner. The President of India appoints them for tenure of six years, or up to the age of 65 years, whichever is earlier. They enjoy the same status and receive salary and perks as available to Judges of the Supreme Court of India. The Chief Election commissioner and other EC members can be removed from office only through impeachment by Parliament.

   The two senior most officers known as Deputy ECs and a separate secretariat consisting of about 300 officials (directors, principal secretaries, secretaries, under secretaries and deputy directors), assist the EC.

Each state has a Chief Electoral Officer (CEO) under the supervision, direction and control of the Election Commission. These CEOs in turn have District Election Officers in each district. At the district and constituency levels, district election officers, electoral registration officers and returning officers, who are assisted by a large number of junior functionaries, are responsible for conducting the elections. Most of this staff are from the central, state and local governments and autonomous institutions work directly under the control of the EC during the elections. The EC appoints a large number of election observers to monitor the elections and to ensure confidence in the minds of contesting candidates and political parties in the fairness. Election expenditure is being monitored by the Observers who keep checking the amount that each candidate and party spends on the election.

Source: Election Commission (EC), 2004.

2. Committees on Electoral Reform

   The important committees on electoral reforms in India are: The1972 India Joint committee on amendments to the election law submitted to parliament, Committee on Electoral reforms (Dinesh Gosawami Committee), the Committee on State fund in Elections (Indrajit Gupta Committee, (170th Bast Commission Report on Reform of Electoral Laws) etc.

3. Laws Governing Elections in India

   The most important provisions in the Constitution relating to elections are:

   Articles 54-58, 62, 66-68 and 71 which prescribe the terms of office and manner of electing the president and the vice-president [1].

   Articles 80-83 lay down the composition and duration of the Rajya-Sabha [2] and the Lok Sabha.

   Article 84 prescribes the minimum qualification for a member of parliament in terms of citizenship and age [3].

Article 101 states that no person can be a member of both houses of the parliament or of the parliament and a state legislature.

Article 102 lays down disqualification for membership of Parliament [4].

Articles 168-173 and 190-192 contain similar provisions for the Constitution, composition, duration and qualifications and disqualification for membership of state legislatures.

Article 324 provides for the appointment of the Election Commission and its functions [5].

Article 326 provides that elections to the House of the People and to the Legislative Assemblies of the States shall be on the basis of adult suffrage i.e., citizens of minimum 18 years of age (this was reduced from 21 years by a constitutional amendment w.e.f. 18th March, 1989).

Article 329 lays down a bar to interference by courts in electoral matters in as much as any law relating to delimitation of constituencies or allotment of seats cannot be questioned in a court of law and no election to a House of the Legislature can be called in question except by an election petition.

6 Electoral Reforms : Making Democracy Relevant

V. Vijaya Balan &
Lakshmi Vijayabalan

"Elections are held to delude the populace into believing that they are participating in government"

-Gerald F. Lieberman

Introduction

Does this statement hold true in the context of our country which is the world's largest democracy? Or are elections (which are acclaimed to be a part and parcel of the democratic process) still trusted by the ordinary citizens of our country as being the primary means by which they record their political preferences and hold decision-makers accountable for their actions? While elections in India may have that latter as its objective, sad to say, the electoral processes in its operation have failed to meet the expectations of the common man.

India's electoral process for its representative system of democracy has many peculiarities: principle of universal adult suffrage[1], they are supposed to free, fair and periodic with an independent election machinery to oversee the process. So ingrained is the principle of free and fair elections in the country's democratic set up that the apex court has held it to be one of the essential elements of the basic structure to the Constitution of India[2]. Therefore, any attempt to subvert this basic feature could threaten Indian democracy.

Admittedly, the present election scenario is a clear warning sign that the Indian democracy is at crossroads. On the one hand, we have various fissiparous tendencies at work to destabilise the Indian Union and on the other terrorism continue to strike at our core values like democracy, human rights and rule of law. While the Indian economy continues to grow at a rapid pace, the broad-based "inclusive growth"[3] as envisaged in the 11th five year plan continues to be elusive with the consequence that the gulf between the rich and the poor continue to widen with each passing day. Consequently in our country many people feel alienated from the present systems of election management. There are several reasons for this. First, the ordinary citizen feels disempowered in relation to the election process as it is bureaucratic and time consuming. Even getting a person's name registered in the electoral roll is cumbersome. Though computerisation efforts are being implemented vigorously, they are yet to pass the test of being truly citizen friendly. Second, the system is yet to achieve the transparency that is required to promote good governance. Even though the ordinary citizen can now request candidate affidavits from returning officers and district election officers or even access them online at the Election Commission of India (EC) website, the way in which the system functions to check electoral malpractices, points out that the system has failed to meet the ordinary citizen's expectations. Suggestions and complaints about electoral malpractices are either ignored by the EC or in most cases they do not have sufficient teeth to take action. Accordingly, if Indian democracy has to remain relevant certain radical changes are essential.

Electoral reforms are the need of the hour, if we wish to ensure that democracy in India survives and remains vibrant in at least a workable form, if not in its ideal form. There has been several numbers of committees, commissions and countless number of seminars has been held to articulate strategies for electoral reforms[4]. The most notable one is the 15the Law Commission's 170th report which undertook a comprehensive review of the Representation of People Act, 1951, (RP Act) and associated legislations with object to strengthen democracy by making the electoral process more fair, representative and transparent.

This paper will discuss the current challenges that face the Indian electoral system and will forward certain reforms which may be considered while developing a strategy aimed to renew the interest and trust of the Indian electorate.

1. Curtailing the Escalating Costs of Elections

The importance of money in fighting an election has increased manifold time and it is estimated that more than a crore of rupees is required for a candidate to fight in an urban constituency and perhaps half this amount is needed for a rural one. It has been reported that money and liquor are distributed in large quantities during elections[5]. India's election expenditures have always drawn international attention. The New York Times reported that for the 2009 general elections "candidates and parties spent \$3 billion on everything, including transportation, advertising, celebrity endorsements and cash bribes over the course of the campaign,... In comparison, the last United States presidential campaign cost an estimated $2.4 billion"[6]. All these figures should be assessed against the strictures by the EC capping the amount of money that can be spent by a candidate on his/her election.

It is imperative that there be proper audit of the funds that are available to political parties and expenditures incurred by them both during elections and in normal times should be made available to the public. The source of funding and the amount, the manner of expenditure needs to be brought to the public domain through an effective audit system. In this regard, the state funding of elections can be considered as an alternative to check the influx of black money during electioneering.

2. Preventing People with Criminal Antecedents from Contesting Elections

It has become a norm in the country's electoral politics that even people with criminal records are nominated even by leading political parties to contest in elections. The Supreme Court (SC) in 2002 held that a voter's speech or expression in the case of an election includes the right to know in full the particulars of a candidate who is to represent him in parliament. The court further held that the EC has the jurisdiction under Article 324 of the Constitution to implement its orders and accordingly directed the EC to seek information from candidates regarding their criminal records, assets and liabilities, and educational qualifications in the form of affidavits to be submitted by them along with their nominations[7]. The EC amended the statutory rules and the format of nomination papers, to give effect to this ruling. As well, the EC has ordered all candidates to clearly state in an affidavit the number of cases pending against them. Voters now have access to information regarding a candidate's criminal record, educational qualifications, personal wealth, etc. In addition, media exposures of the criminal antecedents of a candidate have actually pressured parties against including such candidates on their lists. Though these measures have had some impact on maintaining a certain level of purity in elections, more cleansing measures need to be adopted to purge candidates having criminal cases. As it exists, Indian law does not allow those awaiting trial to vote but there is no bar on people fighting elections even from jail if not yet convicted. These anomalies require the urgent attention of the law makers.

Weeding out candidates with criminal antecedents from the electoral process in their entirety may still take some time in India. As stated, presently the law bars only those with an actual conviction from contesting the polls. But few, if any, of our politicians are likely to have spent time in prison. Can we pass on the blame from political parties and the EC to the Judiciary for this trend due to the delay in the criminal justice administration of the country? The slow disposal rate of our courts and the low rate of conviction will only damage the electoral process[8]. In fact, this situation has somehow added on to the perception that one could get away with any crime and does not need to fear about punishment. If convicted, a contestant could appeal the superior courts, the determination of which may take a long time. Thus many elected representatives with criminal background who have enjoyed full tenures without being concerned that their criminal past. Thus, we cannot stress enough for an effective criminal justice administration which can expeditiously dispose of cases pending against candidates so that they are weeded out from the electoral process of holding public office.

In battling against criminalization of politics several commissions and committees including the EC have recommended drastic changes in the law. The judiciary has time and again pointed out the need for proactive legislation. It is mainly the political parties that are indifferent in engaging themselves for any consistent reforms. Accordingly, the loop holes in law are amply used by criminals to contest elections, for buying votes, and for engineering defections.

3. Need to Restrict the Phenomenon of Paid News which Harms Parliamentary Democracy

Even though media has been instrumental in safeguarding and ensuring free and fair elections, the recent pernicious practice of publishing "paid news"[9] by some newspapers and television channels, particularly during the 2009 elections[10] has threatened to undermine the very foundation of democracy. Media houses aggressively sell their space for sponsored news items that favour candidates. Prospective candidates not only buy space, but also buy these newspapers in bulk and circulate it in their constituencies to influence voters. This practice adulterates news, thereby blurring the distinction between news and advertisements. It deceives voters and impairs the prospects of the candidates with limited resources. In the long run, these candidates loose against those who fight elections paying millions to the media. The media industry is not only venturing a niche market but is increasingly becoming instrumental in circulating disinformation amongst the voters.

One cannot blame the EC for its slowness in action but here citizens also have to share the blame as it is they who encourage this trend by becoming consumers of such misinformation. This raises the question as to where lies the responsibility? There is an urgent need to safeguard the public's right to correct and unbiased information. Could this be another interest that needs protection under the freedom of speech and expression enshrined in the Constitution as a fundamental right? How will courts safeguard the public's right to unbiased information given that freedom of the press is not explicitly guaranteed by the constitution?

One such dilemma arose in relation to the publication of pre-poll and exit poll surveys during elections where political parties were clamouring for its ban on the ground that they impair free and fair conduct of elections by swaying voting patterns. The EC recently decided to ban publication or telecast of opinion/exit polls 48 hours before the last hour of polling in single-phase balloting. Thus, restrictions on this form of freedom of expression have been imposed to protect the integrity and fairness of the electoral process[11].

At present, the Press Council of India (PCI) in consultation with the EC is examining the setting up of a mechanism to look into complaints of paid news. This will be one area which may require stringent regulatory steps on the part of EC or even an amendment to the RP Act.

The Commission can deal with publication of campaign advertisements in the form of news under Section 10A of the RP Act. However, its powers are limited to matters connected to election campaigns. Besides, identification of advertisements masquerading as news is not always easy. One cannot also rule out the possibility of frivolous complaints. Despite this, the EC in combination with the PCI and civil society should take strong action against politicians and media personnel for paid news that are used for election publicity.

4. Restrictions on the Use of Glamour to Sway Voters

We are yet to devise any mechanism that can evaluate the impact of swaying of voters due to celebrities (movie, stars, singers, cricket players) endorsing candidates during recent election campaigns. Bollywood celebrities take a lead role in this regard as they continue to be introduced time and time again into the election campaign by political parties to remind voters to make an informed choice[12]. The State of Tamil Nadu may perhaps be the first in the world to have effectively harnessed and used the film industry for political purposes right from the 1940s. With the prevalence of media, this trend has become unstoppable. As it takes the form of a general phenomenon one has to pose the question as to who will regulate the use of charisma to influence the minds of millions – will it be left to the domain of the film industry to self-regulate or will the burden be shifted to the EC. As citizens of India, celebrities also have a legitimate say in the country's election process. However, one has to wait and see the impact that glamour can have on the democratic process of the country. In the rush to favor glamour, real issues that affect the electorate should not be camouflaged.

5. Restricting the Proliferation of Political Parties

Party system is an essential feature of parliamentary democracy. However, there is no direct reference to political parties in the Indian Constitution. Enacted in 1989 the law relating to registration of political parties was quite liberal which resulted in the mushrooming of many parties leading to confusion as to whom the people should vote for. To eliminate the mushrooming of parties, the EC has had to take certain rigorous measures. The Commission now registers a party which has at least 100 registered electors as its members and charges a processing fee of Rs. 10,000 towards administration expenses[13]. Another closely associated trend is the proliferation of small parties with regional or vested agenda. One cannot lose sight of the threats that this development poses to the country's national aspirations in terms of national integration and development. While political pluralism is acceptable considering India's diversity, one has to strongly reassess this trend of regional parties calling the shots so that it does not end up as "too many cooks spoil the broth".

6. Restricting the Deployment of Teachers for Election Duties[14]

Primary and secondary school teachers in government schools are not just expected to teach, but they are also required to be part of many other government sanctioned activities such as conducting surveys, monitoring elections, collecting census data, etc. This is also true of government employees. It is unfortunate to note that despite the SC order in *Election Commission of India v. St. Mary's School*[15], teachers continue to be deputed for poll duty. In 2007, the SC ordered that government school teachers cannot be required to skip classes and undertake non academic activities like election duty, census work or polio drop campaigns. Also that the teaching staff should be put on roll revision and election duty only during holidays and on non-teaching days and only the services of non-teaching school staff should be utilized for such duties. The SC had held that the right to education, being a fundamental right under Article 21A of the Constitution, it was obligatory on the part of the State to ensure that students are not deprived of their teachers. Justice S.B.Sinha speaking for the Court observed that "holding of an election is no doubt of paramount importance. But for the said purpose education of the children cannot be neglected. Therefore, it is necessary to maintain the balance between the two".

Recently in Goa, it was reported that teachers, headmasters and parents were concerned over the deployment of teachers for election duty during the period of school examinations as it could hamper examination work and disrupt academic functioning. It is imperative that the EC should take an active role in stopping such trends by laying down regulations. Moreover, this issue is of a greater concern as the role of a teacher has unprecedently expanded due to the demands of new curriculum based on ICT related training and quality education.

7. Regulating the Use of Electronic Media in the Indian Elections

Media has always been a significant partner in the electoral process because of its power to influence people's thought processes and to shape public opinion. Indian political parties like their counterparts in the U.S are embracing the internet technology to connect to the political process. This is also the larger outcome of the concept of e-governance rolled out in the country under the National e-Governance Plan of 2006[16]. Many political parties and candidates are eager to establish their online presence to target the estimated 81 million internet users[17]. They run official websites or use social networking tools such as Orkut, Twitter and Facebook for political propaganda. The EC is yet to come out with any amendments to its code of conduct for political parties or candidates to regulate the use of the internet for campaigning *via* the internet which can happen even during the day of the poll. This is another area that needs attention since the rules ban campaigning 48 hours before the close of the poll. Whether this can be extended to an online environment is doubtful. It is indeed a technological challenge for the EC to regulate this problem given the elusive nature of technology. But then leaving out this emerging media will not be fair to the traditional media. The problem has another dimension as mobile phone technology is used to reach out to the masses. As former Election Commissioner S.Y. Quraishi observes, "We ensure that bulk messaging through mobile phones is shown as part of election expenditure by political parties or leaders. If bulk messages do go out, we trace the expenditure involved through cellular operators[18]." Interestingly, there seems to be no ban yet on sending text messages from mobile phones even on the polling day.

8. Recognition to Virtual Voting

The problem of non-participation by the Indian electorate particularly the youth can be eliminated to a large extent by the substantial use of the new information and communication technology in voting. Cutting down expenses and fairness in elections should be read equally with the convenience and interest of the voters. If India's experiment with electronic voting machines has been successful, time has now come to take advantage of the benefits of online voting. Whether this will be an answer to the problems of rigging and the coercion of voters during elections cannot be determined as of now. But the experiment is indeed worth a try considering the technological edge India has in comparison to even developed nations. This will provide a great opportunity for the NRIs to exercise their right to franchise. NRIs who retain their Indian citizenship cannot vote in elections because the RP Act requires a person to be 'ordinarily resident' in a particular constituency in order to be registered as a voter there. Only members of the armed forces, paramilitary forces, state armed police and government officials posted abroad are exempted. The United States and Britain are among several countries that allow non-resident citizens to vote[19].

A Bill was introduced by the first United Progressive Alliance (UPA) government in 2006 (which is still pending in parliament) to amend the RP Act to entitle NRIs to vote[20]. Though there are many logistical challenges associated with the implementation of online voting, a major one on which the amendment is silent is on how NRIs will vote. The Government should also start thinking outside the box to experiment with online voting methods on a pilot basis for the NRIs. This could be a starting point for the government to experiment with the working of this new channel. This will also be a good alternative for those citizens serving in the military far away from their homes to vote online instead of sending the ballot by post.

Online voting method is now being experimented in many jurisdictions[21]. It has many merits - firstly, this mode can attract the youth (who are not enthusiastic to stand in long queues for hours to cast their votes). The convenience factor can work in favour of producing more turnouts[22]. Secondly, the mantra of the day is that citizens are increasingly transacting with the government through the internet and online voting is only an extension of this development. Thirdly, if implemented successfully it could economise the polling arrangements[23]. However, before proceeding with such a system many security loopholes are to be addressed to make the system tamper proof[24]. One step could be to implement the government's uniform identification number cards (UID) programme under which the UID Authority of India will issue identities for all citizens[25]. These smart cards are expected to improve the quality of service delivery by the government to all particularly the poor and provide improved access to the citizens. The EC has given full support to the UID project and election commissioners have been allowed to become members of the UID team in various states in the country[26].

Making UIDs compulsory for voting can be an answer to many of the ills that plague voter ids (like bogus addresses, typos in the cards) and electronic voting machines[27]. For instance, recently, the SC has ordered that the purdah-nashin women who do not want to be seen by members of the public have to lift their veil for being photographed for issuance of the voter ids and later at polling stations for identification purpose. These complications can be avoided in online voting by using the UIDs as it is the number and not the photograph that will be proof of identity[28]. Thus it quells any apprehension of offending the religious values of Muslim women and will help to increase their participation in the electoral process. The UIDs using biometric technology will make elections more tamper proof and will avoid the multiple registrations of a single voter[29]. Very soon the world will move away even from online voting to enable voting from portable communication devices like the mobile phones. For India which is second in the world after China to achieve half a billion mobile phone subscribers – with nearly 15 million new customers being added every month this will be yet another challenge for which the nation will have to prepare itself for[30].

9. Reduce Vote Ambivalence towards Elections

The Indian elections are a huge exercise in terms of logistics, security and the sheer size of the electorate. The 2009 general elections had 720 million eligible voters, nearly two-and-a-half times the population of the U.S. with the turnout being a 60 per cent. Surprisingly, the more educated and affluent people in India's cities seem distinctly less interested in elections than their rural counterparts. Amongst the young electorate (which is estimated to be 200 million voters under the age of 25) the interest in elections has been declining with many of them hesitant to show up for polling. Their loss of interest in the political process is due to several reasons – countless number of political parties, aging leaders and candidates with criminal records and corruption at all levels, non-recognition of their interests, etc. But the 2009 elections demonstrated a different level of political engagement by the young. Political parties were successful to a certain extent in mobilising young voters through their creative interventions *via* the mass media and through the internet particularly through the social networking websites – YouTube, blogs and Facebook and influencing them to exercise their right to franchise. The lack of creativity on the part of EC is providing opportunity for internet giant corporations like Google and Yahoo!. They are partnering with local private companies in taking elections closer to the citizens. They established an online resource in English and in Hindi for Indian voters during the 2009 general elections[31]. Allowing multinational corporations to take control of our elections – the key mechanism which sustains our democracy is debatable. Nevertheless, through technology for the first time ever the aspirations of the youth have intersected with politics.

10. Encouraging Citizen Engagement in the Political Process

Just as war is too important to be left to the generals, so is politics too important to be left only to the politicians[32]. Ordinary citizens and the civil society have a major role in the political process and the view that politics becomes the business of a citizen only when he is a politician has to change. If this mistake continues to be perpetuated, it will be no exaggeration to say that it will be the end of democracy. This demands a concerted effort by the government to involve with the illiterate and the literate masses in the political process. One step to achieve this goal could be the use of interactive medium like the Web 2.0 tools and the e-governance process to involve citizens on a continuing basis in the political process than just periodic elections. The Women's Reservation Bill or the Constitution (108th Amendment) Bill which seeks to reserve 30 per cent of all seats in the Lok Sabha and State Legislative Assemblies for the women is a right step in this regard.

11. Re-casting the Role of the EC – Need for Proactivism

The entire electoral machinery in India functions under the EC, which has been granted the freedom to function independent of the executive under Article 324 of the Constitution. Accordingly, any discussion on electoral reforms has to begin from this agency. Holding regular, periodic elections, based on universal adult suffrage in a multicultural and pluralistic country like India with huge population, is not a small and an easy task.

The conduct of free, fair and impartial elections depends much upon the performance of the three elements that converge to form a triangle. They are an independent and impartial electoral machinery; political parties and candidates; and the electorate. Electoral reforms have received the attention of the Parliament, the government, the media and also the EC for several years. The EC periodically apprises the Government on different subjects that require reforms which arises due to the implementation of certain laws or based on certain directions given by superior courts.

Thus, the role of EC in strengthening the largest democracy of the world is humungous. A consistent criticism leveled against the functioning of the EC is that there exists a gulf between the EC and the electorate. Common people hardly know the rules that are made by the Commission despite the existence of an official website with information on their activities. Bridging this gap is essential not only for rooting out undesirable elements from politics but also for the survival of the democratic polity. Thus, transparency and citizen-centric functioning has to be necessarily achieved. Perhaps digital media and the use of Web 2.0 tools can help EC establish interactive links with the common man. Suitable powers, budget and legislative changes to initiate such policy changes in its day-to-day functioning should be a priority.

Another criticism against the EC is that it has not taken effective action against candidates who are alleged to have committed misconduct and for having violated the model code of conduct. The EC has not so far investigated and disqualified a candidate and generally after the din and fury of an election settles, the matter is swept under the carpet[33]. The Union Law Minister Shri Veerapa Moily in addressing the indifference on the part of EC has assured that the government is willing to think of a new law to vest more powers on the EC to give it more teeth for initiating speedier action against the violators of electoral rules and laws. Ultimately enacting new laws do not make any difference, unless the EC enforces the law in all its might[34].

In view of the vastness of the country and the huge electorate, the EC has also made a proposal for the appointment of regional commissions in different zones to reduce its work load[35]. This proposal has to be implemented at the earliest so that there is more efficiency in its functioning.

Consensus is also required in light of the growing demand for replacing the first past the post system with the proportional representation through means of single transferable vote[36]. Again a retirement age for politicians (usually the scenario is that their career starts at the age of 60 when an ordinary government servant is unfit for a job), negative vote to discourage the corrupt and criminal elements from the process - all these will surely strengthen the parliamentary democracy in the country.

Conclusion

The one billion plus strong Indian democracy cannot be weakened by delaying electoral reforms which form the core of any strategy to strengthen the democratic process. Forests have been cleared and much time and money have been spent to discuss the topic of electoral reforms at length. Several strategies and measures have been proposed. However, if these are to come out of the rhetoric, the wealth of information gathered over years warrant immediate implementation. No democracy can never ever claim perfection. But it is possible for a democratic system to evolve over time, building on the experience gained along the way. In this regard, elections are not only about selecting representatives for governing a country, they are also an opportunity for the people to reaffirm their commitment to democracy and their desire to resolve common challenges and conflicts peacefully. This challenge to reform the electoral system has to be borne by each citizen making the responsibility collective more so in this age of prosumers. Passing it on to a few hands is unwise. Let us hope that the Indian election which showcases the greatest democratic carnival on the earth demonstrates to the world that it is in true spirit democracy at work for now and in the coming years

NOTES AND REFERENCES

1. Unlike most Western democracies, where voting rights were extended to women after protracted debate and agitation, they were granted to all women as well all men in India from the beginning. See Ramesh Thakur, "India's Great Election Carnival", *The Canberra Time* (16 April 2006).
2. *Indira Nehru Gandhi v. Raj Narain,* 1975 AIR (SC) 2299.
3. See generally Government of India, Planning Commission, *Towards Faster and More Inclusive Growth: An Approach to the 11th Five Year Plan (2007-2012),* December 2006.
4. *The Tarkunde Committee Report of 1975, the Goswami Committee Report of 1990, Vohra Committee Report of 1993, Indrajit Gupta Committee Report of 1998, Election Commission's Recommendations* till date, to name a few.
5. Trilochan Sastry, "Electoral Reforms and Citizens' Initiative: Some Breakthroughs" (2004) 39:13, *Economic and Political Weekly.*
6. Heather Timmons & Hari Kumar, "India's National Election Spreads Billions Around" *The New York Times* (14 May 2009).
7. *People's Union for Civil Liberties (PUCL) with Lok Satta and Association for Democratic Reforms v. Union of India,* 2003 AIR (SC) 2363.
8. For instance, till the end of 2006, 7, 192, 451 cases were listed in various

High Courts. Out of these 5,999,200 (83.4%) were still awaiting trial. The lower courts scenario is worse.

9. "This coinage does not fall within the nationality of news even by the farthest stretch of imagination. In fact, it represents the epitome of anti-news". See Speech of Dr. S.Y. Quraishi, Election Commissioner of India at the Seminar on Paid News organised by EGI and IWPC on 13 March 2010.

10. The recent complaint against Maharashtra Chief Minister Ashok Chavan is noteworthy. It is alleged that he paid money to newspapers for publishing reports in his favour during the 2009 Assembly elections. J Balaji "Election Commission Seeks Chavan's Reply on Paid News" *The Hindu* (13 Jan. 2010).

11. News, "Elections, and Paid News Syndrome in the Media", Outlook India (22 May 2009).

12. Indian Elections, *Celebrities in Politics: A Step towards the Degeneration of Politics?* <online:<http://www.Indian elections.com/national- issues/ celebrities-pin-politics.html>.

13. See generally Sumandeep Kaur, "Electoral Reforms in India : Proactive Role of Election Commission" (2008) 46:49 *Mainstream.*

14. News, "Teachers Put on Poll Duty Despite SC Order", *The Times of India* (19 Mar. 2009).

15. 2008 (2) SCC 390, St. Mary's School, an unaided school, filed a writ petition in public interest pointing out to the absence of teachers during school hours due to their deployment for duties outside the school including poll duties.

16. For details of the plan, see Department of Information Technology, *National e-Governance Plan,* online: http://www.mit.gov.in/content/national-e-governance-plan.

17. India, *Internet World Stats,* http://www.internetworldstats. com/asia/in.htm.

18. Ruhi Tewari, "New Media can Trump Poll Code of Conduct" (27 Mar. 2009) online : http://www.livemint.com/2009/03/27223101/New-media-can-trump-poll-code.html>

19. Many countries, from the United States and Canada to Argentina and the Philippines, make it possible for their overseas citizens to vote. Editorial, "Voting Without Borders", *The Hindu* (11 Jan. 2010).

20. The proposed amendment in Section 20 (IAA) will read "a citizen of India, who has not acquired the citizenship of any other country, shall be deemed to be resident in India in any constituency of his choice notwithstanding his residence outside India whatever its duration". It also proposes to classify citizens who take up "employment, education or otherwise outside India". See News, "Counting NRIs In" *The Telegraph* (3 Feb. 2010).

21. For the successful use of on-line voting in the Estonian parliamentary elections and the Swiss local elections in 2005. See Mika Mannermaa, *Democracy in the Turmoil of the Future: Societal Influence within a New Frame of Reference* (Helsinki, Finland: 2007) at 80-82. See also Gabby Asare Otchere-Darko, *Kenya Goes E-Voting In 2012, As Ghana Dithers* (23 March 2010) http://www.ghanaweb.com/GhanaHomePage/politics/artikel. php?ID=179076 (Kenya plans to implement e-voting).

22. Many factors keep away the voters on the polling day-safety, geographical barriers. See Indian Elections, *Indian Election Statistics*, http://www.indian-elections.com/india-statistics.html.

23. Statistics reveal that the number of polling stations in the country is 828,804. In the 2004 Lok Sabha elections, there were 687,402 polling stations. This shows an increase of 141,402 polling stations. To run these units is a Herculean task both in terms of safety and finances. See *ibid.*

24. How it works : the voter inserts the ID card in the card-reader and navigates to the official election site, whereupon the voting system recognized the voter. It was possible to vote at any computer provided it had a cardreader. On the basis of the voter's identity number, a description of the candidates standing in his constituency will be provided. The voter makes his choice, which will be encrypted by the system. To finish off, the voter confirms his/her vote by way of an electronic signature, i.e. with a confidential PIN code. When counting the votes, the system will delete the digital signatures given by the electors in order to maintain anonymity. See Mannermaa, *supra* note 21.

25. This card will have 14 biometric features (which include eight fingers, two thumbs, two eyes and full face) apart from demographic details of an individual. News, "UID Card to Have 13 Biometric Features", The Tribune (13 April 2010). See also the Govt. of India, Department of Information Technology, *Information Technology Annual Report 2008-09*, at 82.

26. See *ibid, The Tibune.*

27. Even after electronic voting machines suspicions are raised about the delay in the counting and declaration of election results. For further details, see *Indian Electronic Election Fraud 2009*, http://www.keralamonitor.com/electronicvoting.html.

28. Dhananjay Mahapatra, "Lift Veil for Voter ID, SC Tells Burqa-clad Women", *The Times of India* (23 Jan. 2010).

29. Otchere-Darko, *supra* note 21.

30. Subir Bhaumik, "Remote State in Vanguard of Indian Mobile Phone Craze", BBC News (23 April 2010).

31. Staff Reporter, "Political Issues Rife on Cyber Space", *The Hindu* (13 April 2009).

32. Jagdeep s.Chhokar, "Electoral Reforms: Need for Citizens' Involvement" (2001), 36:42, *Economic and Political Weekly*, 3977-80.

33. EC has been instrumental in giving its opinion to the President that P.C.Thomas, former MP, may be disqualified from contesting elections for three years, under Section 123(3) of the *Representation of the People Act, 1951,* for corrupt practices. J. Balaji, "Disqualification of ex-MP Advised", *The Hindu* (5 May 2010)

34. "Govt. Wants Speedy Action against Election Law Violators: Law Minister", IndLaw.

35. Kaur, supra note 13.

36. Proportional election will be worse as it will strengthen community or caste based propaganda and voting in our special situation. For details see S.R. Sen, "Electoral System: Ugency of Basic Reforms" (1991) : 6 *Economic and Political Weekly*, 282-83 at 283.

7 Mounting Challenges in Democratic Governance

A.D. Damodaran

1. On 25 November 1949, at the penultimate sitting of the Constituent Assembly which drafted Independent India's constitution, Bhimrao Ramji Ambedkar stated:

"...we are going to enter into a life of contradictions. In politics we will have equality and in social and economic life we will have inequality. In politics we will be recognizing the principle of one man one vote and one vote one value. In our social and economic life, we shall, by reason of our social and economic structure, continue to deny the principle of one man one value. How long shall we continue to live this life of contradictions? How long shall we continue to deny equality in our social and economic life? If we continue to deny it for too long, we will do so only by putting our political democracy in peril. We must remove this contradiction at the earliest possible moment or else those who suffer from inequality will blow up the structure of political democracy which this assembly has so laboriously built up".

Giving glowing tributes to all those who contributed for the historic document deciding India's Tryst with Destiny, Jawaharlal Nehru also reminded them that this was *ultimately* to serve the people, "the millions who suffer".

2. Much water has since then flowed down the Ganges and Kaveri and yet the warning words of late Ambedkar continue to ring in our years and also prick our conscience, the challenges of both economic inequality and social inequality threatening at times even the political unity of the struggling nation. Thus,

(a) Even the thought of a caste-wise census sends shivers and distrust among many, knowing only too well that cherished equality is yet too distant a dream. Leave alone the colossal inequality in all respects, even the most inhuman untouchability system is still prevalent in many parts of the country!

(b) Leave alone the earlier period of development at the much-discussed Hindu growth rate of 2-3%, even in spite of the much trumpeted two-and-half decades long economic growth since the 1990s under the New Economic Policies, the hard core ground realities are certainly not supportive of the tall claims of the proponents of the new regime. First consider our international import/export trade front. When we, for example, consider China's and India's balance of payments in terms of Trade Balance, China is in surplus, upwards of $20 billion with the US every month in boom times and still in the region of $10 billion a month. India, on the other hand, struggles with a trade *deficit* but manages to stay within tolerable limits in Bop, thanks to IT exports, remittances and huge capital flows into equity, bonds, bank deposits and real estate, actually building reserves in a negative trade situation. To be specific, the last year for which we have complete balance of payments data is 2008-09 (April-March). During this fiscal, India's total export of goods stood at $ 189.001 billion, while imports of goods were $ 307.651 billion. Therefore, we have a *merchandise* trade deficit of $ 118.65 billion. But on the other hand, India's export of 'invisibles'- which are physically not shipped out from ports – amounted to $ 163.534 billion. Prominent items under 'invisibles' exports include private remittances ($ 46.903 billion), software ($ 46.300 billion), business services ($ 16.445 billion) and tourism ($ 10.894 billion). While export of invisibles' totaled $ 163.534 billion (almost equal to our export of 'goods'), import of 'invisibles' were only $ 73.612 billion, leading to *an invisibles* surplus of $ 89.923 billion. This 'invisibles' surplus (which indicates our relative competitiveness in services) partly offset the huge deficit in 'goods' trade (which indicates our lack of competitiveness in manufacturing), thereby generating an overall *current account* deficit of $ 28.728 billion. In the normal course, this current account deficit should have brought down our foreign exchange reserves by an equivalent amount. But this did not happen because we also had net *capital inflows* of $ 7.246 billion. These inflows mainly resulted from FDI ($ 17.498 billion), portfolio investment (minus $14.030 billion, which meant a net outflow due to pull-out of FII money following the collapse of Lehman Brothers) and external commercial borrowings ($ 7.941 billion). The *capital account surplus* of $7.246 billion further offset the *current account deficit* of $ 28.728 billion to produce a net foreign exchange reserve

depletion of $ 21.482. In earlier (*i.e.*, preglobal meltdown), our capital account surpluses used to be much higher. It was as high as $ 106.585 billion in 2007-08, reflecting the sheer bullishness among FIIs and other investors on the 'India Growth' story. As a result, our foreign exchanges reserves kept on piling up, despite rising merchandise trade deficits. India is the only country in the world that has accumulated reserves in this manner. Unlike all other nations in the world, India seem to suffer from a unique 'disease' in its currency being a "a tiger abroad and a lamb at home' as one keen observer surmised! All others (China, Japan, Korea, Taiwan etc.) had built up their reserves by exporting goods and as expected, it had in fact parlayed its surplus, month after month, for many years, into a mountain of over $ 2 trillion. Obviously, there's a world of difference between own and borrowed liquidity.

(c) The much acclaimed Arjun Sen Gupta Committee of the Prime Minister has authentically come with the harsh India – Bharat divide with nearly 97% of Indians affording to spend only Rs. 20 on his daily needs on the one side superposed by the significantly large increase in the number of billionaires in our country on the other, the poor being relatively even worse off today than they were when India achieved Independence!

(d) Though there is reportedly good surplus of food grains, thanks to the ushering in the seventies the celebrated Green Revolution, the nation is in extremely serious crisis in terms of hunger and malnutrition in very many parts of the country, with it being increasingly listed with some of the poorest nations of Sub-Saharan Africa!

(e) Indian intellect is highly rated in advanced countries, with one more Indian-born scientist recently added to the list of Nobel laureates. India is accepted as a serious global player in the IT's, even if not of the high-value category, and yet primary education has *only now* been listed as a fundamental right through an Act!

And so on. In other words, India even after six decades of post-independent development is truly in the throes of great human tragedy and deprivation for most of its citizen on the one hand and super-opulence for the few at the top on the other; and amazingly enough its rulers are still soliciting and waiting for others to put her on the high table as a potential super power and a veritable alternative to China!

3. It is not that even in the heydays of the Nehruvian period, things were truly looking up in *adequate measure;* there were serious differences within the political milieu in terms of his policies and programmes, not to forget at all that all around there was adequate hope and trust among the people at large that things would improve for the better under the new development plans through the Five Year Plans. The Left was skeptical, so also many a socialist group. In his monumental 1965 monograph "Economics and Politics of India's Socialist Pattern" the veteran communist leader EMS Nampoothiripad had systematically and critically analysed the Nehruvian dream and concluded at that time that far from building a socialist society as is claimed, the ruling party was building a capitalist society, that "the ever-increasing numbers of the unemployed and the underemployed cry aloud that here is a social system in which those who have no property have no means of honest living" and so on. The rightist groups, on the other hand, championed very many changes in the Nehruvian 'socialist' strategies, euphemistically described as the License-Quota-Raj, and had instead advocated total policy reversals to go in favour of those practiced in the West. Decades later in his article "On Indian Nationalism, From Naoroji and Ranade to Narasimha Rao and Manmohan Singh" in Frontline January 29, 1994, Nampoothiripad had repeated in a way his same views and said, "The economic policies pursued by the Narasimha Rao-Manmohan Singh duo (of which the acceptance of the Dunkel Draft – leading to WTO – is the latest example, would further accentuate all the problems narrated above. *Liberalisation and globalisation—the two ideas running through the Dunkel Draft–would make India the victim of a far more serious "drain of India's wealth' than what Naoraji spoke about a century and quarter ago; the difference is only that, while in Naoroji's time it was the political-administrative power of the British rulers that drained India of its wealth, it is the International power of the World Bank, the IMF, the GATT, and so on, which today forces us to pay a major part of what we earn by exports as interest on and principal of the debts we contract year after year"*. The rightist groups were, on the other hand, obviously rejoiced and were totally supportive of the post-1991 New Economic Policies with also the theory that once there is increasing prosperity all round through rapid growth in GDP, the poor and the disadvantaged would be sucked in into the development bandwagon through the 'trickling down' mechanism! And in spite of the Arjun Sen Gupta Commission reports, many among the neo-liberalists continue to believe that poverty issues can be solved only through more liberalization and globalization!

4. *In other words Indian society has always been a highly fracture society socially and economically and it continues to be so even after six decades of post-independence development; and this in turn has obviously led to untold dissentions in national politics and even divisive and extremist tendencies. These diversities obviously have been getting expressed through widely differing policies and programs propounded by the parties and groups representing them – socially, structurally and consequently politically as well. And they in turn pose innumerable challenges in 'democratic governance'.* At the top of the governance pyramid are the ones resulting from unstable and at times also opportunistic political power-sharing combinations/pressure groups with inadequate if not confusing policies, programs and practices. Concurrent with such political formations in authority, the system has the other two wings, namely, the professionally inadequate 'steel-frame' structures and their decadent procedural practices (which itself were gifted to us by our erstwhile colonial masters) to administer development issues; and adjudicating the total system is the all-winding and cumbersome judiciary and criminal system continually getting caught up between untold legal and procedural tangles and in turn failing to deliver timely and fair justice to the common man. In essence, the credibility of the three-structured authority has been steadily dwindling in the public perception. Thanks to the steadily falling living standards and increasing misery of the masses, divisive tendencies are spreading all round and fanatical/fundamentalist forces are exploiting the situations to their advantage, questioning at times even the fragile unity of the nation. Hence the urgent need that our democratic governance structures are reviewed and corrective steps taken in time.

5. It is true that in a democracy, only the peoples' elected representatives can make any meaningful and long-lasting amendments in the governance system. To that extent electoral reforms per se is perhaps the major challenge on priority facing the country; it is, however, *my submission that the true challenge is in making our democratic governance effective through timely reforms in all the three structures of governance in a synergic mode so that the people achieve their cherished tryst with destiny as envisaged in the Secular, Socialist, Democratic, Republic. And our attempt at electoral reforms must be within such a total perspective, and not just through bits and pieces.*

6. I am not a political activist nor am I an expert in social sciences including economics and politics; I am instead one who has been engaged in hard core S & T for decades in major departments and lately engaged actively also in the pursuit of studies on policy issues related to the

utilisation of modern S&T as an instrument for self-reliance in modernization and national development. Concurrently I must place on record that through my service at different levels of responsibility, I have had some decent level of experience and expertise in bureaucratic/administrative/managerial procedures and over-all governance as well, mostly in the Centre and to somewhat lesser degree in the state. In my working role as a committed 'development technologist' with an avowed objective of championing the use of modern S&T as the key instrument of modern techno-economic development, I have been exposed to serious policy issues related to almost all aspects of modern development itself, including their economic and political aspects. In other words, even though I may appear to be disqualified to speak on electoral reforms per se, my views on challenges in democratic governance deserve, I believe, serious consideration.

7. It is not unusual for democratic nations to *review their governance structures* if they are found inadequate to deliver the constitutionally sanguine benefits to their peoples. One country which had gone through major crises in democratic governance decades ago was France. Afflicted by untold economic and political challenges and the continuing instabilities of successive governments, De Gaulle pushed through his historic Fifth Republic reforms which radically transformed the governance milieu of the nation itself. Rest is history. This is not to say that a similar change over could suit the Indian situation; instead it is mentioned only as an example. After all nothing is more sacrosanct in democratic governance than to make it equipped to make it work in the interests of the majority 'who suffer'. Then only it becomes a government 'of the people, by the people and for the people'.

8. I started my presentation with BR Ambedkar, the father of our Constitution. Our Constitution was formulated by wise people from different walks of life, each representing a microcosm of our complex society. When they drafted our Constitution, they did it on the basis of certain principles that were born out of the ideals of the Freedom Struggle and the aspiration for creating a just society. In the chapter entitled "Ideas of India" of the book "India after Gandhi", Ramachandra Guha gives an exquisite panorama of the deliberations of the Constituent Assembly and its final product, namely, the Constitution of India. "With 395 articles and 8 schedules, it is probably the longest in the world. Coming into effect in January 1950, it was framed over a period of three years, between December 1946 and December 1949 (against a backdrop of food scarcity, religions riots, refugee settlement, class war and feudal intransigence!).....

These volumes (eleven in number, many exceeding 1000 pages) are a little-known treasure-trove, inevitable to the historian, but also a potential source of enlightenment to the interested citizen. In them we find many competing ideas of the nation, of what language it should speak, what political and economic systems it should follow, what moral values it should uphold or disavow". It was these ideals and not any concrete experience of democratic governance under Indian conditions that informed their efforts. The 60 years and more of lived experience of democracy give us sufficient basis for reviewing the functioning of the basic institutions that have underpinned. To start with, look at the judicial system, which clearly does not dispense justice to ordinary people. Equality before law is today a joke, when ordinary people cannot even file FIRs in police stations let alone engage lawyers. The big and mighty, whether the Union Carbides or those who run their BMWs on footpath dwellers, get easily bailed out. If, at all, there is anybody responsible for the growth of Maoism and their way of dispensing summary justice, it is the police and the judiciary. Along with Equality before Law, the other *sine qua non* of democracies is Equality of Opportunity. This again is one area where our institutions have totally failed our people. Today, there is tremendous hunger for education among the lowest classes of our society, just as it was among the upper classes during the late 19th and early 20th century. But the difference then and now is that education those days was affordable. On the other hand, how many Dalits or poor families can afford to pay for getting an engineering or medicine seat today? Unlike 50 years back, even poor people are aware of the need to be educated. Denying them this legitimate aspiration would probably lay the seeds of the next big insurrection threatening the survival of our democracy. Perhaps time has come for us too to call for a fresh Constituent Assembly and once again go for a time-bound review of our triangular governance structure to enable our people to achieve their cherished destiny as enshrined in the Constitution itself and that also matching with the needs, opportunities and challenges of the twenty first century. Undoubtedly for a multi-religious, multi-lingual and multicultural national like ours, and that too with very high societal and economic inequality, there is no alternative than to always treat the secular, socialist, democratic and republican governance as basic features of the Constitution and which cannot be subject to amendment. Within such a basic structure of the Constitution, a fresh and statutory review could be very meaningful since, unlike in the case of the first constituent assembly, the nation has gained much experience of 'democratic governance' *under Indian conditions.* And, happily enough, there are many authoritative reports prepared by experts in the field on suitable changes/amendments on all the three pillars of governance. In other words, the Indian nation has certainly become wiser to undertake such an exercise in more meaningful and effective manner. And the earlier we do this and put the nation on a more people-friendly path of progress, the more prosperous the future would be for its teeming millions "who suffer".

8 Enactments on Disqualification—Office of Profit : Constitutionality and Propriety

K.C. Sunny

The electoral disqualification on the ground of holding of office of profit is a fertile area of litigation since the enactment of the Constitution. The relevant Constitutional provision reads thus:

Article 102 Disqualification for membership: (1) A person shall be disqualified for being chosen as, and for being, a member of either House of Parliament, *(a)* If he holds any office of profit under the Government of India or the Government of any State, other than an office declared by any State, other than an office declared by Parliament by law not to disqualify its holder *(b)* if he is of unsound mind and stands so declared by a competent court *(c)* if he is an undercharged insolvent *(d)* if he is not a citizen of India, or has voluntarily acquired the citizenship of Foreign State or is under any acknowledgment of allegiance or adherence to a Foreign State *(e)* if he is so disqualified by or under any law made by Parliament.

Explanation: 1. For the purposes of this clause, a person shall not be deemed to hold an office of profit under the Government of India or the Government of any State by reason only that he is a Minister either for the Union or for such State.

Explanation: 2. A person shall be disqualified for being a member of either House of Parliament if he is so disqualified under the Tenth Schedule. Article 191 is also similarly couched except for the difference that it would apply to Members of the State legislative assemblies. These two explanations were amended by 52nd Amendment to the Constitution in 1985, restricting the application of this explanation to this article only.

Since the Constitution did not define the term 'office of profit' it has become the duty of judiciary to interpret what is an office of profit and what is not, depending upon the practical situations of each and every case. In order to attract Article 102 (1) (a) or Article 191 (1) (a), as the case may be, the person must hold an 'office' and that 'office' must be an 'office of profit'. An 'office' has been defined as a position or place to which, certain duties are attached which are of public character. Elaborating on this, in order to constitute an 'office', there must be a permanent, substantive position which must exist independently of the holder of the office. There is no 'office' if the employment is only to do a particular work or to perform specified duties and there is an end of the employment after that work or duties are over. An office of profit is an office which is capable of yielding a profit or pecuniary gain. 'Profit' means any pecuniary gain. The amount of such profit is immaterial but fee to reimburse out of pocket expenses do not constitute profit. On the other hand, if a profit does actually accrue from an office, it is an 'office of profit', no matter how it accrues. The earlier judicial decisions reveal that the following factors are material to decide a particular post is office of profit or not.

1. Whether the Government makes the appointment
2. Whether the Government pays the remuneration
3. Whether the performance of functions is for the government
4. Whether the Government Exercises any Control over the Exercise of Functions
5. Whether the Government has the power to remove the person holding the office

When the Constitution of India came into force on 26th January, 1950 declaring that a person holding an office of profit would be disqualified, the explanation to Article 102 clarified that a person who is a Minister (either for the Union or for any State) shall not be deemed to hold an office of profit. However, there existed Ministers of State as also Deputy Ministers in the Union Government who were not specifically exempted from disqualification under Article 102 because the expression 'minister' was construed as referring only to a Cabinet Minister. In order to address this situation, the Parliament (Prevention of Disqualification) Act, 1950 was enacted. Section 2 of the said Act provided:

"2. Prevention of disqualification for membership of Parliament: A person shall not be disqualified for being chosen as, and for being a member of Parliament by reason only of the fact that he holds any of the following offices of profit under the Government of India or the Government of any State, namely, an office of Minister of State or a Deputy Minister, or a Parliamentary Secretary or a Parliamentary Under Secretary."

This was followed by the Parliament (Prevention of Disqualification)

Act, 1951 declaring that certain offices (specified in Section 2 thereof) under the government shall not disqualify, and shall be deemed never to have disqualified the holders thereof for being chosen as, or for being, Members of Parliament. The said Act was given retrospective effect from 26.1.1950.

In 1954, a Committee was constituted under the chairmanship of Pandit Thakur Das Bhargava to study the various matters connected with the disqualification of MP's and to make recommendations in order to enable the government to consider the manner in which a comprehensive legislation should be brought. The Committee submitted its report in 1955. In 1959 the Parliament (Prevention of Disqualification) Act, 1959 was enacted, thereby declaring that certain offices of profit under the government shall not disqualify the holders thereof for being chosen as or for being, Members of Parliament. Section 3 of the Principal Act (amended from time to time) declared that none of the following offices in so far as it is an office of profit under the government of India or the 6 government of any State, shall disqualify the holder thereof for being chosen as, or for being, a Member of Parliament:

"(a) any office held by a Minister, Minister of State or Deputy Minister for the Union or for any State, whether ex-officio or by name;

(aa) the office of a Leader of the Opposition in Parliament;

(ab) the office of Deputy Chairman, Planning Commission;

(ac) the office of each leader and deputy leader of a recognised party and recognized group in either House of Parliament;

(b) the office of Chief Whip. Deputy Chief Whip or Whip in Parliament or of a Parliamentary Secretary;

(ba) the office of Chairperson of - (i) the National Commission for Minorities constituted under Section 3 of the National Commission for Minorities Act, 1992 (19 of 1992);

(ii) the National Commission for the Scheduled Castes and Scheduled Tribes constituted under clause (I) of article 338 of the Constitution;

(iii) the National Commission for Women constituted under Section 3 of the National Commission for Women Act, 1990 (20) of 1990;

(c) the office of member of any force raised or maintained under the National Cadet Corps Act, 1948 (56 of 1948), or the Reserve and Auxiliary Air Forces Act, 1952 (62 of 1952);

(d) the office of a member of a Home Guard constituted under any law for the time being in force in any State;

(e) the office of sheriff in the city of Bombay, Calcutta or Madras;

(f) the office of chairman or member of the syndicate, senate, executive committee, council or court of a university or other body connected with a university;

(g) the office of a member of any delegation or mission sent outside India by the Government for any special purpose;

(h) the office of chairman or member of a committee (whether consisting of one or more members), set up temporarily for the purpose of advising the Government or any other authority in respect of any matter of public importance or for the purpose of making an inquiry into, or collecting statistics in respect of, any such matter, if the holder of such office is not entitled to any remuneration other than compensatory allowance;

(i) the office of Chairman, director or member of any statutory or non- statutory body other than any such body as is referred to in clause (h), if the holder of such office is not entitled to any remuneration other than compensatory allowance, but excluding (i) the office of chairman of any statutory or non-statutory body specified in Part I of the Schedule, (ii) the office of chairman or secretary of any statutory or non-statutory body specified in Part II of the Schedule;

(j) the office of village revenue officer, whether called a lambardar, malguzar, patel, deshmukh or by any other name, whose duty is to collect land revenue and who is remunerated by a share of, or commission on, the amount of land revenue collected by him, but who dies not discharge any police functions."

The issue had become a matter of public importance in 2006 when Congresss President Sonia Gandhi was appointed as the Chairperson of National Advisory Council by the UPA government when she was a member of Lok Sabha. She also held several posts under the government. Complaints were registered against her, and she chose the safe route of resignation. So that she could continue her impression of being the statue of sacrifice and morality.Sonia Gandhi had resigned her membership in the Lok Sabha on the issue of office of profit in 2006. She later contested the Lok Sabha poll and won the election.

Another controversy arose when a Member of the Rajya Sabha Mrs. Jaya Bachchan was appointed as the Chairperson of the Uttar Pradesh Film Development Council on 14.7.2004. A complaint was made that this amounting to the holding of an 'office of profit' on her part and thus, she was not entitled to continue as a Member of the Rajya Sabha in view of Article 102(1)(a) of the Constitution. A Presidential Order was passed under Article 103(1) of the Constitution of India by which the said Member of the Rajya Sabha was disqualified from being a Member of the Rajya Sabha on the ground that she was holding an 'office of profit'. That order was challenged before this Court in *Jaya Bachan v. Union of India*[1], and the challenge was rejected by this Court. Thereafter, it was discovered that a large number of MPs' were holding 'Offices of Profit' and they also would incur the same disqualification. A Bill titled the Parliament (Prevention of Disqualification) Amendment Bill, 2006 was therefore introduced on 16th of May, 2006 in the Lok Sabha and was passed on the same day. On the next day, it was introduced in the Rajya Sabha and was debated on and passed on the same day. The Bill was sent to the President of India for his assent on 25th May, 2006. The President returned the Bill on 30th May, 2006 to the Parliament for reconsideration under Article 111 of the Constitution of India. The Bill was passed again by both the Houses without amendment and presented to the President for assent and the said assent was given on 18.8.2006. Thus, the Amendment Act came into existence.

8. Section 2 of the Amendment Act inserted the following clauses as (ad) after clause (ac) of section 3 of the Principal Act:

"(ad) the office of the chairperson of the National Advisory Council constituted by the Government of India in the Cabinet Secretariat vide Order No. 631/2/1/2004-Cab, dated the 31st May, 2004;"

9. Section 2 of Amendment Act also inserted after clause (j) the following clauses, which were to be deemed to have been inserted with effect from the 4 th day of April, 1959, namely:

"(k) the office of Chairman, Deputy Chairman, Secretary or Member (by whatever name called) in any statutory or non-statutory body specified in the Table;

(l) the office of Chairperson or trustee (by whatever name called) of any Trust, whether public or private, not being a body specified in the Schedule;

(m) the office of Chairman, President, Vice-President or Principal

Secretary or Secretary of the Governing Body of any society registered under the Societies Registration Act, 1860 or under any other law relating to registration of societies, not being a body specified in the Schedule."

Section 3 of the Amendment Act inserted a Table referred to in Section 2(k), listing 55 statutory and non-statutory bodies, following the Schedule in the Principal Act, which was also deemed to have been inserted with effect from 4th April, 1959.

Section 4 contained a special provision as to validation and other matters and it is extracted below:

"4. (1) Notwithstanding any judgment or order of any court or tribunal or any order or opinion of any other authority, the offices mentioned in clauses (ad), (k), (l) and (m) of Section 3 of the Principal Act shall not disqualify or shall be deemed never to have disqualified the holders thereof for being chosen as, or for being, as member of either House of Parliament as if the Principal Act as amended by this Act and been in force at all material times.

(2) Nothing contained in sub-section (l) shall be construed as to entire any person who has vacated a seat owing to any order or judgment, as aforesaid, to claim any reinstatement or any other claim in that behalf.

(3) For the removal of doubts, it is hereby clarified that any petition or reference pending before any court or other authority on the date of commencement of this Act, shall be disposed of in accordance with the provisions of the Principal Act, as amended by this Act."

In *Consumer Education and Research Society* v *Union of India*[2] Supreme Court considered constitutional validity of the amendment.

On behalf of the petitioners it was contended that the amendment that retrospectively exempted certain offices of profit from the disqualification rule was violative of the constitutional scheme of Articles 101 to 104 of the Constitution. It was submitted that the purpose of removal of disqualification by a retrospective amendment to the Act was to ensure that persons who had ceased to be MP's on account of incurring disqualifications would be re-inducted to Parliament without election, and that was impermissible and unconstitutional. It was asserted that several MP's were holding "offices of profit under the Government of India or the State Government, other than offices declared by Parliament by law not to disqualify their holder" (for short `the disqualifying offices of profit') when they were elected. It was further stated that several others had accepted the disqualifying offices of profit, after becoming Members, i.e. during their tenure as Members of Parliament. Hence , it was reasoned that a person holding such office of profit, was disqualified to become or be a Member of Parliament and that such Member's seat would become vacant on the very day when they were elected (with respect to those who were already holding the disqualifying office of profit, when they were elected) and on the day they accepted the disqualifying office of profit (with respect to those who accepted such disqualifying offices of profit during their tenure as Members of Parliament). It was submitted that when a Member's seat had already became vacant by virtue of incurring a constitutional disqualification, his/her membership cannot be revived by enacting a legislation which retrospectively removed the applicable disqualification.

The Court rejected this contention. It was pointed out that the earlier decision of the Supreme Court *Srimati Kanta Kathuria* v. *Manak Chand Surana*[3] has clearly laid down that the power of Parliament to enact a law under Article 102(1)(a) includes the power of Parliament to enact such law retrospectively. In that case, the appellant Mrs. Kanta Kathuria, an Advocate practicing at Bikaner was appointed as a Special Government Pleader. She was subsequently elected to the Rajasthan Legislative Assembly. The respondent therein challenged her election alleging that she was disqualified to be chosen as a Member of the Legislative Assembly since she held the office of Special Government Pleader, which was an office of profit under the Government of Rajasthan. The High Court accepted the contention and allowed the Election Petition. The elected candidate preferred an appeal to the Supreme Court 19 on August 2, 1968. During the pendency of the appeal, The Rajasthan State Legislature passed the Rajasthan Legislative Assembly Members (Prevention of Disqualification) Act, 1969 which removed the disqualification that had been applicable to Government pleaders, Government Advocates and Special Government Pleaders with retrospective effect. The respondent contended that the Rajasthan State Legislature was not competent to remove the disqualification retrospectively. Two opinions were delivered[4] since there was a difference of opinion on the question whether, on the date of her election, the appellant held an office of profit. The minority view was that she did, whereas the majority view was that she did not. However, there was unanimity in respect of the finding that the state legislature was competent to enact a law for the purpose of removing the disqualification with retrospective effect. The Court applied this earlier doctrine in *Kantha Kathuria Case* and observed[5]:

There is no doubt that the disqualification, when declared by the President will become operative from the date the Member accepted the 'office of profit'. It is also not in doubt that the vacation of the seat is consequential. However, the question is whether the seat of the Member become vacant without anything more when a person accepts an 'office of profit'? The obvious answer is 'no'. If the Member does not make a voluntary declaration that he/she has incurred a disqualification and if no one raises a dispute about the same, the Member would continue in spite of accepting an office of profit. There is nothing strange about this position....

When the Amending Act retrospectively removed the disqualification with regard to certain enumerated offices, any Member who was holding such office of profit, was freed from the disqualification retrospectively. As on the date of the passage of the Amendment Act, none of the Members who were holding such offices had been declared to be disqualified by the President, Section 4(2) was not attracted and consequently they continued as Members.

So the Supreme Court upheld the power of the Parliament to enact law so as to exempt an office from the purview of office of profit with retrospective effect. So person who became disqualified by holding an office of profit subsequent to election may be protected from the operation of the disqualification by enacting law and giving retrospective effect to it.

It is submitted that the approach of the Court is erroneous owing to the following reasons. The very moment of accepting the office of profit the person had become disqualified. The fact that either the concerned person or any another person did not point out this fact does not make any difference to this substantive position since the proceedings like complaint to President, seeking of the opinion of the Election Commission, issuing of the order for disqualifying the person etc are mere formalities.

Secondly in certain cases giving assent to the law which exempts a particular office from the purview of office of profit may put the President in a difficult position. For example the bill, which is sent to the President for exempting an office, may be one intending to rescue a person against whom a complaint of disqualification on the ground of holding office of profit is pending before the President. In some cases the recommendation of the Election Commission to disqualify that person itself may be pending before the President at the time of sending the bill for the Presidential assent. In such a situation it may be very difficult for the President to perform his constitutional obligation.

So the correct approach would have been to declare the enactment with retrospective effect to exempt an office from the purview of office of profit as unconstitutional. But the Court took a different approach.

NOTES AND REFERENCES

1. (2006) 5 SCC 266.
2. [2009] INSC 1476 (24 August 2009).
3. [1969] INSC 292.
4. One by Hidayatullah. C.J. (for himself and Mitter J), and another by Sikri, J, (as he then was) (for himself, Ray, J. and Jaganmohan Reddy, J).
5. Supra n.3 para 36 and 37.

9 Electoral Reforms—Are we for Reforms?

P.L. Dharma

The Democratic journey in Indian democracy has a great story to be reckoned with. It is made clear by some of the serious students of India in general and modern India in particular that the journey was primarily planned and organized. Thus adaptation and flexibility could not be adopted at times. However, many have proposed that India wanted a kind of democracy that was in practice in the west, for that the Rights emerges superior to all other existing as part of the modern system. Besides, it must not be forgotten that India had an inbuilt argument that it had the great tradition of democratic experiments. Hence, there was no need to look for an alternative, especially from the west in terms of democracy. Thanks to the nationalist perspective of India that went on eulogizing the Indian existence as superior to all other political systems. Indeed, India was able to build several institutions of democratic content and nurtured democratic political culture that provided the elaborate base for the kind of experiments going on today. However, the journey of Indian democratic experiments has left behind a culture of democratizing both the process of thinking and acting in the larger context of our socio-political life. This does not mean to say that we have democratized every sector of our concern. The democratization process by and large is a continuous one and cannot be achieved overnight. Gradually, we started to feel the system that helped us to know it from its different activities, especially managing the plural character of our society. On the other hand, we have witnessed the absorption of number of socially excluded people who slowly demonstrated their presence if not at all levels but as political supporters. If one looks at the entire democratic activities, it can be understood that there emerged divergent groups either supporting or opposing or being neutral to the democratization process as part of their political right. There may be other groups too with different opinions on the process at times. However, our democratic experiments may have encountered with mixed response from different quarters but they are a new chapter in the Indian history to be approached with care and sensitivity.

Though the result was not satisfactory with every experiment we experimented, the democratic basic in India was getting strengthened on one hand. Social base of the democratic experiments day by day not only got expanded and emerged as plural forces but also began to interpret democracy democratically. This indeed, helped democracy to get a meaningful tag saying that democracy is a way of life.

The elitist traditions that emerged strongly as part of the political process have remarked that the democratic experiments have produced irreparable political trends with the entry of poor, uneducated and socially backward. They substantiate the argument saying that the democratic experiments not only liberalised (democratised) the political space but also closed the door to those who had potentiality to manage the public affairs. Instead of making Indian democracy meaningful, they say it is heading to a series of crises. The popular participation is said to be doing the damage hence, to them the democratic model in India is an outdated practice, having nothing except the politics of appeasing.

In spite of these ups and downs the democratic experiments in India however, have succeeded at two levels. Firstly, it has managed to establish such institutions that helped legalize the participation of people. Secondly, there is a vast opportunity created at the village level for the people that in turn have created a great deal of interest in the public institutions. Thanks to the democratic experiments for being a major influential factor on people who in turn look up to public institutions. The public institutions established here at least legally have healthy spaces for the people of all. They encourage people to be part of the public institutions.

The market forces on the other hand have been nurturing the culture that would help people compromise with political values. As part of the sponsored game, the market forces of different kinds have encouraged people through their culture to disobey the public institutions especially the state. In spite of this, the democratic experiments have attracted the attention of people at two levels. Firstly, the amount of power and capacity of power the elected ones possess in putting the disorder in to orderly way. Secondly, the biggest show in the form of conducting elections for the legislatures.

There are instances that different democratic experiments have constantly engaged in the process of democratisation of society in general and democratisation of relationship between individuals and institutions in particular. Indeed, our democratisation process has attracted the attention of people.

Today, there are a good number of questions posed as to why they did not get the opportunity which is entitled to them? The rise of these questions at the level of people is one of the biggest achievements of democratic experiments in India. However, democratic experiments are not a set of activities that could be achieved overnight. It is primarily a major process of reform involved with number of interconnected activities. Given its design and implementation, it is further more complicated in a society like India where we have seen and experienced different modes of inequality. Even though several initiatives of the democratisation process in India were designed as populist schemes to build political base, they slowly and steadily promoted political awareness.

It is not to read Indian polity from the perspective of only its success story. If it is seen from the larger perspective of nation and national integration, the democratic experiments have proved too expensive. For instance, Caste, religion, region, muscle and money power are the fundamental forces whose influence on the democratisation process has raised fundamental questions. While influencing the same, these forces succeeded in proposing the alternative package and made the democratisation process more complicated. Though the entry of social forces made the state to feel excess, it was considered as the real democratic practice where there is no restrictions on any force entering into the political processes. Besides, our democratic experiments need appreciation at two levels. Firstly, it has encouraged the participation of people at all levels making it a mass-based activity. Secondly, it has slowly and steadily created opportunities based on legal provisions. Both these have helped people to realise their rights on one hand and on the other strengthened the democratic spirit in India. Having created opportunities based on legal frame work, we have attracted the attention of people towards the participation. Though we have not achieved the maximum 'participation target', the people are participating in one or the other activities of their choice. Indian democracy has allowed people even to reject elections. In a way, the decision to reject and not to take part in elections is also a political decision. By rejecting an election, they have also expressed that they too are taking part in the political process. However, the democratization process achieved through the Electoral Reforms has opened up the opportunities to people to act according to their independent decision.

II

Electoral Reforms as Democratising Attempt

Thanks to Electoral Reforms initiated and implemented as part and parcel of democratisation experiments in India. Electoral reforms were primarily a set of measures initiated and implemented to augment the process of conducting democracy. They are primarily manufactured to sell the fundamentals of Indian democracy. They are by themselves appearing as piece-meal engineering as well as a planned patch work. However, the reforms have been also strengthening the democratic language and meaning at all levels. It is interesting that we have travelled less and are ahead of many other parts of the world in some of the major democratic initiatives. One among them was extending voting Rights to all who have completed the age of 18 [we even talk about scaling it down to 16 today]. Indeed, such a bold decision excluding their political tones needed Indian administration to gear up for a chain of actions-like, effective census data, maintaining birth and death documents, implanting agencies to manage the affairs related to reforms and implementing the reformed set actions and a lot more. A single amendment and there after implementing the same is still going on and the same is posing a greater challenge to democratise our experiments.

Besides, our attempts towards Electoral Reforms in general and deciding the accurate group of people having right to vote and avoiding the people without right to vote in particular is a serious work yet to be taken seriously. Both the theory and practice of electoral reforms together stand for a RATIONAL ACTION by a citizen within the existing socio-political reality. It also very strongly argues for a reasonable institutional behaviour. Indeed, electoral reforms have been the most significant components of the Indian Political system. In simple and clear words, electoral reforms are a broadened campaign for absorbing all and to make every qualified citizen to perform meaningfully.

Need for Reforms

Reforms are not a new experiment in India. This is neither a continuation nor a break but an ongoing exercise for that it was necessary and inevitable political action. The students of political studies and research have always looked at it as integral part of a political system. Reforms are as old as the state system. Ever since the study on state was initiated, references on reforms have appeared here and there. Since it takes place within the larger boundary of the state any reform is bound to be called POLITICAL. Thus reforms in general are political.

The political activity being central to every individual cannot escape from the day today activities. People at times may have refused to reforms and proved themselves that they are not for democratisation. While every other things are changing, changing against the plan and expectations one becomes helpless to say no reforms. Accepting reforms, introducing reforms and attaching meaning to reforms are supposed to be seen as democratic duties today. These attempts are not only to reform the existing but also to assess and interpret the capability of producing results.

Reforms at every level are needed. The demand for reforms is emerging from the voiceless and disadvantaged as they understand that the system is not making roads in to their life. Their demand for reforms is generally addressed to state for that it has the capacity to accommodate their demands. Indeed, reforms are everyone's slogan today.

The classical classification of our Society like rich and poor; upper and lower caste; ruling and ruled; Urban and rural; man and women, Schooled and unschooled; empowered and underpowered; employed and unemployed has generated an inbuilt urge to go for reforms. It is thus the political reforms that the electoral reforms promise to deliver.

Globalisation has brought in, rather imposed on us, an urge for reforms. The only crucial thing about reform is that it is emerging with internal dynamics. Reforms expected today are an inbuilt mechanism that successfully satisfies the identified sections of the people. That indeed shows that the reforms expected are not homogenous. Various social groups with the clash of interests add to the complexity of reforms required. However, all of us need reforms and the reforms per se do not reform the society as a whole. Thanks to all the attempts launched through large number of social movements where they show that they are committed for reforms that help society at large. The popular voice expressed at different democratic platforms help us to believe that there are significant numbers of people who work for reforms.

Establishing democracy also involves democratising our practices. Initially, we assumed and believed that we are a democratic society/country hence; reforms will end up in reframing society. But our reforms were not satisfactorily bringing out results as we failed in democratising ourselves. Democracy can exist and survive only when there are reforms in both institutions and their practices as well as with the people. India succeeded in the former and the latter remained the same and at times worst.

When looked at from the perspective of Rights, every group in India has suffered in one or the other way. And, suffering gets defined with the larger frame work of Rights. Thus, every group thinks that aspiring for reforms is nothing but assertion of their Rights. If measured on the scale, it is on the increasing level that reforms are expected to go for changes in what exists.

Argument

Electoral Reforms introduced in India aimed at many changes at different levels. They are primarily a set of 'Means' to bring in expected changes in the existing experiences of life. Depositing on few reforms and refusing to follow up results in the due course of time have ended up in failures. This has been our trial and error method till this date. Thus, reforms of any kind are to be treated as a process. Electoral Reforms cannot take up on their own all that they promise or claim to achieve in a given time until and unless they are correspondingly supported by other sectors where public claims are involved.

For instance, even after major Electoral Reforms we have not been able to get neither 100% voting turn out nor create the interest in public affairs. This subtly suggests that Electoral Reforms are not independent activities. They are related to the educational, social and economic activities of our society. There is no way, where every action of ours must produce the calculated result as long as we isolate other factors influencing the action we have executed. It must be realized that the reforms of any kind ought to be located in the larger context as against what we have been doing for the years till this date.

Large numbers of people are not aware of the significance of voting and those who are aware of it seldom take interest in it. Given this existing fact, one must engage in creating interest among the people who are slowly deserting the political processes in general and voting process in particular. Indeed, Electoral Reforms must prioritize the fact that social reforms can create a meaningful base to the political reform in general and Electoral Reforms in Particular. The political activities in India are not supposed to be seen as the independent activities by themselves. They are one of the inherent expressions of our life that is getting influenced by various factors simultaneously.

More than six decades of experiments and constant vigilance on the activities happening around, the reforms have not fully reformed even the fundamental voting behaviour of the people. Thus, the reforms introduced in India till this date have raised fundamental questions:

1. Whether the Electoral Reforms were attempts to reform the institutions or individuals?
2. Have they been imposed on the individual?

3. Were the electoral reforms political strategies of the ruling government?
4. Whether EVMs have made elections efficient and effective?
5. Are the voters matured enough to exercise their right to vote?

Besides, for whose sake the Electoral Reforms were introduced? A question of this kind deliberately forces us to think beyond the urgency in introducing the reforms even without public debate. If they were introduced to make the activities of the agencies conducting elections easy, it only suggests us that the reforms were suffering from vision. If not, it has to be treated as a matter of concern.

However, in their external outlook, the reforms appear to be the avenues for the individuals to utilize the political opportunities at maximum. In its contents and rationale it only tells us that they were introduced for the sake of making bureaucracy more prominent than the political, therefore the public. Consequently, the administration is emerging as primary than the political so as to make the procedures of reforms complicated. Given this, the existing disturbed and strained relations between the bureaucrats and the political leaders found a different turn when procedures prevailed. If Electoral Reforms were introduced to maximize the participation of the people, there is a strong message for democratization process. Democratisation per se is not just maximizing participation or avoiding the tainted to be fielded as candidates but much more and it has to be much more.

The new political culture under the umbrella of globalisation is suggesting that individuals are increasingly losing interest in politics. There are large numbers of happenings around individuals that attract the attention of people more than politics. On the other hand politics per se has not been able to get the mass attention in spite of the revolutionary reforms.

For instance, every one (a small survey carried out in Mangalore, Karnataka to expose how we have surrendered to technology) is in possession of ATM cards on one hand and the best SIM cards that offer all kinds of benefits in the market today. They have burned candles to possess one or the other cards that helped them to negotiate with the new market. However, hardly people are seen, especially the Urban dwellers in the queue for collecting their voters identity cards. Many have not even registered their name for VICs.

Electoral reforms thus have to address the nihilistic attitudes of the people than taking series of efforts to reform certain rules and regulations to make way for maximisation of participation. The dangerous shift from social democracy to market democracy initiated by the forces of globalisation is not only attacking the public space but also redefining what life ought to be. This situation must work as a framework for Electoral Reforms.

Electoral reforms have to address not just the rural based but the urban based, so called citizens who often fight for consumers' rights rather than rights of the individuals. Indian's growing middle and upper class is completely in the hands of forces of globalization and therefore may completely emerge as apolitical. Electoral reforms have to think beyond mere voters and their behaviour.

Reforms in India today ought to be an integral rather than an independent work.

Part II
Money Power and Muscle Power in Elections

10 Cost of Democracy : Mounting Influence of Money Power in Indian Elections

J. Prabhash

I. Introduction

It is often argued that there is a positive linkage between governance and public opinion, public opinion not as a caricature of elite interests moulded and reflected by mass media, but one which draws sustenance from the concrete life situations of the mass of the people and which is primarily articulated by political parties. This, however, depends on the authenticity of representation, a phrase which denotes the commitment of the elected representatives and political parties to the people. Stated differently, the core problem involved in representation is the relationship that exists between the representatives and the represented [Burke 1986: 28-31], in a sense between state and society.

Though this relationship is predominantly anchored on the legal foundation of citizens' rights (for instance a body of fundamental rights), it also rests partially on the ideology and clarity of moral language of the political society. Implication here is that rights *per se* are incapable of ensuring people the blessings of good governance. While rights have limited usefulness in this regard, what matters most is politicisation of the people through mass mobilisations and struggles by political parties. History had repeatedly testified to the fundamental fact that all meta-narratives of rights for the marginalised were expressed only through the medium of politics.

Thus the success or failure of democracy always depends on the nature of democratic politics or the quality of politics in a democracy. For, the marginalised acquire agency, recover their self-hood and earn self-confidence through politics alone. However it has to be public, pro-active and inclusive so that it could act as a link between state accountability and realisation of democratic rights [*Chandhoke, 2003:2966*]. It is worthwhile to recall here that democracy performs its most salient functions—selection of candidates, mobilisation of electorate, formulation of agenda, and passing of legislations—through parties

[Mehta, 2001:38]. It is here that the political parties and their leaderships figure prominently.

Both ought to have an organic linkage with each other and ultimately with the people *i.e.,* political parties have to mean the people and their leadership, rank and file. They have also to be democratic internally *i.e.,* their internal decision making and recruitment to leadership positions, including electoral positions in the state, have to be transparent and democratic. Only under such a condition popular authorization through votes and public policies through legislation get interlocked in a dialectical relationship making representation authentic and accountability of the state genuine.

The health of institutions, particularly that of legislature and political executive, hinges on this. This makes the criteria for selection of individuals for various elective positions by political parties transparent, principled, rulebound and also open, minimising the interplay of extraneous influences—for instance role of money and muscle power. This has also the anticipated consequence of keeping the electoral system robust and clean to a very great extent. Any discussion on the electoral system and its reform has to be foregrounded on this theoretical premise. This paper seeks to discuss the influence of money power in elections in India against this background.

II. Role of Money in Elections

Influence of money in Indian elections is not a new phenomenon. This was reported even during the Nehruvian period – golden era of Indian democracy – though such influence was much less compared to modern times. This difference in the intensity of influence that money power has in the electoral arena today begs deeper analysis as it is basically related to the somewhat sweeping changes that have taken place in Indian politics in the last four decades. Needless to say, the Nehruvian phase of Indian politics was noted for the following features: unquestioned and charismatic leadership of Nehru within the Congress and the electoral dominance the party enjoyed both in the national and state politics; the moral and political ambience created by the national movement and their influence over the political and civil societies; limited nature of political fragmentation and competition which hardly posed any threat to the entrenched interests of the traditional elites; and a meaningful presence of internal democracy within parties (Congress in particular) and the thorough national outlook of their leadership.

It is true that there was a strong deficit in political mobilisation and politicisation of the masses during this period. The periodic bouts of mass movements and agitations organised by the left parties apart, little attempts were made by other political parties in politicising the electorate. While for a party like the Congress there was no need for this as it was in power continuously, for others like Jan Sangh and Swatantra Party, either they were too elitist in nature and remained marginal to Indian politics or their socio-political agenda had nothing to justify such a course of action. However, this gap was more than offset by the deep faith of the people in the agendum of social transformation and the programme of nation – building put forward by the Nehruvian Congress and by the political education they had acquired through the great pedagogic processes of the freedom struggle. At the other end, intra-party democracy (though restricted in scope and scale) made the process of candidate selection and recruitment to leadership positions within parties moderately transparent. All these taken together accounted for the 'robustness' of the electoral system during the first few decades of Indian politics. Neither the freshness of the freedom movement allowed the civil/ political societies to abandon, totally, ethical considerations from politics nor the looming presence of the ruling party and the electoral marginality of the opposition provided any incentive for them to bend the rules of electoral game beyond a point.

However, things began to change drastically from the seventies onwards. The social base of the once dominant Congress became shaky with many of the marginalised social groups – from Dalits to OBCs and Muslims – shifting their allegiance to other parties and in certain cases, forming their own parties often based on regionalism and ethnicity. The period also witnessed the consecration into politics of a new breed of politicians with little respect for parliamentary etiquettes and democratic values and for whom the freedom movement and the socio-political vision it threw up appeared too remote. Cumulatively this came to have three significant consequences as far as Indian politics is concerned: regionalisation and 'ethnicisation' of the party system; fragmentation of the political society leading to mushrooming of parties making political arena a highly contested domain [*Katju, 2009:9*]; and the subaltern resistance towards monopolization of political power by the traditional elites.

The impact of the above on the political parties and consequently on the electoral system was drastic. Amoeba–like mutation of existing parties and their eventual appearance as new political outfits made politics volatile. The ethnification[1] of the party system further rendered redundant the strategy of cross sectional mobilisation which the Congress had been following for about three decades since independence. According to democratic theory, political parties could address issues like these only by further democratising themselves internally and strengthening their ties with the people by mobilising them around their quotidian concerns i.e., making politics issue-based, public and inclusive – in short making it central to democracy. In the long run this would enable them not only to cross the rubicon of caste/ethnicity based mobilisation but also address the issue of political fragmentation.

Paradoxically, this was not the direction in which Indian politics locomoted. In all the above counts it moved in the opposite direction. As the parties became weak and fragmented, their leadership emerged more powerful dispensing with every trace of inner party democracy that existed. Atul Kohli neatly summarises the situation thus:

> [These leaders] concentrated power in their persons, appointed loyal minions to positions of power, and continued to rule as long as their personal popularity could be maintained....[They] posses a considerable degree of freedom, not in social restructuring, but in creating a top-down political system. The more the second and third tier officers of the party come to be appointed from above, the less independent power exists within the polity and the more centralised becomes the top of the political pyramid. Thus emerges the first important paradox of contemporary India: democratisation of traditional authority, especially in the rural social structure, has proved the way for centralisation of power at the top [Atul Kohli, 2009: 27-33].

This meant that the criteria for basic decisions any party has to take, ranging from candidate selection to party platform, remained/remains either unclear or left to the discretion of one or a handful of leaders [Mehta, 2001:37]. The implication is that moving with leaders rather than working with people became the sole criteria for electoral positions for party cadres who, therefore, shifted their activities from grassroots to party headquarters. This naturally dried up the supply of party workers from the society, ultimately severing the linkage between parties and the mass of the people.

Parties, on their side, tried to make up this deficiency in popular support by entering into indiscriminate electoral alliances, invoking primordial sentiments and even roping in the support of criminal elements. This slowly came to have another important effect – depoliticising the electoral process. When ideological positions, policy preferences and public opinion hardly matter for political parties, governance automatically gets delinked from politics – politics in a democratic sense i.e., public, inclusive and proactive. Economic liberalisation of the nineties has accelerated this process as parties – with the exception of the Left to a certain extent – belonging to various political spectrums began to converge on important questions of public policies, economic and development policies in particular. When different political parties speak the same language of development and use the same idioms and vocabulary of public policies, politics ceases to be a matter of choice i.e., though there are different political formations they do not have alternative programmes and *weltanschauung.* In such a situation we are moving into an era of depoliticization in which even those who call themselves politicians are either themselves depolitisised or have become instruments in the hands of those who have no faith in open politics and none whatsoever in either democracy or the people [Kothari, 1992:17].

The greatest impact of this on elections is that they have ceased to be a contest of ideas and public policies. And when elections are drained of their political content, parties have to look for alternative means to gain popular votes. All these prepare the fertile ground for electoral malpractices of which influence of money is an important one. With the help of money, elections are turned into a great spectacle and the electoral arena converted into a big market space where money mediates between the candidates and the electorate.

II. Nature and Extent of Money Power

Influence of money in elections is not merely confined to overspending and/or purchasing of votes by parties/candidates. Neither is such influence indirect any more. It is now direct as *crorepatis* and corporate interests are becoming representatives themselves. They are no longer content with influencing public policies sitting outside the Houses, but want to call shots and define the contours of state action by being part of the political processes. This has drastically altered the social composition – particularly the class character – of the Parliament as well.

Electoral spending has mounted to such a level that it makes a mockery of all the existing laws. It is stated that on an average a candidate spends anywhere between three to fifteen crore rupees in a single Lok Sabha constituency [Ray, 2009:33]. According to a very conservative estimate, in the 2009 general elections to the Lower House of the Parliament, Congress Party has officially spent Rs. 1500 crore [2], BJP Rs. 1000 crore; BSP and NCP Rs. 700 core each; DMK Rs. 400 core and

AIADMK rupees 300 core[3] [Ibid:36]. It is common knowledge that a portion of this money has gone to the purchase of votes. The survey conducted in 2009 by the Centre for Media Studies (CMS), a Delhi based think-tank, is revealing in this respect[4]. According to it nearly one-fifth of the voters across the country had stated that candidates or party workers offered them money to vote in the past decade [Ibid: 32].

Interestingly state spending on the conduct of elections has also increased phenomenally. While it was just 10.45 crore in 1952 during the first general elections, it has reached an all time high of 1300 crore in 2004 during the 14th Lok Sabha elections (Table 10.1). An important point worth noting is that increase is really noticeable since 1991 *i.e.,* with the inauguration of the neo-liberal economic policies. Though there is hardly any correlation either between state spending and neo-liberal economic policies or state spending and expenses incurred by political parties and individual candidates, still it helps students of Political Science and Psephology to understand the escalating cost of democracy in contemporary times.

Table 10.1
State Spending for the conduct of Elections – Lok Sabha (1952-2004)

Year of election	*State Spending (Rupees in Crore)*	*Increase/decrease from the previous elections (Rupees in Crore)*
1952	10.45	NA
1957	5.90	-4.50
1962	7.32	+1.42
1967	10.80	+3.48
1971	11.61	+0.81
1977	23.04	+11.43
1980	54.77	+31.73
1984	81.51	+26.74
1989	154.22	+72.71
1991	359.10	+204.88
1996	597.34	+238.24
1998	666.22	+68.88
1999	880.00 *	+217.78
2004	1300.00**	+420.00

* Approximate ; ** Provisional.

Source: Ravindranath, 2009:16.

Change in the economic profile of the Members of Lok Sabha also makes interesting reading as it shows the extent to which and the manner in which money power is creeping into the House (Table 10.2). Percentage of increase in the total assets of the members between the Fourteenth and Fifteenth Houses is 186.01 i.e., it jumped from Rs.1273.07 lakh in the Fourteenth House to Rs. 3641.30 lakh in the Fifteenth House. Interestingly, this is the highest for regional/state political parties with BJD registering an increase of 792.56 per cent, DMK 333.12 per cent, BSP 286.05 per cent and Shiv Sena 103.36 per cent. An important observation made by Sanjaya Baru that 'regional parties..... have been most active in States, where regional business groups have been dynamic and assertive' [Baru, 2000:243] needs restatement here though the increase in assets of MPs belonging to these parties could hardly be taken as a conclusive proof to justify it. Among the national parties, BJP has the highest increase (217.27 per cent) followed by the Congress (102.11 per cent).

Table 10.2
Average Assets of Lok Sabha Members: (14th and 15th Houses)

Parties	*Assets : 14th House (rupees in lakh)*	*Assets : 15th House (rupees in lakh)*	*Percentage increase*
Congress (I)	310.76	628.08	102.11
SP	153.78	241.43	57.0
Shiv Sena	151.29	308.43	103.36
BSP	119.83	462.60	286.05
DMK	105.06	455.04	333.12
BJP	96.91	307.47	217.27
RJD	56.19	136.58	82.95
B J D	53.51	427.62	792.58
CPI	25.40	25.50	3.94
CPM	22.95	37.98	65.49
Others	177.39	610.57	244.20
Total	**1273.07**	**3641.30**	**186.01**

Sources: 1. Paul and Vivekananda, 2004: 4629.
2. *http://myxata.info/fs2009/national* election watch.

Note: For the 14th Lok Sabha assets of only 535 MPs were available whereas this is 543 for the 15th House.

Looked at individually, the average assets of a Lok Sabha member currently is Rs. 51 million and that of a Cabinet Minister Rs.75 million[5] [Sainath, 2009]. That in a country where 836 million human beings have a per capita wage of less than Rs. 20/- a day, there are 306 'crorepatis' in the Lower House – an increase of 98 per cent between 2004 and 2009 [Ibid] – speaks volumes about the mismatch between the representatives and the represented.

III. Political Corruption and Assets and Income of Parties

This change in the financial status of the MPs could not be viewed in isolation. Actually it forms part of the changing economic profile of the parties themselves and the mounting instances of political corruption. The assets of political parties for which data are available show that, except for the organized Left – that too to a certain extent only – the same has increased drastically for others over the years. Between 2002 and 2006 this has increased by 249.55 per cent for the Congress, 456 per cent for Samajwadi Party and 303.48 per cent for the BSP (Table 10.3). Even for a party like the CPM, the increase is not insubstantial at 104.22 per cent.

Table 10.3
Assets of Political Parties (2002 – '06)
(Rupees in crore)

Parties	*2002*	*2004*	*2006*	*Percentage increase between 2002-06*
Congress	65.37	135.85	228.50	249.55
SP	13.86	26.56	77.07	456.0
CPI (M)	52.83	84.99	107.89	104.22
BJP	81.41	155.42	111.80	37.33
BSP	10.92	43.69	44.06	303.48
CPI	5.53	5.50	6.25	13.02

Source: Ravindranath, 2009:17.

Notably, at the other end, on their own admission, the income of political parties from membership fees is coming down and from that of donations is correspondingly mounting up. Except for the Left and Samajwadi Party, for all others collection from membership fee has drastically slided between 2002 and 2006 (Table 10.4) with donations constituting their major source of income. This is mainly so in the case of Congress, BJP, and SP with 99.58 per cent, 94.78 per cent and 89.05 per cent respectively of their income coming from donations.

Writing on the wall is thus clear: there is a growing gap between the representatives and the represented in terms of their class position; the assets of political parties and their income from sources other than membership collection is spiraling and both the candidates and parties are spending huge sums during elections than they are legally permitted. The million dollar question here is the source from where this galactical sums come. No doubt they come from corporate contributions and corruption. Though for the former, we don't have any systematic account, the ever increasing instances of corruption scandals involving politicians throw some vague hints at the latter. (Table 10.5)

Table 10.4
Income of Political Parties: 2002 – '06
(Rupees in crore)

Parties and Nature of income	*Period*		
	2002	*2004*	*2006*
Congress			
Donation	134.70	146.87	109.49
Membership Fee	20.40	10.80	00.46
BJP			
Donation	27.16	67.50	25.07
Membership Fee	0.53	5.26	1.38
CPM			
Donation	80.70	14.77	17.90
Levy/Membership Fee	6.39	11.64	16.99
CPI			
Donation	00.47	00.26	00.97
Levy/Membership Fee	00.07	00.07	00.09
BSP			
Donation	4.00		2.55
Membership Fee	1.00	9.95	3.55
SP			
Donation	7.16	14.61	40.35
Membership Fee	00.82	00.03	4.96

Source: Ravindranath, 2009:17.

If one looks at the major political scandals for the last two decades one would be surprised not only by the enormity of the amount involved, but by the geometrical progression in the scale of corruption as well. This has been particularly so since the economic liberalization of 1991 during which period money swindled by the political class is pegged at a mind-boggling Rs.73 lakh crore compared to which the greatest pre-liberalization scam – Bofors (64 crore) - pales into insignificance [Dasgupta, 2009:41]. Except on three occasions (1994, 2002 and 2003), the amounts involved touched four digits and upwards. A part of this amount naturally goes to the electoral arena.

IV. Business Representation in Parliament

It may be recalled that the mainstream discussion on the influence of money power in elections hardly takes into account the growing presence of business interests in Parliament and State Legislatures. While this is partly due to non-availability of statistics in this regard, it also stems from the belief that this has little relevance as far as the issue at

Table 10.5
Major Corruption Scandals (1992 – 2009)

Year	*Amount (rupees in crore)*	*Increase/decrease from previous year*	*Percentage increase/ decrease*
1992	5,000	Not applicable	Not applicable
1994	650	-4350	–87
1995	5,700	+5050	–776.92
1996	2,383	-3317	–58.19
1997	3,474	+1091	+31.40
1998	8,000	+4526	+130.28
2001	6,645	-1355	–16.94
2002	600	-6045	–90.97
2003	172	-428	–71.33
2005	19,141	+18969	+110.28
2006	1,675	-17466	–91.25
2008	1,25,095	+123420	+7368.36
2009	13,630	–1,11,465	–89.10
Total	**1,92,165**	**Not applicable**	**Not applicable**

Source: Dasgupta, 2009:41.

hand is concerned. It is high time that we changed this attitude as direct representation of business in legislature has much more serious consequences for policy making than influencing it through funding parties from outside. It is only a matter of conjecture the likely impact of a business tycoon like Vijay Mallya (owner of Kingfisher Airlines) acting as a member of the Standing Committee of the Ministry of Industry or as a special invitee on the Consultative Committee attached to the Ministry of Civil Aviation[6]; or a media baron like Vijay Darda on the Standing Committee attached to the Communications, IT and, Information and Broadcasting Ministry; or an industrialist like R.P.Goenka on the Consultative Committee of the Finance Ministry.

Table 10.6 indicates the growing presence of business representatives in both Houses of Parliament. Interestingly their representation is highest in Lok Sabha than in Rajya Sabha. Fourteenth Lok Sabha had 22.33 percentage businessmen as its members against 15.90 percentage for the current Rajya Sabha. Significantly, for the last twenty years, the presence of this class in the Parliament has been showing an upward movement with the Lower House registering an increase of 7.26 per cent between 1991 to 2009 and Rajya Sabha registering 6.02 per cent increase from 1994 till date. This shows the extent to which the business class has now come to put a premium on direct representation in Parliament in the era of economic liberization. Though, in the absence of serious studies, one could not put forward a straight forward and cogent argument that there exists a linkage between the growing presence of business in Parliament and the changing nature of public policies – economic policies in particular – of the Indian State, still such a hypothesis could not be ruled out as a figment of imagination. Rising tide of corporate funding of elections, advancing level of assets of elected representatives and the enveloping presence of businessmen in Parliament taken together definitely point towards the possibility of such a connection.

Table 10.6
Business Representation in Parliament (1991-2009)

House	*Business rep.*	*Non-business rep.*	*Data not available*	*Total*
Lok Sabha 10th House	82(15.07)	440(80.88)	22(4.04)	544(100)
11th House	109(20.19)	421(77.96)	10(1.85)	540(100)
12th House	78(14.80)	441(83.68)	8(1.52)	527(100)
13th House	99(17.43)	449(79.05)	20(3.52)	568(100)
14th House	119(22.33)	393(73.73)	21(3.94)	533(100)
Rajya Sabha 1994	8(9.88)	69(85.19)	4(4.94)	81(100)
1998	31(12.60)	211(85.77)	3(1.22)	246(99.59)
Current House	38(15.90)	192(80.33)	9(3.77)	239(100%)

Source : Sinha, 2010:472.

Note : Figures given in brackets indicate percentage distribution.

Therefore, the impact of the influence of money power in elections is not as simple and moderate as it was a few decades back. Today it is no longer restricted to obtaining a couple of import licences or tax concessions or subsidies for corporate houses or rich farmers (the so called vices of the licence–permit – raj), but has a much wider ramification which is potent enough to redraw the rules governing political economy of the country. Interestingly, paradoxically too, all these have come at a time when the electoral participation of the subaltern groups has increased significantly and the consequent 'expansion of democracy has enabled them to gain access to political power' [Fernandes, 2007:175]. The elite sections of various hues and shades have now invented new means to perpetuate their monopoly of political power and even to expand it. As a result, the electoral process is ceasing to be a reflection of the will of the people, or even the will of the political parties on whom the outcome of elections is supposed to rest [Kothari, 1992:16; Bhambhri, 1994:237]. This also means that the system of representation which is the chief instrument of social transformation – a model with which the country has started – is facing severe crisis [Kothari, 1992:15]. This is simultaneously a crisis of representation and that of governance, in a sense a crisis of democracy itself. As such, unless this issue is squarely addressed, democracy cannot become meaningful.

V. Conclusion

Many solutions are offered by various studies for preventing the influence of money in elections. This ranges from state funding of elections, declaration of assets by candidates, putting a cap on election spending, to auditing the source and amount of funding of parties and their expenditure, both during elections and after. A case is also made for including the money spent by parties for campaign purposes in the electoral expenditure of the respective candidates. Some of these suggestions are implemented by the Government as well. However, these measures, *per se,* are not capable enough to address the issue at hand comprehensively. This is not to deny the importance of such measures, but only to emphasise that the issue has also to be addressed politically. Further these legal/ administrative solutions could not tackle the problem of growing political corruption or the increasing business representation in law making bodies and in the political executive.

Needless to say, depoliticisation is often identified as a major cause for the entry of people from non-political class (including business leaders) into the structures of political power. When governance process is thus drained of its political content, societal issues appear as non-political needing for their redressal managerial solutions which could best be articulated by representatives from outside the political fraternity. This along with the decline of ideological politics, rampant corruption of politicians and their overall failure in various fronts, have given a new found legitimacy to the bureaucrat/businessmen–turned – politicians in the eyes of the people. As a consequence, political parties, slowly but surely, become the refuge of these sectional interests ultimately reducing the recruitment of masses to political roles in the system.

In a situation like this, when depoliticisation becomes the foundational cause for some of the most significant ills of the electoral system, the problems has to be confronted primarily through the counter logic of politicisation. People have to be continuously mobilized politically around their quotidian concerns by the political society–political parties, trade unions and even civil society organisations. This not only trains people for political roles but also makes them socially/politically aware and see through the designs of the prophets of depoliticisation. In short, this will help in 'extending' voting rights beyond the confines of institutionalised electoral arenas to an effective struggle against social and economic exploitation [Jalal, 1995: 48]. There cannot be a greater check against electoral pitfalls like money and muscle power than such a course. Legal remedies can only be a back-up to this. Any solution which does not take this long term perspective into account will hardly become an effective remedy to the problem.

NOTES

1. This refers to a process whereby voters vote according to their caste/ethnic affiliations making it very difficult for political parties to transcend their respective social bases.

2. This included rupees one crore it has spent on acquiring the right of the Oscar winning film Slum Dog Millionaire's song, 'Jai Ho' from its copy right holder, T-Series!

3. Those belonging to the organized Left were the only parties to have spent less in the election. The CPM and its allies spent a modest amount of Rs. 250 crore.

4. The survey points out that in states like Karnataka, Tripura, West Bengal, Kerala, Tamil Nadu and Andhra Pradesh nearly half of the voters testified affirmatively to this. Surprisingly in a metropolitan city like Delhi this was 25 per cent.

5. We have a Cabinet whose assets come close to Rs. 5 billion, on its own admission. And this figure covers only 64 of the 79 ministers. The other fifteen are Rajya Sabha members whose updated assets are yet to be computed. Further, these figures are also skewed by the fact that the top five ministers alone are worth Rs. 2 billion [Sainath; 2009].

6. There is already an allegation that Vijay Mallya had lobbied among fellow Members of Parliament to sign a petition demanding that Kingfisher Airlines owned by him be allowed to fly to foreign destinations [Banerjee, 2006:3839].

REFERENCES

Banerjee, Sumanta (2006): 'Salvaging an Endangered Institution', *Economic and Political Weekly*, Vol. XLI, No. 36, September 9 – 15.

Baru, Sanjaya (2000): 'Economic Policy and the Development of Capitalism in India: The Role of Regional Capitalists and Political Parties' in Francine R Frankel (ed.), *Transforming India: Social and Political Dynamics of Democracy*, Oxford: Oxford University Press.

Bhambhri, CP (1994): *Indian Politics Since Independence*, New Delhi : Shipra.

Burke, Edmund (1986): 'Speeches to the Electors of Bristol', cited in John Buchan (ed.), *Burke's Political Writings*, London: Thomas Nelson and Sons.

Chandhoke, Neera (2003): 'Governance and the Pluralisation of the State, Implications for Democratic Citizenship', *Economic and Political Weekly,* Vol. XXXVIII, No. 28, 12-18 July.

Dasgupta, Debarshi (2009): 'After the Burial, At The Wake', *Outlook,* Vol. XLIX, No. 46, 23 November.

Fernandes, Leela (2007): *India's New Middle Class: Democratic Politics in an Era of Economic Reforms,* New Delhi, Oxford University Press.

Jalal, Ayesha (1995): *Democracy and Authoritarianism in South Asia,* Cambridge : Cambridge University Press.

Katju, Manjari (2009): 'Election Commission and Changing Contours of Politics', *Economic and Political Weekly,* Vol. XLIV, No. 16,18 April.

Kohli, Atul (2009): *Democracy and Development in India – From Socialism to Pro-business,* New Delhi: Oxford University Press.

Kothari, Rajni (1992): 'Area of darkness', *Seminar*, No. 399, November.

Mehta, Pratap Bhanu (2001): 'Reform political parties first', *The Seminar,* No. 497, January.

Raveendranath, P.K. (2009): 'Elections funds: from where, to whom', *Power Politics,* Vol. II, Issue 3, April.

Ray, Shantam Guha (2009): 'Offer Valid Till Votes Last', *Tehelka,* Vol. 6, No. 17, 2 May.

Sainath, P (2009): 'The age of the aam crorepati', *The Hindu*, 20 June.

Sinha, Aseema (2010): 'Business and Politics' in Niraja Gopal Jayal and Pratap Bhanu Mehta (eds.), *The Oxford Companion to Politics in India,* New Delhi, OUP.

11 Elections in India-Influence of Money and Muscle Power

K.M. George

This paper tries to examine the problem of the influence of money and muscle power in elections in India. The study mainly concentrates around the general election to the Lower House of Parliament, the Lok Sabha, because it represents the scenario of election to the State Assemblies also. It is divided into five parts: (I) 'Introduction', (II) 'Money Power', (III) 'Muscle Power', (IV) 'Democracy in Crisis', and finally (V) 'The Way Out' that gives some suggestions to reduce the gravity of the problems, most of which, the author acknowledges, are usually shared by the concerned citizens.

I. Introduction

Free India adopting universal adult suffrage as the fundamental principle of elections to the Lower House of Parliament and state legislatures, based on multi-party system, went to the first general elections to Parliament and State Legislatures in 1951-52 in which 173 million voters exercised their franchise in over 196,000 polling stations spread over the length and breadth of the country. The country had undergone through 15 general elections. In April-May 2009, the general elections to choose 543 members of the 15th Lok Sabha took place, involving 714 million electorates, 828,000 polling stations, 1.37 million electronic voting machines and 5.5 million polling officials. Elections in India are the largest popular democratic political process in the world. The efficacy of the system is obvious from the fact of unseating sitting prime minister and chief ministers on several occasions through elections by the people disappointed with their performance or policies. But despite this fact, the extent of free and fairness in elections are matters of serious concern, which if not addressed to and proper remedial measures not taken, will eventually lead to the collapse of the democratic system itself, which we, the people of India, have given to ourselves as the Preamble of the Constitution of India expressly states. In this context, the political rights of the people to freely choose the political executive to govern them have to be emphasised both at the national and state level.

The Constitution of India under Article 326 envisages universal adult suffrage for election of representatives of the people to the House of the People and to the Legislative Assemblies of States from which the political executives for governance of the Centre and States respectively are chosen.

Many international covenants also recognise the electoral rights of citizens in a democracy to participate in government through fair and free election. For instance, the Universal Declaration of Human Rights, to which India is State Party, under Article 21 states:

1. Everyone has the right to take part in the government of his country, directly or through freely chosen representatives...
2. The will of the people shall be the basis of the authority of government, this will, shall be expressed in periodic and genuine elections which shall be by universal and equal suffrage and shall be held by secret vote or by equivalent free voting procedures.

In addition, the International Covenant on Civil and Political Rights, ratified by 148 states of which India is a signatory, the regional treaties viz., the African Charter on Human and People's Rights, the American Convention on Human Rights and the European Convention for the Protection of Human Rights and Fundamental Freedoms guarantee the electoral rights and right to freedom of the citizens. As to freedom, for instance, the International Covenant on Civil and Political Rights (ICCPR) in its Article 19 guarantees:

1. Everyone shall have the right to hold opinions without interference.
2. Everyone shall have the right to freedom of expression; this right shall include freedom to seek, receive and impart information and ideas of all kinds, regardless of frontiers, either orally, in writing or in print, in the form of art, or through any other media of his choice.

Now, the question arises how far the above said provisions of our Constitution and the international covenants regarding electoral rights and "the right to hold opinions without interference" which should be reflected in the electoral choice of representatives are observed in India? In other words, though we have the universal adult franchise, periodic elections and independent election machinery, and the Representation of People Act (hereinafter called the RP Act) that provides the modus operandi for conducting elections, are we successful in conducting free and fair elections that expresses the untainted choice of the people for the democratic governance of our country, where rule of law reigns but not reined. In short, could our elections guarantee us a true representative democracy? The litmus test for these is the very election of the people's representatives, which we shall examine under money power and muscle power below. But before proceeding with that the changing phases of political scenario in the country should be borne in mind.

The political scenario in the country can be divided broadly into two phases: the period till 1970, when the Congress Party was the dominant one with large social and political base, and the period since 1970s when the dominant position of the Congress became weak because of the shifting allegiance of the marginalized social groups to other parties and of their forming of own political parties based on regionalism or ethnicity and the entry into politics of a new breed of politicians with little concern for democratic values[1].The cumulative effect of which is to make the political arena a highly contested domain and highly volatile[2]. As parties became fragmented and weakened, the existence of a party and its strength in the electoral arena depended upon the clout of its leader; and the position of its workers depended upon their loyalty towards the leaders and not on their work at the grassroots level. This has resulted in the centralization of political power, the erosion of inner party democracy and the eventual alienation of political parties from the masses which is depoliticization. The gulf between the representatives and the represented had widened more since the onset of liberalisation, that is, the authenticity of representation now poses a big question mark in the electoral politics in the country. In the light of this background, the influence of money and muscle power in election is dealt with below.

II. Money Power

Money power over elections perverts the free and fair exercise of the will of the people in their franchise. Though Sections 77 and 78 of the RP Act requires that every contesting candidate has to keep correct accounts of all his election expenses, provides that it shall not exceed the prescribed maximum and that the account has to be lodged with the District Election Officer concerned, Explanation-1 to Section 77(1) clarifies that the ceiling applies only to the election expenditure incurred by the candidate or his agent, not by his party or anyone else. Under the guise of this provision big money bags could freely spend for their candidates or parties which they undertake after obtaining guarantees for adequate returns. This not only affects the level playing ground between parties and candidates but also the polity and the economy.

In this context, it should also be noted that a change in the financing of political parties by the business houses has taken place since liberalization. Though initially they considered regular financing of political parties as investments with good returns in the form of licenses, permits, contracts etc., since liberalization, as the license-raj had gone, they have switched over to a strategy of making payments per deal. Further they themselves have entered into the election fray rather than depending on their protegees.

Though, the above law on expenditure has undergone a thorough change since 2003, by virtue of which all expenditures incurred or authorized by political parties, friends and supporters of a candidate have to be considered as part of the candidate's own expenditure, except the expenditures on travelling of leaders of his political party. Still money power plays a crucial role in elections in our country. This is borne out by the assets–position of the MPs. According to the report compiled by the Association for Democratic Reforms (ADR), based on the affidavits filed by candidates during election, whereas in 2004 (14th Lok Sabha), the number of MPs with assets over ₹1 crore was 156, in 2009 (15th Lok Sabha), it increased to 315, that is, 60% are millionaires; and the average worth of assets of an MP increased from 1.86 crore to 5.33 crore during 2004-2009. Quoting Pritish Nandy, Journalist and ex-Rajya Sabha Member, it states that the average assets of 304 MPs in the 14th Lok Sabha who re-contested in 2009 had grown by 300%.[3] How much an MP can amass is discernible from the incredible increase in the asset of a single M.P, Jaganmohan Reddy whose asset has increased from 77 crores in 2009 to 365 crores in 2011[4]. The following Table 11.1 gives the average of assets of MPs party-wise.

Table 11.1. Average assets of MPs in Lok Sabha (in lakhs)

Parties	*14th House*	*15th House*	*Increase%*
Congress (I)	310.76	628.08	102.11
SP	153.78	241.43	57.0
Shiva Sena	151.29	308.43	103.36
BSP	119.83	462.60	286.05
DMK	105.06	455.04	333.12
BJP	96.91	307.47	217.27
RJD	56.19	136.58	82.95
BJD	53.51	427.62	792.58
CPI	25.40	25.50	3.94
CPM	22.95	37.98	65.49
Others	177.39	610.57	244.20
Total	1273.07	3641.30	186.01

Note: For the 14th Lok Sabha assets of only 535 MPs were available whereas for the 15th Lok Sabha assets of 543 MPs are available.

Sources: 1. Paul and Vivekananda, 2004.

2. http://myxata.info/fs2009/national election watch.

The corporate funding of elections, the change in the asset position of the MPs and the growth of their assets, the enveloping presence of businessmen in the Parliament, especially in the 14th and 15th ones, not only show the influence of money power in elections but also the change in the representative character of the 'people's representatives,' and that too in a nation where the proportion of population below poverty line is 32% and the effective literacy rate is 74.4%. The influence of money in winning an election, the change in the economic profile of the candidates/ winners, the attempts to recover the election expenditure incurred, and the members' objective to maximize their income and wealth during their term are also reflected in their individual and collective exercises in the Houses to hike their pay, perks, pensions and allowances which they themselves collectively decide and pass. This can be understood from Table 11.2 given above. Here it is to be noted that till 1968, the monthly salary and daily allowance of an MP were 400 and 31 respectively which during 1969- 1985 became 500 and 51 respectively. In 1985, the salary

Table 11.2. Salary and allowances of M.Ps (in Rs.)

	14th House	*15th House*
Monthly salary	16,000	50,000
Daily allowance to attend Parliament or committee meetings	1,000	2,000
Constituency allowance per month	20,000	40,000
Office expenses per month	20,000	40,000
Washing allowance for sofa covers and curtains once in three months		
Furniture allowance per annum:		
Durable		60, 000
Non-durable		15,000
Interest-free loan for vehicles	1,00,000	4,00,000
Road mileage rate for vehicles /kms	13	16
Free telephone calls	100,000	150,000
Accommodation in Delhi with free water and electricity every year up to		4000kl 50,000 units
Reimbursement of expenses incurred on tiles in kitchen and bathrooms		
Monthly pension	8,000	20,000
Pension for every additional year	500	1,500
Further, MPs can travel anywhere in the country by rail, first class + 34 free air tickets for themselves and for companion.		
Travel for spouse by train: unlimited.		
By air: earlier limited to two trips in the Budget Session and one in other sessions. Restrictions removed.		

Source: Business Standard, August 21, 2010.

was revised to 1,500. Pension was introduced in 1977; now an MP is entitled to pension even if he has spent only one day in Parliament while an employee is eligible for pension only if he has put in service for a period of minimum of 15 years. The increase in the salaries of MPs and pension to former MPs cost the exchequer an additional 103.76 crore every year; and the increase in the daily, constituency and office expenditure allowances an additional 38.50 crore every year.

No doubt that the office of an MP has become very covetable both in terms of money and power, and that is why a candidate on an average spends three to fifteen crore rupees in a single Lok Sabha constituency[5], a portion of which goes to the purchase of votes. The Centre for Media Studies (CMS), in its survey conducted in 2009, has found that nearly one-fifth of the voters across the country in the past decade were offered money to vote in an election either by the candidates or by the party workers. In this context, the estimates made by the Centre for Media Studies (CMS), based on its survey on the month long general election to the State Assemblies that began on 16.04.2011, is noteworthy. According to it the National Election Commission and state governments spent about 20 billion for organizing the actual polling, and the official parties and the individual candidates spent about 80 billion of which 20 billion was for the purchase of votes. In other words, the statutory limit that no party should be allowed to spend more than Rs. 10 lakhs for State elections or Rs. 25 lakhs for Central elections during campaign more or less remains in paper only.

III. Muscle Power

The law disqualifies a person from contesting election only on the ground of conviction under Section-8 of the RP Act. In K. Prabhakaren v Jayarajan[6] the Supreme Court observed that the purpose of enacting disqualification under Section.[7]: "... is to prevent criminalization of politics. Those who break the law should not make the law." But conviction by which court? a trial court or a court of final appeal still remains a controversy. Also a person sentenced to imprisonment for more than six years was free to contest elections after the period of six years from the date of his conviction. This was amended in 2002 by virtue of which under S.8 (1) of the Act the disqualification is for a period of six years from the date of conviction where only fine is imposed. If the sentence is imprisonment for any period, the disqualification starts from the date of conviction and will continue for a further period of six years since the release of the convicted person.

But despite the above said law and in spite of all the efforts made by the Supreme Court and the Election Commission making it obligatory for candidates to disclose information about criminal cases pending against them, the number of legislators with criminal background is ever increasing in both Houses of Parliament and State Legislatures There are umpteen number of cases of persons charged with serious and heinous crimes like dacoity, murder and rape contesting elections pending their trial, getting elected and occupying ministerial positions.

Here, it is to be stated that in the early stages of our elections criminals were lending support to politicians in expectation of money or favours like protection against the processes of law. Politicians wanted black money to finance their political activities, elections, and for themselves for which they banked on the criminals who rendered their help in rigging in elections, booth-capturing, intimidating voters to vote or from going to polling stations and for victimising those voters who defy their diktats. In course of time, the politicians became subservient to the criminals, and the criminals realised the value of their money and muscle power in elections. This has resulted in the politicisation of criminals whereby law-breakers themselves become law-makers. Criminals contest, win elections and become legislators so that they can enjoy the privileges of legislators and perpetrate their nefarious activities with more immunity. Their long arms extend even to the judiciary. Cases against them may remain pending for years, witness against them may not turn up, may turn hostile or may get eliminated and finally the cases may get dropped. The data given below depicts the sordid scenario of representation of the people in the two Houses at the Centre, nay to speak of the State Legislatures.

For instance, in the 14th Lok Sabha there were 125 members i.e., 23% of the total members, with criminal background involving serious charges of murder, rape, kidnapping, extortion etc. In the present 15th Lok Sabha 150 MPs face criminal charges against them, 73 of them face serious cases ranging from rape to murder; and the two main national parties, the Congress and the BJP have 41 and 42 MPs respectively facing criminal charges.[8] The position in some States is much worse, for instance, Uttar Pradesh has 31 MPs facing criminal charges out of its 80 MPs.[9]

IV. Democracy in Crisis

The crisis in the Indian democracy is that, especially since 1970, money power and muscle power determine the electoral outcomes and these increase in every election. The free and fair elections to choose representatives of the people and a government of the free-will of the people have become a mirage. The multiplication of parties at the national and regional levels and their ethnic or casteist orientation of late has aggravated the problem, because each one wants to carve out a space in the polity by whatever means.[10] The consequence is that, election results being determined by money and muscle power, the credibility of election loses its value in the true democratic sense and hence the representative character of democracy.

The changing phase of the polity the recent electoral politics brings forth is that the survival in power and physical protection of the politicians depend upon the criminals and instead of the professional criminals paying protection money to the politicians it has become the other way round. The development of the nexus among criminals including smugglers of arms and narcotics, extortionists, mafia gangs, terrorists, and politicians, police, bureaucrats and businessmen in running the state apparatus forebodes the demise of the democratic system in our county, unless imminent counter measures are adopted. In this context, it is to be noted that the Vohra Committee quoting CBI report states that "all over India, crime syndicates have become a law unto themselves. Even in the smaller towns and rural areas, muscle-men have become the order of the day. Hired assassins have become part of these organisations. The existing criminal justice system, which was essentially designed to deal with the individual offences/crimes, is unable to deal with the activities of the mafia; the provisions of law in regard to economic offences are weak; there are insurmountable legal difficulties in attaching/confiscating the property acquired through mafia activities". It further adds:

The mafia network is "virtually running a parallel government, pushing the State apparatus into irrelevance." And that "... in certain States these gangs enjoy the patronage of local politicians cutting across party lines and the protection of the functionaries. Some political leaders become the leaders of these gangs/armed senas and over the years get themselves elected to local bodies, state assemblies and national Parliament. Resultantly, such elements have acquired considerable political clout seriously jeopardizing the smooth functioning of the administration and the safety of the life and property of the common man causing a sense of despair and alienation among people." which is an issue raised by the Election Commission from 1998 onwards.

Thus it becomes obvious that a sizeable number of representatives of the people in the Parliament represent their power of money and muscle rather than the free will of the people in elections. The surging phenomenon shows the evolution of a curious autocracy based on money and muscle power; instead of periodical elections strengthening democracy, it strengthens the power of money and muscle and hence weakens democracy; the mere change of representatives and political executives will not strengthen democracy. The crisis elections bring forth in our polity is that the free will of the people and their true choice get subdued under the forces of money and muscle; the House loses the real representative character and the constitution of the government will not be in accordance with the real choice of the people.

The consequence is that, once a candidate gets elected by means of money and muscle power, he will shred away his people's interests and will carve out policies and decisions to suit his group's special interests, and the laws may reflect this, and if ever any laws are against his interests it will be implemented with laxity or amended to the extent possible. This means a de-facto alienation of the Houses of the People from the people as a post-election scenario, resulting in the loss of faith of the people in true democracy.

Further, money into politics has become an investment. Several industrial houses give huge donations to political parties as a form of investment in order to gain political favours from them. This keeps at bay a healthy democracy because people who have money get primary dominance in elections, merit becomes sidelined.

Because of the domineering influence of the rich and the criminals in the Houses, the middle class and others being averse of the prevailing politics desist from contesting in elections and in exercising their voting rights; and thereby the possibility of the houses getting infused with noble social democratic values is missed. The fact that in all elections a significant percentage of the population abstains from voting bespeaks of the malady of the democratic system in our country. For instance, it can be observed from the Table below that in all elections to the Lower House of Parliament, the total voting percentage is only in the range of (55.42 -63.56), in the 15th Lok Sabha it has declined to 56.97% from 57.65% of the preceding House.

If in a legislature the rich constitutes the majority, as is given in Table-1, it will develop a class character in the law-making body that is biased in favour of the rich; and if legislators with criminal records are many, as discussed above, it will develop a criminalist character. It is of grave concern that in the House of People in India both dominate. This binds both the rich and the criminals together and the House of the People would acquire truly a non-political character; more than the political ideologies that are

Table 11.3. Voting Percentage in General Elections to Lok Sabha

General Election	*Year*	*Male*	*Female*	*Total*
First	1952	N.A.	N.A.	61.2*
Second	1957	N.A.	N.A.	62.2*
Third	1962	63.31	46.63	55.42
Fourth	1967	66.73	55.48	61.33
Fifth	1971	60.90	49.11	55.29
Sixth	1977	65.63	54.91	60.49
Seventh	1980	62.16	51.22	56.92
Eighth	1984	68.18	58.60	63.56
Ninth	1989	66.13	57.32	61.95
Tenth	1991	61.58	51.35	56.93
Eleventh	1996	62.06	53.41	57.94
Twelfth	1998	65.72	57.88	61.97
Thirteenth	1999	63.97	55.64	59.99
Fourteenth	2004	61.66	53.30	57.65
Fifteenth	2009	N.A	N.A	56.97

Source : Election Commission of India, New Delhi.

Note : Sex-wise break-up of electors is not available for first and second General Elections.

N.A. : Not Applicable.

* : Calculated on the basis of valid votes polled.

of interest to the society's collective interests, issues of the moneyed (for instance, the acquisition of farmland for Special Economic Zones) and the criminals would be considered as of paramount importance and debated in the Houses and decisions on them would be passed off as society's collective will. The passing of many bills in the Parliaments with little discussions will establish the 'concern' of the legislators as to people's causes.

If this trend goes on at its present pace and our electoral process does not become strong enough to 'nip in the bud' such tendencies, it will not be long for our democracy to collapse into a "functioning anarchy;" and that too at huge cost of resources to the society, where poverty, infant mortality, illiteracy, unemployment, gender inequality etc. still remain as burning issues for the people. This naturally raises the question: democracy for whom and at what cost?

V. The Way Out

The most important predicament of the Indian democracy is that the prevailing electoral politics does not ensure us a majority democracy; 70% -80 % of all MLAs and Lok Sabha MPs are elected by minority of votes polled. There are legislators who get elected by less than 15% of the votes polled, though 85% or more of the electorates have clearly voted them out. If we can ensure that the electoral process is such that a candidate gets elected only if he has secured more than 50% of the votes polled the influence of money and muscle power could be reduced to a great extent. For that, if necessary, a second round of contest between the two highest polling candidates of the first round should also be conducted. Here it is also to be noted that the low percentage of voting should be viewed with serious concern to ensure majority democracy.

At present the political parties are categorized and recognized at the state and national levels. As there are many small groups functioning as political parties which work as pressure groups in our political scenario and take undue advantage and create chaos in the political system, their influences should be restricted. For that, in addition to the state and national level registration and recognition, there should be one more layer at the local or regional level within a state. For their registration, a condition should be imposed that it should have not less than 10% memberships of the total electorates at the local regions.

The multiplicity of political parties is a fertile ground for the exercise of money and muscle power in elections and for horse trading; besides these, are the privileges a political party/candidate can enjoy. There are at present 1200 registered political parties, but only six were recognized as National Parties and 36 as State Parties during the general elections in 2004.10 In the 2009 Lok Sabha elections, 369 parties contested fielding 8070 candidates; but 333 contesting parties did not win even in a single constituency, and 19 parties won only in three or less number of seats. A large number of non-serious political parties and candidates make our election process a mockery. The law needs to be changed so that the Election Commission is bestowed with ample powers to derecognize parties.

Multiplication of parties has to be checked to curb its vicious influence in elections. The split in a political party is usually not based on ideological grounds, but for the reason that a seat is denied in election to a party worker or because one is not made a minister. For that, a condition can be imposed for registering and recognizing a new party formed by split in a parent party. The condition shall be that, if a party is formed out of split in a party, the newly formed one should have not less than 10,000 or one-tenth of the total number of members in the original one, whichever is less. That is, if a party has one lakh members and if it undergoes any split the newly formed one should have not less than 10,000 members, the members can be either of the parent party or of new ones.

Election Commission should have the details of the membership (the use of biometric identification number system will be of immense use in this regard) of each political party and should publish either the membership list or the number of members of each registered/non-registered party annually. This will give the electorate an idea as to the political base of a party and incentivize the parties to increase their political base that would help the politicization process among the electorates. These will help the voters to take informed decisions while exercising their right to franchise.

The accounts of all parties must be audited by the Election Commission and they should be published in leading dailies and put on the electronic media.

The political parties of all hues are now undertaking many business activities like running shopping malls, amusement parks, tourist resorts, hospitals, financial services, publishing houses and commercial media, which are carried out with the objective of gaining maximum profits. They are now evolving as corporate enterprises. This aspect along with the enveloping presence of businessmen, criminals and the rich in the legislative bodies has to be viewed with serious concern as it puts obstacle to the delivery of common good to the people. Hence the undertakings of business activities by political parties have to be prohibited, for the welfare of the people they should concentrate on politics and social activities, not on business profits.

It is quite curious that the parties that clamour for democracy do not have internal democracy in their parties. Elections within parties should be made mandatory for a party to contest in elections. Then the candidate's loyalty to the people would become more important than the blind loyalty to the leaders to rise to positions. This will promote the politicization process in the society, and will reduce the role of money and muscle power in winning an election.

It is also to be noted that the contests of non-serious candidates in election are also a big problem that reinforces the play of money and muscle power. For instance, during the general election to Tamil Nadu Legislative Assembly in 1996, there were 1033 contesting candidates in the Modakurichi Assembly Constituency, for which the ballot papers had to be printed in a booklet form.

To reduce criminalization of politics, the Election Commission's suggestion, concurred by the Law Commission, is that persons involved in serious offences with imprisonment for five or more years should be disqualified even during the pendency of the trial, if the competent court of law has taken cognizance of the offence and framed charges against the accused. It also suggested that persons found guilty by a Commission of Enquiry should also stand disqualified from contesting elections. But political parties oppose this on the basis of the doctrine that a person is presumed to be innocent until he is proved guilty and that those in power can foist false cases and implicate their rivals.

The Commission reiterates that keeping a person who is accused of serious criminal charges and where the court being prima facie satisfied frames charges against him, out of the electoral arena would be a reasonable restriction in greater public interests and that this would help in cleansing the political establishment from the influence of criminal elements and in protecting the sanctity of the Legislative Houses. However, as a precaution against motivated cases by a ruling party, it suggested that only those cases which were filed prior to six months before an election need be considered. As one's contest in an election is not a fundamental right, reasonable restriction on contests in the larger public interest can be imposed. Hence the Commission's suggestion in this regard is to be welcomed. In this context the author makes the following suggestions:

At present, the time taken from the date of filing nominations to the conduct of poll is very short, giving little time for the electorates to study the conduct and character, commitments and abilities of the candidates. This time frame should be extended to a period of one year. The filing of nominations and the affidavits should take place one year before the date of the poll.

The Election Commission should have an investigative/intelligence machinery under it to scrutinize the affidavits filed before it by the candidates, including their credentials, criminal involvements etc. It should report its findings before the District Election Commission and based on that the Commission shall raise its objections, if any. Then it should hold sittings and has to pass judgments considering the investigation reports, the averments made by the candidates, their opponents and those interested. The entire process shall not take more than one year. Further, as to the criminal cases involving the candidates who have filed nominations the Election commission shall refer their candidature to the Courts concerned for expeditious disposal of them according to law. The expected outcome is that when the final lists of contestants are published, one year after from the date of filing of nominations, there should be no criminal charges outstanding against any candidate.

Further, a Special Court of the Election Commission shall be constituted for time bound expeditious trial of the cases referred to it in respect of the candidates against whom criminal cases are charged after the publication of the final list of candidates. Based upon the decision of this Court, the Commission shall be vested with powers to disqualify any candidate whose nomination was already upheld on scrutiny. The RP Act has to be amended in this regard. Cases of candidates standing for bye-election shall also be referred to this court.

To restrict the expenses to the ceiling limits, physical limits as to the number of vehicles, mass meetings, use of media, number, size and quality of posters, banners etc should be prescribed and monitored by the Commission.

It is a common scene that persons with mental disability are intimidated or influenced in registering as voters and in voting, though the RP Act in Section 16, subsection (1) states: "A person shall be disqualified for registration in an electoral roll if he...(b) is of unsound mind and stands so declared by a competent court..." Hence all such persons of mental disability should be removed from electoral rolls and if ever any such person happens to be registered as a voter his companion should not be permitted for voting on his behalf.

As to blind and infirm voters, it is to be noted that many feign as blind and infirm under coercion or under the influence of money and their companions cast the votes. Hence before registering them as voters, a certificate from the Medical Board of the Commission as to their blindness and infirmity should be made mandatory and also as to the fact whether they need assistance. It is also to be stated that the inclusion of blindness and infirmity of an elector in the UID under the Adhar Scheme could reduce many an issue that arise during the course of poll in a booth.

The House of the People should consist of representatives on whom people can repose their trust and confidence, but the electoral process in vogue is unable to guarantee that. As a result, the House get alienated from the people, and instead of being "of the people" it becomes "off the people." When the House abdicates its duties people will resort to movements which poses challenges to the elected governments like the Naxalite armed movements and Anna Hazare's Satyagraha movement. The challenges are sustainable so far as there is democratic space for such movements. This is because, though the legislature and the political executive are formed out of the electoral process where money and muscle power play their critical role, there exists the third pillar of democracy, the judiciary, which is supposed to be less affected. But if that also succumbs to the pulls and pressures of the House and the political executive, democracy will collapse, resulting in anarchy and eventually to dictatorship. Hence strengthening of judiciary is essential for strengthening democracy in the nation.

The crux of the above argument is that any reform of the electoral process is infructuous unless and until the criminal judicial system in the country is reformed and strengthened. The undue delay in disposing of criminal cases and the abysmally low conviction rate gives room for candidates with criminal backgrounds to contest in elections and become victorious as legislators. To strengthen judiciary the number of courts and the outlay on it has to be increased taking into account the size of the population. In this context, it is to be noted that in terms of gross national product (GNP), the expenditure on judiciary in India is hardly 0.2 percent, whereas it is 1.2 percent in Singapore, 1.4 percent in United States of America and 4.3 percent in United Kingdom. The mounting arrears of court cases have to be contrasted with the grossly inadequate allocations to meet the requirements of the judiciary. If judiciary is strengthened and made efficient, the influence of money and muscle power in elections can be significantly reduced.

The electorates should be given the right to recall their representatives who are found corrupt because it will always remain as a Damocles' sword over their representatives in their misuse of office and abuse of power.

As courts are handicapped in establishing constitutional governance suo moto, vigilante movements and enlightened citizenry have to play a crucial role in the political governance of the nation. The clamour for legislation of a strong Lok Pal Bill led by the Gandhian Anna Hazare, the Public Interest Litigation on black money lying before the Supreme Court etc. give glimpses of hope for the future of democracy in the nation.

NOTES

1. Prabash, J, 'India: Mounting Influence of Money Power in Elections and the Crisis of Representation', Asia-Pacific Journal of Social Sciences, Special Issue No.1, 20.12.2010
2. Katju, Manjari, 'Election Commission and Changing Contours of Politics' *Economic and Political Weekly,* Vol. XLIV, No.16, 18 April, 2009.
3. The cost of India's MPs www.infochangeindia.org last visited 20.07.2011.
4. Times of India, April 16, 2011, 'Jagmohanan Reddy declares 365 crores.
5. Ray, G.N, 'Role of Money Power in Elections,' Inaugural Address: Seminar

on Role of Money Power in Elections, Kerala Journalist's Union, Palakkad, 08.08.2010.

6. AIR 2002 SC 3393, JT 2002 (7) SC 507, 2002 (3) KLT 521 SC.
7. http://ibnlive.in.com/news/150-new, 'law makers-accused of breaking law'.
8. CNN-BN, 'UP keeps its share record: 31MPs accused of crime', 18-05-2009.
9. Supra note 2.
10. Political parties that wish to contest local, state or national elections are required to be registered by the Election Commission of India. For state level recognition a party must have had political activity for at least five continuous years, and send at least 4% of the state's quota to the Lok Sabha, or 3.33% of members to that state's assembly. For national level recognition it should have recognition in four or more states.

REFERENCES

ADR, 'Corepati MPs double in Lok Sabha; Average Assets Tripled,' Delhi News Agency, 22.11.2009.

Andhra News. net 23.3.2011, '20 to 40 percent legislators have criminal records says embarrassed Chief Election Commissioner.'

Benziger, T.Joseph, 'Criminalization of Politics in India', Dynamic Youth, http://www.dynamicyouth.org, last visited 30.08.2011.

Husain, Maybe, 'Election Without Money and Muscle Power', Financial Express, Dhaka, 24.4.2008.

http://national debate.nic.in, 'Electoral Reforms: Republic 50 Debate', last visited 7.17.2011.

Indian Times, 21.7.2011, '300 Corepati MPs as House Gets Richer.'

Kashyap, Subash C, 'Criminal-Politician Nexus Getting Stronger', The Tribune, 15.8.2007.

Krishan, S.M, 'Without Money and Muscle Power, Very Tough To Win Elections', http://asiantribune.com/news, 15.02.2010

Ray, G.N, 'Role of Money Power in Elections,' Inaugural address: Seminar on Role of Money Power in Elections, Kerala Journalist's Union, Palakkad, 08.08.2010

Sen, S.R, 'Vote Power and Lobby Power', Economic and Political Weekly, 13.08.1994.

12 Electoral Reforms and Compulsory Voting

M.A. Hussain and
Venkatesula Reddy

Introduction

India has had 15 general elections since independence. Electoral reforms are necessary for the success and survival of parliamentary democracy in our country. The reform of electoral process in India has been engaging the attention of many thinkers, political parties and general public.

The Election Commission of India is one of the pillars of Indian democracy. In recent times, the jurisdiction of the Election Commission in India is expanding to the extent of being a supra-governmental authority in the country. The architects of the Indian Constitution attached highest significance to independent electoral machinery for the conduct of elections by giving wide-ranging powers to the Election Commission in Article 324 of the Constitution of India.[1]

"Article 324" Dr. B.R. Ambedkar contended, "Proposed, to centralise the election machinery in the hands of a single commission, to be assisted by regional commissioners working under the supervision, direction and control of the Election Commission". The centralisation of electoral administration was done to prevent injustice being done by the provincial governments to people other than those who belonged to the provinces racially, linguistically and culturally.

A general election in India is a herculean task, equivalent to conducting of polls in Europe, the United States, Canada and Australia put together. The 2009 Lok Sabha election was enormous not just in size, but in cost as well.

The Election Commission in India has considerable autonomy of action as it derives its authority directly from the Constitution. The Election Commission is also vested with residuary powers by the Supreme Court to take decisions on its own on issues where the enacted laws were silent or the provisions were inadequate to handle any electoral issue.

In popular perception also, the Election Commission is fulfilling in a commendable manner, its prime responsibility of the smooth conduct of elections and this is worthy of high trust. Hence people find it trust worthy and not loathsome as they find the others, especially the police and the bureaucracy.[2]

Initiatives Taken by the Election Commission

To fulfil the objective of discharging its constitutional duty sincerely to conduct free, fair and peaceful elections in the world's largest democracy, the Election Commission made some appreciative efforts in terms of taking several innovative and proactive measures in recent times[3]:

(i) Preparing computerized electoral rolls

(ii) Issuing elector's photo identity cards

(iii) Procuring personal particulars of candidates on affidavits

(iv) Using Electronic Voting Machines (EVMs)

(v) Deploying three types of election observers (namely, general observers, expenditure observers and special observers)

(vi) Deploying extensively adequate security personnel to safeguard polling stations and the staff.

Inadequacies of our Electoral System

Under the present system of "first-past-the-post" (FPTP) a candidate can get elected even on a minority of votes. No candidate should be declared elected unless he or she secures more than 50% of votes cast. In case no candidate gets this, it should be followed by a run off election. With electronic machines, it should be possible on the next day. The push button plan may help to solve the problem.

Winning on a Minority Vote and the Question of Representation

The fact that most legislators in India win on a minority vote has attracted debate. The situation is that our first-past-the post (FPTP) system is tailor made for victories resulting from less than 50% of the votes cast in any election.

Proportional Representation System or The List System

The objective of this approach is to generate better representation by providing seats to recognized political parties in proportion to the votes obtained by them. Basing itself on the approach, the Law Commissions report on Reforms of the Electoral Laws (1999) suggested that the number of MPs in the Lok Sabha should be increased by 25% and this additional number of MPs should be made up of candidates pre-nominated by political parties in proportion to their share of votes polled.

The reason for this suggestion is the fact that most governments in India have ruled on a minority vote and that as much as 2/3rd of the votes of the electorate has been wasted in the sense that these were cast for losing candidates and therefore these were not represented at all.

The fact that no government at the centre has ever received over 50% votes in the post independence history of India strengthens this argument. They have suggested that the strength of the Lok Sabha should be increased to 688, which means that about 138 candidates will be nominated on the basis of lists to be provided by various political parties.

To further consolidate votes, the Law Commission of India also suggested that political parties that secure less than 5% of the valid votes cast in Parliament or Legislative Assembly would not be entitled to any seat of the "list" in that legislature. It was also suggested that while bigger states would constitute a territorial unit for this purpose, the smaller states should either be clubbed together for forming a territorial unit for elections to the Lok Sabha.

A variant of this suggestion is that voters be asked to vote on two ballot papers one pertaining to candidates and the other to political parties. The votes polled by political parties would be considered for selecting their candidates on predominated lists.

Compulsory Voting: Will Alter Caste, Religious Equations

In a democracy, people must participate in the democratic process by voting in elections. This is an important part of the democratic process. How can India be an exception to such a proposition?

Compulsory voting will "strengthen" democracy. Voting cannot merely be a right but some argue that voting should be made a fundamental duty. The passage of the mandatory voting bill in the Gujarat Assembly is the first step towards making voting as much a right as a duty.[4] On the 16th of December 2009 Gujarat Government announced that it will pass an Act on the Gujarat Local Authorities Laws Amendment Bill 2009. It will apply to all qualified voters of Municipal Corporations, Municipalities, district, talukas and village panchayats. Failure to vote will bring penal consequences for defaulters. But the Gujarat governor returned the Gujarat Local Authorities Laws Amendment Bill, 2009 which contained provisions for compulsory voting in elections to local bodies. It allows negative voting. The manner of negative voting and its impact on other candidates will be worked out by the State Government through special rules framed later. It is also under consideration that all candidates will be disqualified if negative voting is the highest.

Advantages of Compulsory Voting

Most of the arguments advanced by opponents of the idea are shallow, flawed and premised on wrong presumptions. The Gujarat Government wants to achieve through this land mark bill:

1. The intended legislation is a serious attempt to eliminate passive voters who do not go out to vote but crib about politicians. By bringing them to the polling booth we want to ensure maximum participation in the democratic process. This will benefit all and cause harm to none. The measure will also to some extent alter the caste equations in politics that currently dominate India's polity from the bottom level to the top. It will also help in eliminating money and muscle power that is increasingly used by politicians in elections and plays a decisive role at many places.
2. It will help eliminate the communal aspect of politics as everybody's vote will decide the fate of candidates, not just the minuscule votes of one or another community. We have seen low turnouts in many elections in the country. When the polling is only 40% a person who gets just 21% is elected although the remaining 79% may be against such an individual. Such a skewed arithmetic of politics will undergo a transformation when mandatory voting is introduced.[5]
3. The compulsory voting does not mean you have to vote under any circumstances. There is several escape routes available if a person is genuinely not able to exercise his/her franchise, such as being away on work. To say that mandatory voting violates personal freedom is not true because it does not force you to vote for a candidate.
4. You can also choose the "none of the above" option. Rules shall be framed about this. Compulsory voting is a revolutionary change for India.

Several countries have compulsory voting, out of 32 countries which have laws of compulsory voting, only 19 countries enforced the law and of these, only Belgium has a punitive section. Many countries like

Australia, Belgium, Greece, Argentina, Brazil, Chile and Egypt to name a few have compulsory voting[6].

Compulsory voting is not a new concept. Some of the first countries that introduced mandatory voting laws were Belgium in 1892, Argentina in 1914 and Australia in 1924. There are also examples of countries such as Venezuela and the Netherlands which at one time in their history practised compulsory voting but have since abolished it.

To most democratic governments, participation in national elections is a right of citizenship. Some consider that participation in elections is also a citizen's civic responsibility. Some countries even impose sanctions on non-voters.[7]

In Australia voting is compulsory both at federal elections and at elections for the state and territorial legislatures. Inspite of compulsory voting there are about 10% of enrolled voters who fail to vote at most elections. In Australia they are asked to explain their failure to vote. If no satisfactory reason is provided (for example, illness or religious prohibition) a relatively small fine is imposed ($20 to $70) and failure to pay the fine may result in a court hearing.[8]

In India there is no harm in experimenting with it. It will strengthen our democratic process.

Compulsory Voting
Right to Vote = Right Not to Vote

The passage of the mandatory voting bill in the Gujerat Assembly is the first step towards making voting as much a right and as a duty.

The Gujerat Governor returned the Gujerat Local Authorities Laws (Amendment Bill, 2009) which contained provisions for compulsory voting in election to local bodies. Though the Chief Minister Narendra Modi appears keen on this, the Governor gave three reasons:

1. Compulsory voting violates the citizen's Right to Freedom of speech and expression guaranteed by Article 19 of the Constitution;
2. To punish voters who fail to vote violates their fundamental freedom in the matter of voting; and
3. Experience of other countries shows that it is difficult to implement compulsory voting.

The Supreme Court declared in the People's Union of Civil Liberties

(PUCL) case that "Vote" is a form of speech, as the voter indicates his preference for one of the contesting candidates silently. The court was concerned about the voters' right to know the antecedents of the candidates. Article 19(1) says that all citizens shall have the Right to Freedom of Speech and Expression. *The Freedom to Vote includes the Right not to Vote.* This right is subject to any law made by the state which imposes reasonable restrictions in the interest of the sovereignty and integrity of India, the security of the state, friendly relations with foreign states, public order, decency or morality or in relation to contempt of court, defamation or incitement to an offence. Compulsory voting does not fall with in the above category. The former President R.Venkatraman had suggested compulsory voting, but there were no takers.

Arguments Against Compulsory Voting

Let us consider the arguments against voting being made compulsory.

It is undemocratic to force people to vote – an infringement of liberty. The "ignorant" and those with little interest in politics are forced to the polls. It may increase the number of invalid votes and encourage reckless voting behaviour.

Resources must be allocated to determine whether those who failed to vote have "Valid and Sufficient" reasons. It causes concern over Governance. It represents a failure of democracy.

It is unfair to force a voter, who is not attracted to any candidate to vote. It rewards dishonest electors who turn up and vote informally only to escape penal action. Compulsory voting has made life easier for the political parties.

Compulsory Voting Impossible, Says Election Commission

The Election Commission made it clear that it is impossible to have compulsory voting in India, given the large scale workforce in the unorganized sector. In a vast country like India, it is not just possible for the Election Commission to implement compulsory voting.[9] The Chief Election Commissioner Navin Chawla said in a News Conference held in Bangalore on May 13, 2010 that compulsory voting has not succeeded in those countries where it is practised. The election authorities in those countries received large number of medical certificates from people who did not vote. In India compulsory voting is not yet implemented mainly because a large part of the population works in the unorganised sector. Democracy is rule by consent of the majority of voters who exercise their franchise. If the candidates set up by political parties at elections are not acceptable to the voters because of their criminal background or antecedents, corrupt background or incompetence, which are common complaints in India, it would be oppressive and unethical to compel voters to vote.

The concept of compulsory voting has been defeated in the Lok Sabha which rejected a Private Member's Bill moved by a Bharatiya Janatha Party Member on April 29, 2005. The Supreme Court also rejected in 2005 a petition seeking to make voting compulsory and the question of inclusion of "none of the above" in the ballot paper is pending before the Supreme Court.[10]

The Government of Gujerat is thus not the first to come up with the concept. On April 17, 2009 the Supreme Court of India had dismissed a plea to make voting compulsory.[11] The plea was filed by Atul Sarode from Savda district in Maharashtra. He wanted to make voting compulsory for all elections. His plea also mooted the idea of not allowing any one to represent a constituency unless he/she fails to get a minimum of 51% of votes. If that does not happen then there should be re-elections. We cannot choose the best from the worst. After all, it is a matter concerning our constituency. We do not want some random persons to govern us. We want responsible people. Why can not we have re-elections? Some say that is too expensive. If he/she is going to govern us then we definitely should take all precautionary measures available to see to it that we choose only the best. This plea also mooted the idea of e-voting.

A bench consisting of former Chief Justice K.G. Balakrishnan and Justice P.Sathasivam dismissed the plea and observed that a greater voter turnout could be ensured only by increasing people's awareness. They also observed that voter turnout of 60% was satisfactory.

The Right to dissent is basic to democracy. It is a basic Human Right, which includes the right not to vote although this cannot be compared with right to life which cannot be waived. In the case of voting, the issue is of freedom to vote. Freedom necessarily implies choice and includes the opinion not to vote. Already our courts are overburdened and unable to enforce criminal justice speedily. If failure to vote is made an offence, it will be impossible to implemented. The better way to ensure high polling is by choosing candidates of character and competence with a record of public service.

In the ultimate analysis, the real victory of our democracy lies in those heart-warming, instances when voters pour out, inspite of terrorist or other threats, and cast their votes reaffirming their faith in democracy, such as the recent turnout in the Jharkhand and Arunachal Pradesh bye polls.[12]

REFERENCES

1. Rakahari Chatterji (ed.); *Politics India: The State-Society Interface* (New Delhi: South Asian Publishers Pvt., Ltd., 2009), p.121.
2. *Ibid.*, p.122.
3. Venkatesh Kumar, B., *Electoral Reforms in India : Current Discourses* (Jaipur, Rawat Publications, 2009), p.198.
4. *Deccan Chronicle*, Hyderabad, dated 22nd April, 2010.
5. *Deccan Chronicle,* Hyderabad, dated 4th January, 2010.
6. *Ibid.*
7. Compulsory Voting: To be Nor Not to Be-Srinivas Katta – Internet Publication dated 21-12-2009.
8. *Journal of South Asia Politics,* New Delhi, April 2010, p.52.
9. Chief Election Commissioner Navin Chawla's News Conference held in Bangalore on May 13, 2010.
10. *Deccan Chronicle,* Hyderabad, dated 22nd April 2010.
11. The Concept of Compulsory Voting, Internet Publication, posted by: Phonix on April 11, 2010.
12. Dr. P. Rathnaswamy, *Electoral Reforms: Law and Institutions of India and World.* (New Delhi: Book Well Publishers), p.107.

13 Democracy and Good Governance : Does Electoral System Matter?

T.M. Joseph and
Jos Chathukulam

Democracy is an ideal which often assumes concrete dimensions for the vast majority of people through the electoral system. For many, an election marks the only occasion of any form of political participation as it is the only tangible evidence of what it means to be a citizen in a democratic society. Electoral system, therefore, is the most fundamental aspect of every representative democracy.

Electoral systems can be understood as the mechanisms by which the preferences of citizens are translated into seats in representative institutions. It shapes the rules of the game among political parties and individuals and can affect who is elected and which party is elected to power. It also determines the broader political culture, the way in which political parties and their representatives behave. The electoral laws determine how citizens cast votes, how votes are aggregated, and how aggregated votes are converted into positions of governmental authority.

More significantly, the way in which an electoral system translates votes into seats in elected assemblies may influence the degree of public support for the democratic system itself. If, for example, citizens perceive that their preferences are not adequately reflected in the legislature, their support for the system in general is likely to decline. Turnout during elections will drop off, respect for politicians and elected representatives will fall and laws enacted by government will not be seen as fully legitimate.

The global urge for democratic governance in the 1980s and 1990s stimulate a new urgency in the search for enduring models of appropriate representative government, along with a fresh evaluation of electoral systems. This process has been encouraged by the widespread realization that the choice of political institutions can have a significant impact upon the wider political system – for example, it is increasingly being recognized that an electoral system can help to "engineer" coorperation and accommodation in a divided society. Electoral systems design is now accepted as being of crucial importance to wider issues of governance and as probably the most influential of all political institutions.

Different electoral systems produce different results and different types of representatives. The electoral system also does have an impact on the nature and extent of voting behavior. In this context, the present paper looks into whether the 'first-past-the-post' (FPTP) system in India in truly representative and examines whether alternative models are available which can make our democracy more representative and meaningful.

We may begin by distinguishing electoral laws from other kinds of law. If we agree that 'laws' generally are authoritative rules of conduct enacted and enforced by the holders of governmental authority, then 'electoral laws' are those authoritative rules which pertain to the conduct of elections. "Electoral laws are those which govern the processes by which electoral preferences are articulated as votes and by which these votes are translated into distributions of governmental authority (typically parliamentary seats) among the competing political parties" (Rae 1967 : 14)

A number of concomitant questions are then asked with regard to the electoral laws. Are the voters asked to choose between men or parties? Does the candidate or party with more votes than any other win outright or is the victory divided among the contestants in proportion to their vote? Does the voter express a nominal preference or is he asked to rank his preferences among a number of alternatives? Does each constituency choose a single legislator, or does it select a number of them?

The answers to these questions are interdependent; an answer to any one limits the answers the law may reasonably give to the others. For example, single-member constituency system and elaborate rules for proportionality, at least at the constituency level, are incompatible. It is this interdependence which leads political scientists and politicians alike to regard the total pattern of electoral laws prevailing for a particular country's general election as an organic whole-an "electoral system" (Rae 1967 :14-15). Different countries do have different electoral systems.

Now it is pertinent to examine what kind of electoral system that exists in India. India, being the largest democracy on 'earth, has an elaborate mechanism to make its elections free and fair. The essential characteristics of the Indian electoral system are summarized below.

1. It is First-Past-the-Post System as against Proportional Representation

This system enables a candidate to win an election when he gets more votes than his strongest single competitor, but has not necessarily polled a higher total than the combined opposition. It is this property which accounts for terms like "relative majority", and "plurality formula". The plurality formula makes an election a contest in which the winner is to outscore the best of the opposition. This, of course, introduce an element of "chance", since the number of voters required to win cannot be predicted from the formula and the vote total alone. Sometimes, a candidate may win with 35 votes, while two opponents get 25 and 30 votes respectively. The term 'first-past-the-post' originated from the analogy of a horse race. For a horse which is first to pass the winning post it is, indeed, a matter of indifference whether it has left one or more horses behind. Thus, it is a strange experience for us to consider that the winner with his 35 votes a smart fellow: he has left two opponents behind him, one at a distance of 5, the other at a distance of 10 votes. The rationale is that the object of racing is just to decide which horse or automobile has travelled the distance most rapidly.

Another difficulty the FPTP is that the votes a candidate gets beyond the minimum requirement are, in a sense, wasted. It makes no difference that a candidate wins by a landslide in a constituency; a hair's breadth margin would do as well. In the same logic, the votes given to losing candidates are also wasted.

2. Ballot Structure is Categorical Rather than Ordinal

In democratic elections, voting is necessarily an act of choice. The function of the ballot is to structure that choice. All ballots ask the voter to choose among the contestants in some way, but they vary in the kind of choice they demand. The ballot structure is of two types: (1) categorical ballots, and (2) ordinal ballots. Categorical ballots ask the voter to decide which one of the candidates he prefers. The ballot forces him to say that he prefers one candidate in parliament as opposed to all others. He cannot qualify his decision; and he cannot divide his mandate among different candidates.

By way of contrast, ordinal ballots allow the voter to express a more complex, equivocal preference by rank-ordering the candidates. He may thus say that he prefers candidate 'A' most, candidate 'C' second, and so forth. The voter need not opt in favour of any single candidate.

The significant difference between these two types of ballot lies in the nature of the role imposed by each upon the voter. Under categorical systems the voter must act decisively, delivering his whole mandate to a single candidate. Under ordinal systems the voter is not required to act quite so decisively, and is allowed to represent even his least powerful positive feelings in small parcels of support for each of several candidates.

In the general elections of 1952, 1957 and 1962 the Congress party had bagged 75% of seats each in *Lok Sabha* with 45%, 48%, and 45% of votes respectively. In 1967 and 1971 the Congress has won 54% and 68% of total seats with a vote share of 40% and 44% respectively. The case is repeated in 1977 when *Janata* Party got 55% of seats with 43% votes. When the Congress party returned to power in 1980, it got 67% of seats with 43% of votes. Even when Rajiv Gandhi led the Congress party to its best ever performance in 1984, it got only 48% of votes but mustered a huge share of seats (77%). Since then no political party could get an absolute majority on its own, but the disproportionality between vote share and seat share continued.

This being a serious flaw of the Indian electoral system, majority of Indian voters lives with a feeling that they are not represented in the parliament. The system does not take care to see that the minority (social and political) groups, women and other marginalized sections are adequately represented in the legislature. This badly affects the quality of representation in Indian democracy.

It is more evident from the following tables which describe the percentage of voter support that the elected MPs got in the 2004 general elections at the national level. It is astonishing to see that there are MPs who get elected with the support of less than 30% of the total votes polled. As many as 322 out of 539 newly elected MPs were returned with less than 50% of the voter support. It indicates that nearly 60% of the *Lok Sabha* does not represent the majority in their respective constituencies.

When we take the case of the total population, the situation is still worse. There are two MPs who have won with the support of less than 10% of the total electorate while there are 91 MPs who are returned with 11% to 20% support. This table indicates that only six MPs in the 14th *Lok Sabha* had got the endorsement from more than 50% of their respective electorates. This is the plight of Indian parliamentary democracy.

Table 13.1. Votes polled by winners as percentage of voters in the *Lok Sabha* elections 2004 at the national level

Groups in percentage	*No.of Winners*
Below 20	00
21 - 30	16
31 - 40	93
41 - 50	213
51 - 60	175
61 - 70	36
Above 71	03
Total	539

Source : Election Commission of India – General Elections, 2004, (14th Lok Sabha).

The perceived drawbacks of the present electoral system, necessarily, need to be corrected. To suggest corrective measures, one should know all the available forms of electoral systems that exist in the world today. Therefore, an attempt is made here to survey the typology of electoral systems.

Typology of Electoral Systems

There are several electoral systems currently in use and many more derivatives on each form, but for the sake of simplicity we can categorise electoral systems into three broad families and 10 sub families.

All existing electoral systems in the world today can be classified under any of these ten categories. Arend Lijphart who surveyed all electoral systems in the world illustrates that, just over half (114 or 54% of the total) of the independent states and semi-autonomous territories of the

Table 13.2. Votes polled by winners as percentage of electors in the *Lok Sabha* elections 2004 at the national level

Groups	*No. of Winners*
Below 10	02
11% - 20%	91
21% - 30%	219
31% - 40%	185
41% - 50%	36
51% - 60%	04
60% - 70	02
Above 71%	00
Total	539

Source : Election Commission of India-General Elections, 2004, (14th Lok Sabha).

Table 13.3. Classification of the Electoral Systems in the World

Family	*Sub-family*
Plurality-Majority	First-Past-the-Post (FPTP) Block Vote (BV) Alternate Vote (AV) Two Round System (TRS)
Semi-proportional	Parallel System Limited Vote (LV) Single Non-Transferable Vote (SNTV)
Proportional	List PR Mixed Member Proportional (MMP) Single Transferable Vote (STV)

world which have direct parliamentary election use plurality-majority systems. Another 75 (35%) use PR type systems, and the remaining 22 (10%) use semi-PR systems, all but two of which are Parallel systems.

When classified by population size, the dominance of plurality-majority systems becomes even more pronounced, with parliaments elected by First-Past-the-Post (FPTP), Block Vote (BV), Alternative Vote (AV), or Two-Round System (TRS) methods representing collectively 2.44 billion people (59 percent of the total). Proportional Representation (PR) electoral systems are used in countries totaling 1.2 billion inhabitants, and semi-PR systems are used to represent just under half a billion people. The seven countries which do not have directly elected national parliaments constitute 1.2 billion people, but China makes up 99 percent of that figure.

Individually, FPTP systems are the most popular, with 70 out of 211 nation-states and related territories giving them 33 per cent of the total, followed by the 67 cases of List PR (LPR) systems (32 per cent). But when it comes to people, FPTP systems are used in countries which contain almost twice as many people as those in List PR countries. The 1.8 billion figure in the table is inflated by India (1000 million) and the United States (263 million), but FPTP is also used by many tiny Caribbean and Oceanian islands as well. The largest country that uses List PR is Indonesia with 191 million people, but it is predominantly a system used by middle-sized West European, Latin American and African countries. Next in order are Two Round Systems (15 percent) and Parallel systems (9 per cent). While TRS systems are used in more countries, Parallel systems are used by more people. This is largely because Russia (148 million inhabitants) and Japan (125 million) use classical Parallel systems.

Table 13.4. The World of Electoral Systems (as on 1st May 1997)

Electoral System	*No. of Countries/ Territories*	*%*	*Total Population (in millions)*	*%*	*Established Democracies*	*%*	*Total Population (in millions)*	*%*	*'Free' Countries/ Territories*	*%*	*'Not Free' Countries/ Territories*
FPTP	70	33	1850	45	11	30	1273	71	35	36	17
BlockVote	10	5	139	3	1	3	1	0.1	3	3	3
AV	2	1	18	0.4	1	3	18	1	2	2	0
TRS	31	15	427	10	1	3	58	3	7	7	11
Parallel	20	9	443	11	1	3	126	7	5	5	5
SNTV	2	1	5	0.1	0	-	-	-	1	1	0
List PR	67	32	968	23	15	42	158	9	39	40	10
MMP	7	3	265	6	4	11	162	9	4	4	0
STV	2	1	4	0.1	2	6	4	0.2	2	2	0
Total	211		4119		36		1800		98		46

NB : 36 established democracies are categorized by Arend Lijphart (1998) in *Democracies,* 2nd ed. Yale University Press, New Haven. Lijphart includes all countries considered democratic now, and for the last 20 years, which have a population of at least a quarter of a million people.

The Block Vote is used in 10 countries and territories (5 per cent), but its 139 million people only represent three percent of the total. Conversely, Mixed Member Proportional (MMP) systems are used in only seven countries, but the collective 265 million people of Germany, Venezuela, New Zealand, Mexico, Italy, Bolivia, and Hungary represent six percent of the total. The Single Transferable Vote (STV) and Single Non Transferable Vote (SNTV) systems are the rarest electoral systems in use today, with only two examples of each. The use of AV in Australia and Nauru mean that 18 million people live under AV systems, while Jordan and Vanuatu's SNTV systems represent only five million people and Ireland and Malta's STV systems four million.

If we look at electoral systems in "established democracies" (i.e., those states with a population of more than a quarter of a million which have held continuing free elections for over 20 years), we find that proportional representation systems are more numerous with 21 (59 per cent) out of the 36 states, but the size of India and the United States still means that 71 per cent of people living in these 36 countries live under FPTP systems. MMP systems are over represented among established democracies at 11 per cent, and in fact are used by four million more people than the more widespread list PR systems. Since Japan's switch over to a Parallel system there are no examples of SNTV in established democracies, while conversely both the world's examples of STV, Ireland and Malta, fall into this category.

Considering the increasing tide of democratization which has occurred through the 1980's and 1990's, it is found that 98 independent states and related territories are ranked as "free", on the basis of political rights and civil liberties. Among these countries the distribution of electoral systems bears a close relationship to the overall pattern proportionately there are slightly more FPTP and List PR systems and around half the number of TRS and Parallel systems, but it is difficult to say that any single electoral system is really any more popular in the "free" world than the world overall. However, among the 46 countries ranked as "not free", there are a disproportionate number of Two Round and Block Vote systems, and considerably fewer PR systems. In all, plurality-majority systems make up 70 percent of the electoral systems of the "not free" world.

Across continents, the distribution of electoral systems is more mixed. As Table five shows, FPTP systems make up approximately 30-45 per cent of the total in Africa, Asia, the Middle East, and the Americas

Table 13.5. Regional Distribution of Electoral Systems

Electoral System	*Africa*	*America*	*Asia*	*CIS &Post Communist*	*Western Europe*	*Middle East*	*Oceania*	*Total*
FPTP	19(35%)	19(40%)	10(45%)	1(4%)	4(14%)	3(30%)	14(64%)	70
BV	1(2%)	2(4%)	5(23%)	0	0	2(20%)	0	10
AV	0	0	0	0	0	0	2(9%)	2
TRS	10(18%)	6(12%)	1(5%)	8(30%)	2(7%)	2(20%)	2(9%)	31
SNTV	0	0	0	0	0	1(10%)	1(4%)	2
Parallel	7(13%)	2(4%)	3(15%)	7(26%)	1(3%)	0	0	20
List PR	17(31%)	16(33%)	3(15%)	10(37%)	17(61%)	2(20%)	2(9%)	67
MMP	0	3(6%)	0	1(4%)	2(7%)	0	1(4%)	7
STV	0	0	0	0	2(7%)	0	0	2
Total	54	48	22	27	28	10	22	211

Source : Arend Lijphart, *Democracies,* 2nd ed., (New Haven, Yale University Press, 1998).

(overwhelmingly North America and the Caribbean). The system is less common in Europe and the former Soviet Union, but relatively dominant in the island states and territories of Oceania. List PR systems are similarly spread through out Africa, the Americas (Central and South America), and post communist Eastern Europe. However, List PR is more dominant in Western Europe (61 per cent), and together the three PR systems (List PR, MMP, and STV) constitute three quarters of all electoral systems in Western Europe. By contrast, almost a third of the Commonwealth of Independent States (CIS) and Eastern Europe use French-type Two-Round systems, while over a third of all countries which use the Block Vote are found in Asia.

Whatever might be the nature of electoral system that countries follow, all democratic theorists accept that there should be fair representation to all social segments in proportion to their strength. That seems at first obvious: if a party receives half the votes in the country it should have half of the seats in the parliament; if it gets only a tenth of the votes it should have one tenth of the seats. With this objective in mind, we have attempted to find a suitable electoral system for India which can correct the inherent disproportionality in the FPTP system. The search makes us to suggest a modified version of the Mixed Member Proportional system that exists in Germany to suit the demands of the Indian situation.

The Mixed Member Proportional (MMP) system which is also called Additional Member system would both remedy the disproportional effects of the current Indian system and preserve the constituency representation system to which the Indians are so attached. An additional input to this electoral system could also take care of the under representation of women in elected bodies.

The German Model

The German system is designed to fill 50% of the *Bundestag* (Lower House) with constituency MPs and 50% with MPs drawn from party lists. The former is elected on an FPTP basis, essentially the same as that in India and with equivalent disproportion in the pattern of results. The latter 50% are allocated 'correctively' so that FPTP distortions are ironed out and the final composition of the *Bundestag* is (with limited exceptions) in proportion with how the electorate cast its votes for each party. There are two central features of the system.

(1) Voters have two votes, both of which are on a single ballot paper. One vote is the 'constituency vote'. This part of the ballot paper shows

the names of all the candidates contesting for election as the Member of Parliament to represent that constituency. The candidate who wins the most of the votes becomes the constituency MP. The second vote is the 'party vote'. This part of the ballot paper shows names of all the registered political parties that have nominated lists of candidates drawn up separately in each region, or Land. Somewhat perversely, it is the 'party vote', which is more important. The 'party vote' determines the final, proportional composition of the *Bundestag;* the first has an impact only in the constituency concerned.

(2) However, a political party has to clear one of two 'hurdles' – gaining at least 5% of the 'party votes' nation-wide or three constituency wins-in order to receive a proportional allocation of seats in the *Bundestag*. Votes for parties, which fail these two hurdles, are disregarded in calculating the composition of the *Bundestag.* If a party does cross any of these hurdles, its total number of MPs will be made up of any constituency MPs it has plus enough list MPs to reach its final share of total membership in the House. If a party crossed the 5% votes hurdle but wins no constituency seats, all its MPs will be list MPs.

It should also be noted that the total number of constituency seats won by independent candidates and by candidates for parties that are not on the 'party vote' are deducted from the total number of seats before seats are allocated according to parties' shares of all the 'party votes'. So in a 100 member House, if 5 independents have won from various constituencies, 95 seats will be available for proportional allocation.

Allocation of Seats

The number of 'party votes' won by each registered party which has submitted a party list and crossed the threshold is used to decide how many seats overall each party will have in parliament. These parties will receive enough list seats to add to their constituency seats to reach the total number of seats to which they are entitled.

To determine the precise order in which all the seats in parliament are allocated to the various parties, a number of statistical methods are in use. The simplest of them is one called *St.Lague* formula. According to this formula, the nation-wide 'party vote' of each of the parties which crossed the threshold is divided by successive odd numbers starting with 1 (i.e. the number of 'party votes' won by each party is divided by 1, 3, 5, 7, 9, 11 etc). The highest resulting numbers (which are called quotients) determine both the number of seats for each party and the order in which they are allocated. This process of division is continued till enough quotients to fill all the seats are found.

The number of quotients received by each party is the number of seats that party is entitled to have in the Parliament. The electoral officer will then deduct the number of constituency seats each party has won and allocate enough list seats to each party to bring the total number of seats up to the number to which it was entitled. The electoral officer will then examine the list of candidates submitted on its party list before the election and delete the names of any candidate who had won a constituency seat. He will then allocate the party's list seats to the remaining list candidates in the order they appear on the party's list. Such candidates will be declared elected to the Parliament.

Implications

The list system is in some respects problematic. Lists are 'closed', in other words defined by the parties themselves, with no possibility for voters to influence either the selection or the rank order of candidates. Even the names of the list candidates do not figure in the ballot paper, though the lists are officially sent to all households and widely published. Given that half the members of the *Bundestag* are drawn from party lists, this may be judged a limitation on democratic choice.

Another problem is that leading politicians often appear both as constituency candidates and – as insurance against failing to win the constituency – in high positions on the party list. The winning candidates from the constituencies will be, obviously, deleted from the party list and the following candidates on that party's list move up.

Another significant qualification to proportionality is the phenomenon of so-called 'surplus seats'. This arises when a party wins more constituency seats than the number it is entitled to take on the basis of party votes cast. If this happens, then that party retains these 'surplus seats' and the size of the *Bundestag* is increased accordingly. No compensatory seats are awarded to other parties to maintain proportionality. It is also possible that a party might not nominate enough list candidates to fill all the seats it was entitled to have on the basis of its share of all the 'party votes' it received. It would then not be able to fill those seats, which would remain vacant until the next election. If that happened, Parliament would have fewer members than expected.

Adopting German System in India

The realization of existing diversities in a large country like India might necessitate some variations from the German model. The nation-wide 5% vote and the seat hurdle could be reduced and made state-wide or district-wide. It would be fair, if the hurdle is set at 5% votes at the state level or one constituency win for the Lok-Sabha. For the State legislature, the district could be taken as a unit and the hurdle is set at 5% at the district level or one constituency seat.

To enhance the representation of women in the legislature, rule can be made to place women candidates in the party lists at winnable positions. It can be stipulated that one woman candidate should be placed for every three candidates on the party list. Thus, it can be ensured that there will be a woman legislator if a party could return three candidates; two women, if the party gets six seats and so on. Considering the fact that the total number of seats is doubled, it is certain that the number of women legislators would, definitely reach 33% or even beyond that. The party lists can also be made use of for distributing tickets to different sections of the community like OBC and minorities.

Adopting the Mixed Member Proportional system would positively influence the participation of voters in the electoral process. The fact that more representatives are chosen in the election, more voters can get identified with the candidates of their choice. This would definitely attract the otherwise indifferent sections of the electorate towards the election process.

Conclusion

Care has to be taken in identifying the relevance of one country's experience for another's reform debate. Institutions such as electoral systems are embedded in a country's wider political tradition and institutional environment and cannot simply be transplanted elsewhere. The German system is of course more complex than the simple FPTP, but there is no real evidence that it overburdens the intelligence of the German electorate. Germany has been practising this system ever since 1949. New Zealand has adopted this system with slight variations in 1993 and it is being actively considered in countries that discuss electoral reforms.

Given that the principle of constituency representation is deeply embedded in Indian politics, an electoral reform process, which abandoned that principle, would not easily take root. The advantage of a German style system would be the maintenance of constituencies and FPTP contests, which select constituency representatives. At the same time, it has its own mechanism to ensure proportionality between the percentage of votes polled and seats won by parties. It also ensure even smaller parties to have representation in proportion to their voter strength. The German system brings stability to political system as it requires the naming of a successor Prime Minister while moving a no-confidence motion (constructive Vote of no-confidence).

If the political pulls and pressures that exist in Indian society are any indication, electoral reforms naturally merit a serious debate. In that debate, the German model is well placed to feature strongly as it ensures stability, allows constituency representation and provides outcomes far more proportional than those generated by the current Indian system. It can also put an end to the prolonged controversy over the women's reservation Bill, if we could make it mandatory for political parties to place women candidates at winnable positions in Party lists.

REFERENCES

Droop, H.R (1881) : 'On Methods of Electing Representatives', *Journal of Statistical Society* 44:2.

Duverger, M. (1963) : *Political Parties : Their Organization and Activity in the Modern State,* New York : Wiley Science Ed.

Joseph,T.M. (2000): 'Proportional Representation as a Means of Increasing Women's Role in Legislatures : A Case for Electoral Reform in India', *Journal of Asian Women's Studies.* 9:1:44-52.

Joseph,T.M. (1999): 'Proportional Representation is the Answer to the Quota Problem', *The Hindu,* February 9.

Lijphart, Arend (1994): *Electoral Systems and Party Systems : A Study of Twenty-seven Democracies 1947-1990,* Oxford : Oxford University Press.

Lijphart, Arend (1998): *Democracies,* 2nd ed. New Haven, Yale University Press.

Moncrief, Gary F., and Joel A.Thompson. (1992): 'Electoral Structure and State Legislative Representation: A Research Note', *Journal of Politics* 54 : 246-56.

Rae, D.W. (1967): *The Political Consequences of Electoral Laws,* New Haven: Yale University Press.

Riker, W.H. and Ordeshook, P.C. (1968): 'A Theory of the Calculus of Voting', *American Political Science Review,* 62: 25-42.

Rule, Wilma. (1987): 'Electoral Systems, Contextual Factors, and Women's Opportunity for Election to Parliament in Twenty-three Democracies', *Western Political Quarterly* 40:477-498.

Welch, Susan, and Donely T. Studlar. (1990): 'Multimember Districts and Representation of Women: Evidence from Britain and the United States: *Journal of Politics* 52:391-409.

14 Pernicious Behaviour of Elected Representatives—An Unresolved Challenge to Indian Democracy

K. Surya Prasad

The legislature, the foremost pillar of the temple of democracy, provides 'the most important forum for representation, interest aggregation and political socialization'. It is also invested with the supreme authority to formulate policies, oversee their implementation and in general to act as a watch dog over the functioning of the government. The most important foundation of parliamentary democracy is the faith of the people in the efficacy of the system to address their hopes, aspirations and concerns in the best way possible. Unfortunately, it seems that, people of India have lost all their faith, confidence and trust in the functioning of our parliamentary democracy and the ability and will of the parliamentarians to uphold popular will because money power, mafia, muscle power, manipulations, stuffing electoral rolls, bogus voting, booth capturing, rigging, undue influence, bribery, pre-poll and post-poll violence etc. have been adopted to make the elections of the people's representatives a farce. Further, the intrusion of a large number of criminals in the electoral process and the close liaison among the legislators, the criminals and the underworld cause serious concerns. Then comes the use of unrestricted and unaccountable black money in elections to defy the popular will. Again, members of the parliament and the state legislatures have become marketable commodities. They have become a subject of sale, purchase, horsetrading and other dubious inducements.

Despite laws against defection, party hoping has become a common practice. Frequent and blatant defection and counter defection by the representatives of people for money and ambition for high offices have raised substantial question of morality and constitutionalism. Besides, the representative character of the elected representatives becomes doubtful. Majority of them are elected by minority of votes polled, more votes are cast against each one of them. Again, the Parliament is not performing with any degree of competence or commitment what it is primarily expected to do. Barring exceptions, those who are elected to the democratic institutions are neither trained in law-making process nor do they seem to have the inclination to develop the necessary knowledge and competence in their profession. All the more reprehensive is the unruly behaviour of elected representatives during parliamentary sessions which render the legislature incapable of transacting even its basic function for days together. Even the parliamentary sessions have been abandoned or frozen for reasons that are unclear. The ugly face of the parliament has shown up in cross-voting, vote-buying, demanding cash for asking questions in parliament, harboring criminals, human trafficking and display of currency notes in the well of the House during debate on trust votes. Disconcerting, indeed, is a report from Patna that an MLA chosen for Cabinet berth could not take the oath because he had been absconding. Fractured verdict and the resultant hung legislatures and coalition politics is another aberration that continue to mar parliamentary democratic process. Above all these, come the frequent intervention in the exclusive jurisdiction of legislatures by judiciary in the name of judicial review and judicial activism and by the executive under the guise of delegated legislation and promulgation of frequent ordinances which go a long way in eroding the authority and dignity of these representative institutions. All these disturbing and destabilizing factors coupled with low level of attendance and trivialization of debates have raised questions about the relevance of parliamentary democracy and its future.

Among these aberrations, the most nauseating of the erosion of democratic and moral values in the parliamentary life in India is the pernicious behaviour of elected representatives inside the Houses. It has crossed all limits and reached a shocking and alarming stage where the Prime Minister was not allowed to introduce his team, the speakers were not able to speak and the Governors were obstructed from addressing the legislatures. What started some time ago as a spontaneous action by a few members, especially from the minority parties, to make their voice heard in the parliament on sensitive issues is now seen by political parties as an ordinary form of protest. Now a days, debates and discussions on important policies and issues have been overshadowed by disruptions, confrontation and such other undemocratic practices which make the legislatures a subject of ridicule inviting public opprobrium. It is a matter of common knowledge that even a single day in parliament is not passed without any walkout, dharnas, shoutings, adjournment and pandemonium. The major political parties are now announcing in advance their intention to stall parliamentary proceedings routinely for days, seriously eroding its sanctity. What is even more worrysome is that even if a single member wants to disturb the proceedings, he can hold the House to ransom.

It has become a fashion of some members to stall the Parliament on non-issues. While doing so, they have conveniently forgotten that the people send them to the legislatures to highlight their grievances in the Houses in a mature manner and not to disrupt the proceedings. Sometime, pernicious behaviour displayed by the members turns out to be what could be described as 'Legislative terrorism' and what happened in the Parliament and different state legislatures in recent times reminds us that it is not an apprehension but a reality. Two examples illustrate the point. The attempt of the NDA Government to introduce the Women Reservation Bill in Loksabha may be cited in this connection. The introduction of the bill was obstructed by certain parties and groups like RJD and SP. One member of SP even went to the extent of snatching from the hands of the then Law Minister, Ramjith Malani, what he believed to be the copy of the bill and tearing it into pieces. The ruckus appears to be over the failure to provide subquota for OBCs and Muslims within the 33% of reservation for women stipulated in the bill. They did not have the patience to listen to the clarification of the Prime Minister that the issue could be decided at the discussion stage.

Equally reprehensible was the conduct of another SP member, Devendra Singh Yadav who, during the proceedings of the House, menacingly moved towards Nitish Kumar, the then Agricultural Minister, taking umbrage at certain derogatory remarks that Kumar had made against his party Chief, Mulayam Singh Yadav. The more disturbing part of it was that the member, despite inviting a stern rebuke from the speaker, had shown no sign of repentance. On the contrary, he was reported to have declared that he would not hesitate to beat up any one who dared to insult his leader.

These episodes are the reflection of the deterioration of the parliamentary ethics and standards in general and conduct and behaviour of the elected representatives in particular. The disgraceful 'riotous' scenes, erosion of all cultural, ethical and moral values are highly deplorable and amount to an attack on democracy which deserve strongest condemnation. Obviously, these members aggressively violated all canons and conventions of parliamentary democracy and failed to understand their duties and responsibilities, rules and regulations and ethics and morals of parliamentary standards and behaviour and demonstrated how consideration of ideology, loyalty and even basic decency have stopped pricking the conscience of the parliamentarians. No doubt, it is an assault not merely on a policy or individual view but on the legislature and the legislative process. It appears that what was constitutionally and democratically appropriate was not politically acceptable to them. Consequently, irreparable damage has been done to our parliamentary democracy by these members by indulging in violent demonstration even after the Prime Minister made it clear that 'the issue could be discussed at the discussion stage. Unfortunately priority was given to their political ambitions over and above the parliamentary propriety. These incidents demonstrated the fact that these members have reduced themselves from the position of respected parliamentarians to the position of mere street fighters or muscle men. These episodes demonstrated the fact that criminal elements are getting into our legislative bodies with impunity. Had it not been the case, Yadav would not have shown that much of courage to declare that 'he would not hesitate to beat up any one who dared to insult his leader, Mulayam Singh Yadav'.

Here it may be stated that, of course, representatives of the people have the right to raise issues and draw attention of the House to every act of commission and omission by the government, what they believed to be retrogressive, antipeople and antidemocratic. It has not been uncommon for the opposition to indulge in agitation and thereby correct the wrong policies and decisions. It is true that there can be no democracy if there is no room for protest and dissent. It is also true that dissent leads to newer and newer ideas, provided it is followed by constructive and meaningful suggestions. No doubt, parliamentarians have to fight for the worthy cause and they cannot and should not remain silent spectators when injustices are being done to the society. But, at the same time, they have an obligation that this should be done straight away with the available weapon under democracy, without placing parliamentary democracy in peril. They also have the obligation of paying heed to the chair and maintaining discipline. We should respect the Constitution and never indulge in violence and protests must be registered peacefully and constructively. If they are carried out to the extent of harming democracy itself, then it becomes self destructive. That is why Gandhiji taught and practised non-violence which he termed as sathyagraha. There should not be violence and fist-fight on the floor of the House. There should be dignity, decorum and discipline on the floor of the Houses. The opposition should help and co-operate with the government to transact the normal business of the House.

In this context the observation of B.R. Ambedkar in the Constitutent Assembly becomes relevant. He said:

> "If we wish to maintain democracy not merely in form, but also in fact, what must we do? The first thing in my judgment we must do is to hold fast to Constitutional methods of achieving our social and economic objectives... It means that we must abandon the method of civil disobedience, non co-operation and Satyagraha..... Where Constitutional methods are open, there can be no justification for these unconstitutional methods. These methods are nothing but the grammar of anarchy and the sooner they are abandoned the better for us". (CAD XII, p. 978).

Dr. Ambedkar was speaking of conduct outside the Parliament. His warning is all the more applicable to conduct within Parliament. Parliamentary tradition recognizes obstruction as a permissible tactic but within the rules (Noorani, A.G. Constitutional Questions in India, p.149). It has 'quite a respectable history', Jennings recalled, 'party war-fare is essential to the working of the democratic system. Yet it will not function if it is carried to extremes. A government in control of both Houses could effectively stifle the opposition. An opposition that would not accept the majority rule could make the parliamentary system unworkable. In practice, government is by consent and opposition by agreement' (Jennings, Cabinet Govt., p. 16).

What Jennings added in the concluding pages of his Classic work 'Cabinet Government' is very pertinent:

> "The function of Parliament is not to govern but to criticize. Its criticism, too, is directed not so much towards a fundamental modification of the government's policy as towards the education of public opinion... the government governs and the opposition criticizes. Failure to understand this simple principle is one of the causes of the failure of so many of the progeny of mother of Parliament and of the supercession of parliamentary government by dictatorship" (Jennings, Cabinet Government, p. 472).

All these observations lead to the inference that dissent and protest should be on merit and resorted to sparingly and always through constitutional, democratic and peaceful means rather than repeated interruption of parliamentary proceedings. Unfortunately, our elected representatives have a different approach to any problem raised in the legislature. The opposition takes pride in opposing anything and everything, totally disregarding their merit, instead of extending co-operative and constructive hand for the benefit of the country and its people. This perception of the opposition must be changed; otherwise democracy cannot take roots in our soil.

The parliamentary misbehaviour of elected representatives is not exclusively the problem of the Parliament. If we analyze the chronicle of legislative behaviour of different state legislatures, it would become evident that in the last few years opposition members have resorted to disruption, leaving the grievances of the common man unaddressed and unredressed. The daily scenes of various state legislatures are really shocking. For instance, in February 2009 in U.P pandemonium prevailed as the S.P. members climbed on the reporters desk and some of them threw paper ball at the speaker's podium. The Congress MLAs climbed on the desk to register their protest. Things turned so ugly in Andhra that Marshals had to physically throw out members displaying unruly behaviour. This, of course, is not the first time that such things have happened inside the state Assemblies. In U.P. itself, 33 MLAs were injured in clashes inside the House in 1993. In 1997 microphones and chappals were hurled at the chair by the opposition MLAs. These are the daily scenes of various other state legislatures. Annoyed with the behaviour of members S.D. Sharma offered to quit office as the chairman of Rajya Sabha when faced with unending unruly conduct and open defiance of the chair by some members. P.A. Sangma, the former speaker of Loksabha, compared the decorum of the House to that of boat club saying he was ashamed to preside over the chamber. He threatened to resign his office in July 1997. He lamented that pernicious behaviour of nation's elected representatives was causing the public to lose faith in parliamentary democracy. Speaker Somanath Chatterjee even went to the extent of expressing his greatest annoyance and condemnation when he lost all hope and patience. He said he hoped 'the people of the country would give a fit verdict in the next elections'. He also said 'public money should not be spent on useless allowances for you. You do not deserve one paise of public money'.

All these perceptions bring out the depressing features of India's degenerating democracy. An independent mass movement is necessary. People should assert their sovereign power as observed by the speaker so that our political leaders may not ignore the people any more.

It is interesting to speculate why such behaviour has been so much a part of the Indian parliament. There are many factors that come to our mind. In a sense this ugly behaviour is a symptom of a deeper disease of deinstitutionalized, demoralized, devalued, and dehumanized politics. Almost all parties irrespective of their ideologies indulged in this ugly game of power politics for the sake of convenience and for the furtherance of their narrow interest even if it may be against national interest. This is evident from the fact that every political party that had been critical of this pernicious behaviour while in power, more or less did the very same thing once they became the opposition. Both the two major national political parties went through this crisis resulting in the ever increasing intensity and proportion of indiscipline inside the Houses.

The pluralist political system has created a collection of intensely parochial and self-interested groups. In their eagerness to score points, they fail to recognize people's welfare. In a larger perspective, these corrosive trends are traceable to the ills affecting the party system itself such as growing criminalization, personality-centered cult politics, absence of ideology and principles, lack of inner-party democracy, lack of training, intolerance to the opponents' view, confrontational politics etc. Growing indiscipline is also the result of a complete erosion of all cultural, ethical, moral values, the ever-rising tide of casteism, communalism and religious fundamentalism, regionalism, himalayan corruption and above all the total lack of inspiring and enlightened leadership commanding support bases throughout the length and breadth of the nation. There is a conviction among legislators that low-profile ethical agitations do not create the desired impact and requisite media coverage. Therefore, they believe that the only option before them is to create disorder in the Houses.

The style of functioning of the parliamentarians is the chief barometer of the contemporary societal values and mirror and strength of leadership. Deterioration of national life cast its deep shadow in the behaviour of elected representatives also. Today politics has eventually degenerated into a struggle for power for personal ends. National interest and well-being of the people is a secondary thing for most of the present-day politicians. Those who are out of power want to acquire power by any means and those who are in power want to retain it by all means. They will not part with the advantages that power brings or even agree to share them voluntarily with others. It is this unending power-hungry opportunistic attitude which persuades them to go to any extent, at any cost, even violating all ethics and morals and forgetting the responsibility to uphold the highest tradition of democracy and the highest standard of parliamentary functioning and this finds reflection in the behaviour and actions of the representatives. It may also be noted that the roots of the problem are founded in the kind of people who get elected. When the political parties select the candidates, their criterion is whether those men and women would be able to win votes and not whether they would make good parliamentarians. Political parties want number, not good parliamentarians. The principle of truth, integrity, efficiency were given a go-by by the politicians of today.

The main reason for this decline, however, seems to be a consistent turn over of membership. In particular, legislatures have undergone a basic transformation of power from the urban middle class. The earlier parliamentarians were remarkable in their own ways. Their visionary and sagacious leadership strengthened the very foundation of democracy. Their conduct on the floor was prim and proper, never disorderly and uproarious, who meticulously observed rules and made the debates and discussion informative. They paid attention to the opposition parties and treated them with respect as an integral part of the democratic process. The opposition parties, in turn, acted responsibly abiding by the parliamentary rules unlike the parliamentarians of today. Today, it is the professional politicians and trade union leaders and persons having nexus with criminals and the underworld who are firmly rooted in the law- making bodies. The major consideration before them is to keep their political career secure rather than looking after the interest of the people. For the furtherance of their objectives they are ready to employ any method including disruptionist and confrontationist attitude. They have contributed to the breakdown of earlier elite consensus and conscientious style of functioning. Similar is the case of industrialists who buy their way into the Houses and then use their parliamentary membership to promote the interest of their own business or of the sections they represent. Members of these categories have come to have an edge in finding their way into elective offices. Further, there has been a growing attractiveness towards politics from other professions. This, in turn, attracted power seekers and persons with vested interests into politics and they get elected to the representative bodies. Earlier, leaders came to politics for doing service to the nation and its people and they had something to sacrifice. Now fortune-seekers and opportunists compete for coming to politics, seeing it as the means to gain authority and power. Mani Shankar Iyer was right when he observed:

> 'There has been deterioration in public life as those who are unemployed are now in politics. The major difference appears to be that while earlier, serving the nation was seen as a privilege and attracted many well-meaning people, now it is the privilege that attracts the politicians'. (*The Hindu,* 14 May 1997).

This has increased the number of vernacular and less cosmopolitan politicians in the legislative bodies who have transformed the institutions. Most of the distinguished parliamentarians of yesterday have either retired from politics or dead or failed to win elections because of the lack of money power, muscle power and mafia power. Attracting the right-talented, honest, well-meaning public-spirited educated persons into the arena of politics is the need of the hour.

Above all, the devices to shorten or avoid opposition scrutiny of the executive have also contributed to the incident of indecent behaviour. Also the great discretion given to the speaker has resulted in more opportunities to contest the speaker's decision and create a new avenue for disorder.

All the above factors are tending to transform the parliament into a non-entity incapable of performing even its primary function. As a result, bills are passed regrettably without discussion and several calling attention motions are left undiscussed. The opposition makes it impossible to hear what the Prime-minister's or ministers' statement is on important matters. And it thwarts every opportunity for a debate. A debate cannot take place though it is scheduled by the Business Advisory Committee to which the opposition is a party. Then, one would be tempted to ask this fundamental question. What is the relevance of Parliament if it is not allowed to function?

The damage or losses caused to the nation due to the unruly behaviour of the representatives is really shocking. A recent study indicated that in the XIVth Lok Sabha 26% of precious parliamentary time has been lost due to interruption and adjournments. During 2007 itself the Loksabha lost 133 hours of its time owing to disorders. The figure was 98 hours in 2006 and 75 hours in 2005. In the one month long monsoon session of 2007, it forfeited 42 hours and 20 hours in the winter session of short duration. During XIIIth Lok Sabha 356 hours have been wasted without transacting any business. Moreover, during 2002-2003, budget allocation worth Rs. 7,68,836 crores have been passed without any debate because of interruption. As it is common knowledge the budget sessions are the most important of the three sessions in a year, as it is during this period that the scrutiny by the parliament of the executive should be at its highest. Further more, the entire winter session in 2011 has passed without any discussion on any issue owing to the dead lock over the 2G spectrum issue. If we take the same position of various state legislatures like A.P, U.P, Bihar etc. we will be surprised! Each minute of parliamentary time costs several thousands or lakhs of rupees. No member of parliament seems to be bothered about it. Should we waste our hard earned money for the selfish and opportunistic interest of politicians and that too for their cheap popularity? This sad and sorry state of affairs led an eminent personality like Harvey-Stockwin to comment:

> 'India faces a serious problem. Indian democracy is being subverted by corruption and there is a dearth of action to truly remedy the situation' (Sudhanshu Tripathi, Electoral Reforms in India, JCPS, p. 62).

It goes without saying that pernicious behaviour of elected representatives is most regrettable since it has seriously damaged the parliamentary system, jeopardized the foundation of the democratic set-up, breeded authoritarianism and weakened the constitutional obligation of the government and undermined the dignity of Presiding Officers. In a sense, the disruption of proceedings in legislatures amounts to disruption of democracy itself. If we do not take concerted steps to remedy the 'crime on the floor', the very foundation of parliamentary democracy may get damaged and the people will lose all their faith and expectation in the credibility and utility of the parliament and consequently they may become cynical about the way the institutions of democracy are functioning. When the temple of democracy is allowed to degenerate into platforms for display of muscle power, no doubt, it will toll the death knell of the democratic structure of the Constitution itself. Therefore, to uphold the highest tradition of democracy and the highest standard of its functioning, it is high time to start some fresh thinking for dealing with this indiscipline. It was with this larger national objective that in September 1992, an All India Conference of Presiding Officers, leaders of political parties and ministers of parliamentary affairs and whips resolved to evolve and observe a code of conduct for the legislators. This has since been reiterated on various occasions- in 1997 at the special session of the Parliament to mark the Golden Jubilee of India's Independence, in June and November 2001 at a follow-up Conference of Presiding Officers and in 2004, at a meeting of the leaders of all political parties in the Parliament.The remedial steps, however, did not materialize because those in power could not muster sufficient courage.

The attempt made by the Commonwealth Parliament Union may also be referred to in this connection. It has drawn up a list of pointer on what the Parliament and parliamentarians can do and cannot and should not do to improve the situation. The most important and the excellent suggestion made in this connection was that the Parliament could facilitate more coverage of its serious business by opening the proceedings of the select and other committees to the media. Another was that the parties should take step to raise the standards of parliamentary debates by striving to elect high-calibre candidates. 'enhancing research support, and encouraging a better awareness of what the media needs.

To arrest the devaluation of parliamentary authority and restore confidence, certain pertinent suggestions are submitted here for deliberation. And it should start with the members. That means political parties should think of 'stricter evaluation' while nominating candidates for election. The candidate selected should have good conduct and character, and reasonably be expected to behave decently when elected. Laws that prevent those convicted of criminal offences from standing for elections would be necessary but they themselves do not solve the problem. A more positive approach will be needed from parties at the time of candidate selection. So that those suspected of moral turpitude, even if not convicted in a court of law, are not selected. Political parties violating such norms should be derecognized by the Election Commission. In this context, the latest decision of the Supreme Court is a welcome development as it is based on rational thinking and also in accordance with democratic spirit. On 13 March 2003, the Supreme Court in a leading and milestone judgment said that 'the voters have the fundamental right to know about the criminal, financial and educational background of those they elect. The Court observed that survival of democracy depends upon free and fair elections. Elections would not be fair if the voters are unaware of the antecedents of candidates contesting elections. The court direction to the Election Commission is not based on the assumption that at present voters are ignorant of candidates' criminal past. But it is hoped that official disclosure of information relating to candidates' criminal background would help to make a rational choice on the basis of facts. Thus a citizen can X-ray a candidate's past. The court's attempt to empower the voters would be in vain if the duty to X-ray the candidate is not maximized to expose, evaluate and eliminate candidates. If the verdict is implemented with true spirit as envisaged by the Court it will go a very long way to stamp out candidates with doubtful integrity and thereby eradicating the evil of pernicious behaviour that has bedevilled our parliamentary democracy for a long time.

In addition to what is stated above, it is also suggested that the candidates selected for contesting elections should have some qualifications. When the constitution was drafted the founding fathers of the Constitution expected that only persons of high calibre and integrity would be entering the legislative bodies as representatives of the people. They had a vision about a true Indian and his duties as clearly envisaged in Article 51A dealing with Fundamental Duties. Unfortunately their dreams have been shattered and nowadays power-mongers and persons with criminal records find their way into the legislative bodies. Their action and speech both inside and outside the legislatures are eroding the dignity of the Houses. The current situation warrants fixing of some qualifications for candidates. Dr Rajendra Prasad observed in the Constituent Assembly thus:

> 'I would have liked to have some qualifications laid down for members of the legislature. It is anomalous that we should insist upon high qualifications for those who administer or help in administering law, but none for those who make it except that they are elected. A lawgiver requires intellectual equipment, but even more than that, the capacity to take a balanced view of things, to act independently and above all, to be true to the fundamental values in life in one word, to have character (see Singhvi, L.M, Ed., Nani Palkhiwala: Selected Writings, p. 80).

Thus there is a valid case for minimum educational qualifications to be prescribed for contesting the elections. President Abdul Kalam made a point when he sought clarifications from the government on these vital issues. How is it that while an applicant for even a peon's post is expected to be qualified, the policy making politicians who influence the lives of more than 1000 millions of our fellow beings, are not required to have any education at all? The argument that any such step will be against the principle of universal adult franchise is both fallacious and ludicrous.

Closely allied with qualification, it is also desirable and essential to specify some disqualifications for contesting elections and holding the post of legislators. Taking into account the compulsion of regional parties, bargaining tendency of coalition partners and the limitations of the political leadership in the selection of candidates for elections, it is better to lay down certain statutory disqualifications. In framing such disqualifications it is necessary to give a definition of the term 'Pernicious behaviour' i.e. what does and what does not constitute pernicious behaviour of parliamentarians. All actions which bring or are likely to bring the legislators in disrepute, reduce their public acceptability' in the estimation of the public, undermine the basic functions of the legislators may also be included in the four walls of the definition. Such a law itself will go a long way to restore the credibility and essence of the institution and thereby increase the common man's respect for the representative institutions.

Another valid suggestion in this direction is that the presiding officers should use their power in the discharge of their duties to the nation. Rule 349 of the Rules of Procedure and Conduct of Business in the Lok Sabha categorically states that a member shall not interrupt any member while speaking by disorderly expression or noises or anything in a disorderly manner, shall maintain silence when not speaking, shall not shout slogans in the House; shall not tear documents in protest; shall not utter defamatory words, shall not use his right to speech for the purpose of obstructing the business of the House. Again, there is another rule that 'whenever the' speaker rises, he shall be heard in silence and any member who is then speaking or offering to speak shall immediately resume his seat. The Rule Book given to the members on the very first day provides the procedure to deal with violation of rules and the established tradition of the House to ensure orderly conduct of the business. It is also provided that any abuse of the procedure and willful persistent disregard or defiance of authority of the speaker are considered grave offence or breach of privilege and contempt of the House. Members violating the rule should be dealt with severely without any fear or favour. They should be asked to leave the House for the day and if they refuse they should be suspended for the session. A second suspension should entail disqualification and termination of membership and the member should be debarred from contesting elections for a specified period. In this regard the observation of C.K. Jain seems to be relevant.

'It is for serious consideration whether the Constitution or the R.P. Act, may be amended to provide for vacation of seats and disqualification for any election in the event of a member having suffered the punishment of serious withdrawals and suspension from the service of the House. This will act as a real deterrent and restore the prestige and dignity of the Parliament and state legislatures facing serious erosion for quite sometime (Jain, C.K. Crime on the Floor, p. 37).

It is high time that the respective presiding officers should exercise this power granted by the statute instead of adopting the strange practice of adjournment so that some dignity and decorum is restored. In this connection, the bold decision of the Speaker Somanath Chatterjee to report 32 MPs to the Privileges Committee is a welcome development. By doing so he has given a strong message to MPs that behaviour in Parliament is non-negotiable. It seems that the speaker was left with no choice other than referring the disorderly behaviour of our MPs to the Privileges Committee. His bold decision can be justified because he is the custodian of the House and also responsible for maintaining the dignity and authority of the House. It may also be stated that to correct the erring members and a firm resolve to adhere to the code of conduct expected from people's representatives, this process of cleaning must continue whenever there arises any such occasion in the future also. This punitive step was overdue as much as it was preceded by several unheeded warning by him and also by earnest appeal by the Vice-President, Hamid Ansari. The privileges committee should deal with the erring legislators without any fear or favour. All the guilty members must be punished on charge of contempt of the Parliament but the Privileges Committee must also take suo-moto notice of the matter and debar the members concerned from contesting any election. Any lenient attitude towards such behaviour will embolden others to indulge in unruly behaviour.

Another proposal that should be implemented is that if any parliamentary time is lost due to disruption by any member, all the members should be made collectively responsible for the 'Crime on the floor'. The pay and allowances due to parliamentarians for sitting in the House should be denied to all. Alternatively, to resume back the lost hours is to extend time for sitting (extra hours) to compensate for the time lost due to disruption of proceedings. During such extended period no privilege (DA or TA) shall be paid to members because running of legislatures costs a heavy burden on the tax payers. In other words 'no work, no pay' applies to members of the Parliament who enjoys holidays during session. In this connection, the decision of the Congress MPs that they would not like to claim their daily attendance allowance – although they were present and signed the registers – as the Parliament was stalled and there was no business transacted is a welcome development. However, The Parliament should take up the matter of 'no work no pay' principle and strive to enact a law to such effect. That alone will lend credibility to their stance.

The Lok Sabha Speaker Somanath Chatterjee recommends a system of 'Right to recall' of legislators as a powerful drug to cure the malady of indiscipline inside the Houses. The suggestion is good at the first sight though not without defects. The defects are real. Therefore, it cannot be accepted in a country like India. At the outset, it may be pointed out that it would lead to chaos and confusion. The possibilities of fractured verdict and the resultant 'hung legislatures' can not be ruled out. It would also lead to successive elections which involve a lot of money, time and energy. It would also cause inconvenience to the voters who are already fed up with frequent elections. Then where does the remedy lie? Surely, the remedy rests with the virtue, intelligence and public spirit of the people. The people should come forward and teach the members a lesson in the next election who routinely disrupt the legislative proceedings. For this purpose they should be given a voters' awareness campaign by public-spirited people and organizations so that healthy public opinion is always there to punish these wrong doers and discourage the possible ones. The information technology could also provide the best opportunity to impart education and information programmes to the Sovereign masters. 'Eternal vigilance is the price of liberty'. As such people themselves must be vigilant to have a strict watch on the performance of legislators.

We have adopted the parliamentary system borrowed from England. Therefore, British conventions and practices may also be of great help to face the challenges opened up by the new situation since India's parliamentary democracy has been modelled after Britain. Recently in British House of Commons, a Labour Party member created disorderly scenes and soon the Speaker named that member and on a motion moved by the leader of the House, the erring member was suspended from the service of the House. It is important to note here that more than 40 members of the Labour Party to which the member belonged supported the motion of his suspension. The Deputy Leader of the Labour Party later told C.K. Jain, the former Secretary General of Lok Sabha (who was observing the proceedings) that in matters of privileges they do not go on party line. In the same manner, our political parties should be courageous enough to bring in such a fundamental and important change in the parliamentary behaviour. Such a standard in the Indian Parliament would to a great extent discourage or put an end to the disorderly scenes.

Every profession requires a period of training and apprenticeship for the new entrants so as to enable them to discharge their duties efficiently. But there is no such requirement for the policy making politicians. The political parties and Presiding Officers have the responsibility to prepare and train new members as soon as they get elected in the legislative bodies. Such training should focus on rules of procedure in the House, the need to maintain discipline and the art and practice of law-making process. It should also impart special knowledge in respect of crucial national issues like defense, foreign policy etc. A committee consisting of senior and experienced Presiding Officers and lawyers may undertake such training.

The mass media working with positive criticism can go a long way in ensuring that representatives of people remain responsive to the hopes and aspirations of the people and carry out their wishes in the best way possible. Since democracy requires an active participation of the people, it is the responsibility of the media to keep the citizens informed of what is taking place in the legislatures. The media should ensure good coverage to objective comments, irrespective of the status and standing of members and sideline the subjective comments. In addition to that, the media should also give adequate coverage to what goes on in parliamentary committees. For this purpose, competent journalists should be assigned the task of covering parliamentary news. However, it seems that propelled by narrow considerations and commercial interests the media has surrendered that larger social goals and have fallen for short term gains as speaker Somanath Chatterjee observed.

It is the well-considered opinion of the author that these suggestions, which will certainly render the legislators more answerable and accountable to the sovereign masters, should be implemented. If these measures are implemented both in letter and spirit, the scope of indiscipline of the elected representatives would be diminished appreciably. The author, however, does not presume that the implementation of these suggestions will bring about a sea-change in the present scenario because of the domination of professional politicians in the legislative bodies. However, it is hoped that these suggestions will generate discussion and be considered seriously by all concerned. All said and done, ultimately, no standards whether constitutional or conventions will ensure a cent percent guarantee for good parliamentary behaviour unless the political parties and the political leadership of the country are committed to the democratic, secular, socialistic and political values. Therefore, what is needed is a good political system with a visionary and sagacious leadership coupled with character, calibre, integrity and statesmanship including moral and spiritual qualities. If these values are lacking, no rules and regulations, no socio political and economic changes, no legal system, no advance of Science and Technology, no defense measures, no subtle ideology and no metaphysical concept can save our parliamentary democracy from further degeneration.

REFERENCES

Books

1. Jennings, Sir, Ivor, (1961): *Parliament,* (2nd Ed., New York: Cambridge).
2. Jennings, Sir Ivor, (1961): *Cabinet Government,* (3rd Ed., New York, Cambridge).

3. Kaul, M.N. and Shakdar, S.L, (1972): *Practice and Procedure of Parliament with Particular Reference to Loksabha,* (3rd Ed, Vol. II New Delhi: Metropolitan Books).
4. Brazier, Rodney, (1998) *Constitutional Reforms,* (2nd Ed., OUP, Oxford).
5. Michael Rush, (1976): *Parliament and the Public* (Longman, London).
6. Noorani, A.G, (2000): *Constitutional Questions in India* (OUP, New Delhi).
7. Singhvi, L.M, (Ed.) (1999): *Nanipalkhiwala: Selected writings* (New Delhi: Viking, 1999).

Articles

1. Sudhanshu Tripathi, 'Electoral Reforms in India: Compulsions and Constraints', *Journal of Constitutional and Parliamentary studies (JCPS),* Vol. 40 (2000) p. 62.
2. Jain, C.K, 'Crime on the Floor', *JCPS* Vol. 33 (1999), pp. 36-37.
3. K. Suryaprasad, 'Electoral Reforms: Plea for a Fresh Look', JCPS, Vol. 35 (2001), pp. 1-24.
4. Sevanthi Ninan, 'Pep Talk in Parliament', *The Hindu*, 2 December, 2001.
5. Subhash, C. Kashyap '50 years of opposition,' *The Hindu*, 14 May, 2000.
6. Pran Chopra "Crimes against Parliament", *The Hindu,* 19 August, 2003.
7. 'Consensus in Parliament' (editorial), *The Hindu,* 25 November, 1999.
8. Kannabiran. K.G., 'A Lament for the Constitution', *The Hindu*, 23 March 1997.
9. Naresh Gupta, 'Politics, Ethics and Democracy', *The Hindu,* 25 January, 2009.
10. Katyal, K.K., 'Political Deterioration', *The Hindu*, 3 April, 2000.
11. 'Declining Parliamentary Standard', (editorial), *The Hindu*, 28 December, 1999.
12. Pattabhiram 'How to Arrest the Decline', *The Hindu*, 18 December, 1996.
13. Rajeev Dhavan, 'The Country of the Blind', *The Hindu,* 3 January, 2000.
14. Subramaniam, 'Reforming the Legislatures', *The Hindu*, 14 April, 1998.
15. Nikhil Chakravarty, 'Wither Parliamentary Democracy', *The Hindu*, 15 December, 1998.
16. Katyal, K.K., 'Political Deterioration', *The Hindu,* 3 April, 2000.
17. Pran Chopra, 'The Twlight of Parliament', *The Hindu*, 24 February, 2004.
18. Pattabhiram, 'How to Arrest the Decline', *The Hindu,* 19 December, 1995.

19. Rajeev Dhavan, 'Democracy for Sale', *The Hindu,* 8 November, 1997.

20. Somanath Chatterjee, 'Parliamentary Democracy and Some Challenges', *The Hindu* 15 November, 2007.

21. Kalyanam, 'How we lose the Magic of Gandhi?', *The Hindu*, 25 January, 2009.

22. Birnder Pala Singh, 'Why Deify Leaders in a Democracy?' *The Hindu* 25 January, 2009.

23. Dharmadan, 'How to Root out Pernicious Practice in Parliament', *Indian Law Report*, 24 December, 2008.

24. Hari.N.Ramkarran, 'Strengthening Parliament's Relationship with the Public', *The Parliamentarian,* Vol. 2008, No. 2.

25. Margaret Wilson, 'Assessing Members Behaviour in New Zealand', *The Parliamentarian*, Vol. 2008, No. 2.

26. 'A Bold Decision', *The Hindu*, 5 May, 2008.

27. Shafi Rahman, 'An Uncommon House', *India Today,* March, 2009.

15 Inclusive Democracy and Indian Elections

C.E. Ajithkumar and
M. Lathika

It is now more than 80 years since "poorna swaraj" was declared "birth right" and an oppressive act (salt act) of the alien and hence illegal government of the Indian sub-continent was confronted with wide-spread mass agitation epitomized in the "Dandi march". Sixty years have passed since the People of India, resolved to become a democratic Republic, and have redeemed their pledge to remain so 15 times since then by sending their representatives to the House of People of the Indian Parliament, through elections based on universal adult suffrage. The argument that they became a more rejuvenated democracy each time the electoral procedure was over - and that too almost in a fair and just manner - and a peaceful transfer of power was ensured, gains increasingly greater acceptance.

The Election Commission's recently concluded quinquennial job of conducting election to the 543 seats of the House of People has, as usual, commanded world admiration. Just like a festival in rural India, the general election was being 'celebrated' with all pomp, 'spice and colour', (Gopalaswami, 2008) and also with a fair spirit of national pride. Being acclaimed as the largest democracy in the world with the participation of maximum number of voters, maximum number of parties, maximum number of polling stations and probably the greatest gaiety that accompanies an election campaign, the general elections in India could possibly be the greatest global man-made event of regular periodicity. Thus, the quest for self rule, the urge for collective indignation and "the battle of the right against the might (of the ruling class)" were not anything new which were brought with Indian independence. Values of democracy, by now, are believed to have been rather deeply implanted in the Indian soil.

Self-governance is the mandate and mantra of elections in India, as it is in any democracy the world over. Neither self-governance, nor self-reliance had been alien to the sub-continent before the British colonial hegemony. However, when the British finally decided, after domineering and ruling the sub-continent for several years, to leave the country and hand over power to the natives, it was genuinely hoped that the power will ultimately come to the poor and the native working class who formed a decisively huge majority of the population, and whose sufferings and will to find alternatives largely ended up in their joining the struggle for freedom and 'swaraj'. The suffering was not only on account of their too-insufficient fundamental or livelihood entitlements to earn a decent living (which was largely due to the centuries-old system of blatantly uneven allocation of hitherto common resources) but was also owing to the social repression and denigration in the name of their caste, gender etc. – all aggravated progressively by the advancement of suzerainty under the foreign aggression. The object of democracy will find its realisation only when the interests of these impoverished people are placed at the top of agenda for administration of the country, as these people form the vast majority of the population, and the mandate of a democratic government is nothing but to execute the will of the majority.

The deliberations of the Assembly formed for framing the Constitution of free India, as a prelude to transferring power to the natives, though represented too less by the oppressed class and only by a single political party, reverberated with the voice for the rejuvenation and socio-economic liberation of the poor. The Constitution of India, especially part IV (Article 36 to 48, which are but non-justiciable) of it, nurtured the hopes and aspirations of the majority who, toiling and suppressed as they had been, wanted freedom forever, not only from foreign aggressors but from native oppressors as well. The franchise for the elected constituencies of provincial legislatures – majority were nominated members - was less than 4 percent of the population and confined only to landlords, industrialists, big traders, lawyers and other educated citizens. Despite poor representation of the poor in the Constitution Drafting Committee which was but chaired by a 'Dalit', and also in the Constituent Assembly per se, the Constitution guaranteed them inclusion.

All the recent post-election studies were unambiguous in their opinion that there is a conspicuous disconnect between the voters' perception on what policies that the state should follow and the policy that the government they elected actually pursued. With this backdrop, this paper attempts to address the following issues:

- How well the hitherto governments of India were represented by the people.

- Evaluate the performance of the governments of India and thereby ascertain how far these governments could comply with the constitutional directives.
- Differentiate the national parties in India in their rigour to achieve the constitutional mandates of policies for inclusiveness.

The study will be based on the secondary data published by governmental agencies or the Indian media. The domain of study is confined to the Lok Sabha elections only, and to the limited parameters for which secondary data is readily available.

Lok Sabha General Elections: Dimensions and Diversity

In India, general elections to the House of People are being conducted once the term of the House (maximum of five years) is expired, or the House is dissolved for want of majority by any group of legislators. Voting in India is a constitutional right for all adult citizens (of age more than 18 years) and by the exercise of it the people are, it is believed, guaranteed self-governance. It is the tool by which the will of the largest number could be expressed and executed/ administered. It is to be assumed, by the operation of our Constitution, that all the Government's decisions bear the stamp of all these adult citizens of India. There are currently 1068 registered parties in the country and 47 of them, distributed over 24 states, are 'State parties'. However, only 7 parties are designated currently as national parties. For the last (2009) general elections, there were 713.78 million electors on the roll (as on March 2009 - an increase of more than 6 percent, from 2004 tally) and they formed 62 percent of the whole Indian population (1149.3 million, as on mid-2008). Thus, the participating population of Indian elections, by its size, almost equals the entire European population (736 million), and exceeds one-tenth of the world population (6705 million by mid-2008) (www.prb.org, May 2009). It is not only the size of participation that makes the event big but the diversity of the participants also, by their ethnicity, religion, language and, of course, socio-economic status. In the 2009 elections, 8070 contestants (with only 6.9 percent females) were in the fray and 4241 of them representing 368 parties (largest number of contestants belong to Bahujan Samaj Party (BSP) - 500, followed by Indian National Congress (INC) - 440, Bharatiya Janata Party (BJP) - 433)) and the rest are 'Independents'. The whole process is carried out in 8,30,866 polling stations spread across the length and breadth of the country, in 5 phases spanning a month, and a large contingent of 46,90,575 polling officials are deployed to manage it. Finally, after the polls, only 37 parties could make it to the Lok Sabha – all (7) 'national parties', 22 'State parties' and 8 'Unrecognised parties'. Four alliances of political parties had been formed prior to the elections, one (United Progressive Alliance – UPA) led by the INC, another (National Democratic Alliance – NDA) by the BJP, yet another (Third Front or Left Front) by the Left parties, and the fourth one by others. The elections in India are not, however, a cost-free affair (eci.nic.in, as on May, 2009). The Union government has allocated 1280 crore rupees in the interim budget (almost 20 rupees per elector) for the conduct of the 15th Lok sabha elections. If we consider the money being siphoned by the candidates for their campaign also, the total per-voter cost incurred amounts to a huge sum.

Indian Elections: Mandate and the Outcome

The framers, while finalising the draft of the Constitution, provided for a democratic system of governance closely following British Parliamentary model with certain fundamental rights to the citizens, which are based on the principle of liberty and equality. But the liberty without responsibilities would lead to its abuse which, in turn, should attract state interference. The voluntary limitation of wants, in other words, the rejection of materialisation or the unlimited pursuit of material satisfactions, is essential for the achievement and the preservation of democracy (Narayan, 2006). However, the Indian Constitution stands out from other Constitutions of like genre in that in India, the Constitution, and not the Parliament, is Supreme; and since the Constitution is an agreement by the People for the People, the People are supreme. This was upheld by the Judiciary as early in 1973 which maintained that the power of the Parliament to amend the Constitution (Article 368) is limited to the extent that the basic structure of the Constitution remains intact (Kesavananda Bharati case, AIR 1973 SC 1461). Thus, 'the people' represented by the Constituent Assembly were the framers of the basic structure of the Constitution, and it is final; lock, stock and barrel.

But, how far the decisions of the government reflect the modal needs (needs of the maximum) of the poor? In a democracy, the only legitimate tool to monitor and control the Executive (Union) by the citizen is his mandate to select his representative to the Lok Sabha from among a panel of contestants (Mayo, 1955) that is made available to him once in a maximum period of 5 years. However, his mandate becomes sterile if either he chooses not to exercise his franchise, or the candidate of his choice does not make it to the constituency defeating others in the fray, or his felt-needs, though expressed, are not effectively championed by his candidate, despite his winning the election. Democracy fails where sterility of mandate prevails. Minority rules when democracy fails. India, now being made a Socialist Republic (Preamble, 42nd constitutional amendment, 1976), the resource allocation and opportunities to growth should be equitable (also Article 39). Indian Constitution contains certain directive principles for state policy that safeguard the interests of its citizens in almost all respects that take care of his livelihood, security and enable him to pursue a decent living.

But, no citizen can approach a court of law for a remedy if he finds that the State had violated the Constitutional directives by not complying with the principles enshrined in it either because he remained starving despite that the Government chose to grant tax concessions amounting to lakhs of crores of rupees (Article 38 (1) & (2), 39 (a, b & c), 43; apart from provision for right to life under Article (21) to the corporate sector that is owned and managed by the rich elite of the country, or because the wages that a female received was lower than that of her male-colleague who did the same job (Article 39(d)), or because she could not complete 8 years of schooling though she was 15 years old (39(f), apart from the right to education under Article 21A as inserted by 86th Amendment, 2002). Notwithstanding that the directive principles are non-justiceable, the state is not absolved of its responsibility of implementing the policies spelt out in the Constitution and administering the state affairs so that the people of the state finally, at the end of a certain period, enjoyed all the benefits as per the targets fixed in the Constitution. The people who are at the helm of the Executive should be held accountable to their delinquency/ incompetence/ lethargy in not meeting the targets. However, the Constitution does not provide, even it was established that the citizen(s) are deprived of their constitutional benefits, for immediate dismissal of the government, or even allow an appropriate constitutional body to proceed with punitive actions against the government, or at least confer the powers to prevent the government from showing further generosity in offering grants and concessions to the rich elite of the country at the expense of the poor and thereby widening the rich-poor divide. Notwithstanding anything contained in the Constitution, no government in a democracy holds the moral authority to continue for the next term, if a substantial number of its citizens are not salvaged from their deprivation of capabilities for a decent living, livelihood, nutrition, health and education. The electoral system of the country should address the issue.

Governments are, in fact, the expression of the will of the people (Jawaharlal Nehru, Constituent Assembly Debates on 13th December

1946). The People of India had asserted by expressing their will fifteen times already to elect their representatives to the House of People who, as was guaranteed by the Constitution and so earnestly expected by the citizens, legislate the laws ostensibly suiting the modal need of the People and execute them to their full satisfaction. But do these elections really churn out the will of the majority? Do they at least represent the majority? Table 1 provides certain parameters on the degree of representation of the People of India on their government, over all the general elections to the House of the People.

The table suggests seven phases in the governance of Indian Republic. The first phase is of a long duration of 26 years from 1951 to 1977 of five terms of Congress rule during which four Congress leaders held the mantle. This was a period of "Congress and Congress only" phase of Indian polity. Congress made it to form the cabinet winning a majority of seats ranging from 283 (in 1967) to 364 (in 1951). Its vote share ranged from 20.19 to 24.89 of the total number of electors during the period. However, if one considers the percentage of votes to the total population the party wielded a much lesser appeal. Its vote share comprised 9.68 percent of the total population in 1951 to 12.07% in 1971, when the party was represented by 352 MPs in Lok sabha. The first jolt to the steady and stable going of the Congress in the governance of India came with the onset of the second phase when a leader of Janata party became the prime minister. The JP-BLD rule was but short-lived though its mandate was huge, winning 41.32 percent of polled votes, 12.4% of the population and about one-fourth of the total number of electors, which was higher than that of any previous governments. The Congress (it contested in another name "INC (Indira)" regained power in the third phase (1980-1984) winning much more seats than what the previous regime won. But its next tenure (1984 to 1989) was the most popular government that Indian Republic had ever seen, though huge sweep in its favour was seen to be due to the "sympathy wave" triggered by the unfortunate killing of the Prime Minister Indira Gandhi in the previous Congress regime. The party won 405 seats, 30.80 percent polled votes and a mandate of 16.41% of the population. Except for the period of the BLD rule, the dominance of Congress party in the polity and the Executive of the nation was almost total till1989. The Congress's mandate among the people dwindled drastically since then – lesser than even the least popular Congress (1967) government till then. But the striking feature is that though the party remained the largest party in the lower house both in terms of the number of seats and in terms of the percentage polled out of the total polled votes, the party could wrest power

Table 15.1. How much the legislature and executive represent the People of India: The outcome of the 15 general elections to the Lok Sabha

Year	Population (Mn)[$]	Suffrage (No. of electors) as % of population	Poll %	No. of voters as % of population	Prime Minister's (First, During the period) party: Name of party	No. of seats won	Poll %	% Representation of population	No. of votes won as % of electors	Party with largest share of votes: Party	No. of seats (with poll %)[#]
1951-52	361.1	47.97	44.87	21.52	INC	364	44.99	9.68	20.19	INC	
1957	413.122	46.88	45.44	21.3	INC	371	47.78	10.18	21.71	INC	
1962	462.78	46.75	55.42	25.91	INC	361	44.72	11.59	24.78	INC	
1967	518.221	48.28	61.04	29.47	Cong (R)	283	40.78	12.02	24.89	Cong (R)	
1971	548.2	50.02	55.27	27.64	Cong (R)	352	43.68	12.07	24.14	Cong (R)	
1977[a]	647.238	49.62	60.49	30.02	JP & JP (S)	295	41.32	12.4	24.99	JP	
1980	688.856	51.71	56.92	29.43	INC(I)	353	42.69	12.57	24.30	INC(I)	
1984-85	751.5	53.28	64.01	34.1	INC	405	48.12	16.41	30.80	INC	
1989[b]	834.094	59.81	61.95	37.05	JD & JP	143	17.79	6.59	11.02	INC	197 (39.53)
1991-92[c]	846.4	60.43	55.71	33.67	INC	244	36.55	12.31	20.36	INC	
1996[d]	949.997	62.38	57.94	36.14	BJP	161	20.29	7.33	11.76	INC	140 (28.88)

(Contd...)

1998	982.223	61.68	61.97	38.23	BJP	182	25.59	9.78	15.86	INC	141 (25.82)
1999	998.056	62.07	59.99	37.24	BJP	182	23.75	8.84	14.25	INC	114 (28.3)
2004	1073.415	62.56	58.07	36.33	INC	145	26.53	9.64	15.41	INC	
2009	1139.809	62.62	58.43	36.59	INC	206	28.55	10.45	16.68	INC	

Source: Compiled or computed from data available in the Election Commission's website.

$:Census data, and data for years other than the initial years in a decennial, population projection estimates by United Nations Population Division, World Population Prospects: The 1998 Revision,1999 given in http://www.un.org/esa/population/pubsarchive/india/yrtrend.htm as on 13.05.09

Note: # - if the Prime Minister's party is not the party with largest share of votes.

Abbreviations of parties: INC – Indian National Congress, INC(I) – INC (Indira), JP – Janata Party, JD – Janata Dal, BJP – Bharatiya Janata Party, JP(S) – Janata Party (Secular)

a - Election schedule for 1976 on the strength of the state of emergency that suspended elections and civil liberties. Two prime ministers ruled the nation during the period, first of JP and then of JP(S).

b – Two prime ministers – leader of JD (VP Singh) and leader of JP (Chandrasekhar Singh).

c – Elections were not held in Jammu & Kashmir at this time and in many elections thereafter.

d – Three parties claimed the position of prime minister during the period - AB Vajpayee of BJP, HD Dev Gowda (1.4.96 – 21.4.97) & IK Gujral (21.4.97 – 19.3.98).

only thrice out of the 7 times the nation went for general elections (including the 2009).

Thus, the most popular government of India had a mass-appeal (number of votes it polled out of the then total population of the country) of only 16.41 percent, and the total vote share (out of the total number of valid voters) had been below 31 percent. No government could represent a majority of the population, or even a majority of the valid number of voters. The will of the majority resided outside the treasury bench. As Jayaprakash Narayan noted, the brick with which the present edifice of democratic polity was constructed was the individual voter and the whole process of democracy rested on the arithmetic of votes. This would result in the transformation of Indian village communities into "atomisation" of society. "The system is based on a false premise; the State or the People can not be an arithmetical sum of individuals". More often than not it is commonly believed, governments elected under universal adult suffrage are minority governments in the sense that they represent a minority of the voters, especially in the case of a multi-party polity. Experience has shown that present day mass elections, manipulated by powerful centrally-controlled parties, with the aid of high finance and diabolically clever methods and super media of communication, represent far less the electorate than the forces and interests behind the parties and the propaganda machines. (Narayan, 2006). Each member of the Indian Parliament has equal measure of prerogative in making laws. But executing the laws is largely the prerogative of the council of ministers which is nominated and headed by the prime Minister, as long as the prime minister enjoys the pleasure of the President who ensures that he/she continues to get the support of a majority of the members in the Lok Sabha.

Indian Socialism

India is a socialist country, by the very preamble of the Indian constitution (since 1976), and by many provisions enshrined in it (Articles 14, 39 (b), 39 (c)). But does this constitutional status of India of being a socialist country really reflect in the development agenda and action of the country? Does its long and sustained tradition of democracy contribute to the parameters of the living standard of its people? This section is an attempt in this direction.

The table presents the Human Development Index parameters for the six south Asian countries including India and the US. In HDI, India ranks 134 as on 2007, placed far behind the developed countries like US (13), and two of our neighbours Sri Lanka (102) and Bhutan (132). The

Table 15.2. Development parameters of India, its immediate neighbours and the US

Parameters	*India*	*Sri Lanka*	*Bangladesh*	*United States*	*Pakistan*	*Nepal*	*Bhutan*
HDI rank HDR 2009	134	102	146	13	141	144	132
HDI Growth-1980-07	1.33	0.58	1.86	0.25	1.3	2.16	..
HDI value 2007	0.612	0.759	0.543	0.956	0.572	0.553	0.619
Life expectancy at birth2007	63.4	74	65.7	79.1	66.2	66.3	65.7
Adult literacy rate1999–2007a	66	90.8	53.5	..	54.2	56.5	52.8
Combined gross enrolment ratio in education% 2007	61	68.7	52.1	92.4	39.3	60.8	54.1
GDP per capita (PPP US$)2007	2753	4243	1241	45592	2496	1049	4837
Children under weight % - for age under 5 - 2000-6	46	29	48		38	39	19
Population below poverty line $1.25 a day 2000-7	41.6	14.0	49.6		22.6	55.1	26.2
Life exp at birth yrs 2007 Female	64.9	77.9	66.7	81.3	66.5	66.9	67.6
Life exp at birth yrs 2007 Male	62.0	70.3	64.7	76.7	65.9	65.6	64.0
GDP per cap Annual growth rate at constant prices (%)1990–2007	4.5	3.9	3.1	2.0	1.6	1.9	5.2
Inequality measures Richest 10% to poorest 10%[c]	8.6	11.7	6.2	15.9	6.7	14.8	16.3
Gini index	36.8	41.1	46.8	40.8	31.2	47.3	31.0

Source : Compiled from UN, HDR 2009.

growth rate in HDI (1980-2007), though higher when compared with the developed countries is but lower than the developing countries like our neighbours Nepal (2.16) and Bangladesh (1.86). Of the 14 parameters presented in the table, India cannot stake claim for top position in any of the parameters considered, among the six south Asian countries studied, though it recorded fairly good growth in many respects like per capita (Gross Domestic Production). The inequality measures are alarming, though other south Asian countries except Pakistan fared worse than India. All these show that India with its long legacy of strong democratic foundations and *dejure* socialistic governance bound by the constitutional directives, could not stake any better claims than other governments which were either ruled by Kings, or by military regime for many long years, or even shattered by internal strife. When compared with these countries India enjoyed the fruits of political stability (except during June 1975 to Dec 1977 when a state of emergency was clamped under Article 352 of the constitution), strong constitutional provisions and unchallenged judicial and executive authority. Yet, its living standard does not seem to have made any marked difference. Indian democracy largely remained exclusive especially since the (Gross Domestic Production) growth was more than 7% for the current plan period and the development index parameters fall far short of the (Medium Domestic Growth) set by UN and the inequality measures showed no marked improvement over the non-democratic nations.

Political Parties and Socialist Agenda in India

Constitutionally, political parties appear to be non-entities, except that the Tenth schedule makes reference to "political party", "legislature party", "original political party" etc. A citizen can become even the Prime minister of the country even without being a member of a political party. However, a candidate for election to the Parliament has to tender an oath or affirmation that he would "bear true faith and allegiance to the Constitution of India as by law established" (Form III in the Tenth schedule of the Constitution). Moreover, section 6 of Representation of People Act (1989) made it incumbent upon any political party registered in India to pledge allegiance to the Indian Constitution. In other words, all the political parties registered in India accepted socialism as a principle for development, and achievement of it is an objective and target for their functioning and justification for their very existence. The command the political parties enjoyed over the Executive while either in power, or out of it, is legitimized and justified only because of this. All the governments in free India are formed by the leader of one political party or other.

Because centralisation of power prevents the citizen from participating in government, the parties, that is to say, small caucuses of politicians, rule in the name of the people and create the illusion of democracy and self-government (Narayan, 2006). Table 3 gives an account of how much inequality still prevails in India, over the regime of various parties that won the elections.

Table 15.3. Gini index for rural and urban India during the period of various governments that won the general election

General Election	*Year*	*Party of the Prime Minister*	*Party with largest mandate*	*NSSO survey year*	*Gini index$* *Rural*	*Urban*
1.	1951	INC	INC			
2.	1957	INC	INC	57-58	33.74	35.9
3.	1962	INC	INC	63-64	29.61	36.54
4.	1967	INC	INC	68-69	30.7	32.9
5.	1971	INC	INC	73-74	28.3	31.5
6.	1977	JP	JP	77-78	31.2	33.7
7.	1980	INC(I)	INC(I)	80-84		
8.	1984-85	INC	INC	83	30.1	33.4
9.	1989	JD	INC	89-90	28.23	35.59
10.	1991-92	INC	INC	1992	29.88	35.55
11.	1996	BJP	INC	95-96	28.97	35.36
12.	1998	BJP	INC	97	30.11	36.12
13.	1999	BJP	INC	99-00	26.3	34.7
14.	2004	INC	INC	2004	27	35
15.	2009	INC	INC			

Source $: Jha, 2000 and NSSO reports.

The table shows that the Gini index did not make a visible turn downward ever since the people of India made themselves a socialist country. Even the emergency period, during which, it appeared, the Congress government had initiated the 20-point programme and made some measures to curtail corruption (Brass, 1994) and contain the trend of concentration of wealth, made the country more inequitable. In fact, the inequity does not seem to have changed perceptibly, over the period of governments of all hues, both in rural and urban areas, though urban inequality is discerned to be slightly higher than that in rural areas. It is seen that the inequality was the lowest in rural area during BJP regime, though BJP is known hardly a socialist party.

To analyse the pattern of concentration of material possession over the different regimes, we present table 4 which has two parts. The first part gives the Gini coeffiticent of household consumption as the basis and the second part gives the Gini coefficient in respect of land holdings.

Table 15.4. Gini coefficients of household consumption as the basis and concentration of land holdings (household) of India

Household consumption[a]			*Land holding*[b]		
Period	*Party of the PM*	*Gini*	*Period*	*Gini (Ownership holding*	*Gini (Operational holdings)*
1980-84	INC (I)	0.314	1961-62 (round 17)	0.731	0.583
1985-89	INC	0.315	1971-72 (round 26)	0.709	0.586
1990-94	JD & INC	0.317	1982 (round 37)	0.712	0.629
1995-99	BJP	0.378	1992 (round 48)	0.710	0.641
2000-04	INC	0.360	2003	0.740	

Source a: WIDER (2005) and World Bank (2006)
b: NSSO report No. 491 p. 12.

The inequality in household consumption, which was hovering around 0.31 points, has taken a sudden surge during BJP rule to 0.378, and made a slight dip during the INC regime that followed. The Gini index of landholding also was almost stable around 0.71 till 1992, had ascended to a level of 0.74 by the year 2003. This table shows convincingly clear that there exists great disparity in the entitlement of land, and despite efforts of land reforms it persists. The tables 3 and 4 amply illustrate that India is not on the path towards socialism, and no political party which ruled India since its becoming a Republic could be absolved of not taking the nation to lesser inequities and greater opportunities for sustainable development (Wagle, 2007).

Secularism and Indian Democracy

India was made a secular country by the 42nd constitutional amendment, though tenets of secularism by way of provision of following any religion of one's choice was already there in the Constitution. It appears that the concept of secularism, though not properly articulated either in the Constitution or in any other authentic document prior to it, is but something which could be cultivated and practised as a way of collective life. However, despite long years of a secular tradition, our faith in secularism is seen doubtful. The degree to which one is secular or non-secular is but hardly a matter that could be calibrated using popular survey tools. Nonetheless, to prove our point, we present the case of general elections in Kerala 2009, as evidenced through the media reports. Malayala

Manorama (Malayalam) daily, after analyzing the trend of election campaigning reported on 15/4/2009 that the electoral destiny of six constituencies in Kerala (out of 20) would be determined by the Muslim votes (or influence of Muslim outfits), and four constituencies (all in the south) would be by Christian, particularly Catholic votes. Hindu votes would be decisive in two constituencies. By any belief in secular society, one can not help dismiss Manorama's assessment as completely baseless, for we have been preaching secularism right from the days when we attained dominion status, and no Indian party could admit that they enjoyed the mandate on communal lines. However, after the elections, the Hindu (dated 26.5.09) had put up the following analysis (National Election Study) of the voting pattern. The NES results match hugely with Manorama's predictions. There was a strong swing away from LDF, draining its vote-base among these communities. Thus, even the LDF – the front led by the Communist Party of India (Marxist) - enjoyed a vote-base on communal basis, though a fraction of it remains oscillatory.

Table 15.5. Social Basis of Voting, Kerala 2009

Social group (Community)	*LDF*	*UDF*
Nair	27 (-14)	33 (4)
Ezhava	57 (-1)	27 (5)
SC	69 (-5)	15 (5)
Muslim	26 (-3)	69 (-2)
Christian	32 (-15)	69 (13)

Source: NES 2009.

Note: values within parenthesis show the swing.

Conclusion

The study contests the widely held perception that democracy is manifested and materialized through the outcomes of general elections. India, by its constitution, is a socialist country and hence convergence among its citizens in their social and economic status, equity in the access to livelihood avenues and opportunities for development of its people should be the mandate and active pursuits for the governments of the country. Specifically, the study sought to ascertain how well the hitherto governments of India were represented by the people. It showed that Indian Republic was always ruled by minority governments, and the will of the majority resided outside the treasury benches. On an evaluation of the performance of the hitherto governments it revealed that India with its long legacy of strong democratic foundations and *de-jure* socialistic governance bound by the constitutional directives, could not stake any better claims than other governments in the region which were either ruled by Kings, or by military regime for many long years, or even shattered by internal strife. When compared with these countries India enjoyed the fruits of political stability, strong constitutional provisions and unchallenged judicial and executive authority. Yet, its living standard and inequality measures do not seem to have made any marked difference. Indian democracy largely remained exclusive especially since the GDP growth was more than 7% for the current plan period and the development index parameters fall far short of the MDG set by UN. All these strongly suggest that notwithstanding what the preamble of the Constitution enshrined, the outcome of Indian election can not be considered to be the one which complies with the mandates and principles of democracy, socialism and secularism. In other words, there could be a strong diabolical convergence among the political parties that seek the mantle of governance of the country, in their socio-political attitude and agenda. They seem brutally insensitive not only to the plight of the large majority of the people who granted them the rein of governance of the country but also to the constitutional mandates by which they are inexcusably bound and accountable.

REFERENCES

Banerjee, Mukulika (2007): 'Sacred Elections', *Economic and Political Weekly*. April 28.

Gopalaswami, N. (2008). 'Election, a democratic festival?', *The Hindu* dated May 31 p. 8.

Brass, Paul R. 1994: *The Politics of India since Independence.* (Cambridge, New York).

Jha, Raghbendra. 2000: 'Reducing Poverty and Inequality in India: Has Liberalisation Helped?'

Mayo, H.B. (1955: 256). *Democracy and Marxism*: (New York: Oxford University Press).

Narayan, Jayaprakash. (2006):'A Plea for the Reconstruction of the Indian polity' in deSouza, Peter Ronald and E. Sridharan (Eds) (2006): *India's Political Parties.* (New Delhi. Sage. p. 39).

Wagle, Udaya R. 2007. 'Economic Conditions of the Poor in South Asia: Is the Picture Rosier Today?' *Eastern Economics Association Conference*, (New York, 2007).

www.prb.org, May 2009.

eci.nic.in, as on May, 2009.

Part III
Political Parties and Elections

16 Political Parties and Elections

M. Vijaya Kumar

Political parties are the life line of democracy and any debate on election reform must look at the role and contribution of political parties. Parties connect the people with the government. The parties link the society with the political system. Representative democracy, which is the order of the world today, is unthinkable without political parties. They represent the national interests and societal interests and are responsible for societal transformation. To be sure, it is important to bring socio-political developments and then follow it up by administrative measures.

The real spirit of democracy lies in the participation of the people, both in elections and routine political developments. Keen interest in politics should come up as an instinct and the public must regularly follow political developments. They must be aware of public policies, how the policies are going to affect their lives and future generations. A consistent debate is needed and in a civil society there are many platforms for achieving this goal. Undoubtedly, the strength of democracy lies in the effective participation of the people in the affairs of polity and society. Here comes the term participatory democracy.

The term participatory democracy, it may seem, is self– contradictory. Because one cannot think of democracy without popular participation. It may be recalled that democracy is all about 'governance through popular authorisation'. This was what Abraham Lincoln had meant when he defined a democratic system as 'government of the people by the people and for the people. However if one looks at the democratic countries the world over one could see that this is not the way in which they are run. People's participation in the governance processes leaves much to be desired. De-politicisation, and influence of money and mafia power have reached such a level that all crucial decisions are arrived at by a small group of people.

Today, there is an increasing trend to depoliticize the entire governance process. This is seen in our country, particularly with the inauguration of economic liberalisation. All important economic decisions are taken by following the prescription laid down by international economic organizations like IMF and World Bank. Business corporations influencing economic policies is also not rare. The justification put forward by the government and the ruling class is that economic issues have to be placed above politics. This is similar to the argument that economics and politics are two autonomous areas, and further that politics is a dirty stuff and political parties are dangerous to democracy.

We are forgetting that it is this politics with which we fought the British and gained our independence. We are also forgetting that it is this politics and the political parties which have given – and which still give the poor and down trodden people self respect and the blessings of self government. As Dr B.R. Ambedkar has rightly pointed out 'politics is a great leader. It is only in democratic politics the idea of one man-one vote and one value could be practiced'. Since the poor constitute the vast majority of the electorate of this country, this provides them the only means to participate in the running of the country. Interestingly, the "Angels" of de-politicization knows this too well and it is because of this they try to depoliticize the process of governance. In this context, the ban on campus politics also needs serious discussion. The ban is an attempt to depoliticize 'Politics' itself.

Many factors have paved the way for money and muscle power in the electoral arena. It is not simply that candidates contesting in elections are spending too much during elections. But more important than this is the direct entry of business in to politics. A casual glance at the social composition of our parliament is sufficient to understand that more and more businessmen are becoming MPs. Also the number of business representatives in both the Lok Sabha and Rajya Sabha have increased since the inauguration of economic liberalization. Stated differently, if in the pre-liberalization era moneyed interest tried to control, politics from outside, today it tries to control from inside the Parliament.

Today economic issues are decided by outside agencies and such issues are not even debated in the Parliament. The best example in this regard is the Indo – US Nuclear Deal. Final stamp of approval was given to this agreement without any discussion in our Parliament. The way in which our ruling establishments has allowed the Union Carbide Company to escape from the liability of Bhopal Gas Tragedy and further provided its chairman – Warren Anderson – a safe passage from India are standing testimony to the way governance is conducted in our country without taking people into confidence.

The writing on the wall is clear. Today people hardly matter in the governance process though we speak more and more about decentralization and participatory democracy. Space for popular participation is declining. To achieve this goal, the electoral system of our country is twisted and turned by people with money and muscle power.

Therefore, the greater need is to bring people back to politics. I mean to politicize the people. They should be made to participate in the political process which is the only way we can strengthen the democratic system. It is here that the role of political party assumes significance. On the one side they should take up the responsibility to educate the people and on the other side fight against people with money and muscle power. To achieve this we should also think about reforming the electoral system.

The system needs to be reformed not to depoliticize the people but to politicize them more intensively. This is also the most important means by which we can make democracy participatory and fight against money and mafia power in election.

17 Electoral Reforms in India : Media and Political Parties

S. Sudhakar Reddy

It is always necessary that our democracy should be strengthened and in strengthening our democracy and democratic institutions, electoral reforms naturally play a very important role. Electoral Reforms are not the only method of strengthening democracy; but that plays a very important role. In our democracy, in our electoral system today, there is a big deficiency. In the last sixty years in our experience, there was never a Government with a ruling Party getting 50+1% of the vote in the Parliament. Always, it is with less than 35% of the vote that ruling Parties are coming to power. Of course some times they do not even get the majority of seats. With the minority vote earlier they used to get the majority of the seats in the Parliament. Now a days, only a Front of various political parties including various regional Parties is coming to power. For the last 10 to15 years this has been our experience. There is a possibility that we can reform electoral system and see to it that in the better system, the will of the majority can be reflected in the parliament and state legislatures. Proportional representation is one such. It is not going to be totally foolproof. Krishna Kanth, the former Governor of Andhra Pradesh, made a remark that there is a danger of polarization of the caste vote in proportional representation than the polarization of votes to different political parties. It is true there is such a danger. But the Indian electorate is getting matured. Even today there are several Political Parties based on caste angle. They are trying to polarize their votes in the name of caste. In a system of proportional representation, there will be better representation for the will of the people. Some people say, in our democracy, the policy is 51% is 100% and 49% is '0'. It is not 51%. Some times, it is with 11% or 10% votes that some are trying to represent the entire electorate! Less than 50% of the people participate in the elections. In the multi-party election, sometimes, and with several independents in the fray, a candidate who gets little more votes than the other candidates will get elected and this type of people from very large number of constituencies form the government at the centre and ultimately, that is becoming a permanent practice in our country denying the will of the large number of the people in the country. To reduce the problem of caste-based and other problems, we can think of a different type of proportional representation, which can be only 50% through proportional representation and 50% through direct election of candidates as it is today. It is working excellently in several countries including the newly born democracy of Nepal, where a large number of women also got elected through direct and indirect election.

The second most important reform is about the State funding of elections. It is a very important thing. Not that the cash should be given to the political Parties and candidates. Basing on the performance in the votes which the political parties could secure in the previous elections, the Parties get the financial help in countries like Italy. Indrajit Gupta Committee on electoral reforms has made a recommendation that state funding should be for supply of vehicles, fuel, for organizing meetings, for printing of posters, leaflets etc. All these can be done not only to help the political Parties, but also to prevent the illegitimate spending by multi millionaires to some extent. Still there is a possibility of distribution of liquor, distribution of cash etc. by which they can influence the elections. But the State funding of the election will limit the spending of the candidates and political Parties and it can be controlled more effectively by the Election Commission. This is another important aspect, which should be considered. Then there are several other important aspects for a free and fair election. Election Commission should be above Board. Today, unfortunately the retired Election Commissioners become Governors, Members of Parliament of the ruling party, Ministers, and they take other lucrative jobs. This will raise many legitimate doubts about their accountability towards the people. There should be some sort of a law that the retired Election Commissioners should not take up any political or administrative responsibility for ten years after the retirement or any other such sort of understanding should come.

Regarding the curbing of criminalization of politics, there is a law now. But unfortunately, it has got many deficiencies. In our country, like many other countries also, the ruling Parties try to put false cases on the opposition Party leaders and they will also be treated as criminals. There is a difference between the crime and the agitational activities done by the Opposition Parties. There should be a clarity. There should be a differentiation made. Besides, real criminals are also entering politics.

Today in the Lok Sabha, more that 379 Members of Parliament are hailing from multi-millionaires families or are themselves multi-millionaires. It is becoming commercialisation of politics. We have to find out the methods as to how to stop this. There is a possibility. Earlier, contractors used to help the political Parties. Now the contractors, business people and Corporate house magnates, themselves are becoming members of the parliament and ministers. Recently, we have seen, only two months back, Vijay Mallia got elected from Karnataka Assembly as Member of Rajyasabha. Everybody knows that he shamelessly purchased the votes of hon'ble members of the Legislative Assembly of Karnataka and got elected. There was a candidate in Bihar, from Karnataka, Mr. Uday. He has nothing to do with Bihar. He went all the way to Patna, probably he might have seen Patna for the first time, purchased ten MLAs and filed the nomination for Rajyasabha. 25 lakh he paid to each voter. If this type of thing is allowed, ultimately, the Indian Parliament and Legislatures will be full of such people, Corporate and company magnates and that will be the end of Indian democracy. This is a very dangerous phenomenon that is coming up and we have to think very seriously as to how to curb these types of sections from entering into the Parliament. Criminals, definitely should not be allowed to contest the elections. They should be thrown out of the parliament.

Media plays an important role. But unfortunately media is not that free today. Mostly, print media and electronic media are becoming part of the big business activity. Earlier, they used to have one TV. channel or one newspaper. Now a days, the same company will have six or seven channels and News papers are also being published from almost every district. Of course, in spite of it, there are some limitations. But in the last elections, unfortunately there was a new dangerous development that is called 'Paid News'. I was a victim of it. I was a Member of Parliament twice. I was contesting in the last 2009 Parliament Election. Suddenly I found, for almost a week, there was not a single piece of news about my electioneering anywhere. I was a sitting candidate. I do understand that I will not get big publicity like the major political Parties which were there. But as a sitting Member of Parliament, I thought I will get some news coverage. When enquired, the Advt Managers contacted me and asked whether I had not joined the package. I asked – What is the package? He said "probably our correspondents might have felt embarassed to meet you. But unfortunately, the situation is that now a days, there is a package system in which you are supposed to pay some money for news". How much is it, I asked. According to the circulation of the News Paper, it increases. Of course before the elections I did not tell him. After the elections, my opponent told some people that he paid two crore to print media for purchasing the news! If this type of system is allowed, then it will be very dangerous. I was called by the Press Commission and they made an enquiry at Hyderabad and I found the former Union Minister of State for Home Mr. Vidya Sagar Rao of BJP, also came to represent saying that he was also a victim of the print media package system. This is not going to help.

This is a phenomenon, which should be curbed. In the first part, where the media is controlled by rich people, there is an effort for "manufacturing the consent" in favour of certain political Parties and candidates. In the second part, you will be denying the democratic responsibility of even giving the news of different candidates who are contesting the elections and about the views expressed by them on various issues. Media, of course, is not the final thing which is going to decide the election, but it has got a very big role because it can mould the public opinion in a very big way.

On many issues positively, the media is playing very important role. The English media in the recent period is playing excellent role against the so called honour killings in Haryana. They exposed many misdeeds. They exposed many stories of corruption. Media can rouse the conscience of the people. It will also mould the public opinion during the election. Hence it is necessary that media should be reasonably free. I do understand that media barons, the people who run the media, they will have their own political opinions. But in any democracy they have the responsibility of giving proper importance to all political opinions in the country.

There are several other such instances. Many ideas have came out of several seminars. There is a feeling that because of the multiplicity of political Parties, Indian democracy is in danger. It is not true and there is no country where the number of political Parties is limited by law. By virtue of their popularity, may be that two or three political Parties emerge as the main political Parties. I was surprised at the ignorance of a very senior IAS officer. He was telling that a law should be brought like in England so that only two parties will exist. There is no such law in Great Britian.

There are political Parties even in USA, but to contest for the Presidentship in the election, there is a law by which several thousands of voters have to sign the nomination of the candidate, for the office of President. It is a difficult thing, for fifteen Republics, they have to get the signatures from several lakhs of people. This way it helps to reduce too many political Parties coming without the support of the people. India is a multi-racial, multi-religious and a multi-caste country. The aspirations of the people in different areas, will be reflected through their political Parties. So many regional Parties are coming up. Do not try to curb the number of political parties. That will create more problems. People will take to streets, if they do not have an opportunity even to form a political Party and contest the elections. That will be very harmful to democracy.

18 Need for Change in Electoral System

D. Raja

"WE, THE PEOPLE OF INDIA, having solemnly resolved to constitute India into a (SOVEREIGN SOCIALIST SECULAR DEMOCRATIC REPUBLIC) and to secure to all its citizens:

JUSTICE, social, economic and political;

LIBERTY of thought, expression, belief, faith and worship;

EQUALITY of status and of opportunity; and to promote among all

FRATERNITY assuring the dignity of the individual and the [unity and integrity of the Nation];"

The above is from the Preamble of the Constitution of India. The Democratic Republic of India is six decades old. The journey is one of great triumph of democracy. Thanks to Dr B.R. Ambedkar and the galaxy of leaders, India has not chosen the Presidential form of government or the two party system. But it has chosen the path of Parliamentary democracy and multi party democratic system.

Nevertheless it has to surge forward to realize the objective of emerging as a Sovereign Socialist Secular Democratic Republic.

The Constitution was adopted by the Constituent Assembly on 26th November 1949. Dr Ambedkar, the Chairman of the Drafting Committee of the Constitution, while making his concluding speech in the Constituent Assembly on 25th November 1949 has made the following observation and caution in a very prophetic manner.

"On the 26th January, 1950, we are going to enter upon into a life of contradictions. In politics we will have equality and in social and economic life we will have inequality. In politics we will be recognizing the principle of one man one vote and one vote one value. In our social and economic life, we shall by reason of our social and economic structure, continue to deny equality in our social and economic life? If we continue to deny it for long, we will do so only by putting our political democracy in peril.

We must remove this contradiction at the earliest possible moment else those who suffer from inequality will blow up the structure of democracy which this Constituent Assembly has so laboriously built up."

The objective of one man one vote and one vote one value is yet to be realized. Unless it is realized the democracy however, vibrant it may be, will be always under threats and challenges.

Diamond Jubilee of Election Commission

The Election Commission which draws powers from the very Constitution was constituted on the 25th January 1950. While appreciating the election commission for its role, in attempting to conduct free and fair elections, it needs to be pointed out that the challenges are many.

It is appropriate to quote the Vice-President of India who spoke on the occasion of the diamond jubilee celebration of EC who pointed out the evils of money power, muscle power and even the role of media in the electoral process. "Despite stringent effort, un accounted election expenses constitutes the major expenditure of political parties and their candidates. These related to the distribution of freebies, liquor and cash during elections and the phenomenon of surrogate advertisements, and the extensive media – related mal-practice of paid news and coverage packages". "Each of these is a blot on the democratic process and the objective of free and fair elections. Corrective action by the election commission and political parties is imperative".

India is hailed as one of the largest democracies in the world. A vital component of any representative democracy is the electoral system. The system which India follows today is a Majoritarian Electoral System (MES) as it is being practised in the US and UK.

As against this several countries in the world have already shifted to the Proportionate Electoral System (PES) in order to give full representation to all citizens who vote and to provide level playing field to all political parties.

In India more than 90% of the members get into Assemblies by getting less than half the electors to vote for them. More than 60% get elected with the support of less than 30% voters in their constituencies. It is a fact that the governments in the states and centre and the legislators in parliament and state assemblies do not have the support of the majority, but they become the representative governments and legislators.

Electoral Systems – Experience of India

The first elections to the provincial governments (state governments) took place in India under the British regime in 1937 and 1946 and the electoral method employed was the First-Past-The-Post method. (FPTP)

The electoral method employed influences the Law and the electoral laws are designed to fit into the model. The absence of universal adult franchise and availability of a limited franchise in 1937 and 1946 elections required a plethora of electoral franchise law mentioning in detail the eligibility conditions for every region and for every category of people. The same laws became redundant once the Constitution of India adopted universal adult franchise. The maintenance of separate electoral rolls for certain categories became essential due to the prevailing electoral methods.

The political systems and societal makeup in a democracy determines the electoral method. The British rule in India used electoral methods like separate electorates for religious minorities and special interests and for untouchables it was joint electorates and even reserved seats for women in the FPTP system. Till 1950 the reserved seats for scheduled castes had two rounds of elections. The first was a Primary election – with a separate electorate if in case the contestants were more than 4 and it would return a panel of 4 candidates. The regular secondary or final election was under the joint electorates in which both Scheduled castes and others on electoral roll voted. The reserved seats to Scheduled castes had double member constituencies (or even 3-4) till 1961. 1950 Constitution dispensed off with special electoral rolls that were required for separate electorates under Article 325.

Article 325 of the Constitution

No person to be ineligible for inclusion in, or to claim to be included in a special, electoral roll on grounds of religion, race, caste or sex . There shall be one general electoral roll for every territorial constituency for election to either House of Parliament or to the House or either House of the Legislature of a State and no person shall be ineligible for inclusion in any such roll or claim to be included in any special electoral roll for any such constituency on grounds only of religion, race, caste, sex or any of them.

The Indian law makers used different electoral methods in the electoral system. While in the case of elections to Lok Sabha seats and seats in State assemblies it is FPTP, in the case of elections to the offices of the President and Vice-President and to Rajya Sabha and State

Legislative Councils it is though Proportional Representation through single transferable vote.

In the case of Presidential election under the Indian constitution it is through a special method of PR system. Article 55(3) of the Indian Constitution requires that the President should be elected in accordance with the system of proportional representation by means of single transferable vote. The Electoral college comprises of the members of both houses of parliament and State Assemblies and the value of the vote is according to the strength of population of that state.

In the case of election of the Vice-President it is by an electoral college consisting of the members of both Houses of Parliament through the electoral method of proportional representation by means of the single transferable vote.

Election to the Rajya Sabha is through the best known form of Proportional Representation - that of the "Single Transferable Vote", which means that each elector has only one vote, irrespective of the number of seats to be filled up. For instance, if there are six seats to be filled up, the elector does not cast six votes but indicates six successive preferences, by marking his first preference and the succeeding preferences with the appropriate numerals against the name of candidates printed on his ballot paper.

Changes in the electoral system or amendment is slow and a difficult processes since the parties in power generally do not want to tamper with or change a system that has been returning them.

Proportional Representation System's (PR) basic focus is that the proportion of the votes received by a party will be translated into seats unlike in FPTP where a party might get 10-15% votes and may end up with no seats. The PR system requires more than one member constituencies. PR system is practised in two variations: List PR and Single Transferable Vote (STV). Out of the 72 countries which use PR only two countries use STV and others use List PR with slight variations.

In Israel and Netherlands multi-member constituencies are in vogue. In a large country like Argentina and Portugal in Europe there are several contituencies. PR system dominates in Latin America (Brazil; 18 others). Africa (South Africa; 15 others) and Europe (Spain, Austria, Denmark; 25 others).

Reserved Seats

Many countries give due consideration to women representation. Electoral laws require political parties to place women candidates in their lists. In Namibia, Peru and Bolivia it is one-third. In Argentina 30% of women are to be in winnable position on the list and in Belgium, the top two candidates in the list must be from each sex. Afghanistan which follows the FPTP system has 25%, Uganda 18%, Rwanda 30% and there is 50% in India's local body and PRI elections.

In Columbia (black communities), Croatia (European minorities); Jordan (Christians and Circassians), Niger (Tuareg); New Zealand (Maori); India (SC and ST), Pakistan (non-Muslim minority); Palestine (Christians) and Slovenia (Hungarians) there are reserved seats.

What is the Remedy?

1. The position taken by Communist Party of India is to support the Proportional Representation system and the party desires that the best model should be adopted. This can strengthen the multi party democratic system in our country. Since India is a country of tremendous diversities, it cannot afford to have a bipolar system. It is all the more necessary that all parties have due representation in the legislative bodies according to their influence and support.
2. It is high time that the state funding of political parties as recommended by the Indrajit Gupta Committee be discussed in parliament and adopted as government policy. This can provide a level playing field for all the political parties.
3. Efforts must be made for comprehensive electoral reforms to fight criminalization of politics and politicization of criminals and to clean up the electoral system.
4. Review of People's Representation Act and suitable amendments in this regard need to be considered in the light of our experiences so far. This is imperative for a comprehensive electoral reform.

19 Electoral Reforms and Constitutional Changes

R.L.M. Patil

Reforms in the electoral system of the country are not going to be exercises in isolation. The Election Commission, political parties and the Parliament have to accept changes in their functioning if reforms are to be of any meaning. Of course, there are numerous and oft-repeated proposals of reform. Not all of them merit attention. Some of them are held out mostly because they have become fashionable, like the recall of the elected representative. A proposal of this kind is simply not implementable in our country where – unlike in Switzerland where it is practised albeit rarely – the signatures of those who are a party to a petition of recall cannot be verified or authenticated at all. Likewise the idea of introducing the proportional representation in lieu of the present first-past-the-post method is fraught with possibility of a cure being worse than the disease. Pt. Jawaharlal Nehru in an interview to Michel Brecher (Nehru, 1959, OUP, p. 424) shot down the proposal saying "I can think of nothing more conducive to creating a feeble ministry and a feeble government than this (proposal)". He was right absolutely. If proportional representation was to be adopted here, the story of Pakistan's instability would have repeated here as well. The Congress Party which has been the main ruling party would not have managed single-party government at all even in the Nehruvian days. In fact this party has never received 50% or more number of popular votes in any general elections to the Lok Sabha.

The remedy to the electoral system's defects does not lie in applying off-the-shelf medicines. Some people have suggested that we should switch over to the Presidential (US) system in place of the present Parliamentary System (UK). This too begs the same question. Perhaps it would fare worse than the existing system.

What, then we require to do is to impose certain conditions through law and the Constitution to check the misuse and abuse of the loosely structured provisions and institutions related to the elections.

First of all, the Election Commission should be given the power to register and deregister political parties which wish to contest elections. No independent candidate should be permitted to contest the elections: if anybody wishes to do so he must be required to open a party to suit his convenience and get it registered properly. The parties which do seek registration with the Election Commission have to necessarily fulfill a number of simple conditions. They must have a well-publicised document governing their structure and functioning through democratic and open method. Their finances must be annually audited and thrown open for public scrutiny. Their nominees for electoral positions anywhere should be such that their credibility to represent the public is acceptable (No criminal charges, no outstanding public loan, no pendency or evasion of taxes, sufficiently educated and having a minimum of social/public service).

This above condition is not difficult to be enforced by the Election Commission if small changes are made in the Representation of People's Act. However to allow time to scrutinize the credentials of candidates the parties should nominate their candidates five years in advance! Once of the advantages of this novel suggestion was that one would work hard at least five years prior to the elections! Secondly, there would be avoided a mad rush for and unpredictability of getting party tickets by aspirants.

If general elections are to be held at regular and specific time, the above suggestion may work out. However, if in an unseen circumstance a sudden election is ordered, suitable modifications could be made in the requirements. The Election Commission should be empowered to call for nominations in general anytime.

The Constitution of India does not specify anywhere that we have to follow the British model of parliamentary democracy. Yet, we are doing it, without following the spirit of it. Party-loyalty is something conspicuous by its absence. Splits and marriages of convenience are often observed in the making of and functioning of ministries. The number of ministries is unlimited. Often political horse-trading as witnessed in Jharkhand, Meghalaya, Goa, Bihar, UP or Haryana has brought a bad name to democracy in our country. One or two dissident members of a ministry are enough to bring down the government of the day.

To check this prospect a suggestion may be made that as in Switzerland or in the US federal system, in our country, too, we can fix the number of ministries. In Switzerland this restriction is made through Constitutional provision while in the US this objective is achieved through

Congressional Law. We have proliferated our Ministries to 75 in a state like Uttar Pradesh, 70 in the central government, and in Meghalaya almost all the MLAs of the ruling (or even the opposition) party had a chance of becoming a Minister as if by a method of rotation through changes in the composition of the ruling (?) alliance.

To overcome this problem, first of all the number and nature of ministries need to be mentioned in the Constitution or by law. There is no justification to have 75 Ministries in one state and ten in another. Depending upon the size and specific requirements of a state, the ministries may be instituted without scope for manipulation. Secondly, the Central Government should necessarily have only those ministries which deal with subjects allocated to the Centre by the Constitution. There should be no place for Cabinet Ministers at the Centre for Panchayat Raj and Rural Development. Thirdly, there should be developed consciously among the leading political parties the practice of setting up a shadow – Cabinet or an alternative government in the waiting. If an MP or MLA is put in charge of a subject of a Ministry he may train himself in all respects to tackle the subject efficiently either as an opposition member or a ruling/treasury bench member. What we witness now-a-days, however is anybody can become a Minister and fail to make any impression).

Politically or even Constitutionally the government of the day is answerable to the Lok Sabha or Vidhan Sabha. It is not mentioned anywhere in the Constitution that the government should be made up of only one party. So, sometimes, a coalition or alliance of parties have formed the government. And some other times, even a 'minority' party (meaning not having a majority number of MPs on the floor of the House) has run the government. Smt.Indira Gandhi and Shri P.V. Narasimha Rao were adept at this practice. However, for want of an assured majority, many a Governor has dismissed ministries at the state level. Defections, re-arrangements of parties in alliance etc., have been witnessed at various levels. Though immoral, these have been justified as being politically correct and Constitutionally tenable. To avoid this unseemly spectacle a suggestion can be made which looks unconventional but answers to political and constitutional needs. This is to allocate years/months of rule to the major parties which are represented in the Lok Sabha or Vidhan Sabha. If a has won 55%, 60%, 75% of the seats in the House, it can function as a ruling party for 55%, 60%, 75% of the tenure of the House. This is even more relevant and meaningful when no party has secured 50% of the seats. The parties aspiring or dying to form government would make unethical compromises just to stay put in power because of uncertainty of number. Instead of this risky exercise, they can all form governments, one another, for a reasonably fixed period without let or hindrance. After all one has witnessed in the case of Karnataka a combination of Congree and JD (S) ruling for some twenty months followed by a combined government of JD (S) and BJP for the next twenty months. If so, why not allow JD (S), Congress and BJP twenty months each to rule the state without being thrown out by the 'opposition'?

If one examines the electoral manifestos of all political parties, one finds that most of them say the same thing: clean (i.e. corruption-free) administration, roads, hospitals, education, water and electricity! If the Congress and BJP's words and their practices were to be examined with respect to economic policy, telecom policy, foreign policy, defence, Kashmir, Telangana, administrative and judicial reforms, one would find a "virtual identity' of views of standpoints! Then, why not allow them to rule one after another? The present practice of one party almost monopolizing the 'ruling' and another party or parties almost monopolizing 'opposing' reminds one of Aristotle's observation that some are born to rule while other to be ruled (or to oppose).

If 'coming to power' is all that there is to election, democracy cannot survive for long in its true spirit. Corruption in the form of desire to occupy seats of power, would spoil the entire body politik. It has been truly well said that while power corrupts, lack of power corrupts absolutely.

The aim of the elections should be a sportive competition to serve the public. And elections should not be the be-all and end-all of democracy. True democracy lies in the spirit of accommodation, discussion and healthy cooperation between the opposing parties. An alert public opinion, strong judiciary and independent media are indeed the touch-stone of democracy, not electoral outcomes.

20 Electoral Systems and Modern Governments

Aruna Sivakami

The debates on electoral reforms revolve around the practical consequences of changes in the statusquo of political parties. Underlying the arguments is the concern for realization of fundamental principles of representative democracy. The heart of the argument is in finding whether it is the absolute power which is important in running the government or the inclusion of minority voice that is essential as a characteristic of democracy.

As argued by western scholars there is a direct relationship between a country's party system and its electoral system leave alone the voting behaviour and stability of governments. 'The simple-majority, single ballot system' wrote Maurice Duverger 'favours the two party systems.' Of all the hypotheses that have been defined, this, most nearly is the proper approach to a true sociological law. "The simple majority system with the second ballot and proportional representation favour multi-party system". So the greater multiplicity of political parties in India should have a system of proportional representation or a run off system in which there is a second ballot. But this has not been adopted. Can India be an exception to Duverger's Law and be explained by the existence of deep social cleavages and social divisions generating multipartism, reinforced by federal constitution.

India's Electoral system is outlined in its Constitution and in the two major Acts of Parliament, the Representation of the people's Act 1950 and the Representation of People Act 1951. The electoral system created by the Constitution and enlarged by the acts of Parliament, provides for a system of universal adult suffrage. Direct elections are provided for the house of the people in New Delhi and for state assemblies. Of the total seats, some percentage is reserved for scheduled castes and scheduled tribes, both in the Parliament and Legislatures.

The Indian Electoral System, with its simple majority and single ballot, has the usual consequence of giving any party a disproportionate number of seats both in the state legislatures and Parliament. It reduces the number of seats to the smaller parties. Mostly the smaller parties win no seats. With only 45% or even less the bigger parties like Indian National Congress secure a comfortable majority and forms a government. A smaller party like the Socialists used to get 10.6% of the votes but got only a negligible number of seats. There is no seat for very small parties as seats are not apportioned on the basis of proportion of the votes secured. The net result is that there is no representation of minority social groups. Such political systems under represent social groups in terms of class, race and gender. Political parties concerned about this issue have adopted several strategies including gender quotas and other affirmative actions considered fit by parties. Affirmative actions are possible when applied to balancing the social composition of party lists. That is designating every other position on the list for male and female candidates or balancing the list by region, occupation or religion. The other mechanisms can also serve minorities based on regional, ethnic or religious cleavages although the effects depend upon the spatial concentration of such groups. Otherwise there is a coalition government at the centre and state, which has become the order of the day. Indian coalitions produce weaker governments with not much of muscle power in the parliament.

Another feature of Indian Electoral system is that it encourages fragmentation and wastage of votes. When it is seen in the context of multiplicity of political parties, candidates with only 30% of valid votes are declared elected as 70% of the votes are distributed between the umpteen smaller parties, and they are left without representation. How representative the candidates with 30% are of the entire electorate does not require much imagination.

For proponents of majoritarian system the most important criteria is the effectiveness of governments. A perfect example of "First past the post" system is the Westminster Model, with the twin virtues of strong and responsive party government. Strong means a single party government, not coalition government. Cohesive parties with a majority of parliamentary seats are in a position to implement their policies without engaging in post-election negotiations with alliance partners. Single party majority government can legislate comfortably on any subject necessary during their term of office, so long as they can carry the backbenchers along with them. A manufactured majority is created by translating a relatively small lead in votes into a larger lead of seats in parliament. Again responsive governments are able to give responsive and accountable government. In an easily inflammable situation even a small swing in the popular vote would be sufficient to defeat the government or make its chances in next elections questionable. The situation is highly tricky as it is a pulley and weights mechanism: a modest pull on the electoral rope produces a disproportionate displacement of weight. So a responsive and accountable government tries to maintain an equilibrium always considering the strength of the opposition parties put-together in the parliament. In contrast if there is a coalition even if public becomes dissatisfied with particular parties they have less power to determine their fate. The process of coalition building after the result not the election perse determines the strength of the government. Indian democracy from 1970 is characterised by coalitions or support from outside. Again, in simple-majority systems disproportional outcomes results in polarization and the extinction of smaller parties and the emergence of two or three party system. Thus the number of political parties should have got reduced due to mechanical and psychological reasons also.

If this is true Indian political situation should have reduced the number of minor and smaller parties. But it has not. Why? Indians do not agree with one another for too long a time. There are and there will be only groups and factions within a bigger party or small parties whose existence do not count in parliament or normal social life. One has to agree with Sartori that strong electoral systems reduce the number of parties through strategic voting. But the formation of coalitions by the elites in countries with weak electoral systems give rise to numerous parties.

Our system was considered conducive to maintain bigger parties in spite of the dissidents and factions which were the characteristic feature of Indian political system. Smaller parties would have withered away from the political scene. This is also the reason for the mergers of smaller parties with a bigger party. But, now it is electoral alliance that is much preferred. It is unlikely that all the opposing parties would unite as a single front as Indians can never remain united for too long a time. Further the political parties show greater concern for ideology. Existing evidence suggests that it is not because of the electoral system that India is destined with a multiplicity of political parties but because it is advantageous for the major national and state or regional parties to have and work this system of elections. No serious attempt to reform the electoral laws or processes has taken place in spite of some serious efforts like that of Indrajit Gupta, Dinesh Goswami, T.N. Seshan and others from time to time.

Recruitment of party members appears to occur largely in the cities and is conducted for the most part, among office employees, shopkeepers, members of profession and others in the middle classes. Mostly parties seem to recruit from similar groups. The Baratiya Janata Party for example, attracts students and young people from towns and cities. The Left parties and the communists are also seen to be more active in urban areas but in different localities. It is true that some of these groups, especially the communists have expanded to rural areas, but the recruitment of rank and file members is still largely from urban centers.

The process of recruitment has been from urban centers because it is only there that the breakdown of the traditional order has taken place. It is understandable that where there has been a break from the traditional pattern there you see a concomitant desire for more status than given by the traditional order. One can surmise from this that youngsters are often caught in the craze for westernisation. The process may seem abstract, but it operates on the most personal and human level. Having moved from the village to city, broken physically or spiritually with his family and caste, the young person feels that loss of his role of family and its importance, his status from his home community, and values with which he judged the world, resulting in the loss of individual self identity. The person who has wholly or partly left this traditional system is in search of new values and a sense of belonging. In India the frustrations of a rapidly changing social system are compounded by the lack of economic opportunities for young people and by widespread educated unemployment.

Those who join a political party in India invariably become members of a faction. A faction can be defined as a group with an articulated set of goals, operating within larger organisations but not created by or with the approval of the parent body. The faction may range in size from several dozen members to several hundred. It is generally characterized by a uniformity of goals and basic values and usually sufficient permanence to allow members to develop sense of identification with the faction. There is little movement into and out of faction. Except in its formative stages, it does not generally recruit members openly. A person who joins a political party in India apparently feels the need to be a member of a tightly knit face to face group. This need is not confined to political joiners. Every school and college in India contains a large number of student cliques. These groups are usually closed to outsiders; the members provide their own social life and have their own leaders. Groups of students who are members of the politically dominated student organization might later become a faction within a political party.

The faction assumes many of the functions of the traditional joint family, caste system, and village organisation. Indian parties are like castes, since they often regard each other as untouchables. In most of the ways the factions are like traditional organisations. The party members even talk to the faction head their personal problems in the same manner that in older days one would confide to a caste head. So the affections between the party member and faction head become deeper and real. What keeps the factions working together within the same party. Firstly it can be attributed to the figure of the party leader as a unifier. His detachment but control over the factions is his ability to hold the party in tact. A second unifying factor is the level of tolerance which one faction has on another. Next is that an Indian opposition party is generally united by a consensus on the basic party thesis which cuts across factions. As long as this unity continues, the factions are likely to remain within the party. Lastly there is an agreement on the common party ideology.

This electoral system is conducive as revealed only to popularize personality cult and make bigger political parties stand in the political arena ably but it is not conducive to the stability of the parliamentary government as there are only coalition governments in the centre for the past few decades as well as in the states. The responsibility of the government is also sacrificed at the altar of convenience. The opposition is neither strong to form or run the government as in other two party democracies. In such a situation no government can be held accountable also. Above all the public is unruly, indiscipline, non-cooperative and mostly behaves as mobs and in the absence of a community, the society has become a mass society and so politics is that of the mass and not that of educated, or that of elite or of the intelligentsia in the society.

The Hare System and the List System: Even the very idea of representation is in jeopardy. Problems may be somewhat different under the two major modern types of proportional representation, namely, the hare system and the list system. Let us now briefly discuss the differences between the two.

Under the hare system the voter casts his ballot for individual candidates. He gives his first choice to the man whom he likes best, his second choice to the candidate whom he likes second best, and so on. To be elected a candidate is supposed to obtain a certain number of votes, the "quota", which may be a number fixed by the law or may differ according to the number of votes cast and the number of candidates to be elected. If a candidate obtains first preference votes in excess of the quota, the surplus is attributed to another candidate to whom his supporters gave their second preferences. If, by following through with this process, not enough candidates have obtained their quota yet, the weakest candidates are eliminated, and their votes are transferred to the stronger ones, until ultimately the successful candidates have been determined.

So far as the list system is concerned there are two rather important variations: the "rigid list" and the "free list". In the first case the competing lists are drawn up by party committees, who arrange the candidates in a certain order. After the counting is over, it is first determined how many seats each party obtains; when this has been done, those candidates are declared elected who are at the top of the list. If, for example, a party obtained five seats, the first five candidates of the party list are selected. The voter can also be given the opportunity to express individual preferences for one or more candidates; sometimes he is allowed to give his preferences to candidates of more than one party list. The electoral law determines how much weight is to be given to these preferences. It might be provided, for example, that after the number of seats to be given to a party list has been determined; those candidates are elected who have obtained the highest number of personal preferences, irrespective of the places given to them in the list of their party.

If we try to compare these two systems of proportional represenation it is necessary to establish a proper basis of comparison. In England and in the United States the supporters of proportional representation usually advocate the hare system, and call it the "best system of proportional representation" and the list system "an inferior system" are subjective value-judgments, without scientific meaning. The only standard with the help of which we can decide about the claim for perfection made on behalf of the two systems is in relation to the logical premises of proportional representation The question must be asked: representation of what and in proportion to what? There is no doubt that the objects for which "representation" is sought are, as mentioned above, parties or "opinions" or something similarly impersonal, and proportionality simply means that these bodies of "opinion" share the seats in an elective body in proportion to the votes cast for them among the population of that country. The person of the "representative" is, in this process, fully subordinated to that more objective entity. Whoever glances through the literature written in defense of proportional representation will not fail to realize how strongly the majority system is attacked for the very reason that it emphasizes the "subjective" element of parties. The hare system, however, if it operates as intended, focuses the attention of the voter on persons rather than on parties. For this reason it is an illogical form of proportional representation whereas the list system, which makes elections primarily an option among parties, is its most logical form. However the public and the election machinery of U.K. is now puzzled by the three party system that has emerged there. It raises questions about the efficacy of list system.

India can also adopt any one of the other systems based on electoral formula that determines how votes are counted to allocate seats from among the three types:

1. Majoritarian formulas (including plurality, second ballot, and alternative voting system);
2. Semi-proportional systems (such as the single transferable vote, the cumulative vote, and the limited vote);
3. Mixed systems (like the additional member system combining majoritarian and proportional elements).

To reduce money power in our elections to some extent India can insist on the money managers as in west where the source and amount received and the manner and disbursement of the money is to be accounted for by each candidate. This can only mitigate the problem to degrees and not substantially. Restoring section 77 of the Representation of Peoples Act, 1971 so as to control the expenditure must be made compulsory.

We need reforms that would secure socially responsible and ethical parties. For the prevention of entry of criminals in the legislature, the Election Commission can insist on clean record of the nominations filed by the political parties. There should be no court cases or convictions not only for the candidates but any member in the family that should suffice to disqualify the candidate. The political parties should come to evolve a code of conduct. The internal working of political parties must be democratised. Of late, the middle class that won India's independence seems to have abdicated electoral politics considering it rough and dirty. It is not the politics of the upper class any more but the middle class, so they have to participate in large numbers. Too much education weakens a stomach for politics and legislative business.

The recommendations and reforms of the Lyngdoh committee include prevention of Surrogate advertisements after elections have been announced, restrictions on the number and publishing of opinion polls so as to prevent an undue influence in public voting, and 50% of votes + 1 to be made a requirement to declare a candidate a winner. The idea of legislation and legislatures are as old as the Greeks and Romans.

Legislative institutions are an integral part of democratic forms of government. From the 16th to 20th century the structure of the legislature along with legislation had undergone changes along with the idea of representativeness of the legislatures. The legislative institutions are powerful in parliamentary and presidential forms of governments, but not in popular democracies, guided democracies and candillo type fascist regimes where their representative character becomes doubtful. The world today has only two types of legislatures-parliamentary and presidential. The types of governments, are presidential or parliamentary and collegiate types.

The crucial element in the parliamentary model is that the executive is selected by the legislature from among its own members. The government thus formed becomes ultimately responsible to the legislature and to the nation. To day the legislatures are deprived of their dynamic role because of their utter subservience to the executive. Interest groups too have a free play and try to get the independent members vote to the advantage of the ruling party or the opposition.

However not only the structure, but also the political forces shape the legislative decisions. The use of scaling and cluster bloc analysis has made possible comparison of the votes of every member of the body on a set of issues with those of every other member. The roll call vote does not reveal vast portions of the legislative process. What finally happens on the floor may be simply the ratification of agreements or policies negotiated elsewhere through bitter disputes.

The complexity in law making, legislative techniques and greater unity of outlook between legislatures and executive resulted in executive guidance of legislation. Special procedures in financial legislation and budgets have reduced the role of parliament in over all legislation. Its place has been taken by two other functions, day to day control of governmental operations and the formalized, highly resonant expressions of the grievances and aspirations of groups. Powers of the legislature have been further fragmented by delegated legislation and secondary legislation. It was K.C. Wheare who observed that legislatures have not declined in power but in efficiency.

21 Electoral Reforms to Immunise Local Bodies Against Party Politics

M.N. Prasad

Introduction

In a democratic republic like ours, the national political parties have an important role to play in shaping the country's future, based on the mandate given to them by the people through elections to the parliament. Each party is supposed to have its own philosophy and ideology and, if voted to power, formulate its policies and plans accordingly, along with such new legislations as may be needed. Ideally, the top leaders of all parties, whether in power or in the opposition, ought to be statesmen with vision who can contribute effectively to the process of collective decision-making.

Similar is the case at the State level as well, where the mandate to rule is based on elections to the State Assemblies. There is, however, one distinctive feature in that, besides national parties, even regional parties may have a relevance at that level.

In sharp contrast to governance at the national and state levels, the institutions of local self-government, ie., the 3-tier Panchayats; the municipalities and the corporations, are mainly concerned with day-to-day administration at the local level, side by side with welfare and planned development, both social and economic. They have neither any law-making to do, nor any policy-formulation, and are only required to follow the central and state laws and policies. Party politics, therefore, has little relevance in the local bodies.

It is a well-known fact that, over the past four decades, political party rivalries and power struggles have become a regular feature, both at the centre and in the states. This has led to several unhealthy trends, like heavy spending on election campaigns (wherein lie the roots of governmental corruption at all levels), the resultant nexus between politicians and business houses, persons with criminal background gaining entry into political parties or enjoying their protection, fragmentation of political parties and unprincipled coalitions of parties with disparate ideologies for the sole purpose of capturing power, ceaseless efforts of opposition parties to destabilise the elected governments through agitations, hartals, etc and frequent disruption of business in the parliament and state assemblies. In this way, what should ideally have been governments "of the people, by the people and for the people" have, over the years, turned into *governments of the political parties, by the political parties and for the political parties.* The people do have the power to vote, but the choice of the voter is limited to whichever candidates are put up by the parties.

Political activities in the LSG institutions gained considerable momentum consequent on decentralisation of governance under the Panchayati Raj Nagarpalika Act, implemented in Kerala about 15 years ago. As a result, many of the adverse effects of party politics, as mentioned above, have been in evidence in the local bodies as well, impairing their performance and public image. *(This, in fact, was something that the author had foreseen much earlier, even while the draft bill was being debated upon. In a public discussion held in Thiruvananthapuram, he had pleaded for addition of a proviso to eschew party politics from elections to local bodies; but this was vehemently opposed by the politicians present. However, soon after the new LSG institutions came into being in Oct. 1995, the author had ample opportunities to observe things at close quarters, while actively engaged in the People's Planning campaign launched in mid-1996, which further strengthened his conviction about the need to free the local bodies from party politics.)*

In retrospect, we now find that notwithstanding the great strides that India has made on various fronts during the past sixty years as a Republic, the gap between the rich and the poor has widened, which in itself ought to be a major cause for our concern. Unfortunately, any change in the present system will need strong political will, as well as a broad consensus among the major parties. It can best be achieved through electoral reforms, starting with the elimination of party politics from elections to the local bodies. This, in fact, ought to be the very first step for cleansing of the whole system, working from the bottom upwards.

Adverse Implications of Party Politics in Local Bodies

The following are the major problems commonly encountered in LSG institutions on account of party politics:

1. The party in majority is considered as the "ruling party" and the rest as the "opposition", in the same way as in the State legislature. This is a mistaken notion, since every local body is an institution

of governance where the power is to be shared by all the members, regardless of their party loyalties. Once elected, they ought to function as a team, with the most competent among them being elected as President, or Chairman, or Mayor, as the case may be. *(This would be quite analogous to the concept of a "national government" formed of all major parties, or the more commonplace example of a State football team where players selected from different clubs gel together as a team under one able captain, casting aside their traditional rivalries at club level.)*

2. The animosities between the so-called "ruling party" and "opposition" sometimes lead to coups and toppling of the elected leaders.
3. There is wasteful spending on election campaigns, in the same manner as for Assembly elections which in turn leads to perpetuation of corruption at all levels, contrary to the professed goal of total transparency in the local bodies. (Since the candidates are all local persons, known to most people of the electorate, there is no real need for any expensive campaigning).
4. Party-based elections deter independent persons like retired professionals, teachers and public servants from offering themselves as candidates.
5. Panchayat members and ward councilors who are active workers of political parties tend to devote their time and energies more for party work than for looking after their wards.
6. Because of political animosities the wards represented by members belonging to the so-called "opposition" tend to receive step-motherly treatment in the matter of inputs for development.

How Freedom from Party Politics Will Help

All the problems listed above can be ameliorated if party rivalries at the level of the local bodies are eliminated through electoral reforms, on the lines indicated below:

(a) For elections to local bodies every candidate shall contest in his/her individual capacity, regardless of whether he/she belongs to a political party. No party symbol shall be used, either for campaigning or in the polling process.

(b) There shall be no gender bias in the choice of candidates, which should be based on individual merit, like character, competence and service spirit. (33% reservation for women, first adopted in the 1995 elections, may be dispensed with at the end of the third five-year term, by which time all the electorates would have got covered, bringing women candidates to the fore).

(c) Campaigning shall be confined to speaking at meetings at one or more venues, depending on the size of the electorate. All the candidates shall be given equal opportunity to address these meetings. Posters shall be avoided but personal canvassing on a door-to-door basis may be allowed.

(d) All those who are elected to a local body shall function as one team in sharing the task of self-governance, as in the State cabinet. Any discrimination on the basis of party loyalties shall be forbidden

(e) Election to various offices like President/Chairman/Mayor in the Panchayat/Municipality/ Corporation, as the case may be, shall be based on merit, with no gender bias.

If the above norms are observed it will not only ensure healthier functioning of the LSG institutions, but also encourage more of able and upright persons with no party label to come forward and get elected, thereby improving the character and competence of the elected bodies. This will go a long way in cleansing the system and ushering in a new development-oriented work culture. In the long run, it may even pave the way to betterment of governance at the state and central levels.

Part IV
Media, Civil Society and Elections

22 Role of Media in the Democratic Process

Sashi Kumar

As we know, the free press is a *sine qua non* of a true democracy. Our democratic trajectory was forged by robust journalism. Those who led our freedom struggle were either lawyers or journalists or both. Gandhiji himself best exemplified this synergy. It could broadly be said that while the Gandhi of South Africa was more a lawyer, in the later Indian phase, when he led the independence movement, it was the journalist in him that stood out.

In fact, Gandhiji himself acknowledges that his journalism was not only an agency to communicate the myriad strands of his moral-political movement; it was actually *constitutive* of his unique and potent political weapon: Satyagraha, as he wrote, "I used to pour my heart out in the columns of the Indian Opinion and in that process I was thinking aloud, I was also constituting the weapon of satyagraha."

The Navjeevan Press in Ahmedabad was state of the art for those times. Gandhiji ran four or five publications which were all germane to the causes he took up and the struggles he led. In and through his writings in 'Harijan', Satyagraha', 'Indian Opinion', or 'Young India', he evolved and elaborated on his political philosophy and his personal credo. He was up as early as 1.30 am every day to write his column in one or more of these journals. As he travelled a lot by train, what he wrote was often dropped off at stations en route and carried back by couriers to the Navjeevan Press at Ahmedabad. His assistants, notably, Mahadev Desai, were constantly engaged in correcting the proofs of Gandhiji's articles for his journals. While travelling, these corrections were often sent as telegrams back to the Press.

Gandhiji always took this journalistic work very seriously. Even in 1913 when he asked all settlers of the Phoenix farm in South Africa to go to jail, he exempted those responsible for producing Indian Opinion from that directive. He was always alive to the power of the press. In that sense he was no savant who sought refuge from the glare of the media. He was very clear about what he wanted from the press. He set and dictated terms to the press. The media corps following Gandhi during his Bengal padayatra in the wake of the Noakhali riots were given regular set briefings and were expected to publish only what was officially communicated to them, almost always in writing. Gandhi also had his priorities when it came to the news media. Indian journalists were at times irked with him for privileging the foreign media. He would explain to them that it was more important for him to be heard and read overseas, in the heart of Britain, rather than in India.

Gandhi's finest media coup in India was perhaps the Dandi march. On March 2, 1930, Gandhi and a band of 78 followers set out from Sabarmati Ashram in Ahmedabad to Dandi, some 230 kilometers away, to defy the salt law. The whole event and every bit of the march was widely covered by the native and the international media and culminated in the iconic image of Gandhi defiantly scooping salt at the seashore in Dandi.

The media was an organic part of the struggle for independence. The framers of our Constitution subsumed the freedom of the media in the larger freedom of expression, assembly and movement. The freewheeling powers of the media accrue from Article 19(1) in the fundamental rights chapter of the Constitution, particularly clauses (a) and (g) which speak about freedom of expression, freedom of movement and freedom to practise any profession. These are rights, with reasonable restrictions, granted to any citizen of India. The freedom of the Press is therefore inferred from these rights and is not prescribed or stipulated *per se* in the Constitution; unlike, say, in the Constitution of the United States, where the first amendment specifies that Congress shall make no laws which abridge the freedom of the press. The moral and constitutional high ground the news media enjoy in India are a construct built on the faith reposed in them by the people at large and by successive verdicts by the courts of the land. There have been phases – all of them passing, except for the Emergency under Indira Gandhi in 1975 when the Press was gagged – when the freedom of the Press was under duress, pitted against legislative privilege or judicial intolerance expressed in terms of the threat of contempt of court. In every such situation, the Press emerged with its rights intact because it was considered, in the popular mind, the true agency of democracy. It was almost universally and implicitly accepted that censorship of the press would be tantamount to curtailing democracy. The state stepped warily when it came to dealing with the press.

Let me digress for a moment here to address the general impression that a free press is a mismatch in a socialist society. The historical experience may unfortunately bear this out because the track record of the news media in the USSR or the socialist bloc in East Europe or subsequently in China or Cuba leaves a lot to be desired from the point of view of press freedoms. Amartya Sen has pointed out how the absence of a free media was responsible for a man made disaster like a famine claiming millions of lives in China because the leadership was fed only what it liked to hear from the levels of the hierarchy below it and, in the process, the actual situation on the ground was grossly underreported or not reported at all. The presence of a free and objective news media would not have allowed this make-believe of normalcy to take hold of the upper echelons of the party when famine was stalking the land. On the other hand, the theoretical argument against a free press in a socialist regime is/was that since socialism by definition fulfilled the collective and productive aspirations of the people there was no need for a critical, inimical force running loose within the system subverting the peoples' faith in it.

What is significant is that this experience of press freedom in socialist regimes is at odds with the exposition of it by Marx himself. Karl Marx was a champion, as fierce as they come, of the free press. As Editor of the *Rheinische Zeiting* and *Neue Rheinische Zeiting,* he fought passionately against censorship of the press by the Prussian state. He has written at length and in considerable detail arguing forcefully for the freedom of the Press. *Censorship,* Marx declared, *is never ethical even when it is legal, just as slavery is never ethical even if legal* (as it was in his days). This categorical equation of censorship with slavery was apparently lost on subsequent socialist practice and what transpired must at best be seen as an un-Marxian aberration. Marxism, in its theory and best expression, is an unambiguous advocate of the freedom of the press.

As it has turned out, liberal democracies with free market are no longer safe havens for Press freedom either. The market, which has become acutely aggressive and acquisitive in this phase of advanced capitalism, has literally hijacked the news media and made it another commodity, subject solely to the laws of supply and demand. The media now are manifestly accountable not so much to the people, but to the advertisers, who bring most of their revenues, and, therefore, to the market. The *reader* and the *viewer* have been reduced to the amorphous *consumer.* Media coverage also reflects this commercial obsession. Real issues affecting and afflicting the mass of the people receive short shrift. What we get, instead, is an orchestrated fare continuously whetting middle class consumerist and apsirational appetites. This raises fundamental questions about the very *raison d'etre* of the news media. If the thrust of the Press is profit maximisation, if it is merely a player in the market place, not a catalyst in the public sphere, why should it continue to enjoy the protection and privileges it has been accorded by society at large as an instrument of democracy? Does the news media, as a sheer product of the market, deserve any special entitlements?

The commercialised, consumerist news media whose mantra is to make profit and whose discourse sub-serves that end cannot, naturally, be expected to report the world faithfully or meaningfully for us. As if that were not bad enough, the press today sets the agenda in its own narrow terms and for its own selfish ends. In other words, it no longer *describes* the world for us; it *prescribes* it for us. There is a Sumerian saying, dating back to 3000 BC, that what is not recorded does not exist. Its modern equivalent would be: if it hasn't happened on TV, it hasn't happened at all. This totalising role of the Press (whether print, television, radio or internet) gives it unprecedented power over our lives. It has, at the same time, becoming more activist and interventionist, often weighing in on the side of anti democratic and anti people measures. The media today are part of the problem. Not that one expects the media to be part of the solution; but surely they cannot become part of the problem! They are like fire fighters who set the blaze on fire, and then go through the motions of dousing it. Their 'do-not-kill-the-messenger' plea, every time they are taken to task for their sins of commission or omission, does not wash any more because the message is, increasingly, their own concoction.

The business of the news media lends itself peculiarly today to a hybrid form of *political capitalism.* We have seen how Sylvio Berlusconi or Thaksin Shinwatara rode to power in Itay or Thailand on the strength of their dominant media empires. In India we have numerous instance of political parties floating their own TV channels in various languages. They are market enterprises with a Party agenda and in their own way make a mockery of the values of journalism and freedom of the Press. In some states like Tamil Nadu the leading political parties literally dominate the media sphere: The DMK and the AIADMK parties in the state both have their own TV channels and it looks like the two are talking to one another – the public is left trying to figure out the objective news from this partisan cross talk. Indeed, objectivity in the media, as we have traditionally understood it, may not really be relevant or viable any more. As the media scholar Robert McChesney recently pointed out, masquerading as the objective may be more dangerous than the subjective recognised and accepted as such. May be the way forward is, to parody Mao, to let a thousand subjectivities clash and hope you will find the golden mean subjective when and if the dust settles down.

The media, then, are undergoing a transformation and what will emerge remains a question mark. The growing disconnect of the news media from the public they are meant to inform and empower does not augur well for the freedom of the Press. The growing credibility gap in the news media is making them redundant as an instrument of democracy. The Italian philosopher, Umberto Eco, puts his finger on the essential paradox of the news media in a democracy like India today. The three organs or pillars emerging after the separation of powers in a democracy – namely the Executive, the Legislature and the Judiciary – are each, institutionally or constitutionally, accountable to the people. The Executive is obviously accountable to the people through a Parliament. The Legislature has to go back to the people every four or five years to seek their mandate afresh. Even the Judiciary is accountable to the people at one remove because a Judge can be impeached with two thirds majority in both houses of parliament. It is only the fourth pillar of democracy – namely the Press – says Eco, which is not so formally or structurally accountable. And indeed, he argues, that is the way it should be, because, if the fourth pillar, or the fourth estate, is to be so accountable, one of the other three pillars would have to bring it to heel. Such a Press would not be really free; nor the political system it operates be truly democratic. Thus the fourth pillar, or fourth estate, must essentially not be subject to the control of any of the other three pillars. Therefore, it behoves the fourth estate, argues Eco, to put itself in the dock every once in a while and ask itself whether it is acquitting itself in terms of its *dharma* to the public. It must, based on honest introspection, correct and reset its course as a determinant of democracy to continue to enjoy the trust and confidence of its constituency of readers and viewers. Failure to do so may prove its undoing. For, it is any body's guess whether the next time the state seeks to bring a draconian law against the Press, the people at large will come out on to the streets, as they have done in the past, in defence of its freedom. A mere consumer product in the market does not demand that kind of popular solidarity.

23 Media, Civil Society and Elections

B.R.P. Bhaskar

When Edmund Burke, Henry Fielding, Thomas Carlyle and William Hazlitt used the term 'the Fourth Estate' to denote the newspapers, they were acknowledging the emergence of the media as a power centre outside the establishment in 18th century Britain. Since then newer media forms have come up and together they have emerged as a powerful element—for good or bad.

Civil society is composed of myriad voluntary civic and social organizations which remain outside the power structure but interact with all the four estates on a continuing basis and often influence them, on the strength not of numbers but of the justness of the causes they espouse.

What role do media and civil society play in our democratic process, especially in the elections? When we seek an answer to this question in the context of the need for electoral reform, it is necessary to take a close look at the way our democracy works.

Barring the Emergency period, when the life of the Lok Sabha was extended by a year, parliamentary elections have been held regularly without fail. Elections to the Assembly have been put off from time to time in several states using the expediency of President's rule. After the Supreme Court laid down parameters for use of this constitutional provision, the Centre has been unable to invoke it recklessly as before. In the early decades of Independence, many states habitually delayed local self-government elections taking advantage of the absence of any compelling constitutional provision. After the Constitution was amended to make local elections mandatory, they have been held at stipulated intervals in most states. Thus elections are now a regular feature of Indian democracy at all levels. However, the democratic process remains deficient in as much as the citizen's role in it does not extend beyond exercising the right to vote when called upon to do so. In the long interval between one election and the next, he remains a passive spectator at the mercy of the political system. To use a term familiar to us from the working of the market economy, he is a mere 'consumer' of governance.

The law as it now stands provides for holding of meetings of the gram sabha (village assembly) which all citizens residing in a specified area are entitled to attend, at regular intervals. This is the only forum to which a citizen has free and direct access. To begin with, people turned up at the gram sabha meetings enthusiastically, ready to use the opportunity they provide to question those responsible for management of day-to-day affairs. Soon they realised that the powerful elements, social or political, which dominate life in the area are able to limit their role. Consequently they lost interest in the institution of gram sabha. Today in many parts of the country, the gram sabha does not function in the intended manner. Officials are compelled to hold its meetings with a captive audience – in Kerala, women belonging to the Kudumbasree self-help network are the chosen victims — or to fabricate records to show that the sabha has met.

It is against this background that we must examine the performance of the media and the civil society, two institutions which have the ability to augment the content of the democratic process, at election time as well as during the interval between elections.

In the early years of Independence, the large metropolitan newspapers in English came under the control of business houses. In the first General Election, the Congress helped the owners and editors of some newspapers to enter Parliament and the State Assemblies. There was only one metropolitan newspaper owner among them: Ramnath Goenka of the Indian Express, who was elected to the Lok Sabha from Madras state. Two decades later, he re-entered the house, from Madhya Pradesh, as a Jana Sangh candidate.

Even when the Indian newspapers, which had been following the British pattern, started adopting the ways of the US press, they steered clear of the American practice of endorsing a party or candidate at election time. However, when J.B. Kripalani took on V.K. Krishna Menon in the North Bombay constituency in 1962, the big business press did not hide the fact that its sympathies lay with the former. Frank Moraes, who was the Editor of The Indian Express at the time, joined the "Defeat Krishna Menon Committee" formed by right-wing elements.

As literacy spread and reading habit grew, provincial newspapers in English and several Indian languages emerged as major players in their respective regions. The owners of many of these newspapers cultivated political links. Some entered politics directly and sought public offices, but most of them were content with the influence they wielded by virtue of their proximity to the political establishment. Apart from owners, some editors and working journalists also sought elective posts or other political favours. Thus a cosy relationship developed between politicians and media persons. Rajiv Gandhi made M.J. Akbar, a rising media star of the time, a member of the Lok Sabha but he did not remain in the political arena for long. More recently the Shiv Sena sent Pritish Nandy to the Rajya Sabha. What is common to them? It appears, by and large, the relationship between the media and the political parties has been of the wheel-and-deal kind. Recent revelations about "paid news" indicate that it has now metamorphosed into a commercial one.

Apart from attempts to trade favours, there have also been attempts to browbeat each other. There have been instances in which newspapers which invited the hostility of the political establishment were penalized. Media offices and media persons have come under attack from Kashmir to Kerala.

Several parties and politicians have their own media organisations. To begin with, the party newspapers did not aspire to anything more than the status of a political organ. Lately, however, there have been efforts to establish and sustain newspapers and television channels on a commercial basis. Some politicians have acquired control of long established newspapers or started new ones in recent years.

Do media organisations influence the voting pattern? This question needs to be looked at carefully. The pronounced anti-communist bias of the Malayalam newspapers, which hold sway in Kerala, did not prove an insurmountable obstacle to the Communist Party of India in its successful bid for power in the state in 1957. While there has been no marked change in the attitude of the large newspapers — the state CPI-M alleges they are part of a media syndicate which is conspiring to destroy it — the Left Democratic Front which it heads has been coming to power in alternate elections.

The experience of other states is no different. Both the Dravida Munnetra Kazhagam and the All India Anna DMK rose to power without any support from the large newspapers of Tamil Nadu. The BJP probably got some push from sections of the press in the north but Mulayam Singh Yadav and Mayawati rose to the top in Uttar Pradesh and Lalu Prasad Yadav in Bihar overcoming the indifference or even scorn of the media.

Andhra Pradesh has a different story to tell. The Telugu newspaper Eenadu was primarily responsible for N.T. Rama Rao's sensational electoral triumph there within a year of the formation of the Telugu Desam party. Its owner-editor, Ramoji Rao, with the help of his correspondents in the state, had identified candidates with a winning chance for the fledgling party. His tactics worked because circumstances were favourable. He could not repeat the performance later.

Over the past two decades, television has emerged as a more powerful medium than the newspaper across the country but there is no evidence so far to conclude that it is able to influence the outcome of elections.

Lately the major political parties have been enlisting the services of public relations and advertising agencies at election time to mount media campaigns. The impact of these campaigns remains questionable. The BJP sought a renewal of mandate in 2004 with a pithy slogan "Shining India", coined by an ad agency. In 2009, it tried an even bolder slogan "Strong leader, decisive government". Neither slogan worked.

James Mutti, a Fulbright scholar who was in India last year to study the media's role in the democratic process, observed that it was not playing a significant public service role. He wrote, "The media may do a good job of providing news to the estimated 300 million members of the Indian middle class – in fact, coverage of political issues tends to be quite good – but as long as over 700 million Indians are sidelined from the media's gaze by their inability to conspicuously consume, the media's role as public service is severely limited."

Mutti said the country needed a new media model which balanced its profit motive with coverage of issues relevant to the poorer, voting classes, and which could serve as a model for the entire developing world.

Electoral reform has figured in the media sporadically and the major newspapers have extended editorial support to the concept in general terms from time to time. The media enthusiastically endorsed the Law Commission's reform proposals of 1999. When Tehelka exposed political corruption, the Times of India pointed out that "any solution aimed at cleansing the system must address the issue of *electoral* reforms". The media also supported the limited efforts made by the Election Commission to improve the working of the system.

However, no media institution has made serious and sustained efforts to mobilize public opinion in favour of electoral reform. Civil society, which lacks the reach and resources of the media, has been striving to fill the breach. Tarun Tejpal, Editor of Tehelka, draws an interesting contrast between media and civil society. "The media," he says, "has become a purely commercial construct. Civil society, in contrast, is not. There is no money to be made out of the activities that civil society is involved in. I think this has become the fundamental difference between the media and civil society organisations."

Several national and international civil society organizations have been campaigning for or extending support to electoral reform. Notable among them are the Association for Democratic Reforms (ADR), Lok Satta and People's Union for Civil Liberties, whose public interest litigation resulted in the Supreme Court order of 2003 requiring disclosure of the criminal, financial and educational background of all contesting candidates. The National Election Watch has been gathering information filed by candidates about their assets and criminal antecedents and giving wide publicity to it. Such activity has not inhibited the parties from offering tickets to criminals. Nor has it prevented criminals from getting elected. Quite obviously the campaign needs to be continued with great vigour. There is reason to suspect that some of the affidavits filed by the candidates are not truthful. NGOs working at state and local levels must come forward to verify their statement and initiate legal action against those who have made false declarations.

Transparency International, Amnesty International and the Asian Human Rights Commission are among the international NGOs which have called for reform of the Indian electoral system with a view to eliminating malpractices and cleansing the democratic process.

At the root of the malaise is the emergence of money power and muscle power as major elements in the electoral exercise. Various ideas to tackle the problem have been before the country but the political establishment has been unwilling to initiate purposeful measures to check the twin menace. The media is a beneficiary of democracy in more than one sense. The democratic set-up allows it to function freely. It also helps them commercially: newspaper circulations grow and channel ratings rise at election time. In the circumstances, it has a duty to play a pro-active role in the efforts to ensure the well-being of the democratic system.

24 Elections and Journalist's Dilemma

T.N. Gopakumar

When we look at elections, we also have to realise what goes into the process of elections. For example, from where you get your first voter's identity card; what are the issues which prevent you from getting that first identity card which enables you to vote? Do you think that 70% or 80% of the votes that are cast in India were real votes? Do you think that among those voters all are legitimate voters? Are you sure that there are other voters who are chewing up the real voters and the real voters when many times they visit different polling booths, are unable to vote? We have been saying it for years and years in different media.

Even before the advent of private television channels in India, I remember, how booths have been captured by the local mafia dons, who are on the pay roll of the politicians, business houses and there were no serious changes in the years that passed by.

I am talking about 1980s. From 1980, how much India has changed? Not much, we have been getting reports. We notice that the media is not making an aggressive campaign on this basic issue. At one point of time, T.N. Sheshan tried to do something innovative and tried to make sure that the office of the Election Commission is stronger and has its own Constitutional authority. That itself has eroded now. The media here today, apart from all the other things, shows frivolous concerns about the issues of society. Keeping all those things apart, the media at least, if you run a 24 hour channel, you can give at least two minutes of this kind for burning issues. It is not a question of camera travelling to a rural area and bringing in the inputs of the problem. It is not the question of entire world media going to 'Kinaloor' or other issue based areas at a particular point of time and forgetting it later. Those are primary issues. We have been fighting this kind of faults from the days of Silent Valley in Kerala and in other parts of India. But an entire village is denied voting right. What is the role of the media? Is the media going there? I think that is happening everywhere. I find that where there are less number of votes, they are un-addressed. If there is only 300 votes in a small rural area, they don't care about those 300 votes. The candidate even does not bother to go there and waste one day because of the travel problem. You will have to climb three bridges or go by boats for 300 votes. You will waste time. How to bring these issues into the main stream? There is no temple involved, no church involved, there is no mosque involved, there is no organised fishermen community involved. Even politicians do not bother about that.

When we talk about elections, remember that we also have election results which say that candidate won by 80 votes, 90 votes. So to canvass these 300 votes from a particular colony, which is in a small island, it causes them some inconvenience. Is it not worth it?. Instead of that, it is better to focus on those areas where there is good strength. Shashi Tharoor won the election from Trivandrum. Why is it so? The new middle class, the new young generation wants Shashi Tharoor elected looking at the flamboyance and background of that man. He campaigned only in that way. He won by around one lakh votes here. He was only looking at the main stream. Do you think that any Kerala media gave enough attention to the other poor opponent candidates? No. It is because of other compulsions.When you assign a reporter and camera man you will give him enough money and he will go where? If it is UP elections, he will go to Rai Bereli, Amethi and such other places. It does not mean that Rai Bereli or Amethi is the real India. These are compulsions we have been facing as journalists. There are occasions when Indira Gandhi fought from more than one Constituency. So did others. Focus was only on that Media cannot be faulted there. But I fault the media for this omission, the side lined people, the marginalised people, the people who are Indian citizens, who are living in a literary State like Kerala right in the city of Trivandrum, two kilometers long, do not have a pathway to walk down, who have been given promises and all the money is spent. Money that has been funded by the Centre is swindled by one person and money funded by the State Government is swindled by another person. This is the reality. This reality, if it is not properly looked at by the media, it is a huge omission. This is one aspect of it. Another thing is in the name of electoral reforms; there are quiet a few things being talked about. Intention of government through the Parliament is uncertain and unclear. They are planning legislations and regulatory measures to suit them. We went through a national emergency period. What should come in the media was not decided by the journalists then. They were prevented from going to some areas. There were attempts to compel us to go to certain other areas.

During the period of emergency, everything was paid news. Reference was made to “paid news”. Would you prefer emergency period or new generation corporate paid news period? In a comparison, one would prefer the new period. One will prefer the new corporate period rather than the emergency period, if there is a choice involved. But there is no such choice. We have been talking about it within our own systems, with our colleagues and other media.

How to evolve a mechanism by which we can bring up these issues constantly. Every effort made in terms of social interventions have to be projected better. Some channels are doing justice to those kind of processes. At the same time, one cannot but agree that in those issues that have been pointed out, the media is failing. The level of sensitivity of the new generation journalists have to be enhanced. It is easy to say that you are going after and what can bring your ratings etc, whereas, one can say that on the other side you would also see that ultimately only the fighters survive in a kind of media market we have today. Will any of us settle for a situation where only Dooradarshan is the available channel with all commitment to civil society and civil aspects? We will not settle for that. We will carry this effort. But the truth is that television is still a very very young medium in India. Twenty years new generations television, is a very young medium and the persons who are handling it are relatively new in the field and those persons are fast in making decisions and at the same time facing challenges. At the same time, we are trying to reach as many numbers of viewers in terms of that as many numbers of readers. It is a huge threat. It is dangerous when the nexus between media and business reaches a point where no right media activity is possible. That threat is there all over India. There are two options for journalists. To fight it. In the process of that fight, leave the responsibility. The other option is fight and make compromises and in that process we are losing out our time and we are also unsure whether those persons who have gone to step into the shoes that I am leaving, will be strong enough to fight either of these things. One is how strong is to amend himself to the compromises or how strong is to fight the management, which is demanding two things. If the management demands three things, it is O.K. Tell us to increase the revenue – it is fine. Tell us to increase the rating, tell us to increase better programmes, tell us to get revenue. At the same time, do not tell us to do all the things together. I belong to a community of journalists which believe we can not do all the three things together.

25 Media and Elections in India

Mirza Asmer Beg

The media occupies a central place in a democratic society. The abdication of its responsibility to report "serious" news and bring the government to account is disturbing. But with the media becoming more diverse and all-pervasive, the actual situation has become more complex. Today, newspapers are estimated to reach about 240 million people. Terrestrial television reaches over 50 per cent of the Indian population, and 80 per cent of the urban residents, cable and satellite television figures are 20 and 46 percent respectively. Popular culture is media culture, as a consequence, there is even greater temptation by those who can manipulate the media to their advantage, to actually do so.

Today, we are witness to a dangerous phenomenon of a growing number of elected representatives funding their poll campaigns with corporate backing. A large number of people, with a big business background have ventured directly into the electoral arena.

The last Lok Sabha election has been the culture of "coverage packages" explode across the country. The media have been the biggest winner in these polls, their poll period earnings have been in hundreds of millions. A lot of this did not come as direct advertising but in packaging a candidate's propaganda as "news".

The elections saw the culture of "coverage package" pervades across the country. In many cases, a candidate just had to pay for almost any coverage at all. Issues did not come into it. No money, no news. This effectively shut out small parties and independent voices with low assets and resources.

None of this is new, but the scale is new and shocking, and the brazenness of it is alarming. And the game has now moved from the petty corruption of a few journalists to the structured extraction of huge sums of money by media outfits.

On the other side, the media in general has shamelessly defended the advertising packages as the bread and butter of the industry. They are however, dismissive of its effects on India's electoral democracy. With the media and money power in a tight embrace, the smaller and less expensive voices are completely blacked out. The sad part is that the Election Commission has not taken any significant deterrent action in this regard. Prakash Singh Badal, while speaking in a Seminar, expressed disappointment over the role of the media in the last Lok Sabha elections. He observed that "expenses on media constituted major part of election costs incurred by parties and candidates. Media has the power to highlight as well as pull down a candidate". He was speaking the truth. He quoted the example of a Punjab daily. This newspaper made available two full pages to antagonistic parties led by Badal himself and Amrinder Singh. These two pages, he said, are a historic example of selling news space and antagonistic perceptions and contents against each other on the same day and in the same paper. In a newspaper, news is considered sacred, objective and non-partisan. Advertisements are placed giving a clear understanding that it is not news. But these articles written by correspondents give the impression that they are sacred.

An important factor is that readers pay very little attention to advertisements as compared to news. According to a study, news items carry eleven times more credibility. Publicity hungry candidates are desirous of getting a news item with eleven times weightage, instead of an advertisement which would be barely noticed. P. Sainath, a veteran journalist, wrote in The Hindu, about a series of corrupt practices in the media, of selling news space. He gave mines of researched information of corruption in media. He wrote in The Hindu on December 6, 2009, that "Maharashtra Chief Minister Ashok Chavan spent a mere Rs. 5,379 on newspaper advertisements during the recent State Assembly Election by his own claim. And he spent another Rs. 6,000 on cable television advertisements. These figures are clearly at odds with the unprecedented media coverage the Chief Minster got during the election campaign." He added that "The Hindu has gathered 47 full newspaper pages, many of them in colour, focused exclusively on Chavan, his leadership, his party and government. These appeared in large newspapers including one ranking amongst India's highest circulation dailies. However, these were not marked as advertisements."

How money can get the better of ideology, was amply demonstrated in Maharashtra before the 2009 general elections, the Aurangabad-based *Lokmat* group which is promoted by members of the Darda family who are important politicians belonging to the Congress Party, carried a number of allegedly "paid for" articles that heaped high praise on candidates of the opposition Bharatiya Janata Party (BJP). Banwarilal Purohit, managing editor of *Hitavada,* Nagpur's most widely circulated English newspaper, was a BJP MP but his newspaper published many articles in favour of the Congress candidates and the Congress Party. Money obviously was the driving force in these cases.

When confronted with circumstantial evidence that substantiate allegations of "paid news", the standard reaction of individuals and representatives of the accused media organizations was to pretend that nothing untoward has happened. Since the evidence is circumstantial in nature the allegations cannot be further pressed. The typical response of representatives of political parties as well as media organizations who have been named and against whom specific allegations of corruption have been levelled was to flatly deny these allegations. In private, however, these very people acknowledge that the malaise of "paid news" has spread deep into the country's body politic and needs to be attended to urgently.

Only rarely have the newspapers in question acknowledged publically that there is something wrong with their reporting. For example, on 30 April 2009, the day of the elections, the Varanasi edition of the *Hindustan* newspaper carried an article that looked deceptively like a news item on top of its front page. The headline suggested that there was a clear wave in favour of the Congress. The following day, the newspaper apologized to its readers. The representatives of *Hindustan* told the Press Council of India that when they realised their mistake they promptly pointed this out to their readers the following day, but interestingly by then the, polling was over. This was a rare instance of a publication acknowledging before the PCI's subcommittee that it had made an error.

The second example is of a candidate who acknowledged publicly that he had paid money to a publication for favourable coverage. Parcha Kodanda Rama Rao of the Loksatta Party said that he had paid a sum of Rs. 50,000 to a representative of *Eenadu* for favourable coverage. He, however, did not receive a receipt. Quick to deny that any money had been accepted, Ramoji Rao, who heads the *Eenadu* group, told the PCI that the problem of "paid news" was part of a larger problem which needed to be tackled.

Recently, Umlesh Yadav, The Rshtriya Parivartan Dal, MLA from Bisauli constituency in UP was served a notice by the Election Commission following a complaint by one of her rivals, that she resorted to paid news in the 2007 Assembly election (TOI, June 27, 2010). Her rival Yogendra Kumar had alleged that two Hindi dailies carried news items to favour

Yadav in the form of an advertisement, in lieu of money. The Press Council which went into the complaint found the two newspapers guilty of ethical violations and cautioned the media to refrain from publishing news masquerading as advertisements and vice-versa.

Modus Operandi: In the last Lok sabha and Assembly Elections, a number of genuine advertisements appeared 24 hours before the election code of conduct came into force. After that the term 'advertisement' disappeared. The items became 'news'. There was another flurry of advertisements just before the candidates began filing their nomination papers. This happened because individual expenses of candidates come under scrutiny from the day she filed her nomination. Both these methods enabled the rich candidates to spend huge amounts which did not figure in their poll expenses. Moreover, the same 'news' appeared in print, on TV and on the net. This was package journalism at its very best. As more and more candidates took this option, real advertising, interestingly, fell in some newspapers.

Reputed PR companies and advertisement agencies, were at the service of rich candidates, making up their items, to neatly fit in the concerned newspaper. They also customized the news to make it seem exclusive. Through 'paid news' the reader/viewer was made to believe that what was basically an advertisement, was actually independently produced news content. Moreover, by not declaring the expenditure made on the 'news item', the candidates were in violation of Conduct of Election Rules, 1961. On the other side, the concerned media organization by not accounting for the money received from the candidate, was in violation of the Income Tax Act, 1961, and the Companies Act, 1956.

Absence of issues: Issues in the election are now reduced to fights between individuals. Issues of hunger and backwardness are now projected as stand-offs between candidates- heroic or villainous. The media billed the 2009 Lok Sabha elections as one without issues. There were actually a spate of issues in the country, but they were not glamorous enough for the media. The dominant media was not at all sincere in covering pressing issues like rising food prices. The visual media's obsession with film stars and star politicians pushed the real issues to the sidelines. Actually, issues retain space in the media only when they are acceptable to the media barons and their sponsors.

The disease of 'paid news' is now all-pervasive and highly organized. What started as an exercise by the rich candidates to influence the media in their favour, has turned into a more dangerous game, where the media are into a sinister cycle of extortion of candidates. The candidates, who do not want to antagonise the media, have no option but to play on.

Way Ahead: The most important role in curbing this menace can be played by the Election Commission. It should be open to all complaints in this regard and initiate action as and when a *prime facie* case is established. It is also imperative that the press council should be given more powers to discipline media organizations. The legal framework also needs to be strengthened so that the erring individuals or organisations may be brought to book.

We also need to think in terms of enacting better and stricter laws to plug the loopholes in the process of electoral finance. Perhaps we could take some ideas from the American system, where they have been constantly involved in devising better campaign finance reforms. This is not to suggest that the American system is the best and should be emulated. What is required is to just see how they have been trying to face the menace of money in elections and to what extent they have been able to deal with it.

It has been observed that surrogate advertisements appear in print media, especially newspapers for and against particular political parties and candidates during election period. As per Section 77(1) of the Representation of the People Act, 1951, expenditure involved in such advertisements in connection with the election of any candidate has to be added to the account of election expenses of the candidate, required to be maintained under that Section. Further, Section 171H of IPC prohibits incurring of expenditure on, inter alia, advertisement, circular or publication, for the purpose of promoting or procuring the election of a candidate, without authority from the candidate. The surrogate advertisement defeats the purposes of the aforesaid provisions of law. Although the Election Commission has been making efforts to regulate such advertisements by urging all Newspaper establishments, to follow the requirements of Section 127A of the Representation of the People Act, 1951, in the matter of advertisements related to elections, but substantive results have not come forth. For this purpose, Section 127A of the Representation of the People Act, 1951 may be suitably amended, adding a new sub-Section (2A) to the effect that in the case of any advertisements/election matter for or against any political party or candidate in print media, during the election period, the name and address of the publisher should be given along with the matter / advertisement. Sub-section (4) should also be suitably amended.

According to Rajdeep Sardesai, President of the Editor's Guild, curbing paid news in newspapers will be the prime focus of the Editors Guild in 2010. "The code is being drafted and letters will be sent to all the newspapers and television channels to follow it. We will isolate organisations which do not follow the code," he said. To drive greater transparency, newspapers and television channels will have to clearly distinguish between news and advertisements with proper disclosure norms so that the reader or viewer is not tricked, Sardesai said. The Guild will also push for transparency in news companies' private treaties business, which involves the barter of equity in unlisted companies for advertising space or minutes. The Guild mandates that news organisations should disclose their commercial and equity interests in such companies for the benefit of their readers and viewers.

Taking a lead in this connection, on 8 June 2010, the EC issued a circular to the chief electoral officers of all states and union territories directing their attention to the "recent phenomenon" of "paid news" which had become "alarming" as a "serious electoral malpractice". The EC's principal secretary Tapas Kumar wrote that "there is near unanimity" that necessary steps should be taken to halt such malpractices which unduly influence the free will of the voters, encourages the role of money power in a covert manner and disturb the level playing field in elections. The EC directed that "maximum vigilance" be exercised to ascertain and investigate instances of "collusion" between a candidate or a political party and publishers or broadcasters when articles or reports appear that either praise or denigrate a particular candidate or a party. "Such collusion would, however, have generally no transactional evidence of payment of consideration in cash or kind", the circular pointed out, adding that it is mandatory for the publisher of an election advertisement or a pamphlet or any other document to print the name and address of the publisher as well as the printer. Failure to do so attracts a penalty of imprisonment up to two years and/or a fine of Rs. 2,000 under Section 171 H of the Indian Penal Code (IPC). The EC suggested that district committees should keep a watch on election-related news and features in the elections media.

The EC's directives were put to test in the first election which was held after its issuance, i.e., in the Bihar assembly elections of October-November 2010. There, Akshay Rout, director general of the commissioner, has gone on record saying that during this election, over 100 show-cause notices were served on candidates who were later "forced" to officially disclose the expenditure incurred on "paid news". What is not known, however, is whether any action has been taken or is expected to be taken against the recipients of funds for inserting such "paid news" and whether such transactions have at all been disclosed. In Bihar, the EC had appointed a committee headed by a retired officer of the income tax department for the purpose of identifying "paid news" and tracking the flow of funds but it is difficult to tell how effective this committee has been.

However, all these efforts would yield little unless the media persons and organisations themselves realize the onerous responsibility which rests on their shoulders as the fourth pillar of democracy. We all were a mute witness to the manner in which the 'Tahelka group' and its leader Tarun Tejpal were hounded by the NDA government at the Centre as they probably were trying to actually act as the 'Fourth Estate'. This case provided the cue to other media organisations to fall in line. Hence, when the NDA regime sang 'India shining', the Indian media joined the chorus. The immense influence and power which the media enjoy is actually because of the faith the people of India have in their objectivity and non-partisan behavior. The day this faith- which has slowly started to erode- is shaken, it would really sound a death-knell for Indian democracy.

The way the Press Council of India has acted in response to this problem was sad and would go a long way in undermining the democratic electoral process in a profound way. Initially, after the scandal of paid news rocked the media, the Press Council suo motto set up a sub-committee to probe this phenomenon. Its two-member sub-committee, which was constituted to go into this phenomenon, presented an exhaustive and excellent report. But when the PCI came out with its 'final' report, the sub-committee's exhaustive report, which exposed the guilty, was not even attached as an annexure to the final report. The final report only mentions it in the footnote, saying that "it may remain in the record of the council as a reference document". It was not even placed on the PCI website, and consigned to the archives. So the same media, which is out to expose names in all other scandals, when it came to exposing its own people who were perpetrators of paid news, decided to shield them from public exposure. Thus, the body entrusted with the task of preserving the freedom of the press has acted as the stooge of the powerful media barons. This indeed is a sad commentary on the manner in which the rich and powerful publishers' lobby control the media in India.

Nevertheless, the saving grace is that it is not essential that those who spend money would necessarily have an upper hand in Elections. In the last Assembly Election in UP, of the about Rs. 700 crores spent by political parties and their candidates, according to the Centre for media studies, BSP's share was the least, around 10 percent. SP, on the other hand spent four times more, BJP and Congress about 35 percent. The BSP hardly spent on media publicity and paid news, which constitutes, around 40 percent of all poll expenditure of political parties. In fact, what other political parties had spent in this poll in UP was as much as what the Government's expenditure was for the general elections in the entire country. Instead, the BSP leaders and cadres concentrated on their own pockets or constituencies, and they were amply rewarded. The BSP had actually made progress in UP compared to the 2004 Lok Sabha elections (21 seats against 19) and was still, by far, the first party in terms of valid votes, 27.4 per cent in UP, 3 percentage points more than in 2004, and 10 more than the Congress. Although, the popular media had created an impression that BSP was basically a rural based party, actually it got the maximum votes both in rural and urban areas. Moreover, to say that Mayawati's rise is rooted in caste factor alone, and is, therefore, transient is again not correct. When the electorate was asked in the National Election Survey conducted by the Centre for the Study of Developing Societies, as to which party was better in curbing corruption, 27 per cent of the voters preferred the BSP, while 22 per cent went with the BJP, 19 per cent with the Congress and 16 per cent with the SP. When asked about their choice of the Chief Minister, 28 preferred Mayawati, 27 per cent Mulayam Singh Yadav, 12 per cent Rajnath Singh and only 4 percent chose Rahul Gandhi. When asked which party was better for maintaining law and order in UP, 27 percent said BSP, 22 per cent preferred the Congress, 19 per cent BSP and 16 per cent SP. This, certainly is, good news for Indian democracy.

26 Role of Civil Society in Electoral Process

S.S. Sreekumar

Introduction

The idea of democracy subsumes participation of the 'demos' in political life. A fully participatory democracy is perhaps a myth[1]. But it expresses a basic condition of self-rule, people must have control over matters that vitally affect their individual and collective existence. Lincoln's definition of democracy as "rule of, by and for the people" points to this important principle. The term democracy as it is used today always signifies a government constituted indirectly by elected representatives. Democracy in modern times represents political system which accepts no other authority than the will of the people and their freely given consent as the basis of governance. It is this freely given consent at frequent intervals that constitutes the ground of *legitimacy* of the political system. It is also this freely given consent that keeps alive the myth of sovereignty. The state has to continuously renew its legitimacy not only because a democratic government is supposed to be based on popular consent but also because in the absence of popular support forthcoming at least from a large section of people, democratic regimes will find it difficult to play their role well. As such, the renewal of legitimacy at frequent intervals acquires crucial importance in a democratic political regime[2]. The governing power should be derived from the will of the people. It is the people who give legitimacy to a Constitution. Government acquires its authority both from the Constitution and the people who elect it. The following four characteristics of democracy are worth mentioning:

(a) democracy is a government which is derived from public opinion and is accountable to it;

(b) the public opinion must be overtly and freely expressed;

(c) for the overt and free opinion of the people, some opportunity and machinery so as to make that opinion implies some kind of suffrage, some kind of voice or vote; and

(d) in matters of contention between sections of public opinion it is the majority opinion that prevails[3].

In direct democracy, the people can control collective decision through equal rights to vote on law and policy in person. In large and complex societies, they have chosen to do so indirectly, through elected representatives to act for them. The shift to representative democracy has been necessitated due to vast population, enormous social and economic problems of nations which cover greater areas. Viscount Bryce opines that democracy proceeds on two basic assumptions[4]. (a) Popular sovereignty in the sense that the country should be governed by representatives of the people; (b) there should be equality among the citizens in arriving of decision affecting them.

The representative form of democracy postulates popular control over decision makers indirectly and hence requires a complex set of institutions and practices to make the principle of participation effective. Thus, *election* is the effective instrument of ascertaining the popular will. Similarly in the case of political equality, it is assumed that there exists equality of votes between electors, an equal right to stand for public office. Hence universal franchise is part of democracy. Political freedom requires congenial conditions i.e. equality in the conditions for making one's own voice heard freely[5].

The test of popular control can be studied from four inter-related segments. The first is the popular election to the legislature and to the office of the head of government. This ensures effectiveness of popular control and also degree of political equality. There should not be any discrimination on the ground of religion, race, caste, sex, place of birth or any of them. In brief, there should be ample scope for conducting "free and fair elections". The second criterion of popular control is what Finer termed as "open and accountable government"[6]. Continuous accountability of government to the electorate is equally relevant. The third one is the guarantee of civil and political rights or liberties, the freedom of speech, association, assembly and movement and the right to due legal process. These rights are necessary if citizens are to communicate and associate with one another. The fourth dimension concerns with democratic society as a whole. There should be equal opportunity for self-organisation or association, equal access to the media, political awareness of citizens, the democratic culture and required education[7]. It can be summarized that public control over the government through periodic free and fair elections based on political equality, an accountable and responsible government, rule of law, decision according to majority rule, supremacy of constitution and welfare of the people are essential to a constitutional democracy. The process of election is termed as the corner stone of any democratic system as it is the political means through which political opinion and awareness of the people are promoted.

Like other democratic political systems, India has also adopted a constitutional democracy. A look at the Indian Constitution gives the following description. Under an elected President who is nominal or formal head of the state, government is led by prime minister whose Party has been given a parliamentary majority by a mature electorate which has participated in free and fare elections. The prime minister and his cabinet is responsible to the elected representatives *i.e.,* to Lok Sabha. Similar arrangement is made for the states where governor is the head of the state and chief minister and his council of ministers run the government. The government is accountable to state legislature. Thus the concept of democracy presupposes the representation of the people in Parliament and state legislatures through elections.

Part XV of the Constitution and the statutes and rules made there under, instructions issued and exercised by the government and Election Commission constitute the package of electoral law governing the parliamentary and assembly elections in the country. The Representation of Peoples Act, 1951 and the Indian Penal Code, 1860, contain well defined provisions relating to corrupt practices and electoral offences.

In the context of the above mentioned theoretical and constitutional background, let us examine the scenario in India and how far the situation is congenial for the conduct of free and fare elections.

Political Scenario : Indian Context

1. There is a distressing new trend in the Indian public life. It is the *growing cynicism about politics and politicians*. The public do not even care to cast their votes at the time of elections. The voter turnout in parliamentary polls shows a declining trend. For *e.g.,* in 1996 elections, in states like Gujarat, Rajasthan, Uttar Pradesh and Jammu and Kashmir, the percentage votes polled was less than fifty percent. A sizeable section of the voters do not know the value of vote. The women, especially from villages are not in a position to cast votes in the way they ought to. This issue is most serious for powerful individuals and groups even in advanced political systems like the U.S.A. According to 1996 post election survey, only 50.6 percent of registered Black voters and 26.7 percent of registered

Hispanics reported that they had actually voted[8]. The general public seems to be *apathetic towards political life.*

The political awareness of common man is guarantee for the purity of the system. However, it is a pity that an average citizen in India is indifferent to free and fare elections. He is feeling himself irrelevant and directionless. Although the aim of the Constitution is a classless society and an equal right of franchise, the use of voting right is invariably not identical among the upper and lower strata, elitist and common man. For him, the balloting is fruitless and unprofitable. He has scant regard to his sacred and social duty cast upon by virtue of being a citizen of the country to participate in the task of electing a representative governing machinery.[9]

2. In a democratic polity, political parties are assigned the role of the prime movers of society. One major problem facing the Indian political scene is that finest men of calibre and vision, knowledge and character are not getting opportunity to be involved in politics. There was a semblance of morality in public life. Political parties are not fulfilling their functions. They are pre-occupied with struggle to remain in power. They find less time to address the problems of people.

3. Parliamentary democracy is not merely representative democracy. It is participatory democracy too. The responsibility of voters does not stop with casting their votes. Continuous and active involvement of people in the political process is a prime requirement. A less privileged voter, though he participates in election, his participation terminates with marking of his ballot. The electoral game is for privileged and affluent persons and not for the honest, sincere and devoted social activist[10]. The common man should not be influenced by the promises made by the politicians and the parties. Many empirical researches show that people especially in the rural areas lack a sense of participation in political affairs i.e., *they lack participatory approach.*

There has been a sharp *erosion in the respect* people have for politicians. Politics has been criminalised and crime politicized. Governments have lost their credibility, legitimacy and even their representative credentials.

People have been losing faith in political parties and in the promises of their leaders. Free and fair election constitute the foundations of parliamentary democracy. The framers of the Constitution have given a fool proof electoral mechanism to ensure free and fair elections. However, some factors have shaken the foundation - increase in the use of money-power, reliance on muscle power at the time of elections, kindling the caste and communal prejudice of the voters and the misuse of official machinery.

Before examining the role of civil society in the Indian context, the concept of civil society may be examined.

Civil Society : A Conceptual Framework

Right from the time of scholars like Cicero, the term civil society was used inter changeably with political society. For Marcus Tullius Cicero (106-43 B.C.) it stood for a society whose members lived together as citizens, abided by civil laws and led a civilized, cultured and dignified life. Seventeenth century English philosopher John Locke (1832-1704) equated civil society with political society. He observed that when people relinquish state of nature, set up government for the protection of their natural right to life, liberty and property, they enter into civil society. Thus, civil society is a means to establish discipline, order and security for the humanity community. Eighteenth century French Philosopher Jean Jacques Rousseau (1712 – 78) also treated civil society and political society as co-terminus. It provides for legal equality of all citizens who thus become equal in the eye of law in spite of their natural differences.

Hegel was the first philosopher to develop a recognizably modern notion of civil society in this 'Philosophy of Right'. To Hegel, Civil Society was identical with private and particularistic and characterized by the conflicting and avaricious striving of individuals and classes for largely material ends, while the state was seen as the embodiment of universal ethical values and rational civilisation[11]. Antonio Gramsci characterized civil society as the realm of culture and ideology or more concretely as "associated realm". For Gramsci, civil society exists as a kind of intermediary, linked both with the economic structure and with the state[12]. Herbert Marcuse argued that Hegel's distinction between civil society and the state was particularly significant for an analysis of the problem of contemporary society. He observed that under modern capitalism civil society had eclipsed the state whereas under modern communism, the state eclipsed the civil society. We must secure independence of both institutions in order to restore civil liberties of the citizens.

Civil society is defined as the sum of individual and collective initiatives directed towards the pursuit of common public good[13].The civil society is recognised as a non party political sphere where individuals come together and form associations voluntarily to promote public good.

The civil society, can thus be viewed as a spontaneous group of citizens who interact independently of the government, while collaborating with it sometimes and opposing it at others. The contours of civil society can be looked into three different ways[14]. First, civil society is a space that is free, open and accessible. It is the space for ideas where values, perspectives and norms are debated and developed and plan for action formulated. Second, it can be seen as a movement for advancing various causes. Thus, civil societies promote causes like tribal rights, women's and children's rights and protest against powerful national and international players which ordinary citizens cannot do. Third, civil society is a set of organisations of mutual help and support group such as neighborhood associations, village councils, local sports and cultural groups, trade unions, cooperatives, who get together and look after common interests.

The civil society in common parlance refers to network and relationship of those groups that are not organised or managed by state. In terms of membership and constituents, it includes all types of associations. For *e.g.,* academic institutions, community-based organisations, consumer protection bodies, environmental campaigns, human right fora, labour unions, relief organisations, professional bodies, religious institutions, women's network, youth campaigns and even business associations fall under civil society. Civil society comprises collectivity of those social organisations that enjoy autonomy from the state. The growing emphasis on "state minimalism" has created a space which needs to be filled by the civic institutions that could function with welfare, social justice, economic equality and human development as their goals.

In the contemporary discourse, the term civil society is used to describe intermediate associations between individual and the state. It serves as a channel of communication between individual and the state. A strong civil society directly supports democratic participation, ensures the rights and probity of the citizenry and contributes towards the deepening of accountability for policy decisions.

In developing countries, the civil society is making its presence felt to promote and facilitate participative development projects and create conditions for people's empowerment. It is expected to identify major problems in society, articulate current issues, empower the disadvantaged, serve as an independent voice in strategic debates and provide a constructive forum for exchange of ideas and information between the key actors in the policy process.

Role of Civil Society

In a matured and rational polity, the problem of governance have to be addressed through participation of citizens in the political process. It is the right of citizen to join political party, articulate the interests of the society, seek elective public office, and bring about necessary changes. This political process is seen perverted in India. Political process has become inaccessible to the best men and women in the society. Consequently political parties have ceased to be agencies of political socialisation. In this context, the civil society can play a crucial role in socialising the people. Political socialisation of the general mass especially in the rural areas is an urgent need of the day and the task has to be taken up by civil society organisations.

One of the challenging problems facing developing countries is illiteracy. Even after five decades of growth, we could not attain reasonable level of standards regarding literacy. Informed citizenry, active citizenship and collective assertion are civil society functions in democratic set up. Civil society organisations in collaboration with concerned Departments of the Government can take up programmes to eradicate illiteracy. Besides general awareness, political education has also to be inculcated to the public. This will help them to participate in the political process.

Yet another role of the civil society is in the field of *political recruitment*. People with calibre and ability are not attracted to participate in the political process. The civil society organisations which are active in various fields can identify able leaders especially youth from rural area and help in the process of political recruitment. The opinion of the *middle class* regarding the electoral reforms and other political reforms can be better reflected only through civil society organization.

Even in the context of the implementation of the RTI Act, many *crucial issues and problems are not highlighted*. The civil society organisations with the help of mass media can throw light on various issues and problems faced by the Government. This can create awareness among the masses which enable them to take a right decision and rational choice. Some of the major issues facing electoral process include the high cost of election attracting unethical and illegal funding, misuse of religion and caste in the process of political mobilisation of group identities and participation of many candidates and political parties. The existence of civil society organisations and their active role in creating awareness and public opinion on these issues to some extent work *as a vigil to the working of electoral process*.

The present scenario of our electoral democracy depicts that there is a need for *strengthening party organisation* especially at grass root level, formulating norms for inner party democracy, finding out non legal and non formal ways of enquiry in political parties. In this context, the task can be taken up by civil society organisations. Strengthening civil society organisations is an important condition to have check on electoral process.

Civil society organisations have to attend the task of inculcating democratic values so that they develop participatory approach towards political process. *Awareness campaigns* are to be conducted before the commencement of elections. The Election Commission should be provided with enough funds to make the campaign successful.

Elections are intended to open up channels between society and the polity, between masses and the elites and between individual and the government. Elections are the sources of political socialisation and participation. Dr S. Radhakrishnan aptly pointed out: "Our constitution has adopted adult suffrage. It is the most powerful instrument devised by man for breaking down social and economic injustice and destroying the walls that imprison men's minds. This can be achieved only if our people are aware of their rights and responsibilities and this is the task of dedicated leaders to teach the people."[15]

Concluding Observations

Civil society organisations have to perform mainly three roles. First is to create favourable and congenial environment for making general public especially youth politically conscious and inculcate democratic values leading to political socialisation. The second role is to identify able men and women to participate in the democratic process leading to political recruitment. In our society, social and political mobilisation is not taking place in an effective manner. Majority of the rural mass are unaffiliated to any formal organisation. Hence, an emerging need is to develop social capital for which civil society organisations have to play a dominant role.

Civil society treats citizens as basic building blocks capable of acting collectively through network and associations .Thus, as democracy takes deep roots in the country, civil society can act as a vital player in making citizens' voice felt in governance. Civil society organisations are sine qua non of efficiency and effectiveness and legitimacy of the government in a democracy. Through the above mentioned tasks, the civil society organisations would be able to develop a political culture based on democratic values so that legitimacy can be created and thereby play a role in transforming the subject political culture into participatory one.

REFERENCES

1. Ramashray Roy, *Captive Vision, Ideas as Weapon*, Aganta Publications, Delhi 1993, p.19.
2. Angana Kaw Bhagat, *Election and Electoral Reforms in India,* Vikas Publishing House, New Delhi 1996, p. 4.
3. S.E. Finer, *Comparative Governments*, The Penguin Press, Allen Law, 19702 pp. 63-68.
4. Viscount Bryce, *Modern Democracies,* London 1921, Vol. II, p. 9.
5. *Ibid.*
6. S.E. Finer, *op.cit.*
7. H.W.R., Wade, *Constitutional Fundamentals,* ELBS, 1980, pp. 24-40.
8. Richard J Schaefer, *Sociology,* Mc Graw Hill, 2001, p. 428.
9. E. Smith, *Elections in Developing Countries,* Macmillan, London, 1960.
10. Hardwari Lal, "Twilight of Democracy". *The Hindustan Times*, Dec. 23, 1995, p.11.
11. Karlson, Nils, *The State of State: Invisible Hands in Politics and Civil Society,* Transaction, SA 2002.
12. Gideon Baker, *Civil Society and Democratic Theory, Alternative Voices,* Routledge, London.
13. Rajesh Tandon and Ranjita Mohanty, *Civil Society and Governance,* Samskriti, New Delhi, 2002, p. 6.
14. Rajesh Tandon, "The Civil- Society Governance Interface", in Rajesh Tandon and Ranjitha Mohanty (eds), *Does Civil Society Matter,* Sage Publications, New Delhi, 2003, pp. 64-66.
15. L.K. Advani, *et al.,* (eds.) *Electoral System in India: Need for Reforms,* Panchnad Research Institute, Chandigarh, 1987.

27 Electoral Reforms : A Human Rights Perspective

P.S. Vijaya Natharaj

India is the largest democracy in the world. Her democracy hinges upon the principle of political equality that is evident in free polls and in multi-cornered electoral contests. Political equality is maintained through *one man, one vote and one value*. To ensure free, fair and periodic elections, the Constitution established a multi-member Election Commission as per the Constitution Amendment Act, 1993. The democratic experiences in India so far proved to be quite encouraging despite weaknesses and challenges.

Democratic system do function only when the rule of law and human rights exist along with a popular government. The foundations of democracy are strengthened by the existence of human rights and their enjoyment by the people. Human rights ensure dignity of human beings which form the life blood of democracy. The success and survival of democracy would therefore depend to a large extent on the degree to which rights are available to the people. Democracy does not merely mean a majority rule but a majority rule coupled with human rights. Democracy endangers when human rights are not guaranteed. Both democracy and human rights go together on the same track. No doubt, the reform packages so far introduced with the motive of strengthening democracy widen the scope for human rights protection and human development.

Elections constitute the signpost of democracy and serve as a medium through which attitudes, values and beliefs of the common men towards the political system and the governance of the country are reflected. However, over a period of time, India's political system underwent challenges of a lose of value and the resultant decadence of democracy. Election Commission has often expressed its concern and anxiety over the emerging trends of obstacles in guaranteeing free and fair elections. It also has made a number of recommendations to the Union Government and repeatedly reminded the urgency of changing the existing system in order to check the electoral evils and malpractices, and thereby protecting political rights and aspirations of the ordinary voters.

The Election Commission in its annual report to the Parliament in the year 1985 had suggested a number of proposals towards electoral reforms such as elimination of non-serious independent candidates, ban on contesting the elections by a person in more than two constituencies, disqualification of persons with criminal records, measures to check the evils of booth capturing etc. The Union Government too in its part has set up many committees in order to cleanse the elections. The reports of the Tarkunde Committee 1975, the Goswami Committee 1990 and Indirajit Gupta Committee 1998 etc. have made comprehensive recommendations for electoral reforms. The report of the Sarkaria Commission on Centre-State relations suggested the adoption of necessary measures to overcome the emerging undemocratic practices in the existing electoral system. The need for electoral reforms has been thus a priority agenda for the successive governments. The recent decades witnessed remarkable efforts being made by the Parliament, Election Commission and the Supreme Court in the direction of electoral reforms.

India is the land of frequent elections, ranging from Local Self Governments to the state legislatures, the Parliament and to the Head of the Nation. One of the positive effects of this is that it contributes to nation building. There are also some negative aspects of this. Often elections widen the scope for causing damage to life and property. No election so far has proved violence free. No election is hundred per cent free, fair and transparent. The threat of boycott of elections is always there. No election is free from the play of money and muscle power. We also see the presence of persons with the charges or records of corruption in elections. The practice of booth capturing, blackmailing and intimidation of the voters has become a regular feature. Indian democracy survives even in the midst of such undesirable practices. Every electoral process starts and ends with varying degrees of violations of human rights of the ordinary voters. Loss of life of kith and kin, parents, sons and daughters and bread earners; political assassinations of leaders and causing damages to crores worth of public property are the common features in election all over the world including in India.

During the 2009 Lok Sabha elections in India, there were incidents of organised violence in the strongholds of Maoists and Naxalite groups and stray and isolated incidents brought home by party loyalists in many other parts. In the first phase of election on 16th April itself there were reports of killing of 19 people including five poll officials and 10 security personnel, setting fire to voting machines, attacks on voters and polling workers and destroying election vehicles. During the third and fourth phases, on April 30 and May 7 respectively, there were reports of bomb attacks in West Bengal, killing and causing injury to voters and paramilitary forces there. Cases of stabbed to death over clashes between rival party workers were reported both in Tamil Nadu and in West Bengal. There were numerous cases of voter omission from the electoral roll as reported in Tamil Nadu and in Kerala and thereby materialised denial of right to vote. Election Commission ordered repoll in 46 polling stations in different parts of the country on varying reasons including violence. One of the positive steps taken by the Election commission to the successful conduct of election was the arrangements made for special transport to shuttle the refugees of Kandhamal district of Orissa from the refugee camps to the polling booths, and thus making a high voter turnout.

Recent Electoral Reforms and Right Protections

The first and concrete step towards cleansing India's public life in the form of a comprehensive amendment to the electoral law was taken up by the enactment of Anti-Defection Law on 31st January 1985 through 52nd Constitutional Amendment Bill. The law is the culmination of series of efforts made by successive governments. The effort was in response to the resolution passed in the Lok Sabha for a move initiated by a Congress member Sri. P. Venkatasubbiah. On 11th August 1967, the Government constituted a committee under the chairmanship of Y.B. Chavan to suggest the feasibility to control the political defection. As a result, the 32nd Amendment Bill or Anti-Defection Bill was introduced in Lok Sabha on 17th May, 1973. However the Bill lapsed following the dissolution of the House in January, 1977. The debate to curb defections was still on the stage when the Janata Party came to power in 1977 which too set up a committee comprising Morarji Desai, Charan Singh, Jagjivan Ram and L.K. Advani to examine as to how political defections could be prevented. But the government itself encouraged defection in Rajya Sabha to command its majority in the House. 1960s and 70s were the two decades that spearheaded defection politics in India. For instance, between 1967 and 1970, 138 members of Lok Sabha defected. In the case of MLA's it was 1504 for the same period.

A turning point emerged in the direction of electoral reform when Rajiv Gandhi assumed power with thumping majority in the 1984 election. One of the major contributions of his government was the enactment of Anti-Defection Act, 1985. The Act was widely welcomed, because defections had made democracy a mockery for decades. However, there were many loopholes in the Act that gives a fresh meaning to the concept of defection. The Anti-defection Act 1985 was amended again in 2003 taking into account of the experiences over a period of two decades. The Amendment provides a limited scope for political defection of the types of 'aya rams' and 'gaya rams'. The Amendment made the elected members obligatory to act in a reasonable way of the voters, to whom they are responsible. The will and desire of the voters are made supreme against the elected ones. The Amendment confirmed that the elected members shall have loyalty to both the voters and to the party to which they are elected

Direction to furnish information about the past records, revealing economic assets, and liabilities and the criminal antecedents of the contesting candidates became the second most important step followed by the enactment of anti defection towards electoral reform. In a judgment on May 2, 2000, the Supreme Court of India held that "the little man of this country would have basic elementary right to know full particulars of a candidate who is to represent in Parliament and in the State Legislatures". The content of the view is that the voter has the right to have a clear and correct information before making his choice. On June 28, 2002, the Election Commission issued a directive enforcing the candidates to furnish all their liabilities, assets, previous convictions and the cases in which criminal charges had been framed against them. Against the contention of both the Supreme Court and the Election Commission, an all party meeting was held on July 8, 2002 which decided that the Election Commission's Order should not be allowed to be implemented. The matter became further serious when the Parliament made an Electoral Reform in August 2002 overruling both the opinion and the directive of Supreme Court and the Election Commission respectively.

The provisions of the reform were a clear breach of voter's right to know about their candidates or representatives. Petitions were filed again in the Supreme Court against the reform as it violated the voter's right to know. The three member bench of the Supreme Court ultimately, declared that the reform made by the parliament was unconstitutional and reaffirmed that a voter has a fundamental right to know the criminal antecedents of the contestants. Accordingly, the Election Commission has directed all the Returning Officers to display the copies of nomination papers and affidavits filed by the candidates to the general public and to the media, free of cost.

As an impact of this reform, the ordinary voter now is able to know the economic assets, liabilities and the criminal records of the people who are to be adorned as members of the Parliament of the world's largest democracy. Statistics reveal the number of crorepatis, criminal records and other assets of the candidates in the light of the reform. To be specific, the number of crorepatis in the 15th Lok Sabha has increased by 98 % against the 14th Lok Sabha, that is from 154 in 2004 to 306 in 2009. Of the crorepatis, four have assets more than Rs 100 crores. The total assets of all the 543 members reach to Rs. 3075 crores, making an average of 5.12 crores. The average assets of a minister in the 15th Lok Sabha are Rs. 7.63 crores. No doubt, ordinary voter knows that India shines with corepatis in the 15th Parliament. Until 2004 election, the voter had been in the dark and not aware of the criminal history of the candidates. The number of members with criminal records increased. If in 2004, the number was 128, in 2009 it was 150. In 2009, there were 72 MPs with serious criminal records ranging from the case of rape of women to murder. One can find fault with the political parties which put up candidates taking into account of their winning chances. Voters right to know the background of the contestants is thus protected by the concerted efforts of the court.

The introduction of Electronic Voting Machine (EVM), issuing multi-purpose voter identity card and reviewing electoral roll with photo of the voter are the other recent applaudable reforms of the Election Commission that guarantees voter's right from the threat of invalidation and impersonation. The EVM was first applied on an experimental basis in a constituency in the state of Kerala during the assembly elections in 1982. In 2004 Lok Sabha elections, it was used all over the country. This is a major initiative taken by the Election Commission to make the electoral process simple, quick and trouble free. EVM was introduced with a view to reducing malpractices and improving efficiency in the conduct of elections. By this system, counting of votes becomes fast and accurate. One of the major advantages is that the EVM facilitates for no invalid votes, as every vote recorded in the machine is accounted in favor of the candidate for whom it is voted.

Prior to the introduction of EVM, the score of invalid votes, both protest invalid votes and ignorant invalid votes, went on to increase election after election despite improvements in literacy rate and political awakening. For instance, the 1989 Lok Sabha elections recorded a total of 76.3 lakhs invalid votes against the 29.5 lakhs in 1957 elections. More interestingly, invalid votes are not only confined with the ordinary voters but also with parliamentarians. The presidential election in 1992 recorded 67 invalid votes, making a value of 17199 votes. In 1991, The High Court of Kerala, while giving its verdict on an election petition, held that the "improper reception of void votes and the improper rejection of valid votes" had materially affected the actual result of the elections in *Kovalam* and in *Edakkad* assembly constituencies in Kerala. In a civic state, the improper rejection of valid votes strengthens the cases of violation of the right of political equality. The little man's vote was not given due value on technical and flimsy grounds. The political and muscle powers determined the validity of little man's vote when the circumstances of doubtful marks prevail in the ballot paper. Introduction of EVM in Indian election guarantees the voter's right against the threat of invalidation of their votes and against the impressions of the little man's votes by muscle men.

In an attempt to improve the accuracy of the electoral rolls, the Election Commission in August 1993 ordered the issuance of Electors Photo Identity Cards (EPIC) for all the voters. Despite the EPIC was introduced to reduce the electoral malpractices, there are complaints in every election regarding improper inclusion and improper exclusion of voters from the electoral roll, and enrolling name in the roll and voting in more than one polling station illegally. The alleged voter's inclusion in and exclusion from the electoral roll in a by-election for the state legislature in Kerala in 2009 created a great concern among the public and there by the election commission took precaution and conducted the election with the help of Para military forces. Also in order to prevent impersonation of the voters and to eliminate bogus entries in the electoral roll, the election commission has taken a Himalayan task of publishing electoral roll with voters photo. Lok Sabha elections 2009 were held with the electoral roll with photo identity of the voters. In the past, impersonation was a common feature. There had been many cases of tendered votes and the arrest of persons at the polling stations while trying to impersonate the actual voter. These changes in the electoral system helps the poll administrators to conduct the election free and fair and ultimately guaranteeing the right to vote with no fear of impersonation. Despite introducing historic and revolutionary changes in the system over a period of decades, India needs some more changes in the system in order to strengthen democracy

Need of Compulsory Voting

Voting at the elections is both a constitutional and human right in a democratic system. In a liberal political system, the decision to vote or not to vote is the choice of the citizen. It is a known fact that in many of the nations including India that a considerable number of voters do not vote at all. As a result, the person who is elected with a fraction of votes in a multi-cornered contest, does not represent the majority of the voters in the constituency. In the process of cleaning the electoral system both rights and duties have equal responsibility. In ancient Hindu Society, Manu's Dharma Sutra relates all rights to duties. A notion of human rights within Hindu tradition requires duty consciousness. Based on the Hindu Tradition, Gandhi stressed that the very right to live occurs when we do the duty of the citizenship of the world. The voter shall hence consider his right to vote as his duty. When all the eligible voters voluntarily come forward or otherwise compelled to enter into the polling stations, the entry of unwanted persons in the law making bodies can be reduced to a great extent. It is reported that the statistics of voter turnout is not impressive in India and the rate continues to exist at two-third varying from 61.70% in 1951-52 elections to 61.33% in 1969, 60.48% in 1977, 60% in 1999 and 58.4% in 2009 election. In other words, the rate of 'not voting' is increasing election after election.

To overcome this menace, voting should be made mandatory or compulsory with a limited exemption in appropriate cases of persons who are seriously ill. As a step towards extending voter participation, the representation of the people's (Amendament) Act 2010 was enacted to allow an Indian citizen residing abroad to enroll in voter's list and exercise his franchise. The act came into force on 10th February 2011. For the first time the NRIs were able to vote in the Assembly election held in April 2011 in Kerala, Tamil Nadu, Puduchery, West Bengal and Assam. However the first experience of NRI votes in Kerala in 2011 Assembly Election makes a little impact. Of the total 8820 NRI s registered, only 4639 (52.60%) exercised their votes. Total participation guarantees good governance by the man of honesty and efficiency. Good governance is a desired end of the voter to ensure all-round development. The Bill passed in the Assembly of Gujarat making vote compulsory is no doubt a forward step. However, the Bill was returned by the Governor to reconsider some of the contents in the Bill. There are many arguments for and against compulsory voting. Taking into account of the general will for good governance, sense of duty is also equally important. In politics, voting is not only a right but also a duty of the citizen and thereby it shall be compulsory.

Need for an Absolute Majority of Votes

The system of voting in vogue in India is simple majority under which a candidate securing the largest number of valid votes among the contestants is declared elected. In fact, in the context of multi-cornered contests and the low level of voter turn out, a candidate with a small number of votes, even below one-third of the total valid votes, gets elected against the will of a good majority of voters. The trend is reflected from the past experiences that only 33% of the Lok Sabha members in 1952 won with absolute majority and it was 39% in 1967 and 48% in 1989. A study in1999 election in the states of South India revealed that, of the total 131 seats in four states and in two Union territories, a majority (76 seats) won the election with a minority of votes ie below 50% of votes. In 2009 Lok Sabha election in Kerala, of the total 20 seats, twelve won with a minority of votes. In actual practice, the government is formed with the support of minority voters while the majority is with the members of the opposition benches. In simple majority system, a party with a majority of seats in parliament may not have the support of the majority of the voters. It denotes that the will of the majority has not been represented or its voices have not been heard in the governance of the country. The system is against the principle of democracy and thereby weakens the democratic rule. An electoral reform is to be made to ensure that the consent of the majority as is practiced in many countries prevails.

Need for Negative Vote

Constitution of India guarantees the citizens the right to cast or not to cast his vote in the elections. It is already referred that more than one-fourth of the voters do not go to the polling stations and cast votes. Migration, ill health, out of station on the polling day, political apathy, cynical attitude against government or the system etc are the common reasons for keeping away the voters from voting. But for those who decide to vote for, are forced to vote to any one in the ballot paper or in the display of the voting machine. No alternative option is provided to him to vote against all the candidates who may be enlisted in criminal records or corruption charges or anti-social and national activities, financial liabilities or are good for nothing. This is a clear violation of the rights of voters to do according to their conscience.

Therefore, there shall definitely be a provision in the ballot paper or in the electronic voting machine to express their disapproval of the contestants altogether. Prior to the introduction of EVM, at least few had shown their disapproval by making invalidation of their votes by striking off the ballot paper top to bottom, or making vote to none or writing something against the candidates in the ballot paper etc. In the EVM such dissent are not possible. By including a column in the EVM for exercising negative vote, not only the voter's option is guaranteed but the rate of 'not voting' also can be reduced. Currently a sizeable number of voters do not vote at all due to their disenchantment with the candidates put up by the political parties. This is reflected in the decreasing trend of turn out. Democracy is strengthened when voters have a choice to mark their likes and dislikes instead of being forced to select.

Need for a Ban of Non-Serious Independents

The Goswami Committee was very much concerned about the proliferation of non-serious independent candidates in Indian elections. With the influx of their number, electoral process has been made a mockery. Since 1967 elections, their strength began to swell in an abnormal manner. For instance, there were 2694 independent candidates contested the election in 1980 election and it was 3746 in1984, 5230 in 1991 and 3289 in 2009. Of the total candidates, independents form 62.09% in 2009 against the 53.97% in 2004, 63.04 in1991 and 28.44^ in 1952 election. At the same time, the percent of the independents elected to the Lok Sabha was decreasing from 7.13% in 1952 to 1.23% in 1971, 0.32% in 1980, 0.02% in 1991, 0.92% in 2004 and 1.66% in 2009 elections. In a study conducted in Tamil Nadu Assembly Election in 1977, 1980, 1984, 1989 and in 1991, it was found that the number of independents who polled below 100 votes each increased considerably from 17 in 1977 to 1058 in 1991. Of the total 5667 independents for the said five elections, 90.33% polled below four digits of votes while just 1.66% polled above 10% votes to the total votes polled in the respective constituencies including those who saved their deposit amount and won the election. In 2009 Lok Sabha elections in Kerala, of the total 217 candidates, 105 were independents who jointly received 1.31% votes. And of them, around 30% received below 1000 votes each. To make maters worse, it is observed that many of the independents were sponsored by the major political parties to get the rival candidates defeated. Also the defeat of some serious candidates were ensured and materialised by sponsoring independents into the election fray who bear almost similar name of the rival party candidate.

No doubt, the constitution guarantees the right to contest the election on any label. But it is unethical to agree such contests making mockery of democracy with poor performance repeatedly. A study in Tamil Nadu proved that non-serious independents did not improve despite their repeated contests. For instance of the 154 independents who repeatedly contested the Assembly Election in the same constituencies in both 1989 and in 1991, 98 secured lower votes in their second attempt. Indian politics provides no scope for non-serious independents. While hearing on Rajiv Gandhi's election to the Lok Sabha in 1980, The Supreme Court held that "... the situation causes anxiety to us and we hope that the parliament will device ways to end the onslaught of democracy by the independents". Free, fair and correct choice is the fundamental right of the voter. But creating a deliberate confusion among the voters by the contest of independents, either voluntarily or sponsored by the political parties, reflects a way of exploitation of the voters. A constitutional ban of the contest of non-serious candidates becomes worthy to democracy and an exercise of political rights with appropriate choice.

India, the world's largest democracy, earns the credit of experiencing innumerable reforms aimed at cleansing the electoral system ever since the first general elections. Electoral polities of India successfully passed through may stages of development, despite many challenges and weaknesses. Many of the emerging nations learn things from India's experiences. The laws and reforms concerned with free and fair elections thus assume significance from a human rights perspective also.

REFERENCES

1. Advani L.K, 'Electoral Reform: Excluding Non-Serious Candidates' *Indian Express,* Nov 9, 1991.
2. Chimanbhai Mehta, 'A New Electoral System' *Indian Express*, August 4, 1990.
3. Ganesan K, 'Electoral Reforms' *The Hindu*, Dec. 2, 1997.
4. Institute of Management in Government "National Seminar on Electoral Reforms" held on 17th September, 1991 at Thiruvananthapuram.
5. Maitreya Buddha Samantaray, 'Election Commission and its Role in Electoral Reforms', *Employment News*, Vol. xxxviii, No. 33 Nov. 15-21, 2003.
6. Malini Sehadri, 'The Real Electoral Reform' *Indian Express*, Jan. 16, 1991.
7. Malayala Manorama, March 17.2003,
8. Prem Chopra, 'For Better Governments' *The Hindu,* Jan 21, 1992.
9. Rajeev Dhavan, 'Electoral Law' *The Hindu*, March 21, 2003.
10. Ritu Rao, 'Assessing the Electoral System: A Positive Verdict' *Economic and Political Weekly,* Dec. 18, 2004.
11. Rodney P. Stiefbold 'The Significance of Void Ballots in West German Elections', *American Political Sciences Review*, June 1965 pp. 391-407.
12. Sonu Trivedi, 'Human Rights under Democracy' *Mainstream*, Dec 13, 2003.
13. Sumandeep Kaur, 'Electoral Reforms in India: Proactive Role of Election Commission' *Mainstream* Vol. XLVI, No. 49, Nov 25, 2008.

14. Venugopal KK, "De-democrating the Electoral System" The Hindu, 9 April 2009.

15. Vijaya Natharaj P.S, 'Indian Electoral System and Invalid Votes' *ISDA* Journal Vol.3, nos. 3 & 4, 1993, pp. 258-261.

16. _____________ 'Independent Contestants and the Elections in India: With Special Reference to Tamil Nadu' *Punjab Journal of Politics*, Vol. xviii, No.1., June 1994, pp. 29-42

17. _____________ 'Voter Turn out in Indian Elections' *Loyola Journal of Social Sciences,* Vol. xiii, No. 2 Jul-Dec 1999 pp. 192.197.

18. _____________ 'Right to know and Indian Electoral Reform' *Mainstream* Vol. XLIII No 43 Oct 15, 2005, pp. 23-27.

19. _____________ 'Lok Sabha Election, 2009: Kerala's Experiences' *Holistic Thought*, Vol. VIII No.1 82, Jan-Dec 2009, pp. 133-144.

Part V
Agenda for Electoral Reforms

28 Agenda for Electoral Reforms

P.J. Alexander

Electoral Reform in this country is not the result of a single piece of legislation, but the outcome of sustained pressures and persuasion put up by activists and civil society groups over the years. From the bold foray of Sukumar Sen in the 1950's till today we have traversed extensive ground. However, electoral reforms is an unfinished national agenda. I do hope and wish that the deliberations of the present Seminar would bring about further necessary changes in our electoral system.

It is not the attempt of this paper to catalogue with mathematical precision, the many deficient areas in our electoral process; the attempt is only to identify the most glaring and deleterious, while pressing home, the crying need to commit ourselves to eternal vigilance against the system sliding into old ruts or vested interests neutralising through clever political ploys, the gains of reforms effected. It is our sacred commitment to make our electoral system as perfect as we can. It is remembered that no human institution can ever be perfect; yet the struggle for reform and reconstruction should continue without pause, relating itself to the changes taking place in the socio political milieu of this country. A zero-defect electoral system is the very soul of a clean and healthy democracy. The simple message of this Paper is that the struggle for electoral reforms should be carried forward relentlessly and with very strong commitment, till we make it as perfect as human institutions can be.

As we attempt to outline an agenda for electoral reforms, what strikes us as most unusual is the presence of millionaires and billionaires in our legislatures. That in a country which was led to freedom by bapu, clad in just a *dhoti,* not many years ago, in a country, where those below the poverty line still account for nearly 50% of the population and in a country where the beneficiaries of the social justice agenda of the state are quite large, it is shocking that the legislatures and Parliament teem with crore-patis. "In the 2004 General Elections about 1000 candidates out of 5000 had declared assets of over one crore. 136 of crore-patis made it to Parliament. There are about 800 MLA's around the country with declared assets of about one crore"[1]. The data published by the Election Commission and other organizations freely available in the internet give us a graphic picture of their assets at the beginning of their tenure as MLAs/MPs and their present worth. This paper has consciously avoided reproducing those nauseating figures though they would have helped to expose the ground realities. Thus in our legislatures today we have more rich people than poor. It was Jesus who said that "where your riches are, there your hearts would be". So we have many representatives in the legislatures with their hearts in the wrong place. It is doubtful whether it is with "WE THE PEOPLE OF INDIA", who solemnly resolved to constitute India in to a Socialist, Secular, Democratic, Republic and to secure to all its citizens social, economic and political justice along with liberty, equality and fraternity with dignity of the individual.

When we discuss electoral reforms, the massive assets of these rich men, stare us in the face compelling us to ask a number of inconvenient questions. The first of these is 'How do they swamp the Legislatures when we do not find a fair share of our professionals/technocrats/managers/ scientists/ teachers/lawyers and such others who form part of our collective intellectual assets in the legislatures and Parliament?' The Election Commission has laid down guidelines putting a limit to the expenditure that can be incurred by a candidate seeking election to the legislatures and parliament. Can we honestly believe that these Members of the Legislatures, kept their expenditure within these limits? Where did all this money flow in? How does anyone recoup the money so spent in 60 months? Who can afford not to recoup such huge amounts at least in the long run? There are Observers of the Election Commission who visit the Constituencies and look into the range and quantity of propaganda/ canvassing material on display, to determine whether they indicate any ostentatious display of money power. In rare instances the Observers also intervene to remove some offensive material. Are these the heads of expenses on which huge amounts are spent? It is evident to even casual observers of the electoral scene in the different Constituencies in the different States that each State has developed its own strategy to overcome the restraints imposed by the Election Commission. It is widely believed that nominations are secured often by remitting hefty amounts in to the party coffers. From that point onwards, the man with money takes the lead in ensuring that he has the support of the party functionaries, workers and ofcourse voters. The money actually spent is obviously much more than what is permitted. Thus when a rich man and another with less resources contest, albeit with the support of political parties, there is no level playing ground in the electoral contest. There are several parties which mobilize enormous amount of funds, by making hay while the sun shines. 'The sun shine' depends on the portfolios, they handle (d) and also the period they were in office. Collecting funds to face future elections is an article of faith with many political parties. The 'money power' a candidate can flaunt certainly gives him an advantage. And how does such money reach the candidate? Not certainly from legitimate sources. Money power spawns muscle power. Money power breeds corrupt practices, many of which go unnoticed.

This author on the strength of his personal experience as a self appointed observer of elections in different States can assert that money power is employed in various forms and the capacity to spend money at different stages of elections tilts the balance and money power is capable of hyjacking any fair electoral process. Entire villages are served with liquor, food packets, cloth and money to see that the voters favour a particular candidate. These gifts perhaps do not always come from the candidate, but from his promoters who are confident of reaping a rich harvest once he is elected. The Electoral identity cards of the voters of an entire village/community/faction are collected ahead of the polls and are returned to the voters only on the day of the poll along with the voters' slip. It is neither necessary nor possible to detail the various ways in which money power is employed for electoral advantage. It was indicated above that money power brings with it muscle power. Muscle power belongs to organized criminal gangs. The two, money power and muscle power, together make an awesome combination, capable of thwarting any free or fair elections. So the first priority today is to ensure that money power is curbed and expenditure incurred by any candidate/political party is put strictly within permissible limits. How this can be done is a matter for serious deliberation[2]. A suggestion that can be made at this stage is to empower Independent observers/organisations within each constituency to monitor expenditure being incurred by each candidate, his support organisations, his party etc, and be associated with the audit of the final accounts submitted by each candidate. It is conceded that it would be difficult to get such a provision in the Statute, but a beginning can be made by independent observers/organisations faithfully recording all information on expenditure that come to their notice and submitting such information to the Election Commission for its consideration. This would be a beginning and would come to be accepted as a reliable source of information, in due course. After all, we obtained a favourable order to disclose the educational standard and the criminal record of the candidate only by knocking at the doors of the Supreme Court for years. If the observers appointed by the Election Commission in the midst of their non professional engagements (sight seeing, cuisine – tasting or crudely attempting to discipline errant lower functionaries by forcing them to do symbolic acts of penance) find time to interact with the independent observers/organisations, it would lend the efforts, abintio, credibility.

In the background of mounting expenditure on which nobody has any control and the advantage accruing to those who have unlimited resources, it is sometimes suggested that the State should fund elections. This suggestion has several merits and quite a few demerits. The ideal situation is one where it would be possible for any voter who has a track record of clean public service and who has the confidence that he has something to contribute to the government of this country and in building up a just society, to contest an election to the legislature/parliament with the means at his disposal, limiting the expenditure to what is permissible. Would State funding of elections really inhibit those who are rich from spending their money too, besides government funds? A study conducted by an organisation with which the present author is associated, brought out in unmistakable terms that a serious candidate contesting for a seat in the parliament (Lok Sabha) today should be prepared to spend about Rs.25 crores. Despite the vast improvement in communications, it is very expensive to get in touch with the voters and as a result only very rich people can aspire to contest an election to the legislature/parliament. This is thus an issue that should receive our serious attention. If money power can deny a level playing ground to the different candidates in the field, the electoral process cannot be said to be free or fair.

Just like the rich, those with criminal records also contest elections and among our MLAs and MPs those with criminal records are quite a few as can be seen from the data published in the print and electronic media. At present disqualification is limited to conviction for a certain period and it barely affects the large majority with criminal records. It is only too well known that in India, those with political influence can often, if not always, remain out of the reach of the law – by resorting to a number of shortcuts. Involvement in crime and conviction by the courts are two issues which are poles apart. Therefore restricting disqualification to conviction for a certain period does not really serve the purpose of providing for such a disqualification. When some one who is politically powerful commits a crime, silence afflicts everyone, from the victim to the guardians of law. Complainants can be intimidated, complaints can be burked; serious offences can be doctored and substituted by mild /

trivial offences, accused and witnesses can be substituted and FIRs can be kept under investigation for ages and cases can be charge sheeted for sure acquittal. Therefore a conviction for a certain period acting as a disqualification affects only a hand full among the large numbers who practise crime. The state has been in recent times withdrawing a large number of cases awaiting trial, out of political considerations and thereby sparing the accused the rigours of a trial. Police investigation can be politically tampered with at all stages. From the registration of an FIR, the police process is subject to political interference. There are a thousand ways in which those with political patronage can mock the criminal justice process. It is time that we demand that those tainted by involvement in serious crimes are disqualified at the very outset, from contesting elections. If the police are not free from political interference, and cannot act professionally and objectively, disqualifying a candidate on the basis of criminal records would be too unreliable a ground. For instance, if figuring in an FIR would disqualify a political rival, would not FIRs be registered by pliant police officers in collusion with their political masters? Such instances are not uncommon in the public services. Therefore disqualifying a person from contesting the elections on the basis of his record of criminal activities is an area that has to be treaded cautiously. It is for political parties to do the initial sieving to eliminate those with a criminal past. The statute has to be suitably amended to make involvement in crime a disqualification. This would not only strengthen the process for free and fair elections but would also preserve and nurture the rule of law. Short-circuiting the judicial process has become all too common and it has to be stoutly resisted.

Another area that should receive our attention is the stage of pre-poll arrangements – like enlistment of new voters, preparation of electoral rolls, location of polling stations, making available voters list for verification/correction/addition, deployment of police personnel both local and para-military in constituencies vulnerable to violence etc. In fact the last by election in Kannur District provides the material for a case study on pre-poll arrangements. The pre election stage of induction of new voters, transfer of voters from one constituency to another, establishing the identity of the voters and preventing duplication and ensuring honestly and fairly that only those who have unassailable credentials to be in the voters list of a constituency alone are in the voters list, are all very important functions which cannot be left to teachers and lower functionaries of the various government departments in view of their unionization under different political parties and paraded loyalty to one or other political parities. It should be seriously considered whether the entire range of functions, should be out-sourced and entrusted to professionals without any political bias. It also follows that to eliminate arbitrariness and unfairness, the registration of voters should be made as simple as possible and access should be given to members of the public/vigilantes/whistle blowers to inspect such documents without hassle. In the present age of electronic processing of data these measures cannot create either more work or cause delay. It would ensure that all those who are qualified to be voters from a constituency are registered as voters in that constituency. The initiative of the civil society is crucial here[3]. We all look forward to the *16-digit Unique Identification Number* to be assigned by the Unique Identification Authority of India (UIDAI) to make the electoral process free of a lot of malpractices.

When it comes to actual polling, every voter should have the unlimited freedom to come to the polling booth and cast his vote. The conditions required for peaceful polling is both law and order and strict overseeing by the polling officers. True, booth capturing, ballot box snatching and other criminal activities have come down, but not gone altogether. Even in the state of Kerala we hear of "party villages" where no one but the 'party's' candidate is permitted to woo the voters and canvass his candidature. This is a complete negation of the right to freedom. Just as every voter should have the freedom to march to the tunes of any drummer, any drummer should have the freedom to play his tune before any elector. Denying such freedom would make a mockery of free and fair elections. Therefore those who maintain law and order should ensure that every candidate and every supporter of the candidate should be free to approach every voter. Where such freedom is not available, such village/area should go under neutral police supervision and the Election Commission should empower its officers to take necessary steps against such hobbesian state of nature. The location of the polling booths are very important here and we must even consider mobile polling booths for those who are denied the physical freedom to come out and vote, to whom so ever they would like to.

Low voter turnout or 'voter apathy' is a phenomenon, seen all over the country. In many constituencies, the total votes polled are some times less than 50% of the electorate. A number of candidates come in under the flags of different political parties, and there are also a host of independents – persons with names closely identical with that of serious candidates – spoilers – being fielded to confuse the voters, sundry fortune / fund seekers entering the fray, on their own crowd the ballot paper. In this context, low voter turnout can make the first – past – the post system that we have, severely deficient. Where the winning candidate gets the highest number of votes among the candidates, but not sufficiently large a chunk to make him truly representative, it would be difficult to assume that he has had the support of the majority of voters of that Constituency. Therefore ensuring that every voter exercises his franchise is desirable. It may be recalled that at the start of the Republic itself, we had provided universal adult suffrage, without any riders, and later lowered the age limit for participation in the elections to the Local Self Government Institutions. Like various other virtues of a good and responsible citizen, taking part in the poll process should also be taken as a prized – virtue. While one should have the freedom to stay away as a sort of *'conscientious objector'*, to register his reservations on the contestants – till we have a negative vote and the right to recall – increased, voluntary and enthuastic participation in the polls must be part of our enlightened political culture. In fact it should be part of the political socialisation process of the people at large. Political education by political movements as well as political parties should lay strong emphasis on active involvement of the citizenry in the electoral process. On a suggestion from Narendra Modi, chief minister of Gujrat, that participation in voting should be made compulsory, there where sharp reactions, all of which were not entirely objective nor with an open mind. The prejudice against the Chief Minister, it would appear, influenced the range of response. To contend that asking every qualified voter to vote, i.e., once in five years – is a violation of personal freedom is carrying the idea of personal freedom too far. Participation in the electoral / political process should be seen as the exercise of a fundamental right of greater import, than any fancied inroad in to the realm of personal freedom. This is an issue that has to be seriously debated, ignoring the association with Narendra Modi, who is at the best, only a recent spokesman for the proposal. Others have raised the very same issue much earlier[4]. Similarly the question of giving the right to vote to Non Resident Indians (NRIs) also has to be seriously considered, in view of the very high ratio of migration from certain areas in states like Kerala[5].

We have seen that the obstacles in the course of free and fair elections are not uniform in the different States, even in the districts or constituencies. This demands a greater role for the civil society. There is definitely a mood in the country in general to condemn malpractices, high-handedness and blatant violations of the provisions of the Representation of the People Act, the Code of Conduct for Political Parties issued by the Election Commission and the various directions issued by the Chief Electoral Officers. This certainly is the outcome of the vigilance mounted by the Fourth Estate, the electronic media in particular, to which we all owe a deep debt of gratitude. Now the issue is how to keep the media free and independent in the background of 'Prepared Propaganda' being published in the print media for payment, absolving the beneficiary of all liabilities. It is axiomatic that like power, influence also would corrupt and corrupt absolutely. Is not "Eternal vigilance the price of liberty"? Nothing should be left to chance since it is clear that given an opportunity those who handle power would manipulate it to ensure that they continue to enjoy the fruits of power. The pre-election preparations are therefore as important as the preparations on the day of the poll and the post poll arrangements.

NOTES AND REFERENCES

1. See Liberty Institute, New Delhi, empoweringindia.org/eci.nic.in.
2. In an Article in the *Mathrubhumi* Weekly (April 11-17, 2010) the well known journalist and commentator B.R.P. Bhaskar has discussed this issue while analyzing the proliferation of political parties in the State.
3. For a strong plea on increased involvement of the Civil Society, see the author in 'Free and, Fair Elections and Beyond: The Case for People's Initiative in India, Yesterday and Today', T.P.S. Nair, (Ed) Trivandrum, 2009.
4. In Australia for instance voting is Compulsory; failure would invite a stiff fine and an explanation from the voter.
5. This suggestion appears to be welcome in Kerala. The Indian Lawyers' Congress has suggested that the names of all Indian Passport holders residing continuously aboard for six months or more would be included in the Voters List (See *The Hindu*, Trivandrum, June 25, 2010). The thinking of the Government of India also appears to favour the idea.

29 Electoral Reforms—How it can be Done

Jayaprakash Narayanan

I know many of you say that there is a lot of corruption, but you have to come to Hyderabad and Bangalore to see what corruption really is. Kerala is definitely not entirely touched by political decay. Naturally, Keralites do not understand the enormity of the crisis in this country. This environment insulates or relatively sanitises us from what is going on in the rest of the country. I came from one State and I flew through another State (Andhra Pradesh and Karnataka) both of these arguably are the best examples of what today's politics is. Another State which is almost as bad is Tamil Nadu. It would be utterly illogical to argue that the people of India, because of the lack of values, are more corrupt, or more unfit for democracy.

We have a strong civilisation ethos, a great history and I am sure you know all about it. What is wrong is not values alone. We should have institutions to sustain these values. It is like water in a bottle. The values are the water and you have them. But suppose, there is no bottle to keep a check, the water spills over. It evaporates and in no time, disappears. It is the container that gives the water its shape and makes it useful. Institutions are "the containers". Yes, we require values, but never forget the importance of Institutions. Therefore, people who are questioning laws are really questioning the constitution and in turn questioning the existence of governance.

In our country, far too much confusion arises in a variety of areas. There is no logical consistency or clarity; we mix A with B. With a few people, a lot has been done but everything is mixed up. This is not right. If we are all really together in the pursuit of fundamental change in this country that we desire, then Kerala, the intellectual nerve centre of this country must look at things with more clarity and with more logical consistency. That we require values is undeniable. But we also require institutions to nurture and sustain those values; that are what laws are for. A law cannot merely be a statement of intent. It ought to be a mechanism to enforce values and to sustain them. It is this institution that is to give the right kind of incentives and the right kind of behaviour and it is in this spirit that I am going to discuss on electoral reforms.

What are the incentives? What are the institutional mechanisms that will help alter our behaviour? In our anxiety to look for what is wrong, we often miss what is right with our democracy. Notwithstanding our woes and traverse, we have actually done reasonably well in our democracy and its evolution over the last sixty years or so. Myron Weiner, the late sociologist and political scientist, wrote extensively on democracy and ofcourse about the democracy in India. He came out with four postulates to determine whether or not a country is a functioning democracy. The general rule is, if a country in its title has the word 'people' or 'democratic', that country is by definition 'undemocratic' and 'autocratic'. There is not a single country, which once included the word "people" in its title, which is actually democratic. So we must not go by self-deceptions. We must go by certain objective yardsticks. Prof.Weiner developed four yardsticks. First thing is "competitive elections". It is actually true competition for power. Almost every State in India has this intense electoral competition therefore, we score high. Second is "political freedom". Competition without the freedom to articulate, communicate or mobilise the public is meaningless. Again nobody can dispute this and it is a fact that India has enormous freedom for its people. The third is that the winners do not punish the losers merely by virtue of the fact that they lost the elections. You often see, in Bangladesh and Pakistan and a few other countries, the former President or Prime Minister is beheaded, shot, executed or incarcerated. In India, you do not see this. One does not lose his head or his liberty merely because he has lost elections. It is an important thing but we take it for granted because it is so ordinary for us. It should be realised that it is a very important ingredient of a functioning democracy. Without this, the elected government is only a cipher, a Junta or a coterie in its governing. The fourth postulate of the theory is that the elected governments are not figureheads; they exercise power and make policies and are "only" accountable to the electors. Our country seems to essentially satisfy all these postulates so then, is there true democracy in India?

By these four yardsticks, we are doing pretty well, in fact, admirably well. That is why the rest of the world is in awe of India. Even with our diversity in languages and culture we do satisfy the thresholds. It is unbelievable what we are accomplishing as a country. Look at Belgium a tiny country with just the Flemish and French linguistic groups. How hard is it for both these wings to live in peace with each other? Our own neighbour, Sri Lanka has seen a civil war and enormous strife, for the past twenty five years. Just two languages and yet they could not accommodate. We have definitely done pretty well in a lot of ways but the reason why we are still concerned with reforms is, we can do much better. Let us look at some other things that agitate us. I will only mention them because we all know these issues. The first is an inexhaustible appetite for illegitimate funds in elections and in politics. My opponent in Andhra Pradesh for elections to the State Legislative Assembly has spent Rs. 30 crore. You talk of four crore rupees for Parliament. Here is another news, A candidate from a rural constituency in Andhra Pradesh spent twenty five crore rupees. He told me by his own admission. Twenty five crore rupees for a losing campaign and mind you, I am only talking about State Assemblies. Here is yet another incident. In a village called Dacheppalli in Guntoor district in Andhra Pradesh, the Panchayat sarpanch (the panchayats here, unlike in Kerala, are bigger, about 10000-15000 population) spent four crore in the panchayat election. Unlike in Kerala, Panchayats are inconspicuous in Andhra Pradesh. Power has not been given to them. local government is not very important and yet four crore has been spent. The money spent is astronomical. There is an inexhaustible appetite for illegitimate funds.

I am proud to say that Lok Satta Party was the one that started the whole disclosure of criminal antecedents of candidates. In 1998-99, when this disclosure started it created a sensation in the country. Nobody thought that we would be able to list out the names of murderers and criminals in politics. We lived to tell the tale. I fought valiantly to get the law in place, but I know, it does not mean much now. Yet, I believe it is a symbolic victory of the people in this country. It was said that 800 MLAs of India are crorepatis and therefore, things are going wrong. That is not wrong at all. The people should ask these "crorepati MLAs" to disclose their assets and show whether the acquired wealth is legitimate or illegitimate. The problem is this un-disclosed illegitimate wealth. By that yardstick, I should say that there is not a single legislator, who is not a multi crorepati. So these disclosures, I mean, pretending that we have got a fantastic framework in place and if we come out with such data and do nothing, is a big shame. Because, the problem is not that people with money come into politics though it has been true throughout the history but that, people come to politics for making illegitimate money. We are barking at the wrong tree. It does not matter, if a multi crorepati comes into politics. It matters a great deal if somebody comes into politics with intention to make money through public office. The tragedy of India is not crorepatis coming into politics, but the fact that people come to make crores through politics. Let us not confuse the issues. Every distinguished member is opposed to this for political reasons. I disclose money because I make money legitimately. I am in a very, very competitive profession. Perhaps one of the best in the country. I have invested wisely. A colleague of mine, whose name I would not like to mention, has made an income disclosure of Rs. 50,000 per year. Most people in India know that he has assets worth a few thousand crore and yet his disclosure is only Rs.50,000. So do not get carried away by such disclosures. As the author of "Disclosure Law", as the man who fought for it for ten to twelve years now, I believe that, and now I say it, disclosure is just a tiny little symbolic step in politics. It does not necessarily mean anything. If you make your assumptions and come to the conclusions on the basis of that data, you are completely wrong. In Andhra Pradesh, for instance, one man is said to have made around Rs.20,000crore in public office in a span of five years. They are talking about hundred-thousand crores and we could not bring him down. I have a simple yardstick when somebody mentions a number. In terms of corruption, I bring it down by a factor of five immediately because there is lot of exaggeration in India. So the twenty-thousand I mentioned earlier is after bringing it down. This is the tragedy of India. Much of the money is not spent for campaigning. Many people including Prime Minister Manmohan Singh believe that the common people are very fond of the folly of public funding of elections. With all due respect, I give it one word 'rubbish'. The money spent is not on campaigning. The four crores are not spent for campaigning. I fought an election in Hyderabad City, possibly the biggest constituency of Andhra Pradesh against three candidates, who spent crores of rupees. My expenditure was Rs. 4.5 lakhs. At least I could break the taboo that if Mahatma Gandhi contests in a State like Andhra Pradesh, he would lose the deposit because he would contest honourably. Apart from the fact that I could win the elections with Rs. 4.5 lakhs, the real issue is that reaching out to people does not cost much money. It is a lie; it is a big myth that you require four crore to communicate. But it is true that you require four crore or forty crore in Andhra Pradesh for Parliament in order to buy the vote, distribute liquor, hire criminals and bribe policemen in every election.

If it is the illegitimate expenditure through illegitimate funds that needs to be challenged, then that can never be addressed by legitimate funding for campaign. Public funding of elections assumes that poor and good people are coming in, who have no money to campaign and fight the elections and they require that money. This is not the reality. The reality is radically different. Right now, in Andhra Pradesh, a big 'tamasha' is going on. One man, whose claim to fame is the fact that he is "the son of somebody" who has made tones of money in public office, is challenging the establishment. Many people in Andhra Pradesh watch and believe the television news. Almost all the Telugu channels retain some sanitary hope. But if you watch TV in Andhra Pradesh today, every channel is full of this man and his political tours. They claim that this is the making of a "political wave". Once upon a time we had the *zamindari* and *jagirdari* systems and like them, today, each constituency/district is the empire of such politicians and they are the unchallenged kings of the constituencies and districts in a rigidly democratic India. There is a causal link between each of these points that I am describing. Nothing is new in Andhra Pradesh, each of the things I told you about. May be some of the numbers are startling you. But I want you to see the causal link and therefore, the consequences.

What now? What about the people? Why are the democratic citizens, the free citizens in a Republic, who are the sovereign, failing themselves? They are failed not by somebody else but themselves because a vote is substantially delinked from public good. In the minds of the people it does not matter who is elected because no matter who is elected, things will roughly remain the same. Therefore, the only benefit you get out of voting is not better governance and better future, but a day's money and liquor and may be freebies for tomorrow. That is the reason why, increasingly, in many parts of India, free rice, free power, free colour TV, a sum of Rs. 2000 a month etc. have become the currency of elections. It is not a misconception and I say this because we have not shown the people that something different is possible. We have not ourselves demonstrated that electoral outcomes can make difference in their lives in a significant way. In a way, they can see, they can understand, they can measure, they can taste, they can relate to. If the Governments are elected authentically and relatively decent people are in Legislatures it is nothing short of a miracle.

In almost all States, save Kerala and to some extent West Bengal, honesty and survival in public office are no longer compatible. Even if you clean up the elections, say, by a miracle, and all nice guys come in through a revolution, given the present situation it is tough for an honest Chief Minister to survive in office even for hundred days. Narendra Modi, is perhaps the one significant exception. Whatever be his other political angularities, his personal honesty is generally respected, this considering only certain factors. Probably to a significant extent Nitish Kumar of Bihar is another exception and of course, Delhi's Chief Minister is yet another example. I am assuming Bengal and Kerala are of a different league. But otherwise, honesty and survival in public office are not compatible or at least increasingly incompatible. We have to address that too. There is no point in giving moral lectures if you do not create a frame work in which these can improve because after all, as Gladston said, "the purpose of a Government is to make it easy for people to do good and difficult to do evil." That is what the Government should do. This is what the Constitution, the law and the institutions are all about. Social divisions are exacerbated. If things like money and liquor fail in elections there are always the eternal caste, region, religion and language factors. You divide people on a river water dispute like Andhra Pradesh and Karnataka, Tamil Nadu and Karnataka or on the basis of sub castes like the differences among Kammas, Reddys, Kapus etc in Andhra Pradesh and of course, Hindu – Muslim differences never end. We can always incite people on caste, religion, region, language. Divisions are exacerbating. Electoral reforms have to be looked at with this in mind. Therefore, what is that we have to do? I will now come to a brief list because I have already got an analysis, though it is not exhaustive but just illustrative. Let us call it a bird's eye view. I will try to look at the issues with some clarity. But first we must address one issue, the Election Commission and its role. Today, for me, much of how elections are being observed by observers from IAS or non-IAS from this state or from other states etc. is inconsequential. Election Commission is an over-glorified institution. I am making a controversial point here. We are glad that it has been by and large independent and reasonably effective. It is solely technical, bureaucratic and administrative.

It is doing reasonably well, but not exceptionally well. We are grateful. But is the Election Commission the answer to India's political problems? It is not. In fact sometimes it can well be the cause of the problems. I do not want to go into details. The commission is a creation of the Constitution and law. The commission can operate within the boundaries of law. The commission knows very well that the money spent in elections in most parts of India is an average of 20 to 30 Cr., for Parliament and 5 to 10 Crore for the Assembly. The Commission knows fully well. But what can the Commission do? Nothing. If the giver and the taker, both are content, the Commission can do precious little. There is actual evidence, like for instance, the paid elections which has been in news for the last five six years. There is enough evidence and it is also proven, but what has the election commission done- "nothing". Let us not pretend that election commission is the answer, just because somebody says that the election commission has fifty television cameras in and around it.

Rama Devi, was the only lady who served as the Chief Election Commissioner, for a short span of time. It is a male-dominated institution. I do not remember any senior official, who was a woman, in the commission so far. Just because somebody is listening, evidently, media is exaggerating and giving it a lot of importance. But the Election Commission is not the answer to India's problems. It definitely is not. I have seen something deeper. Therefore, coming to the specifics of the agenda in the contemporary situation, the first is the disclosure of candidate details. Let us not overstate its importance but use it to the extent that we can. The media can actually go into the details of the disclosure particularly the financial antecedents and to see to what extent they are verifiable and then bring pressure on the system asking for an improvement. But unfortunately for us, the media is incompetent and thus a void is created. Simply repeating what has already been said is not the job of media.

As far as political parties are concerned, it goes without saying that we have to democratise our political Parties. The argument that finances are a part of a political party's "internal affairs" is absolutely wrong. If you are running a civil society organisation, an NGO, as defined under Art.19 (1) (c) of the constitution of India - a group of free citizens forming an organisation in pursuit of their own goals, as long as the goals are not unconstitutional, as long as the methods are not illegal, nobody has a right to touch them. They can do what they want. They can sleep, work or do anything under the sun. That is exactly what liberty is about. But being a political party is different. They have the power to make laws, to influence the behaviour of people and to regulate it. So, the moment somebody comes asking for "the power" to govern you, remember that his liberty ought to be curtailed. Your future is far more important than his liberty. Do not get confused. The freedom that is available to a society is different from the freedom that is available to a political party. The parties must be regulated by law. It is absolutely certain. Many countries have this mechanism. Germany has a federal law on membership, and on leadership choice. This mechanism works.

On the choice of candidates and of course on accounts, *i.e.,* raising of funds and utilisation – a very rigorous legal mechanism with accountability is essential. But there should not even be a remote attempt to look at their policies. It is their business. The problem is that the moment you regulate, the regulators become crooks, either being directly corrupt or partisan. So, the trick is, how do you create this mechanism? It is with public awareness that you regulate it. The only question that should be asked is "how" and not "what" because "what" a political party is doing is only his business but "how" it is doing it is what concerns us as citizens. These are two different things. A policy is said to be decided in the market place of ideas, which is what elections are for. Therefore, there must be clarity on where to recall and to what extent.

"Money power" - I do not know, how many of you are aware but India has an exceptionally sound law on political funding. I should know. I am one of the authors of that law. In 2003, this law was enacted by a bi-partisan consensus in Parliament. I know, many will disagree with some of the elements, but I will strongly stand by that. This law provides an incentive to the donors to make contributions to legitimate political activities. Therefore, for the first time in India, individuals and corporates get a tax exemption for political contributions. The problem is not that they get a tax exemption but that this regulation is not being utilised. The problem is that many political parties take money "under the table". This money is not accounted for. I can once again proudly say that Lok Satta is the only political Party that is accounting 100% of the contributions and guaranteeing the tax exemption. No other party is doing that and I say this with complete candor. All that is being shown is a small amount. The rest is underhand.

We require a law that is applicable to all political parties, not just the recognised political parties, but for the unrecognised parties as well, with strong penalties for deviation. This law must be effectively implemented. For instance, say, if I gave a political party one lakh rupees unaccounted, put me in jail. I believe that nobody is ready to both give money as well as go to jail for doing so. You change the terms of disclosure. Give consent for parties to get funds, but also give a strong penalty in case of violation. Right now, there is no penalty and the parties are making money. The second element of that is the media ought to give free time to political parties for campaign. The law in India provides for that. Ours is one of the few countries in the world that provides for it. But this part of the law is not implemented because the rules have not been framed.

For years, I had written to the existing prime cinisters, chief election commissioners and law ministers, all in vain. But for the past three years I have stopped writing because we became a political party. This particular thing applies to recognised political parties and until we become a recognised party, I do not see why I should give my rivals all advantage, if they do not want that advantage anywhere. So, I stopped writing to them for the past three years. But really speaking, to reach out to people what is the cost in modern elections? It is television. You like it or not. We have increasingly become a television driven society. If that is taken care of by a legal mechanism in India, then the actual campaigning costs are next to nothing. But this has not been implemented. The real question is why people are willing to spend 25 crore rupees on a losing election. It is amazing. Nowhere in the world can one see this. The highest expenditure ever recorded in America, for a Congress man was ten million dollars. Highest ever! Typically, it takes more than a million dollars or half a million dollars for campaigning in the American Parliament, a country whose GDP is a lot more times higher than ours. Even today, America's GDP is 12 to 14 times as that of India. Texas State alone has more revenue, more expenditure and also more GDP than the whole of India. Texas Legislature meets once in two years. Nobody knows when they meet. Nobody knows who their MLA is. They are inconsequential.

We have to change the incentives in politics dramatically. The heart of the issue is the First Past poll system'. One extra vote: you win. Lack of one vote: you lose. This will always remain an anxiety. Look at Kerala. Two or three percentage point of change of voters and suddenly there is a dramatic change in the political fortune. There is no link also between representation and the voting. But what happens? There is always desperation to get more votes. Marginal votes become very important. Do not ever think that politicians of these parties are all crooks. If that is so, your assumption is completely irrational. They are just responding to a situation. They are compelled to do so. If not, you must be content with some humiliation, disappointment and complete disconnection from power. Therefore, you must make it possible for people to get into power through legitimate means. And as long as it is in an objectively poor country like India, first past poll system operated without a problem. You may ask about other countries. There is news for you. There are very few countries with first past poll system in the world. We only look at Britian, USA and former British Colonies. In fact, except those countries, no country has the first past poll system and they took centuries to evolve and to improve. They must have delayed. We should not take centuries. Australia started with first past poll system. Eventually Australia gave up this system and now it has a very sophisticated system, 'alternative voting', where you give preferences. New Zealand too gave up the first past poll system and now it has 'mixed proportional representation' like in Germany. In Britian, except for House of Commons, the rest of the bodies are elected either by proportionality or some other model is used. In the local elections, they adopt proportionality. Scotland, Wales and Northern Irelands practice proportionality. In London City – there is direct election to the office of Mayor, and yet he is an empowered Mayor. What is left is the House of Commons. Even that may change with the current coalition government – liberal democrats' main agenda is to push for a referendum asking for a proportionality model. We in India are the only ones sticking to this because we Indian's want to believe that we are the last living English men. Ironically, the English themselves have substantially changed their system of elections. We adhere to this for no good reason. Just that we are used to it. It is ridiculous.

The second part is how to ensure that the executive branch of government is separated from Legislative Branch and the elected Legislators do not become Maharajas. Today, Legislators in most parts of India are Maharajas. When one refuses to be a Maharaja, there are a lot of problems one has to face. The expectation is that an MLA should function as a disguised executive. When he says transfers or police cases are not his business, it is horror. When a legislator does not want to interfere in temple committees, it is horror in Andhra Pradesh. This is absurd. You are not elected to be an Executive. You are separate. The reason why legislative office is so powerful in India is not because people want to sit in the Legislature, make laws, and shape politics but because they are almost a part of the Executive. That is what we see. Separate them, at least at the local level and State level; for a direct election for the Head of the Government, not at the National level because there is North-South, Hindu-Muslim, Hindi-Non-Hindi and too many fractures in India. Central government is not where the real change is required now. It is in the States because power has decisively shifted to States in India now. Separation of Executive from Legislature and direct election of the Head of the Government, must receive urgent consideration.

Votes and public good have been de-linked. You need not go very far. Kerala is an outstanding example of the attempt to link vote with public good and that is local self governments. A three tier federalism- empower the people. Empower the communities. Transfer all powers, all authorities and as many resources as possible and then hold a big stick to keep a check. Have an independent Ombudsman to make them accountable for there is always going to be a fellow like the one I told you about, who would be willing to spend Rs. 4 crore to become a Sarpanch. If we give him all the power without accountability, that person will do the same thing to become MLA tomorrow. Therefore, hold a stick to ensure accountability decentralisation. Not mere decentralisation. The third tier of Federalism. You do know we require independent anticorruption institutions. The struggle of Santhosh Hegde in Karnataka, right now for instance, is an example. The Government has today apparently offered this. A news item in the Headlines Today read, *"Officials can have suo moto powers, but MLAs and Ministers have not, or are dead bodies"*. You require independent authorities with independent prosecution, independent time investigation, special courts, and confiscation of properties. Will this work? Of course, it will. Look at Hong Kong. Thirty five years ago there was phenomenal corruption in Hong Kong. They created an independent anticorruption Commission. Within three years, corruption drastically plummeted. Risk and reward along with the system may bring change in politics and elections. The moment you know that a fellow who made illegitimate money will go to jail and will lose office and money, ninety nine out of hundred will abstain from corruption, not because they are moral giants, but because they know the outcome. We require that. The answers are self explanatory. We gave a report. I was a member of the Second Administrative Reforms Commission along with a great son of Trivandrum Mr. Ramachandran. We gave a very solid report, a well considered report. A thorough report on probity in public life. We do not know what has happened to that today. The Government knows what should be done. It is just that we do not do it because we do not have incentive to do the right thing.

Finally, Criminalisation, in Kerala, you do not have this problem, but in many parts of India, notorious murderers, gangsters and criminals are all in politics. You have to do four things. The reason why these goons are a part of politics, the reason why they are actually prominent in public life is because there is no justice in India available. The *gundas* are seen by the people as the undeclared judges dispensing rough and ready justice. If justice is not available to the poor and weak easily, you will always have to find extra-judicial mechanisms. We need Rule of law. The second is interference in crime investigation. The main job the MLAs seem to be doing these days is to calling the Police Stations and instructing them, *'in ko arrest karo, in ko nikalo'*. The moment crime investigation is truly independent and yet accountable, these thugs have no incentive to be in politics. By being outside public glare he might as well do his business silently rather than being noticed by people. The third essential is that you must ensure that the electoral system is changed. That is what the fight is about. The anti-social element is invited by the political parties and politicians because he is the most likely winner. He has the money power, he has the muscle power and he has the capacity to get things done. Therefore, he is electable. And the fourth is you must have a governance system which actually is flexible and not wooden. The system should be responsive to people. Today it is a *gunda* who can get things done. A *gunda* can fight even for illegitimate things and therefore, people vote for them. You remember, in Madhepura, even a man like Lalu Yadav lost, but Papu Yadav, a notorious murderer, won, not because people are bad, but because people believe , be whoever he is, at the end of the day he is going to go ahead and get things done, because legitimately getting things done has practically become impossible. Once you change all these, you will definitely see the end of criminalisation.

To conclude, it doesn't mean we have to despise politics. I am a great optimist. I believe India is ready for a fundamental transformation. In the past ten to twelve years, a lot of good things have happened like the funding law, disclosure, and voter registration implementation. This is also a reason why I am angry with the Election Commission. The voter registration is entirely in the hands of Election Commission. No politician or parties are stopping them. Then why have the Commission successively failed? It is not for want of effort on our part. We have done enormous work, be it making the post office nodal agencies for voters' registration on a permanent basis or transforming them into citizen friendly, accessible, transparent and bringing in technology that you have access to. But basically there is no desire. You have to push and push repeatedly even for the slightest improvement to happen in a place. This is not good. The Commission has to stand before the bar of public opinion and answer to us. It does not mean that the political parties and politics are guilty. The Commission has actually failed to execute where it has the power. Balance must be restored in this country, in our public institutions. You must get them into action. I have said this in the presence of the Chief Election Commissioner. The public institutions must stand the scrutiny of the public. They must respond to our urges and change things. They cannot simply give us pious proclamations. They are there to change things and to use their authority for the benefit of the people of this country. Things will surely change. But they will not change without our effort. Some twenty years ago there was a very famous story in the former the Soviet Union.

In Moscow City, in front of a ration shop hundreds of people were waiting in a queue for a few crumbs of bread. They waited for hours and hours but there was no bread inside. One young man lost his temper. He said he was sick and tired of the wait. The country was supposed to be a super power and yet there was no bread for its children who were hungry.

"I will go and kill the General Secretary in Kremlin" he said and stormed off in protest. The others still waited patiently for the midnight clock/stock/knock. This young man came back two hours later and they all asked – What happened? Have you killed the general secretary or the convener of this store? He replied, *"I went there to kill him, but there is a much longer queue waiting there"*. This story is recounted in every household in the Soviet Union in all the Republics. People laughed, but they did nothing about it. They all hoped for change, but did not act for change. They did get change, but a disastrous one in 1991. Positive Change is possible, but only if we work for that with clarity, with conviction, with commitment and collectively setting aside our differences. There may be a hundred issues on which we disagree, but there is always a core issue on which we all agree. Let us fight together to change the country. I am sure, we can do that. Every country went through these travails. Some of them overcame, some of them did not. We too can. There is no reason to blame ourselves. There is nothing particularly wrong with us or self flagellate about Indians. Of course, there are many things wrong, but they are nothing different from those in any other country. It is that we built an institutional framework, which simply is sometimes self-defeating. But, look at that, analyze and ask hard questions, come up with sensible answers and implement them ruthlessly, and together we will fight for it.

30 Electoral Reforms in India : Some Critical Issues

D. Jeevan Kumar

An essential feature of a democratic polity is elections at regular intervals. Elections constitute the signpost of democracy. As Sumandeep Kaur points out, elections are the medium through which the attitudes, values and beliefs of the people towards their political environment are reflected. Elections grant people a government and the government has a constitutional right to govern those who elect it. Elections are the central democratic procedure for selecting and controlling leaders. Elections provide an opportunity to the people to express their faith in the government from time to time, and change it when the need arises. Elections symbolise the sovereignty of the people and provide legitimacy to the authority of the government. Thus, free and fair elections are indispensable for the success of democracy.[1]

Jaytilak Guha Roy brings out the significance of 'Free and Fair Elections' in three well-argued observations:[2] First, elections are the most important and integral part of politics in a constitutionally ordained democratic system of governance. While politics is the art and practice of dealing with political power, elections represent the process of legitimization of such power. Purity of elections is therefore the key to the success and sustainability of democracy and democratic institutions.

Secondly, democracy and Rule of Law are intimately inter-linked. Rule of Law presupposes that a democratic government ought to be a representative, responsible and responsive government. Accordingly, the political institutions of governance in a democracy such as Parliament and State Legislatures must possess the three R's: Representativeness, Responsibleness and Responsiveness. In a parliamentary democracy such as ours, free and fair elections ensure that all those elected in the legislative bodies are the *true representatives* of the people, as also *responsible* and *responsive* to them. In other words, free and fair elections ensure the legitimacy as well as the sanctity of the political institutions of governance in a democracy based on the values of Rule of Law.

Thirdly, a democratic government needs to be based on the trust of the governed. Free and fair elections are considered as the first and foremost step to ensure the trust of the governed. Fair election contemplates that the voters should be well-informed about the contesting candidates and, as such, they must have the right to know the full particulars of a candidate who is to represent them in Parliament or any other legislative body.

Since 1952, the country has witnessed elections to the legislative bodies at both the national and state levels. However, the reality is that our electoral system is plagued by a variety of defects and deficiencies. Such maladies cast a slur on the very system of Parliamentary Democracy. Many a time, the Election Commission has expressed its concern and anxiety for removing obstacles in the way of free and fair polls. It has made a number of recommendations and repeatedly reminded the government the necessity of changing the existing laws to check electoral malpractices. Apart from the Election Commission, the issue of electoral reforms has been taken up by numerous government committees in the recent past, like the:

- Goswami Committee on Electoral Reforms (1990);
- Vohra Committee (1993);
- Indrajit Gupta Committee on State Funding of Elections (1998);
- Law Commission on Reform of the Electoral Laws (1999);
- National Commission to Review the Working of the Constitution (2001);
- Election Commission of India – Proposed Electoral Reforms (2004);
- The Second Administrative Reforms Commission (2008); and the
- Core Committee on Electoral Reforms of the Ministry of Law and Justice of the Government of India (2010).

A nation-wide consultation process has recently been initiated by the Ministry of Law and Justice of the Government of India, in consultation with the Election Commission of India, to take a comprehensive look at electoral reforms. In this connection, a Background Paper, prepared by a core committee on electoral reforms, was released in December 2010. The background paper looks at seven issues, namely:

1. Criminalisation of Politics;
2. Financing of Elections;
3. Conduct and Better Management of Elections;
4. Regulation of Political Parties;
5. Auditing of Finances of Political Parties;
6. Adjudication of Election Disputes; and
7. Review of the Anti-Defection Laws.

There has also been a great deal of substantive work on the topic of Electoral Reforms undertaken by various civil society groups, which have contributed significantly to the public discourse on the subject. This Paper looks at four critical issues with which any serious discussion on Electoral Reforms should begin with, namely:

1. Criminalisation of Politics;
2. Financing of Elections;
3. Curbing Electoral Offences and Malpractices; and
4. Regulation of Political Parties.

The above issues represent a cross-section of the Electoral Reforms suggested by the Core Committee on Electoral Reforms, based on the recommendations made by several government committees, referred to above.

1. Criminalisation of Politics

The criminalisation of our political system has been observed almost unanimously by all recent committees on politics and electoral reform.[3] Criminalisation of politics has many forms, but perhaps the most alarming among them is the significant number of elected representatives with criminal charges pending against them. Two measures recommended by previous committees have been discussed, in detail, by the Core Committee on Electoral Reforms in its 'Background Paper on Electoral Reforms', namely, enforcement of the disclosure of criminal antecedents of candidates, and eligibility restrictions for candidates with criminal cases pending against them.

The Vohra Committee Report on Criminalisation of Politics was constituted to identify the extent of the politician-criminal nexus and recommend ways in which the menace can be combated. Chapter 4 of the report of the National Commission to Review the Working of the Constitution, cites the Vohra Report as follows: "The nexus between the criminal gangs, police, bureaucracy and politicians has come out clearly in various parts of the country" and that "some political leaders become the leaders of these gangs/armed senas and over the years get themselves elected to local bodies, State assemblies, and national parliament." This point becomes self-evident when one looks at the number of elected representatives with pending criminal cases against them at all levels in our federal system.

According to Madhav Godbole, over 20-25% of MLAs and MPs have had a criminal record in successive elections.[4] Quoting from successive reports of the Lok Sabha's Committee on Absence of Members from the Sittings of the House, he lists the names of 'honourable' members who were granted Leave of Absence by the House so that they could be taken into judicial custody!

While several of remedies have been proposed by various committees on the criminalization of politics in the country, two of them deserve careful attention:

1.1 Disclosure of Criminal Antecedents of Candidates

Currently, Rule 4A of the Conduct of Election Rules, 1961, prescribes that each candidate must file an affidavit (Form 26 appended to Conduct of Election Rules, 1961) regarding:

(i) Cases, if any, in which the candidate has been accused of any offence punishable with imprisonment for two years, or more, in a pending case in which charges have been framed by the court, and

(ii) (ii) Cases of conviction for an offence other than any of the offences mentioned in Section 8 of Representation of the People Act, 1951, (hereafter, R.P. Act, 1951) and sentenced to imprisonment for one year or more.

In addition to this, pursuant to the order of the Supreme Court, the Election Commission on March 27, 2003, issued an order that candidates must file an additional affidavit stating:

(i) information relating to all pending cases in which cognisance has been taken by a Court;

(ii) assets and liabilities; and

(iii) educational qualifications.

The affidavit is given in a form prescribed by the Election Commission of India.

Section 125A of the R.P. Act, 1951 prescribes penalties for withholding or providing incorrect information on Form 26, which amount to imprisonment of up to six months, or fine, or both.

However, in spite of the above, the Election Commission of India notes that not only do candidates leave some of the columns blank; they also give grossly undervalued information!

Relevant Recommendations

- In its report on Proposed Election Reforms, 2004, the Election Commission of India recommended that an amendment should be made to Section 125A of the R.P. Act, 1951 to provide for more stringent punishment for concealing or providing wrong information on Form 26 of Conduct of Election Rules, 1961, to minimum two years imprisonment and removing the alternative punishment of assessing a fine upon the candidate. It also recommended that Form 26 be amended to include all items from the additional affidavit prescribed by the Election Commission, and to add a column requiring candidates to disclose their annual declared income for tax purpose as well as their profession.
- The Law Commission of India Report on Reform of the Electoral Laws, 1999, suggested that an amendment be made to the R.P. Act, 1951, to insert a new Section 4A after Section 4 to make declaration of assets and criminal cases pending against the candidate part of the qualifications necessary for membership to the House of the People.

1.2 Eligibility of Candidates with Criminal Cases Pending against Them

Section 8 of the Representation of the People Act, 1951, provides for disqualification of candidates from contesting an election on conviction by a Court of Law. In Subsection (1), it lists certain crimes and stipulates a disqualification period of six years from the date of conviction. In Subsection (2) it lists a different set of crimes and provides for the candidate to be disqualified from the date of conviction and for a period of six years since his release. In Subsection (3), it provides that any candidate convicted for a crime for which the minimum imprisonment is two years shall also be disqualified from the date of conviction and will continue to be disqualified for six additional years after his release.

Relevant Recommendations

- The Election Commission proposed in its 2004 report that Section 8 of the R.P. Act, 1951 should be amended to disqualify candidates accused of an offence punishable by imprisonment of 5 years or more, *even when trial is pending*, given that the court has framed charges against the person. In the report the commission addresses the possibility that such a provision could be misused in the form of motivated cases by the ruling party. To prevent such misuse, the Commission suggested a compromise whereas only cases filed prior to six months before an election would lead to disqualification of a candidate. In addition, the commission proposed that Candidates found guilty by a commission of Enquiry should stand disqualified.
- The report "Ethics in Governance" of the Second Administrative Reforms Commission concurred with the recommendation of the Election Commission.
- In Chapter 4 of its report, the National Commission to Review the Working of the Constitution proposed several measures. Firstly, it proposed that Section 8 of the R.P. Act, 1951, be amended such that a candidate accused of an offence punishable by imprisonment of 5 years or more be disqualified on the expiry of a period of one year from the date the charges were framed against him, and unless cleared during that one year period, he shall remain disqualified until the conclusion of his trial. It also recommended that in case a candidate is convicted by a court of law and sentenced to imprisonment of six months or more, he shall be disqualified during the period of the sentence and for six additional years after his release. Candidates violating this provision should be disqualified, and political parties putting up such a candidate with knowledge of his antecedents should be derecognised and deregistered. Thirdly, the Commission has stated that any person convicted for any heinous crime such as murder, rape, smuggling, dacoity, etc., should be permanently barred from contesting political office. Finally, the Commission proposed the establishment of Special Courts to decide cases against candidates within a period of six months or less. Potential candidates against whom charges are pending may take the matter

to the Special court, which can decide if there is indeed a prima facie case justifying the framing of the charges. Special courts would be constituted at the level of High Courts and decisions would be appealable only to the Supreme Court.

- The 1999 Law Commission of India Report took a separate stand, suggesting that Section 8 remain unchanged. It suggested, however, the addition of a new section – Section 8B, which would provide a separate set of penalties for electoral offences and offences having a bearing upon the conduct of elections under Sections 153A and 505 of the IPC and serious offences punishable with death or life imprisonment. The proposed Section 8B would provide that framing of charges shall be a ground of disqualification but this disqualification shall last only for a period of five years or till the acquittal of the person of those charges, whichever event happens earlier. If a candidate is found guilty, he would automatically be disqualified under Section 8.

1.3 Negative or Neutral Voting

The criminalisation of politics, widespread corruption in the system, and use of violence, voter intimidation, and the like, may result in there being no desirable candidates within those contesting elections in a particular constituency. Currently there is no way for voters to express their dislike for all candidates. The lack of such a provision may further contribute to the decay in the system in such cases by encouraging only those voters who support such compromised candidates to vote, returning those same leaders to power again and again.

Relevant Recommendation

- Both the Election Commission and Law Commission of India recommend that a negative or neutral voting option be created. Negative/ neutral voting means allowing voters to reject all of the candidates on the ballot by selection of a "*None of The Above*" option, instead of the name of a candidate on the ballot. In such a system there could be a provision according to which if a certain percentage of the vote is negative/neutral, then the election results could be nullified and a new election conducted.

2. Financing of Elections

The Core Committee on Electoral Reforms put it rather mildly by stating that "it is widely believed that in many cases, successfully contesting an election costs a significant amount of money that is often much greater than the prescribed limits."[5]

A Consultation Paper to the National Commission to Review the Working of the Constitution, 2001, noted that "the campaign expenditure by candidates is in the range of about *twenty to thirty times* the legal limits".

There are many negative social impacts of this high cost. Chapter 4 of the Report of the National Commission to Review the Working of the Constitution, 2001, notes that the high cost of elections "creates a high degree of compulsion for corruption in the public arena" and that "the sources of some of the election funds are believed to be unaccounted criminal money in return for protection; unaccounted funds from business groups who expect a high return on this investment; kickbacks or commissions on contracts, etc." It also states that "Electoral compulsions for funds become the foundation of the whole super structure of corruption".

2.1 Official Limits on Campaign Expenditure

Currently, limits on campaign expenditure are fixed at certain amounts depending on the nature of the election. However, it is believed that these limits are violated with audacity. This is mainly attributed to the fact that the actual cost of running an election campaign is often much greater than the prescribed spending limit.

Relevant Recommendations

- The National Commission to Review the Working of the Constitution, 2001, recommended that the existing ceiling on election expenses for the various legislative bodies should be suitably raised to a reasonable level reflecting increasing costs. The ceiling is currently Rs. 25 lakhs for a Lok Sabha seat and Rs 10 lakh for an assembly seat. In order to cope with rising expenditures over time, this ceiling should be re-fixed by the Election Commission from time to time and should include all the expenses by the candidate, as well as by his political party or his friends and well-wishers, and any other expenses incurred in any political activity on behalf of the candidate by an individual or corporate entity.
- A Consultation Paper to the National Commission to Review the Working of the Constitution, 2001, entitled "Review of the

Working of Political Parties Specially in Relation to Elections and Reform Options" largely concurred with the above opinion but also suggested a much bolder one:

Either the statutory limit should be scrapped altogether and replaced by a selective ban on certain kinds of expenditure. Or

(b) the existing provisions should be amended to provide for:

(i) much higher ceiling than what currently exists;

(ii) regular revision of the ceiling before every general election;

(iii) all the expenditure, irrespective of who paid for it, to be brought within the purview of this provision;

(iv) mechanism for routine verification /auditing of the return of the expenditure; and

(v) publicity of the returns filed by the candidate in the local press.

- The Election Commission of India recommends that the ceiling on election expenditure be rationalized from time to time.

2.2 Disclosure Audit of Assets and Liabilities of Candidates

On March 27, 2003, the Election Commission of India issued an order, in pursuance of the Supreme Court judgment dated March 13, 2003 in the *Peoples Union for Civil Liberties and Another Vs. Union of India* case, that candidates for electoral office must submit an affidavit disclosing their assets and liabilities.

It has been noted by the Election Commission of India in its report, 'Proposed Electoral Reforms', 2004, stated that "there have been many cases where the candidates are alleged to have given grossly undervalued information, mainly about their assets."

Relevant Recommendations

- The National Commission to Review the Working of the Constitution recommended a follow-up action to the declaration of assets and liabilities by candidates - that the particulars of the assets and liabilities of both candidates and political parties should be audited by a special authority created specifically under law for this purpose. Accounts of candidates and parties should be monitored through a system of checking and cross-checking through the income tax returns filed by candidates, parties, and their well wishers. At the end of the election each candidate should submit an audited statement of expenses under specific heads.

- In 2004, the Election Commission recommended that an amendment be made to Form 26 of Conduct of Election Rules, 1961, to include disclosure of assets and liabilities by candidates. To enforce complete compliance by candidates on Form 26, the Commission recommended that Section125A be amended such that there is more stringent punishment for concealing or providing wrong information on the form. The amendment would provide for minimum two years imprisonment and removal of the alternative punishment of assessing a fine upon the candidate.

2.3 Curbing the Cost of Campaigning

It has been noted by several committees that in order to remedy the negative impact of the excessive cost of elections, the first step should be to reduce the cost of elections themselves.

Relevant Recommendations

- It was observed by both the Indrajit Gupta Committee on state funding of elections, 1999, and the National Commission to Review the Working of the Constitution, 2001, that many of the tools used for campaigning – such as wall writings, rallies on public property, using loudspeakers for campaigning – are not only costly, but are also a public nuisance. Curbing these activities can both reduce the public nuisance caused by them and also reduce the amount of money needed to fight elections. For this purpose the Committees suggested that a suitable law should be enacted providing penalties or reasonable restrictions against damaging or desecrating public or private property by candidates, political parties, or the agents, through painting of slogans or erecting cut-outs and hoarding or putting up banners and buntings, wall writings and hoisting of flags (except at party offices, party offices, public meetings and other specified places).

- In addition, the National Commission to Review the Working of the Constitution, 2001, suggested the following measures: (i) State and Parliamentary level elections, to the extent possible, should be held at the same time; (ii) The campaign period should be reduced considerably, and (iii) Candidates should not be allowed to contest election simultaneously for the same office from more than one constituency.

2.4 State Funding of Elections

A major concern associated with the high cost of elections is that it prevents parties and candidates with modest financial resources from being competitive in elections. It is also feared that if candidates need to raise funds from a variety of sources, then their policy decisions after being elected as policy makers may be somewhat biased in favour of groups that fund them. State funding of elections (in various forms) has been proposed as a potential solution to this problem.

Relevant Recommendations

- The Indrajit Gupta Committee on State Funding of Elections, 1998, backed the idea of state funding of elections on principle, stating that "The Committee see full justification, constitutional, legal, as well as on ground of public interest, for grant of State subvention to political parties, so as to establish such conditions where even the parties with modest financial resources may be able to compete with those who have superior financial resources." It added two limitations, namely (i) such funds could not be doled out to independent candidates, and only to national and state parties having been granted a symbol and proven their popularity among the electorate, and (ii) in the short-term, State funding may be given only in kind, in the form of certain facilities to the recognised political parties and their candidates. However, despite strongly backing full State funding of elections, in principle, it stated that only partial State funding would be possible in the short-term, given the prevailing economic condition of the country.

- The 1999 report of the Law Commission of India concurred with the Indrajit Gupta Commission, stating that "it is desirable that total state funding be introduced, but on the condition that political parties are barred from raising funds from any other source". It also agreed with the Indrajit Gupta Commission that only partial state funding was possible at the present time, given the economic conditions of the country. Additionally, it strongly recommended that the appropriate regulatory framework be put in place with regard to political parties (provisions ensuring internal democracy, internal structures and maintenance of accounts, their auditing and submission to Election Commission) before state funding of elections is attempted.

- The Report "Ethics in Governance" of the Second Administrative Reforms Commission also recommended that "a system for partial state funding should be introduced to reduce the scope of illegitimate and unnecessary funding of expenditure for elections."
- The National Commission to Review the Working of the Constitution, 2001, did not comment on the desirability of State funding of elections but reiterated the point of the Law Commission that the appropriate framework for regulation of political parties would need to be implemented before proposals for State funding are considered.
- The Election Commission is not in favour of state funding as it will not be possible to prohibit or check candidate's own expenditure or expenditure by others, over and above that which is provided by the state. The Election Commission's view is that for addressing the real issues, there have to be radical changes in the provisions regarding receipts of funds by political parties and the manner in which such funds are spent by them, so as to provide for complete transparency in the matter.

It cannot be denied that accountable and legitimate political party expenditure is at the heart of the fight against corruption. A law to this effect, having far-reaching consequences, has seen the light of day. The *Election and Other Related Laws (Amendment Bill, 2003) (Funding Reform Bill)* was a crucial change proposed in the Indian electoral process. The Lok Satta Movement, the Centre for the Study of Developing Societies and Lok Niti had been advocating funding reform and direct state funding of elections. Except for public funding, most of the key provisions proposed by civil society groups found place in the Bill introduced first in the Lok sabha on 19th March 2002. The revised Bill was introduced in Parliament on 13th May 2003, after incorporating changes recommended by the Parliamentary Standing Committee on Home Affairs. The *Election and Other Related Laws (Amendment) Bill, 2003* was approved by both Houses of Parliament in August 2003 and became law in September 2003, with the assent of the President. The law has the following key provisions:

- Full tax exemption to individuals and corporate on all contributions to political parties.
- Effective repeal of Explanation 1 under Section 77 of the Representation of the People Act, 1951 – Expenditure by third

parties and political parties will now come under ceiling limits; only travel expenditure of leaders of parties is exempt.

- Disclosure of party finances and contributions over Rs. 20,000.
- Indirect public funding to candidates of recognised political parties, including free supply of electoral rolls (already in vogue) and such items by the Election Commission as are decided in consultation with the Union Government.
- Equitable sharing of time by the recognised political parties on the cable television network and other electronic media (public and private).[6]

3. Curbing Electoral Offences and Malpractices

According to the Election Commission of India, the size of the electorate for the 2009 elections to the 15th Lok Sabha was more than 714 million. The National Commission to Review the Working of the Constitution, 2001, noted in its report that "the holding of general elections in India is equal to holding them for Europe, the United States, Canada, and Australia all put together." Successful administration of the electoral process requires more than 50 lakh personnel and almost 1 million (10 lakh) polling booths. Millions of security personnel are required to promote a peaceful and incident-free voting experience.

Electoral reform committees have recommended several changes in the conduct of the electoral process to properly address the challenges posed by electoral offences and malpractices. Major problems, and proposed solutions, are outlined below:[7]

3.1 Irregularities in Polling

Irregularities in polling procedure have been identified as important issues that need to be addressed in our electoral system. Rigging of elections have become common facets of our electoral system.

3.1.1 Importance of Electoral Rolls

The National Commission to Review the Working of the Constitution, 2001, rightly noted that "The electoral process begins with the preparation of electoral rolls. If the rolls are incomplete or defective, the whole process is vitiated." A Consultation Paper to the National Commission to Review the Working of the Constitution noted that "political parties and influential persons manage large-scale registration of bogus voters, or large-scale deletion of names of "unfriendly" voters." The Goswami Committee on

Electoral Reforms stated that irregularities in electoral rolls are exacerbated by purposeful tampering done by election officials who are bought by vested interests or have partisan attitudes.

Aside from intentional tampering, the structure of the system set up to create electoral rolls may contribute significantly to the widespread inaccuracies. In the current system, the Election Commission prepares electoral roles for parliamentary and assembly constituencies, and the State Election Commissions prepare electoral rolls for local elections. While some states have coordinated their electoral rolls with those prepared by the Election Commission, there are still some States that significantly modify them. Some States even have different qualifying dates for the State rolls from the Election Commission rolls, which is inefficient for both the Commissions involved and confusing for the voter. The duplication of essentially the same task between two different agencies is also an unnecessarily costly affair.[8]

Relevant Recommendations

- The National Commission to Review the Working of the Constitution recommended in its 2001 report that an automated online database should be created by the Election Commission. In such a system, each voter would be provided with a unique bar-coded ID number, assigned for life. This bar-coded ID card and number could be verified at the polling booth by a handheld device. The electoral rolls in this system could be prepared at the panchayat or district level. Along with this, the commission also recommended that the task of electoral roll preparation should not be duplicated as it is now, possibly by entrusting it to an outside agency under the supervision of the Election Commission. A centralised, computerised system could provide for the easy public availability of the electoral rolls as well.
- In its 2004 report on Proposed Electoral Reforms, the Election Commission concurred with the National Commission to Review the Working of the Constitution that there should be common rolls for all elections, with the parliamentary and assembly rolls adapted to suit the needs of local bodies elections. This is primarily recommended by the Commission for the purpose of saving on expenditure and to make the process more efficient.
- The Goswami Committee of 1990 recommended that Post Offices should be the agencies for preparation and maintenance of

electoral rolls. This solution may well be outdated in today's society where efficient computerised systems can be created. The Committee, did however, recommend a multi-purpose ID somewhat along the same lines as that proposed by the National Commission to Review the Working of the Constitution.

2. Rigging through Muscle Power and Intimidation

Rigging of elections is possible not just through tampering of booths, ballots, and electoral rolll, but also out of sheer 'muscle power' and intimidation of voters.

Relevant Recommendations

- The Goswami Committee Report of 1990 recommended that the Election Commission should be empowered to take strong action on the report of returning officers, election observers, or civil society in regards to booth capture or the intimidation of voters.

- The National Commission to Review the Working of the Constitution recommends that the Election Commission should have the power under Section 58A of the Representation of the People Act, 1951, to order a fresh election, void the election results, or order a re-poll in such cases. It further recommended that the Election Commission should make use of electronic surveillance equipment as a deterrent to booth capture or intimidation of voters.

3.2 Proliferation of Candidates

To say that there is a proliferation of candidates in Indian elections would be an understatement! According to the Election Commission of India, "too many candidates in the election fray puts unnecessary and avoidable stress on the management of elections and increases expenditure on account of security and maintenance of law and order, apart from the requirement of extra numbers of balloting units of voting machines, and the like". It has been observed that a large number of candidates in the fray are non-serious candidates, which according to the Law Commission of India, makes elections "cumbersome, expensive and unmanageable – indeed farcical in some cases." The National Commission to Review the Working of the Constitution notes that out of the 1900 independent candidates who contested the general election of 1998, only six actually won!

Relevant Recommendations

- The Election Commission of India, Law Commission of India, and National Commission to Review the Working of the Constitution all recommend measures to check the proliferation of non-serious candidates. In their reports, all the committees mentioned recommended increasing the security deposit of candidates. The recommendations of these committees were enacted through the Representation of the People (Amendment) Act, 2009, which increased the amount. The Election Commission further recommends that it be given the power to prescribe deposit amounts prior to each election so that repeated amendments to the Representation of the People Act are not necessary.
- The Law Commission of India Report on Reform of the Electoral Laws goes even further and declares that independent candidates should be debarred from contesting elections to the Lok Sabha.
- The National Commission to Review the Working of the Constitution proposed a system of discouraging independent candidates from running for office, by implementing the following measures:
  - (i) The existing security deposits for independent candidates should be doubled;
  - (ii) The deposit should be doubled every year for those independents who fail to win and still keep contesting elections,
  - (iii) If any independent candidate fails to win five percent of the vote or more, he should be debarred from contesting as an independent for the same office for six years,
  - (iv) An independent candidate who loses election three times consecutively for the same office as an independent should be permanently debarred from contesting election to that office.

3.3 Restrictions on Government- Sponsored Advertisements

It has been noted by the Election Commission that on the eve of election, the Central and various State Governments are able to advertise for the purpose of influencing elections, justifying it by providing information to the public. The expenditure on such advertisements is generally incurred from the public exchequer. The Election Commission feels this practice allows the misuse of public funds and provides the ruling party an undue advantage over other parties and candidates.

Relevant Recommendations

- The Election Commission proposes that where any general election is due on the expiration of the term of the House, advertisements of achievements of the governments, either Central or State, in any manner, should be prohibited for a period of six months prior to the date of expiry of the term of the House, and in case of premature dissolution, from the date of dissolution of the House. Here, advertisements / dissemination of information on poverty alleviation and health related schemes could be exempted from the purview of such a ban. The Commission also recommends that there should be specific provisions that name or symbol of any political party or photograph of any of the leaders of the party should not appear on such hoardings/banners.

3.4 Restriction on the Number of Seats which one may Contest

According to Section 33 of the Representation of the People Act, 1951, a person can contest a general election or a group of by-elections or biennial elections from a maximum of two constituencies. There have been several cases where a person contests election from two constituencies, and wins from both. In such a situation he vacates the seat in one of the two constituencies. The consequence is that a by-election would be required from one constituency which involves avoidable labour and expenditure on the conduct of that by-election.

Relevant Recommendation

- The Election Commission is of the view that the law should be amended to provide that a person cannot contest from more than one constituency at a time.

3.5 Amendment of Law to Provide for Filing of Election Petition even against Defeated Candidates on the Ground of Corrupt Practice

As per the existing law, election petition can be filed only for challenging the election of a returned candidate. If a defeated candidate has indulged in corrupt practice, there is no provision for filing an election petition against such candidate.

Relevant Recommendation

- The Election Commission has recommended in its letter dated

24th April 2009 that the law should be amended to provide for filing election petitions in cases of commission of corrupt practice by a losing candidate. In the same letter, it was also suggested that the period by which the candidates are required to file their account of election expenses should be reduced to 20 days from the present 30 days, so that more time is available for others to scrutinize the accounts and to take the matter to the court in election petitions in cases of spending in excess of the ceiling. Alternatively, the period for filing Election Petition may be increased to 60 days.

3.6 Restrictions on Opinion Polls

Previous committees on electoral law have debated the possibility of whether opinion polls are misused to manipulate voters on the eve of elections.

Relevant Recommendations

- The Election Commission had recommended that there should be provision in the law putting restrictions on publishing the results of opinion polls and exit polls for a specified period during the election process. By the recent amendment of the Representation of the People Act,1951, a new Section 126A has been inserted in the Act prohibiting conducting of exit polls and publishing results in any manner, during the period starting from 48 hours before the close of poll in an election. In a multi-phased election, the prohibition will last till the close of poll in the last phase.
- However, the amendment does not cover opinion polls. Thus, results of opinion poll can be published even on the day of election polling. Although dissemination of results of opinion polls would be prohibited during the 48 hours period before the conclusion of poll by virtue of Section-126 (1) (b) on electronic media, there is no provision of law to restrict dissemination through print media (since Section126 (1) (b) does not apply to print media). These limitations need to be addressed.

3.7 Prohibition of Campaign during the Last 48 Hours

Section 126 of the Representation of the People Act, 1951, prohibits electioneering activities by way of public meetings, public performance, processions, advertisements through cinematograph, television or similar apparatus during the period of 48 hours before the time fixed for conclusion of poll. Thus, political advertisements on TV and Radio are prohibited during these 48 hours. However, since this Section does not refer to print media, the political parties and candidates issue advertisements in newspapers during this period, including on the day of poll. They also undertake house-to-house visits. The logic behind the restriction on campaigning during the 48 is to allow citizens to decide their option, without being prejudiced by any last moment appeals.

Relevant Recommendation

- The Election Commission recommends that Section 126 should apply to print media as well. Furthermore, it recommends that house to house visits by candidates/supporters should be specifically prohibited during the said 48 hour period. It is the opinion of the Commission that the house-to-house visit/ contact in the last hours provides that opportunity for indulging in malpractices such as trying to bribe electors with cash.

3.8 False Declaration in connection with Elections to be an Offence

Section 31 of the Representation of the People Act, 1950, contained a provision providing for punishment with imprisonment up to one year for making a false declaration in connection with preparation/revision of electoral roll. There is no such provision in the Representation of the People Act, 1951, in relation to conduct of elections. During the course of an election, the Election Commission has observed several cases of such false statements/declarations before the election authorities such as by candidates and representatives of political parties. A provision for punishment for false statement / declaration would be a deterrent against frivolous complaints and petitions.

Relevant Recommendation

- The Election Commission recommends that there should be a provision for penal action against those making any false declarations in connection with an election. Such a provision would provide for a similar punishment for false declarations in connection with conduct of elections, such as false complaints of booth capturing or false complaints about the conduct of election officials.

9. Punishment for Electoral Offences to be Enhanced

Undue influence and bribery at elections are electoral offences under Sections 171B and 171C, respectively, of the IPC. These offences are non-cognizable offences, with punishment provision of one year's imprisonment, or fine, or both. Under Section 171G, publishing a false statement in connection with an election with intent to affect the result of the election is only punishable with a fine. Section 171H provides that incurring or authorising expenditure for promoting the election prospects of a candidate is an offence. However, punishment for an offence under this section is a small fine of Rs. 500.

Relevant Recommendation

- The Election Commission feels that considering the gravity of the offences under the aforesaid sections in the context of free and fair elections, the punishments under all the four sections should be enhanced. This was recommended by the Commission in 1992.

10. Expenditure Ceiling for Election to Council Constituencies

Presently the expenditure ceiling for candidates applies only for the Lok Sabha and legislative assembly elections.

Relevant Recommendation

- The Election Commission has in its letter dated 30th May 2007 proposed that this should also be applicable in the case of Legislative Council elections from the Council Constituencies. The candidate should also be required to submit the account of election expenses.

11. Totalizer for Counting of Votes

Currently votes are tallied by individual EVMs at individual polling stations. This exposes the trend of voting in a particular voting station, making the electorate of that area vulnerable to backlash by candidates or elected officials in retribution.

Relevant Recommendation

- The Election Commission recommends an amendment be made to the Conduct of Elections Rules to provide for the use of 'totalizer' for counting of votes cast at more than one polling station where EVMs are used, so that the trend of voting in individual polling station areas does not get divulged and the electors may not be subjected to any harassment or victimization on that account.

12. Disqualification for Failure to Lodge Election Expenses

Under Section 10A of the Representation of the People Act, 1951, the Election Commission may disqualify a candidate for three years for failure to lodge the account of election expenses, as per the requirement of the law. Thus, the period of disqualification may end by the time of the next general election to that House. Therefore, no effective purpose is served by the disqualification (except that the person cannot contest in the odd by-election that may be held during the three year period).

Relevant Recommendation

- The Election Commission recommends that the period of disqualification under Section 10A of the R.P. Act should be increased to 5 years, so that the disqualified person does not become a candidate at the next general election to the House concerned.

4. Regulating Political Parties

It is very obvious that the party system in India has seen a sharp decline. Not only have political parties declined in terms of their ideological orientations and commitment to the welfare of the people, in recent times they have shown sharp tendencies of factionalism, opposition for opposition sake and agitational, unprincipled politics. So many of the political leaders reveal communal, religious, caste and other biases, and are known to have links with the mafia, criminals and militant/ fundamentalist organizations. Changing party loyalty has become endemic. Parties make and break political alliances just to remain in power.

A consultation paper of the National Commission to Review the Working of the Indian Constitution titled, *Review of the Working of Political Parties Specially in Relation to Elections and Reform Options* identified several areas of concern, of which the most significant ones are as follows:

- Institutionalization of political parties – Need for a comprehensive legislation to regulate party activities – Criteria for registration as a National or State party – De-recognition of political parties.
- Structural and organizational reforms – Party organizations at national, state and local levels – Inner party democracy – Regular party elections – Recruitment of party cadres – Socialization, development and training – Research and policy planning.
- Party funding – Legislation to regulate party funds – Income and

expenditure during non-election and election time – Maintenance of accounts – Auditing and publishing of accounts.

4.1 Registration and De-Registration of Political Parties

Political Parties are registered with the Election Commission under the provisions of Section 29A of the R.P. Act, 1951. This Section, as it stands, suffers from a certain looseness by which just about any small group of persons, if they so desire, can be registered as a Political Party, by making a simple declaration under Section 29A(5). This has resulted in mushrooming and proliferation of a large number of non-serious parties, which causes a considerable systems overload in the management of elections.

By way of example, of the more than 1100 parties registered with the Election Commission in 2009, only about 360 actually contested the general election that year. The motivation for non-serious parties to get registered is to probably give some sort of a distorted aura of their status and standing in their localities, particularly in rural and mofussil areas. The Election Commission feels that election is a serious process and this tendency of small groups of individuals who have no serious interest or desire to contest elections, should not easily be allowed to get the official stamp from the Commission as active political parties.

Apart from this, there is another equally serious problem. In addition to there not being sufficient conditions under Section 29A to deny registration to a political party, the Section also suffers from a serious infirmity in that once registered, a political party would stay registered in perpetuity, even if it does not contest any election over decades of its existence. This is because there is no specific provision to de-register a party. Similarly, certain political parties, which have served their purpose and have presently become defunct, which is normal in the functioning of a democracy, also stay on the rolls of the Commission as functioning political parties.[9]

Proliferation of political parties is stated to be a major concern by several committees.

In its 2001 report, the National Commission to Review the Working of the Constitution states that "it is a desirable objective to promote the progressive polarisation of political ideologies and to reduce less serious political activity."

The National Commission to Review the Working of the Constitution adds that while proliferation of smaller parties creates "confusion", any tightening of regulation on the subject must also take into account "the need to reflect the aspirations of a plural society."

Relevant Recommendations

- The Election Commission proposes that an amendment be made to Section 29A of the Representation of the People Act, 1951, adding a clause "authorising the Election Commission to issue necessary orders regulating registration and de-registration of political parties."
- The National Commission to Review the Working of the Constitution, 2001, recommended that "the Election Commission should progressively increase the threshold criterion for eligibility for recognition so that the proliferation of smaller parties is discouraged. Only parties or a pre-poll alliance of political parties registered as national parties or alliances with the Election Commission be allotted a common symbol to contest elections for the Lok Sabha. State parties may be allotted symbols to contest elections for state legislatures and Rajya Sabha."
- Furthermore, the National Commission recommended that the rules and by-laws of the parties seeking registration should include provisions for:

  (a) A declaration of adherence to democratic values and norms of the Constitution in their inner party organisations;

  (b) A declaration to shun violence for political gains;

  (c) A declaration not to resort to casteism and communalism for political mobilisation, but to adhere to the principles of secularism in the achievement of their objectives;

  (d) A provision for Party Conventions to nominate and select candidates for political offices at the grass root and State levels;

  (e) A code of conduct (which each political party should evolve for itself);

  (f) Some institutional mechanism for planning, thinking, and research on crucial socio-economic issues facing the nation, and educational cells for socialising their party cadres and preparing them for responsibilities of governance;

  (g) Implementation of legal provisions regarding representation to women and weaker sections of society in party offices and in candidacy for elections to legislatures.

2. Regulation of Finances of Political Parties

There is need for a comprehensive piece of legislation regarding regulating both income and expenditure of political parties. As mentioned earlier, the high cost of elections provides a logic for corruption in the public arena. This affects not only candidates, but parties as well.

In an order dated March 27, 2003, the Election Commission of India issued an order, in pursuance of the Supreme Court judgment dated March 13, 2003 in the *People's Union for Civil Liberties & Another Vs. Union of India* case, that candidates for electoral office must submit an affidavit disclosing their assets and liabilities. It is a matter of grave concern that this Order, however, does not apply to political parties.

Relevant Recommendations

- The 2004 report of the Election Commission declared that political parties should be required to publish their accounts (or at least an abridged version) annually for information and scrutiny of the general public and all concerned, for which purpose the maintenance of such accounts and their auditing to ensure their accuracy is a pre-requisite. The auditing may be done by any firm of auditors approved by the Comptroller and Auditor General. The audited accounts should then be made public.

- The Election and Other Related Laws (Amendment) Bill, 2002 (introduced in Lok Sabha on 19th March, 2002) sought to introduce section 29D in the Representation of the People Act, 1951 in this regard. The department-related Parliamentary Standing Committee on Home Affairs while examining the matter desired that the audit of accounts of donation received by the political party may be done through Chartered Accountants appointed by it as at present, as per the provisions of the Income-tax Act (Section 13A). In view thereof the Committee recommended deletion of entire Section 29D in Clause 2 of the Bill.

- In 2001 the National Commission to Review the Working of the Constitution recommended that "audited political party accounts, like the accounts of a public limited company, should be published yearly with full disclosures under predetermined account heads".

- The Law Commission, in its 1999 report, recommended steps be taken to amend the Representation of the People Act, 1951, to insert a new Section 78A requiring the maintenance, audit and publication of accounts by political parties. To enforce compliance, Section 78A would prescribe the following penalties: *(i)* A political party which does not comply shall be liable to pay a penalty of Rs. 10,000/- for each day of non-compliance and so long as the non-compliance continues; *(ii)* If such default continues beyond the period of 60 days, the Election Commission may de-recognise the political party after affording a reasonable opportunity to show cause; *(iii)* If the Election Commission finds on verification, undertaken *suo motu* or on information received, that the statement of accounts filed is false in any particular case, the Election Commission shall levy such penalty upon the political party, as it may deem appropriate, besides initiating criminal prosecution as provided under law.

- In order to further transparency in the funding of political parties, the Election Commission recommends the following measures:

  (i) Any receipt of money by a political party either directly or through the executives or the party functionaries should be deposited in the Bank Accounts of such parties;

  (ii) All payments by the political party exceeding Rs. 20,000/- to a person should be made by crossed account payee cheque; and

  (iii) All contributions or donations or gifts by any person to a party functionary, other than those by his/her relative(s), shall be deemed receipts of the political party and it will be accounted for by the political Party.

A close reading of the above recommendations relating to political parties would clearly reveal that there is a need for a comprehensive legislation to regulate their functioning. This legislation should stipulate conditions for the establishment, recognition, registration and de-registration of a political party. All parties should declare their allegiance to the provisions of the Indian Constitution and to the sovereignty and integrity of the nation, apart from abiding by the spirit of democracy in its internal management and operation, and observing inner-party democracy in its decision-making processes. The law should provide for the holding of periodic elections to various party positions at all levels. It should also be made mandatory for parties to provide for adequate representation to women in organizational positions. Only those parties which are registered under this Act should be allowed to contest elections.

Concluding Observations

Given the complexity of the crisis in our elcctoral and political systems, the reform agenda described in this paper may represent significant milestones, but it is unlikely that they will radically change the nature of our troubled politics. As graphically pointed out by Dr. Jayaprakash Narayan, there are several factors complicating the scenario and perpetuating the status quo:[10]

1. Election expenditures are large, unaccounted and mostly illegitimate. For instance, expenditure limit for Assembly elections in most major states was Rs six lakh until recently, when it has been revised to Rs ten lakh. In reality,average expenditure in most states is several multiples of it. Most of this expenditure is incurred to buy votes, bribe officials and hire musclemen. The implications of such skyrocketing election expenses need to be kept in mind. First, large expenditure does not guarantee victory, but inability to incur huge expenses almost certainly guarantees defeat! Desperate to win at any cost, parties are compelled to nominate mostly those candidates who can spend big money. Such large, unaccounted expenditure can be sustained only if the system is abused to enable multiple returns on investment. This vicious chain of corruption has created a class of political and bureaucratic 'entrepreneurs' who treat public office as big business.

2. As the vicious cycle of money power, polling irregularities and corruption has taken hold of the system, electoral verdicts cease to make a difference to people. Repeated disappointments have made people come to the conclusion that no matter who wins the election, they always end up losing.

3. This situation has bred a class of political 'entrepreneurs' with established fiefdoms. In most constituencies, money power, caste clout, bureaucratic links and political contacts come together to perpetuate the politics of fiefdoms.

4. In a centralised governance system, even if the vote is wisely

used by people, public good cannot be promoted. As the citizen is distanced from the decision-making process, the administrative machinery has no capacity to deliver public services of high quality or low cost. Such a climate breeds competitive populism to gain electoral advantage.

5. Elected governments are helpless to change this perilous situation. As the survival of the government depends on the support of coalition partners, Independents and others, their demands have to be met.

6. The First-Past-the-Post (FPTP) system exacerbates our social divisions, as it tends to over-represent geographically concentrated social groups, and under-represent scattered minorities. This representational distortion leads to ghettoisation and marginalization of the excluded social groups, which then indulge in strategic voting. This gives rise to vote bank politics in which obscurantists become interlocutors of the group, drowning the voice of reason and modernity. This pandering of fundamentalism leads to competitive mobilisation of various groups based on primordial loyalties, leading to communal polarisation and social strife.

7. The need for money power and caste clout to win a plurality of votes in the FPTP system precludes political participation of men and women of integrity and competence. With their exclusion, bad public policy and incompetent governance become endemic, deepening the crisis.

8. Under the FPTP system, only a high threshold of voting ensures victory. Usually, a party needs 35% vote or more to get reasonable representation in the legislature, or social groups with local dominance get elected. As a significant but scattered support pays no electoral dividends, reform groups and parties below the threshold tend to wither away. FPTP thus tends to lead to oligopoly of parties.

Given the complex nature of the crisis, as described so graphically by a renowned scholar-activist turned politician, the electoral reform agenda that is currently being pursued may represent just the tip of the iceberg. Deeper systemic reforms may need to be pursued to transform our procedural democracy into a genuine one.

REFERENCES

Core Committee on Electoral Reforms, *Background Paper on Electoral Reforms* (New Delhi: Ministry of Law and Justice, Government of India, 2010).

Committee on Electoral Reforms (Chair: Dinesh Goswami), *Report of the Committee on Electoral Reforms*, (New Delhi: Legislative Department, Ministry of Law and Justice, Government of India, 1990).

Committee on State Funding of Elections (Chair: Indrajit Gupta), *Report of the Committee on State Funding of Elections* (New Delhi: Ministry of Law, Justice and Company Affairs, Government of India, 1998).

Election Commission of India, *Proposals of the Election Commission for Electoral Reforms*, (New Delhi: Election Commission of India, 1992).

Election Commission of India, *Proposed Electoral Reforms*, (New Delhi: Election Commission, 2004).

Law Commission of India, *Report on Reform of the Electoral Laws*, (New Delhi: Law Commission, 1999).

National Commission to Review the Working of the Constitution (Chair: Justice M.N. Venkatachaliah), *Report on Electoral Processes and Political Parties* (New Delhi: Government of India, 2002).

Subhash C. Kashyap, ed., *National Resurgence through Electoral Reforms* (Delhi, Shipra Publications, 2002).

Madhav Godbole, *India's Parliamentary Democracy on Trial*, (New Delhi: Rupa and Co., 2011).

Jaytilak Guha Roy, *Electoral Reforms in the Context of Recent Supreme Court Judgements* (New Delhi: Indian Institute of Public Administration, 2003).

Jayaprakash Narayan, *Electoral and Political Party Reforms in India* (Paper presented at the Mont Pelerin Society Asia Regional Meeting, 10-13 February 2011).

Sumandeep Kaur, "Electoral Reforms in India: Proactive Role of Election Commission", Mainstream, New Delhi, Vol. XLVI, No 49, 22nd November 2008.

31 Elections in India : An Agenda for Reform

Midatala Rani

Election is the foundation of a democracy. Elections lie at the heart of the democratic process. While discussing the draft Constitution in the Constituent Assembly, Nehru said that in India, Democracy should be in its fullest form. Electoral reforms is a way to achieve the fruits of democracy. Today our democratic deficit is more serious than budget deficit. Where we should have been and where are we? Electoral reforms, I believe is the way out of this chaos. Democracy should not become merely ritualistic. Democracy is the destiny of the nation. Fortunately conducting elections in India is the 9th wonder in the world. Conducting elections in India means conducting elections in Cuba plus Vatican City plus Russia plus Indonesia plus Canada. In Uttar Pradesh alone there are 10 crores of people. Nearly 20 lakhs are illiterates. Still all of them are voters. So conducting elections in Uttar Pradesh is almost like conducting elections in the whole of Europe. Elections have almost become a policing system. In Arunachal Pradesh in a particular area there were only 3 voters – father, mother and son. A helicopter was arranged and a polling station was set up with 5 people. Votes were polled by 5 pm and it was declared that 100 percent polling is over. The report went to the Former Chief Election Commissioner T.N. Seshan and he signed on it. Later when he was briefed he ordered for repoll in the area. But the results were same with father, mother and son voting. Despite all this India can develop only through Democracy. The question of electoral reforms has been engaging the attention of political parties, academia, and leaders of public opinion for many years. Many reforms have been contemplated. Still much has not changed.

Agenda for Electoral Reforms in India in Major Areas

1. Restructuring of Electoral Process

In the present simple majority system i.e. first-past-the-post system whoever gets a majority of votes is declared elected. As a result, large number of candidates get elected by less number of votes. This system will not truly reflect the choice of the voters as a whole. There has been a demand for a long time that we should adopt some kind of proportional representation so that there is correlation between the members of the ruling party and the opposition parties in a legislature in the same ratio as the votes polled by them at the election.

There are three alternatives to the first-past-the-post system:

(i) A system of binary voting. Under this every voter has two votes: one positive and one negative. Positive votes are subtracted from negative votes. It must be ensured that people not only support a candidate but has no enemies. It can arrest communal voting. The former governor of Andhra Pradesh Sri Krishna Kant suggested that the ballot paper should consist of a last column "None of these above". In any elections if none of the above is more, all the candidates must be prevented from contesting future elections. If we have this system the voter will show enthusiasm to vote. But the issue here is whether there is a positive dimension in this solution.

(ii) The second alternative proposed is the use of the German electoral system in which half the seats are directly elected and the remaining half are filled on the basis of votes polled by different parties out of the lists prepared by them. This is a complicated system and may not be suitable for India.

(iii) The third alternative is second ballot. In any election if a candidate gets a simple majority he is declared elected. But to ensure better candidates get elected the winning candidate must secure atleast fifty percent of polled votes, no doubt this is a costly system. But the positive argument is that a little extra expenditure on the second ballot is useful in the interest of making elected members really representative of the majority opinion. The emphasis here is to generate a debate on this issue.

2. Election Commission and its Reform

The appointment of the Chief Election Commissioner (CEC) and other Election Commissioners (ECRs) is done by the President on the advice of the Government in power. The CEC cannot be removed from office except in like manner and on the like grounds as a judge of the Supreme Court. The removal of the other members of the EC was made subject to the recommendation of the CEC. Regarding the appointment of the CEC in order to ensure the independence of the EC and keep it free from any kind of influence it is preferable that the CEC and other ECRs are chosen by a Committee headed by the Prime Minister. The committee should include the Lok Sabha Speaker, leader of opposition in Rajya Sabha, the Law Minister, the Deputy Chairperson of the Rajya Sabha and a Judge of the Supreme Court nominated by the Chief Justice of India.

The provision for removal of other election commissioners is something which needs to be debated at large. The Naveen Chawla episode has brought this into sharp focus. The issue here is can the CEC remove the ECRS if any action of theirs displeases him? Conversely if the ECRS fail in discharging their duties should the CEC ask for their removal? Both these issues need to be discussed in the context of the prevailing political situation.

3. Electoral Expenses

One of the vitiating influence on elections is the money power. State funding of elections and public funding of elections are mooted to control electoral expenses. Today on an average a candidate contesting for an election is capable of spending even above Rs. 50 crores per Constituency. Here it is not just the political dimension but the economic dimension of curbing the black money that is involved. Holding huge public meetings and rallies by *Netas* is a colossal waste of money. Only door to door campaigning must be allowed. So far as State funding of elections is concerned the problem is if the government is giving money how can the government prevent the parties/candidates from spending. Curbing of election expenses is possible only when punishment is too severe. The mass media can also play an effective role in this matter.

4. Poll Violence, Irregularities, Criminalisation of Election Process

A list of all these have made a mockery of our election process. Booth capturing is also a bane on our election system. These could be taken care of by imposing very strict rules on polling days, strict discipline for party workers, curbing a candidate contesting from many constituencies and curbing candidates contesting from outside the state. Criminalisation of election process along with the falling quality of the elected representatives is a serious problem. The architects of the Constitution believed that it was possible to build up traditions for the party system. This has not happened. Alternatively it is necessary to reform the party system by enacting a basic law governing the Constitution and functioning of political parties, making it obligatory for them to register, to maintain regular accounts and come up with guidelines for conducting their affairs on democratic lines and prevent defections.

5. Multiplicity of Contestants and Elector's Participation in Voting

An issue which is assuming an alarming proportion in our elections is the multiplicity of contestants. Added to this are increasing number of independent candidates some of whom may be party rebels contesting the election. In addition to this rightly or wrongly the number of film personalities entering into politics is on the rise. To reform this the security deposit should be increased substantially and each candidate must be proposed by a number of proposers. Secondly the security deposit should be forfeited in the event of a candidate failing to secure ¼ of the valid votes polled and such a candidate should be prevented from contesting elections in future.

The electors participation in voting in small numbers is a matter of big concern. It is very unfortunate that the educated voters are not active in political activity. Statistical figures prove that the lowest voter turn out in most elections is from urban areas. Districts with high literacy rate, have low voter turn out in elections. To reform this, voluntary organisations like Voter's Council or Citizens Forums can play an important and useful role. In addition, polling day should not be declared a holiday and voting should be made compulsory.

6. Dual Registrations and Duplication of Names in Electoral Rolls

At present the EPIC (Electoral Photo Identity Card) issued by the Election Commission is not a mandatory requirement to exercise the voting. Many alternative documents listed out facilitate voting. Also when people migrate to new places they do not get their names deleted from the previous electoral rolls. This paves way not only for duplicate voters and absentee voters but also for bogus voting. To arrest this a multipurpose identity card issued by the government that is mandatory for all citizens for manifold uses will help in removing the menace of dual registrations and duplication of names on electoral rolls.

Electora! reforms should bring in decent election campaigns, issue based election manifestoes and citizen awareness. In recent times election campaigns have become lack luster and abusive. None of the political parties have cared for development issues in their manifestoes. The citizens supremacy is important and needs to be reassured. The mass media should play a responsible and impartial role. As long as each political party uses religion and caste factors as a shield during election campaigns our secular credentials are at stake. It is high time the electoral reforms take note of this.

REFERENCES

Gopalaswamy, N. (2008): 'Election Management and Absentee Electors', *The Hindu*, 10th January 2008.

Manjari Katju (2009): 'Election Commission and Changing Contours of Politics', *Economic and Political Weekly*, Vol. XLIV, No. 16, April 18-24, pp. 8-12.

National Election Study, (2009): 'Themes in Lok Sabha Elections (2009)'. *Economic and Political Weekly*, Vol. XLIV, No. 39, September 26, October 2.

Sezhiyan, Era (2001): 'Appointment of Election Commissioners', *The Hindu*, 21st May 2001.

Special Number on Electoral Reforms in India (1984): *Journal of Constitutional and Parliamentary Studies*, Vol. XVIII, Nos. 1-2.

State of Democracy in South Asia: A Report, (2008) : Oxford University Press, New Delhi.

32 Democratisation of Electoral Reforms in India : Some Basic Lessons and Drastic Measures

R. Sreekantan Nair

1. Introduction

It goes without saying that we are all for protecting and upholding the civil rights of the citizens. Therefore we are deeply concerned with the deteriorating and downward trends found in many areas of our social and political life. General elections are not an exception. Elections are the signposts of democracy. It is the platform through which the political culture of the people is reflected. Elections provide an opportunity to the people to express their faith in the government from time to time and change it when the need arises. It also symbolizes the sovereignty of the people and provides legitimacy to the authority of the government. Thus, free and fair elections are indispensable for the success of any democracy. We are a successful democracy in many respects. One of the reasons why we are said to be successful is that we conduct elections regularly. However this is only a technical part of democracy and therefore we are successful only technically. On the other side, we are not that much bothered about the process of democracy. Irrespective of political ideologies and party affiliations, almost all political parties have a role in diluting the true spirit of democracy. This involve a series of undemocratic and unethical practices resorted to by them.

Indian electoral system was largely free from any major flaw till the fourth general elections of 1967. It was in the fifth general elections (1971) that distortions of any proportions took place and the same got multiplied in the successive elections, especially in those held in the eighties and thereafter. Many a times, the Election Commission has expressed its concern and anxiety for the obstacles that stand in the way of free and fair polls. It has made a number of recommendations and repeatedly reminded the government of the necessity of changing the existing laws to check the electoral malpractices. Committees such as the Tarkunde Committee (1975), the Goswami Committee (1990) and the Indrajit Gupta Committee (1998) produced a comprehensive set of proposals regarding electoral reforms along with the recommendations (1998) of the Election Commission.

As a whole, when one looks at the entire electoral front from the very early phase itself there was a persistent demand for electoral reforms from different quarters. But there was opposition from different vested interests due to obvious reasons. A number of new initiatives have been taken by the Election Commission to cleanse the electoral process in India. In spite of all these precautions, the last general election witnessed a host of negative practices. This gives rise to some basic questions like what lessons do we learn from the past? What all initiatives/cautions should we take for the conduct of free and fair elections? The present paper is an attempt to answer these and related questions.

2. The General Scenario

The general electoral scenario is the true reflection of the general political context of the nation. As there exists many political issues and democratic pitfalls, the general electoral system in India too is disturbed by so many snags and stultifying factors. That explains why the anti-social elements too jump into the electoral fray. Since 1952, in the Indian context, elections took place to the legislative bodies both at the national and State levels. The whole process of election is monitored by the Election Commission (EC) and the Commission is regarded as the guardian of free and fair elections. In every election, the EC issues a model code of conduct for political parties and candidates to conduct elections in a free and fair manner. As such, the first of such was circulated at the time of the fifth general elections, held in 1971. Since then, the Code has been revised from time to time. The Code of Conduct lays down guidelines as to how political parties and candidates should conduct themselves during elections.

A provision was made under the code that from the time the elections are announced by the commission, ministers and other authorities cannot announce any financial grant, lay foundation stones of projects of any kind, make promises of construction of roads, carry out any appointments in government and public undertakings which may have the effect of influencing the voters in favor of the ruling party. These measures have been taken as a general rule and any violation leads to frequent litigation and controversy both in the national as well as state elections. But in spite of these cautious measures, there were larger frequency of violation of election rules by both the candidates and their political parties which subsequently rose to higher proportions.

Despite the acceptance of the code of conduct by political parties, cases of its violation have been on the rise. It is a general complaint that the party in power at the time of elections misuses the official machinery to further the electoral prospects of its candidates. The misuse of official machinery takes different forms, such as issue of advertisements at the cost of the public exchequer, misuse of official mass media during election period for partisan coverage of political news and publicity regarding their achievements and the misuse of government transport including aircraft/helicopter, vehicles. For example, during the 2003 Himachal Pradesh Assembly elections, the Commission had issued strict instructions to the political parties to abstain from the use of plastic and polythene for the preparation of posters and publicity material. But the political parties, particularly the Bharatiya Janata Party and the Bahujan Samaj Party, put up a large number of saffron and green publicity flags made of polythene.

During the 2002 Punjab Assembly elections, an aggressive advertisement campaign was launched by the Congress against Chief Minister Parkash Singh Badal and his son, accusing them of corruption and bartering away the interests of Punjab. The Akali Dal hit back with its own set of equally aggressive advertisements against the Congress leaders.

As a result, the Election Commission of India had to intervene to clarify that under the model code of conduct, personal allegations against individual leaders were not allowed, though criticisms of policy decisions and performance were permitted. Similarly, the EC also held Narendra Modi and Sonia Gandhi responsible for violation of the Model Code of Conduct by making controversial remarks during election campaign in the 2007 Gujarat Assembly polls. The EC expressed its severe displeasure over its violation by the two leaders and expected that both of them in future would adhere to the provisions of the Code in letter and spirit. Despite sincere efforts on the part of the EC to check malpractices, every election in India witnesses violation of the Model Code of Conduct.

3. Disclosure of Criminal Antecedents

The Election Commission in June 2002 issued an order under Article 324 that each candidate must submit an affidavit regarding the information of his/her criminal antecedents; assets (both movable and immovable) of self and those of spouses and dependents as well; and qualifications at the time of filing his/her nomination papers for election to the Lok Sabha, the Rajya Sabha and the State Legislative Assemblies. Though the particular order was based on the directives of Supreme court, the move was unanimously opposed by all most all political parties, in whose view, the Election Commission and the judiciary were overstepping the powers. At the all-party meeting, held on July 8, 2002, representatives of 21 political parties decided that the Election Commission's order should not be allowed to be implemented.

The Supreme Court again interfered with the new developments when the Apex Court gave its judgment on March 13, 2003, basically asserting its previous June 2002 decision, which required full disclosure by all candidates. The particular order made it clear that failing to furnish the relevant affidavit shall be considered as a violation of the Supreme Court's order and as such the nomination papers shall be liable to be rejected by the Returning Officer. Furnishing of wrong or incomplete information shall result in the rejection of nomination papers, apart from inviting penal consequences. The 2004 general elections were, thus conducted under these rules.

The EC's order is an effective step to make democracy healthy and unpolluted. No doubt, Citizens have every right to know about the persons whom they prefer as their representatives. The EC has directed all Returning Officers to display the copies of nomination papers and affidavits filed by candidates to the general public and representatives of print and electronic media, free of cost. This was really an effective step which in turn did bring far reaching implications in terms of cleansing the electoral front. The increase in the cases questioning the veracity of the disclosures of elected candidates is a clear indication that the order was effective in filtering the electoral process.

4. Registration of Political Parties

In a multi-party system like that of India, political parties perform complex roles and responsibilities. At the same time, there is no direct reference of political parties in the Constitution of India. The statutory law relating to registration of political parties was enacted only in 1989 which was quite liberal. As a result, a large number of parties mushroomed and got registered with the Commission. Many of them did not contest elections after their registration. It led to confusion among electors as to whom to vote. To eliminate the mushrooming of parties, the EC had to take some rigorous steps. The Commission now registers a party which has at least 100 registered electors as its members and is also charging a nominal processing fee of Rs. 10,000 to cover the administration expenses.

In order to ensure that the registered political parties practice democracy in their internal functioning, the Commission requires them to hold their organisational elections regularly in accordance with their constitutions. The measures taken by the Election Commission to streamline the registration of political parties have shown effective results. These have lessened the headache of the administrative machinery, as well as the confusion of the electorate.

5. Checking Criminalisation of Politics

Indian political scenario has been witnessing the entry of criminals in the election fray. This is a phenomenon which developed after 1980. After 1980 the nation witnessed the Criminalisation of politics which demoralised the Indian political system. The new trend began in Bihar and gradually spread to every nook and corner of the nation. In 2003, a law was introduced to prohibit the election of criminals to the legislative bodies. However, persons with criminal background continue to hold seats in Parliament and State Assemblies. This leads to a very undesirable and embarrassing situation when law-breakers become law-makers and move around under police protection. During the 13th Lok Sabha elections, candidates having criminal cases against them numbered 12 in Bihar and 17 in Uttar Pradesh. It has been rightly observed by J.P. Naik: "Power is the spoiler of men and it is more so in a country like India, where the hungry stomachs produce power hungry politicians."

The EC has expressed its serious concern over the entry of anti-social and criminal persons into the electoral arena. From time to time, it has set down norms and made recommendations to the government to curb the menace of criminalisation of politics. The Commission has urged all political parties to reach a consensus that no person with a criminal background will be given the party ticket. The candidates to an election are also obliged to submit an affidavit in a prescribed form declaring their criminal records, including convictions, charges pending and cases initiated against them. The information so furnished by the candidates shall be disseminated to the public, and to the print and electronic media.Inspite of these drastic measures and precautions their number continue to be alarming. The last general election repeatedly affirmed this.

It was the Vohra Committee that in 1993 had first exposed the criminalisation of politics. Before that, several reports since independence had highlighted different aspects of corruption. The Transparency International's ratings over the years have not been flattering for India. The 2008 report ranks the country at 72nd amongst 179 countries. Actually, the Vohra committee report had sparked a political discourse. In his address to a joint sitting of Parliament on the golden jubilee of Independence (August 15, 1997), the then President KR Narayanan, said: "Sheer opportunism and value-less power-politics have taken over the place of principles and idealism, relationships between people, groups and parties... And corruption is corroding the vitals of our politics and our society... It seems the people have to be in the forefront of the fight against corruption, communalism, casteism and criminalisation of politics and life in the country."

The Supreme Court issued a directive to the Election Commission in 2002 to the effect that rules must be framed to get candidates seeking election to parliament or a state legislature to file affidavits on any criminal activity, so that "the little man may think over before making his choice of electing lawbreakers as law makers".

The EC complied with the directive despite unprecedented political resistance. The constitutional authority was able to generate popular awareness over the fact that politicians were acting like criminals, and criminals getting space in the Indian polity. It was revealed that 16.28 per cent of the candidates contesting the 2004 Lok Sabha elections had criminal antecedents. Since one-fourth of the MPs elected to the Lok Sabha in 2004 had criminal cases against them, it is obvious that a large of number of tainted candidates won the contest. The National Election Watch, a civil society initiative, reported that in comparison to 18 per cent of tainted candidates winning in the state assembly elections, 20 per cent of such candidates won in 2008.

6. Limits on Poll Expenses

Impact of money has always been one of the challenges to Indian democracy. This became very much implicit when it comes in the context of general elections. During elections the poor public are bullied and often cheated by most of the candidates by offering money and other materials for purchasing vote. This is nothing but absolute cheating of the ignorant and illiterate public. Usually, most of the candidates spend unauthorised and unaccounted money for influencing the poor public. Recently, in order to get rid of the growing influence and vulgar show of money during elections, the EC has made many suggestions.

The Commission has fixed legal limits on the amount of money which a candidate can spend during the election campaign. These limits have been revised from time to time. During 2004 elections, the ceiling limits for Lok Sabha seats varied between Rs 10,00,000 to Rs 25,00,000. For Assembly seats, the highest limit was Rs 10,00,000 and the lowest limit was Rs 5,00,000. The EC, by appointing expenditure observers keeps an eye on the individual accounts of election expenditure made by a candidate during election campaign. The contestants are also required to give details of expenditure within 30 days of the declaration of the election results. However, political parties do not adhere to the financial limits as huge amounts are spent by parties under the garb of their supporters.

Apart from this, the EC is also in favour of holding the Lok Sabha and the Assembly elections simultaneously, and to reduce the campaign period from 21 to 14 days. This, they feel, will lead to lowering the election expenditure. The Election Commission's attempt to impose these measures has been a move in the right direction and the same bore desired results. This would invite strong alternative mechanism to remedy this trouble.

7. Multi-member Election Commission

There was a longstanding demand to make the EC a multi-member body. The Supreme Court in the S.S. Dhanoa versus Union of India case had observed: "When an institution like the Election Commission is entrusted with vital functions and is armed with exclusive and uncontrolled powers to execute them, it is both necessary and desirable that the powers are not exercised by one individual, however wise he may be. It also conforms to the tenets of democratic rule." With the 1993 Constitution Amendment Act, the Election Commission was made a multi-member body. The EC was made a multi-member body by the government in the wake of certain controversial decisions taken by the Chief Election Commissioner, T.N. Seshan.

The Act provided that the decision of three members 'shall, as far as possible, be unanimous'. But in case of difference of opinion among three members, the matter 'shall be decided according to the opinion of the majority'. It was a significant step to remove a one-man show in such an important function as that of conducting elections. A single member EC would have no longer 'unbridled' powers. In view of the large size of the country and the huge electors, the Election Commission also made a proposal for the appointment of Regional Commissions to different zones to reduce its burden. So far the demand for a multi-member election commission has been met. At the same time the issue of appointing regional commissioners are still pending with the policy makers.

8. Use of Scientific and Technological Advancements

The Election Commission of India has been trying to bring improvements in election procedures by taking advantage of scientific and technological advancements. The introduction of 'electronic voting machines' (EVMs) is one of the steps in that direction. The Election Commission has recommended the introduction of electronic voting machines with a view to reducing malpractices and also improving the efficiency of the voting process. On an experimental basis, the EVMs were first tried in the State of Kerala during the 1982 Legislative Assembly Elections. After the successful testing and long legal inquiries of the technological aspects of the machines, the EC took a historic decision to go ahead and start the use of EVMs for certain Assembly elections in November 1998. The Commission selected 16 Assembly constituencies in the States of Madhya Pradesh, Rajasthan and Union Territory of Delhi. Later, in the June 1999 Assembly elections, Goa became the first State to successfully use EVMs in all its Assembly constituencies. In the 2004 Lok Sabha elections, the machines were used all over the country. It is a major initiative taken by the EC to make the electoral process simple, quick and trouble-free. It has saved money, solved several logistical issues and also contributed to the conservation of environment through saving of paper. Another major advantage of these machines is that the counting of votes becomes more fast and accurate. Now there are no invalid and wasted votes at all, as every vote recorded in the machine is accounted for in favour of the candidate for whom it was cast.

The Election Commission has not lagged behind in making use of Information Technology for efficient electoral management and administration. It launched a website of its own on February 28, 1998 which is now a good source to have accurate information about elections, election laws, manuals and handbooks published by the Election Commission. During the 1999 Lok Sabha elections, the Commission's Secretariat was directly connected with nearly 1500 counting centres across the country. The constituency-wise counting results were fed into the Commission's website from those counting centres. These results were instantly available throughout the world.

In order to bring as much transparency as possible to the electoral process, the media—both electronic and print—were encouraged and provided with facilities to report on the actual conduct of the poll and counting. The Commission had, in cooperation with the State owned media (Doordarshan and All India Radio) taken several innovative and effective steps to create awareness among voters. All recognised national as well as State parties were allowed free access to the state-owned media on an extensive scale for their election campaign. During the 2004 general elections, the total free time allocated to political parties was 122 hours.

With a view of preventing impersonation of electors at the time of voting and to eliminate bogus and fictitious entries into electoral rolls, the Election Commission took a bold step. In 1998, it decided to take a nationwide programme for the 'computerisation' of electoral rolls. The printed electoral rolls as well as CDs containing these rolls are available to the general public for sale. National and State parties are provided these free of cost after every revision of electoral rolls. The entire country's electoral rolls are available on its website. Karnataka became the first State to prepare electoral rolls with the photographs of voters in the 2008 elections. The State EC developed the electoral roll management software called 'STEERS' (State Enhanced Electoral Roll System) [The Hindu: 2008] to prevent duplication of voters lists and to eliminate wrong addresses. The EC has decided to introduce photo electoral rolls for proper verification of voters across the country by the 2009 general elections.

In an attempt to improve the accuracy of the electoral rolls and prevent electoral fraud, the Election Commission in August 1993 ordered the issuance of electors' photo identity cards (EPICs) for all voters. A modest attempt to introduce the photo identity cards was made for the first time in 1978 at the instance of the then Chief Election Commissioner, S.L. Shakdher, in the case of elections to the Legislative Assembly of Sikkim. During the 2004 Assembly elections, it was mandatory for people possessing EPICs to furnish it at the time of voting. People who did not possess EPICs had to bring the proofs of identity as prescribed by the EC at the time of voting [Rao 2004: 5438]. During the 2007 Punjab Assembly elections, Parneet Kaur (MP from Patiala), could not cast her vote till late afternoon as she had misplaced her voter card [The Tribune: 2007]. The distribution of EPICs, on the part of Election Commission, was a major step to reduce electoral malpractices. Only genuine voters were listed in the rolls with the issuance of voter identity cards.

9. State Sponsored Elections

Right now the General elections are conducted by the Government. This causes immense expense to the exchequer. The expenditure increases in tune to the nature and extent of conduct of elections. Last time it was estimated that the exchequer had to spent Rs. 818 crore. At the same time, the total amount spent by the government is justified as an effort to protect the democratic system. In this regard, it would be proper to interfere with the sponsoring of the electoral expenses. The entire materials used by the candidates should be issued by the EC where as the commission can fix a fee towards the cost of the materials thus issued. No candidates or their proxies shall not use any other materials other than the one issued by the EC. This would help control the expenses as well as the use of unaccounted money in the electoral front.

10. Peoples Right to Recall

As of now there is heated discussion on whether the people are to wait for the next 5 years to recall their representatives for their non performance. Really it is an intrinsic question. In India, it does not look easy to initiate such measures. At the same time, a mechanism of recall will provide better democratic space where the representatives would become more responsive and people-friendly. According to the Chief Election Commissioner S.Y. Quraishi, the concept of recall carries many impractical hurdles and blocks. He is critical to the proposal and raised objections to the same and said, "It is not possible in India, it will destabilize the country. Everywhere there is discontent, people will start recalling." "Our main fear is that if we start rejecting all candidates, we will have another election and people already complain of election fatigue," he argued in a television interview. "It is not possible at all in India, which is a large country. It exists in smaller countries like Switzerland. It can be there in a panchayat election, but not in bigger elections".

Though the argument of the CEC is right from the administrative and functional context of the system, it should be taken into account that the demand for the right to recall is getting greater momentum in India .This is due to the enormous corruption taking place now a days irrespective of ideological or party affiliations. It has been argued strongly that the people's representatives could be recalled for their non-performance, corruption, lack of development in their respective area, inaccessibility to people and on other issues. This will increase their accountability.

11. Fixed Term for Representatives

Equally, it also looks very much relevant that there should emerge a consensus on the term of office of the representatives in the legislative bodies. In the case of Rajya Sabha members and the President, only two terms should be allowed. An age limit should be fixed. When bureaucrats and other officials retire at the age of 60and 65, Indian politician's career start after the age of 60. For the politician also some retirement age should be fixed. This would help them contribute when they are active. Unfortunately many politicians repeatedly get elected from the same constituency and often they hesitate to vacate the seat for any new comer.

This is undemocratic and authoritarian behaviour. For continuing in offices, they use their ethnic, religious and communal identities.

12. Accountability/Performance Chart of the Representatives

It is quiet common that the representatives often become inaccessible to the people once they get elected. That is why the demand for the right to recall is receiving support in recent times. This undemocratic and anti-people stand could be minimized if the activities of the representatives are systematically coded and a performance chart is prepared and published periodically. This could be done by a nodal agency authorised by the EC or any other officer under the control of the local judicial forums with in the limits of the constituency. Such a performance chart of the representative will help the people understand where the constituency stands in the process of development. This would also help the people to have a comparative look at their constituency as well as the neighbouring ones.

Conclusion

Given the backdrop of the contemporary scenario of the Indian electoral system and the undemocratic and unhealthy practices taking place in many parts of the country, it is high time that drastic measures are taken to protect the interests of the general public. In a democratic system the proposals, for this should come from political parties. But are they willing? We have already seen the hide and seek game played by the political parties when the women's reservation bill was introduced in Parliament. In spite of a theoretical consensus on the imperatives of women's reservation, the bill is yet to be passed. It is intentionally delayed, dragged and suppressed. If this can happen to a bill like the Women's reservation bill, what will happen to other more controversial bills? So, what is at stake is Indian democracy itself. Hence it is high time that the EC should use its powers to bring reasonable restrictions on parties and candidates so that people can enjoy the best fruits of Indian democracy.

NOTES AND REFERENCES

Anjana Kaw Bhagat, (1996) : *Elections and Electoral Reforms in India,* Vikas, New Delhi.

Arora N.D., (1977) : *The Lok Sabha Elections in India; A Study in Statistics,* Prageetha Prakashan, Delhi.

Bhagat Singh and Gurudev Singh (1950) : *Indias Election Campaign 1920-59,* University Book Agency, Allahabad.

J.K. Chopra, (1989) : *Politics of Election Reforms in India*, Mittal Publications, New Delhi.

Rao, Ritu (2004): 'Assessing the Electoral System: A Positive Verdict', *Economics and Political Weekly*, December 18.

The Financial Express (2007): December 23.

The Hindu (2008): February 15.

Mainstream, Vol. XLVI, No 49.

Suman Deep Kaul, 'Electoral Reforms in India: Proactive Role of Election Commission', *Mainstream*, Vol. XLVI, No. 49, November 22, 2008

http://www.electoral-reform.org.uk/

http://eci.nic.in/eci_main/PROPOSED_ELECTORAL_ REFORMS.pdf

http://www.mainstreamweekly.net/article1049.html

33 Evolution of Franchise and the Concern for Quality of Democracy

C.P. John

The will of the people shall be the basis of the authority of governments. This is the rationale of election according to the Universal Declaration of Human Rights by UN in 1948. 'Election' is the gauge of the will of the people.

Modern democracies are relatively new. The democratic elections which we are now practicing emerged only in the 17th century. Though there were elections in the city states of Athens it could not sustain for long. There are still 44 monarchies in the world. More over in the democracies of Common Wealth Countries including UK, monarchies are retained. One party rule and autocracies exist in several other countries like China. Even in the 'Developed' democracies of Europe, women were denied the right to vote for a long time.

In UK, which is considered as the citadel of parliamentary democracy, only in 1920s did women get the right to vote, after prolonged agitations and campaigns. In France it was introduced in 1944, in Switzerland only in 1971. In this regard our constitution proclaimed adult franchise right from the beginning. (Now we are discussing about 33% reservation for women in State and Union Legislatures. Women are already enjoying 50% reservation in the local bodies.)

The first American Presidential election of 1789 can be considered as a landmark in the history of elections. The reform bill of 1832 outlined the fundamentals of modern elections in UK. The inter Parliamentary Union (IPU) was established in 1889. The newly liberated third world countries, like India, opted for parliamentary democracy in the 1940s. The Universal Declaration of the UN gave fillip to the democratic aspirations of people across the world.

But in 1964, the progress of democracy received a setback in Chile where the CIA carried out undemocratic practices for aborting elections. In the UN Covenant of Civil and Political Rights adopted in 1966, the

Human Rights Declaration of 1948 was codified. In the new nation formed after the collapse of Soviet Union in 1990's multi-party democracy was opted. In 1993 the World Council of Human Rights adopted the Vienna declaration on Human Rights.

The 154th session of the Inter Parliamentary Union (in 1994) outlined the basic principles of "Free and Fair Election". The UN millennium declaration too emphasized the importance of democratic elections. Though in our country we have neglected quality of democracy as a millennium goal, the declaration has given ample importance to it (Chapter 5). Quality of democracy is considered as a Human Right.

In recent times, the Democratic wave has been shaking the very existence of monarchies all over the world. Nepal's king had to quit his throne; elections are being held in Kuwait. The monarch of Bhutan also accepted election. The democratic base is expanding. But in Iran and Zimbabwe the elections were rigged. But it does not mean that the trend of democracy is receding. Antonio Marico Costa, a UN expert on 'democracy studies' tried to map the 'level' of democracy in different countries. According to him, the African nations and China which were liberated in 1940's and 50's have not yet attained minimum level of democratic rights. The democratic index of India and the newly formed CIS countries are in the average level. The indexing of the quality of democracy is not an easy job to do, since the parameters are not evenly applicable to the societies spanning from – a forest setting to the most modern city. But the parameters of "Free and Fair" election can easily be applied to any election anywhere in the world. The "Freeness" and "Fairness" constitutes the major fundamentals of the quality of democracy.

Since election is the tool to gauge the 'will of the people' (Which is the basis of the authority of the governments), it will reflect the true will only if the citizen had the unfettered right and opportunity to choose the candidate of his choice without fear or favour; the elections are then considered 'free'. In between his (votes) home and the polling booth there should be a total absence of intimidation. The voters shall not be influenced through any illegal favours. In short, the voter should have effective and equal access to the polling booth. "Fairness" is related to the authorities conducting the elections. They should conduct this in a fair manner providing a level playing ground for all the contestants, respecting the fundamentals of human rights. Fraudulent practices must be legally prohibited and opportunities should be given for appealing against any fraudulent practices.

In the Indian context proper attention has not been given to the 'level' of free and fair election. The quality of elections is not properly defined; often the quantity i.e., the number of voters, booths, money spent etc. are more important than the 'free and fairness' of the electoral process. Out of 575 districts in India, nearly 50 districts are virtually controlled by Maoists, who do not participate in the elections.

In many other districts caste, communal and political issues intimidate the voters. Money is freely distributed to voters (as in Tamil Nadu) by major political parties. Even in the state of Kerala in some places like Kannur district there are many complaints of intimidation and booth capturing.

To improve the quality of democracy several suggestions are being considered in democratic countries. In India too it is high time to start a national level discussion on the improvement of the quality of democracy.

State funding of elections, proper media support for the candidates, empowering the election commission for auditing the political parties and amending the Representation of People Act according to the changed situation are the major points to be considered in the national agenda for a better and high quality democratic polity.

34 Electoral Reforms : A Clever Ploy/A Redherring?

M. Kunhaman

This paper is not about electoral reforms. Instead, it raises the question whether the electoral system, mutatis mutantis, must continue, answering the question, not perfectly convincingly, largely in the negative. The paper does not consider either elections or electoral reforms as urgent and important. Rather, it tries to interrogate the existing democratic politics. However, in conformity with the major theme of this seminar, and also as an interim, short-term measure, it tries to set out a list of reforms for critical consideration. India has been hailed as the largest democracy with the largest electorate in the world. It is widely acclaimed for its "free and fair elections". Many a time, it is cited as a model worth emulating. It is true that the country has perfected its electoral process over time.

Dwindling Voting Percentage

A discerning feature of voting in India has been the progressive decline in the voting percentage and the expansion of the non-electoral political space. The last Lok Sabha (the 15th) election, and the various by-elections corroborate this. Nearly half the populations do not consider it worth their while to participate in the electoral process. Hence, the tendency to abstain from voting is not a middle class phenomenon as is, sometimes, alleged. And given the increasing political consciousness of the people, this phenomenon is attributable to their disillusionment with electoral politics. The disconnect between promises and performance by political parties is the major reason.

It is the candidate getting the largest (not the majority) number of votes that is declared elected. Suppose the winning candidate got only 17% of the total number of votes polled. He does not represent the constituency. Here, victory in election means defeat of democracy.

In parliamentary democracy, election is more important than politics. Non-political persons like business-people, film stars and house-wives can get elected. In the first-past-the-post system winnability is the major criterion for the selection of candidates. Hence, considerations such as religion, region, caste, money and muscle power are used in the selection process. Fraud and chicanery are used, often, with impunity.

Whereas, in non-parliamentary democracy, politics is important, Parliamentary democracy and equality do not go together. For example, in India, there is no equality even among members of parliament. Think about the relation between Sonia Gandhi / Rahul Gandhi, on the one hand, and an ordinary Congress MP, on the other; L.K. Advani and an ordinary BJP MP. In fact, legislators are unindependent persons to a considerable extent. They cannot express their independent views as they cannot deviate from the party position on any issue. In this sense, if by democracy, we mean equality; parliamentary democracy is a contradiction in terms. Democracy may be a desirable idea; but in a society premised on the caste-class-patriarchy axis, it is impractical.

The position that legislature represents all sections of society is a travesty of reality. For instance, in the present Lok Sabha, the rich have their representatives (there are more than 130 crorepati's in the Lok Sabha today), businessmen, cine actors, criminals, farmers, industrialists all have their representatives; but no representatives for (Below Poverty Line) people, beggars or sex workers. The present crop of legislators does not and cannot understand the Indian society which is the most diverse in the world; nor do they understand the Indian economy which is one of the most egregiously unequal in the world. In other words, given the extant socio-economic structure, electoral politics does not suit India. Nor can the country afford such a costly electoral system. Several crores of Rupees are spent on the conduct of elections while several crores of people are starving. Same persons or members of the same family repeatedly get elected. In fact, what we have in India is dynastic/feudal democracy. Given the innumerable structural inequities and inadequacies afflicting the Indian polity, it is not inconceivable that electoral politics will have to yield place to some other political system in the not-so-distant a future. The point is not that democracy is bad, but that what is prevailing in India is not democracy. The political class (an idle and inefficient group) is swelling at an exponential rate, living of the sweat and tears of the toiling masses.

The poor do not get the leaders they deserve while the rich manage to get the leaders they want.

At present, the Indian state is waging a war against its own people. State attention is focused almost exclusively on mobilising the military, paramilitary, police and intelligence and scarcely on the development/ welfare needs of the poor.

Idle academics repeat, ad nauseam that democracy is a government of the people, by the and for the people even as in the post-liberalization era, it is a government of the market, by the market and for the market. In fact, the PREAMBLE TO THE Constitution should be so reframed to say that "we, the rich people of India resolve to work against Liberty, Equality, Justice and Fraternity". The state, instead of protecting the poor, has become the custodian of an unequal and oppressive socio-economic order which is oppressive and exploitative. It is not the rulers but the victims of a system who change the system. The ultimate victory will be that of the oppressed and the exploited. They will restructure the society and rule it.

Any close reconnaissance of the Indian polity will make one venture to observe that India's political future is being built in the growing non-electoral space by the victims of the system. And this process, it appears, is irreversible.

Pending such a denouement, for the interim, the following are suggested for consideration in the context of thinking about electoral reforms.

India is a democratic country without democratic practices.

Parliament is becoming irrelevant. The steeply declining number of working days, legislators' absenteeism, Ministers not attending even Cabinet meetings, the low quality or no discussions-all these make the Parliament a money-guzzling, vegetating and anachronistic organisation.

1. Introduce proportional representation
2. As Indian population is becoming younger, (the country has been taking advantage of demographic dividend), only persons below the age of forty should be allowed to contest elections.
3. Persons should be allowed to become members of legislature only for two terms.
4. After a person from one particular family has served for two terms, no other member of the same family should be permitted to contest elections.
5. There should not be reservation in legislatures. Let legislators come through the route and not through the legislative route.
6. In the context of the three-tier panchayati raj system as well as the increasing acceptance of participatory democracy, the federal structure has become irrelevant and unnecessary. State

Governments have become redundant and an inconvenience (a sixth finger on the right hand), merely a wastage of public money. Hence, they should be disbanded.

7. Coalitions are a bane of electoral democracy. They have become a matter of convenience. Post-poll coalitions, often cobbled just for the sake of forming government and sharing power, must be disallowed.

8. Abolish the Rajya Sabha. A costly leviathan, serving no purpose other than bringing unnecessary (apolitical) and unwanted (discarded by the people) persons into positions. India is in an unenviable position today: it has a Prime Minister (for a second consecutive term, to boot) having never won even a panchayat election.

Index